Cooking Light
COOKBOOK 1994

Cooking Light

COOKBOOK 1994

Oxmoor House

Copyright 1993 by Oxmoor House, Inc.
Book Division of Southern Progress Corporation
P.O. Box 2463, Birmingham, Alabama 35201

Library of Congress Catalog Number: 87-61020
ISBN: 0-8487-1144-0
ISSN: 1043-7061

Manufactured in the United States of America
First Printing 1993

Editor-in-Chief: Nancy J. Fitzpatrick
Senior Foods Editor: Susan Carlisle Payne
Senior Editor, Editorial Services: Olivia Kindig Wells
Director of Manufacturing: Jerry R. Higdon
Art Director: James Boone

Cooking Light® Cookbook 1994

Editor: Cathy A. Wesler, R.D.
Assistant Foods Editors: Caroline A. Grant, M.S., R.D.; Kathryn L. Matuszak
Copy Editor: Holly Ensor
Editorial Assistant: Lisa C. Bailey
Director, Test Kitchens: Vanessa Taylor Johnson
Assistant Director, Test Kitchens: Gayle Hays Sadler
Test Kitchen Home Economists: Beth Floyd, Michele Brown Fuller, Telia Johnson,
    Elizabeth Luckett, Christina A. Pieroni, Kathleen Royal, Angie Neskaug Sinclair,
    Jan A. Smith
Senior Photographer: Jim Bathie
Photographer: Ralph Anderson
Senior Photo Stylist: Kay E. Clarke
Photo Stylist: Virginia R. Cravens
Designer: Faith Nance
Production Manager: Rick Litton
Associate Production Manager: Theresa L. Beste
Production Assistant: Marianne Jordan
Recipe and Menu Developers: Susan S. Bradley; Patricia Coker; Trish Leverett;
    Debby Maugans; OTT Communications, Inc.; Jane Ingrassia Reinsel;
    Elizabeth J. Taliaferro; Grace Wells
Text Consultants: Maureen Callahan, M.S., R.D.; Joyce L. Hendley; Office of the Vice
    President of Health Affairs, University of Alabama at Birmingham: Julius Linn, M.D.,
    Executive Director, and Lisa Latham, Associate Editor
Exercise Model: Judith A. Mason

Cover: *Triple Delight Cheesecake (page 246)*
Back cover: *Steamed Chicken Roulades with Chunky Tomato Sauce (page 73), steamed
    green beans, steamed baby carrots, Crisp Rosemary-Pepper Breadsticks (page 74), and
    Sparkling Berry Cooler (page 74)*
Frontispiece: *Cantaloupe Sorbet (page 236) and Raspberry-Lemon Frozen Yogurt (page 238)*

Contents

Living Well Is The Best Reward   7

Update '94   8

The Food & Fitness Connection   13
    Nutrition Basics for *Cooking Light*   15
    Exercise—The Perfect Partner   18
    Set Yourself Up for Success   22
    The *Cooking Light* Kitchen   24
    What's New in the Marketplace?   26

Healthy American Meals   31
    Breakfast and Brunch   33
    Quick and Easy   45
    That's Entertaining   57
    Holiday Celebrations   75

Light Recipes   93
    Appetizers and Beverages   95
    Breads   107
    Fish and Shellfish   119
    Grains and Pastas   131
    Meatless Main Dishes   145
    Meats   157
    Poultry   171
    Salads and Salad Dressings   183
    Sandwiches and Snacks   195
    Sauces and Condiments   203
    Side Dishes   211
    Soups and Stews   221
    Desserts   231

Cooking Light 1994 Menu Plans   248
Calorie/Nutrient Chart   250
Recipe Index   262
Subject Index   269
Acknowledgments and Credits   272

Living Well Is The Best Reward

Welcome to *Cooking Light Cookbook 1994*. And welcome to the tenth volume of all-new, kitchen-tested recipes reflecting the most up-to-date principles of good nutrition. *Cooking Light Cookbook 1994* is filled with menus and recipes so flavorful you'll find it hard to believe they're good for you. In addition, each year we report results from the latest research on nutrition and fitness. And this year is no exception.

Research shows the importance of keeping fat intake at 30 percent or less of total calories per day, but that doesn't mean every food you eat must contain less than 30 percent of calories from fat. Rather, your goal should be to balance higher fat foods with lower fat ones to create an *average* of no more than 30 percent of calories from fat *per day*. *Cooking Light* demonstrates this message within the menu plans and in the wide variety of recipes. Remind yourself each day—the key to eating healthfully is balance, variety, and moderation.

Variety and moderation also apply to exercise. There's no need to exercise until you drop. Recent studies show that any amount of exercise can help improve your health and decrease your chances of developing heart disease as well as a host of other maladies.

Research also shows that it's important to encourage your children to be active and eat nutritious meals and snacks. The payoff years later will be healthier adults who remain active longer and who require less medical care and spend fewer health-care dollars.

Cooking Light Cookbook 1994 provides the reasons to reduce fat intake and exercise regularly. By choosing a healthy lifestyle, you can make changes in the way you feel today and the way you'll feel years from now.

Eating well is a key to living well, so take the time to relax and relish the refreshing flavor of Fresh Fruit with Sweet Yogurt Dressing (page 184) and Citrus Spritzer (page 106).

Update '94

"Update '94" reports on the latest research results in nutrition and fitness. Although the research has focused on a variety of subjects, including cancer, heart disease, weight loss, exercise, and living longer, three basic rules for healthier living have surfaced repeatedly:

- **Reduce fat in your diet**
- **Eat five servings of fruits and vegetables a day**
- **Exercise at least three times a week.**

Fat and Cancer

Eating less fat and more fruits and vegetables can do more than slim your waist and keep your arteries clear. Researchers at the National Cancer Institute (NCI) report that nonsmoking women who consume lots of fat, especially saturated fat, increase their lung cancer risk five-fold. On the other hand, a diet low in fat and high in fiber provides considerable protection from colon cancer.

Although an eight-year study did not find that eating less fat and more fiber protected women against breast cancer, not everyone is convinced. Last year, the National Institutes of Health (NIH) began the largest study ever of women's health to look more closely at a possible correlation between fat in the diet and a number of health issues, including breast cancer.

Winning at Weight Loss

With commitment, you can win the weight-loss battle by simply reducing the fat in your diet and adding exercise.

If you, like more than 50 million Americans, are depriving yourself of favorite foods or starving to lose weight, you may be setting yourself up for failure and worse.

Recent research has shown that up to 95 percent of people who diet to lose weight will regain the weight they've lost within five years. Worse, up to 98 percent of quick-fix dieters will regain the lost weight after just one year.

Yo-Yo Dieting Increases Heart Disease Risk. It's healthier to maintain a steady weight, even if it's a bit above normal, than to repeatedly lose and regain weight.

When people lose weight quickly by severe dieting, they lose both fat and muscle tissue. The weight they regain is mainly fat tissue, which burns fewer calories than does muscle. And for some people, weight may be lost from the lower part of the body but gained again primarily in the abdomen, which increases the risk of heart disease, diabetes, and stroke.

Exercise slows the loss of muscle tissue and boosts the metabolic rate (the rate at which you burn calories). Dieting without exercising not only burns muscle tissue but also lowers the metabolic rate to protect your body from starvation.

Beginning Early

Efforts to reduce fat intake and control weight should begin early. Currently, one in four teenagers is overweight enough (20 pounds or more) to be at high risk for heart attack, stroke, colon cancer, and other health problems later in life. But don't impose drastic diets on children. (For specifics, see page 15.)

The best approach is to make healthful eating and exercise a part of everyday life for the entire family. Educate your children about the basics of healthy nutrition and lifestyles. You can start by setting a good example.

Education does work, according to studies presented at last year's American Heart Association (AHA) meeting. One study showed that teaching third and fourth graders about heart-healthy eating resulted in changes that dropped their cholesterol levels an average of 13 points over two years. Adding exercise helped even more. Children who learned to combine heart-healthy eating and regular exercise dropped their cholesterol levels an average of 7 points in only two months.

Winning the Cholesterol War

Americans' efforts to reduce fat, saturated fat, and cholesterol in the diet are working. The nation's mean blood cholesterol level fell 6 to 8 percent between 1960 and 1991. The drop from 220 to 205 milligrams per deciliter (mg/dL) brings Americans' cholesterol levels to just 5 points above the desirable mark of 200 mg/dL. Researchers say this substantial change should translate into a 12 to 32 percent drop in the incidence of heart disease. And that's just what's happening. Between 1963 and 1990, the number of deaths from coronary heart disease dropped by 54 percent.

More than half of that drop can be explained by changes in lifestyle—specifically, lowering blood cholesterol levels and stopping smoking.

This encouraging data heralded the second report of the Expert Panel on Detection, Evaluation, and Treatment of High Blood Cholesterol in Adults. The national panel recommended refinements in evaluation of people for cholesterol problems and in deciding who should be treated and when.

The panel continues to emphasize that a high blood cholesterol level is a major risk factor for coronary heart disease. Lowering a high blood cholesterol level, especially a high level of low-density lipoprotein (LDL) cholesterol, will decrease the chances of developing heart disease or of developing more severe problems from heart disease if you already have it.

The Role of HDLs. The panel also underscored the important role of high-density lipoprotein (HDL) cholesterol. HDLs whisk cholesterol away from artery walls, thereby lowering heart disease risk. The higher the HDL level, the better, and the panel says it should be at least 35 mg/dL. In fact, even people with a desirable total cholesterol of 200 mg/dL may be at risk for heart disease if they have a low HDL value.

Encouraging research shows that heredity plays less of a role in determining the levels of HDL than of LDL. This means that by exercising regularly, stopping smoking, and keeping your weight down, you can boost your HDL levels and reduce heart disease risk, regardless of heredity. Researchers have even reported that learning to control stress and curbing hostility can boost HDL levels a bit.

Hidden Dangers in Unsaturated Fats. Recent information shows that unsaturated vegetable fats—when altered for use in margarine, vegetable shortening, and commercially

baked goods such as cakes and cookies—may be no healthier than saturated fat and perhaps worse. Scientists have said for some time that saturated fat, the type found in large amounts in butter, lard, and red meat, is the main dietary factor that raises blood cholesterol levels.

But there is concern now that these altered fats may also raise blood cholesterol levels. The problem may be the trans-fatty acids that form when unsaturated oils are partially hydrogenated to make them better able to thicken foods and resist spoilage. These changes create a more saturated product that raises LDL cholesterol levels just like saturated fats do and also lowers the levels of the good HDLs, which saturated fats don't do.

Can Cholesterol Go Too Low?

It's beyond question that lowering cholesterol levels is worth the effort. Heart disease remains the number one killer of Americans. Men with cholesterol levels over 240 mg/dL are three times more likely to suffer a heart attack than men with levels below 160 mg/dL.

Some studies have suggested, at least superficially, that you can lower your cholesterol too much. Followup on the Multiple Risk Factor Intervention Trial (MR FIT) involving more than 350,000 men showed that cholesterol levels below 160 mg/dL were associated with deaths from stroke, alcoholism, suicide, and certain cancers.

In addition, a major analysis of 19 studies by the National Heart, Lung, and Blood Institute revealed that a person with a cholesterol level below 160 mg/dL was more likely than the average person to die a violent death or die from lung disease or certain cancers. Since cancer, lung disease, and liver

disease drive cholesterol down, they are causes of low cholesterol rather than results.

If there is a risk in lowering cholesterol too much, it seems to be greater when cholesterol-lowering drugs are used. This emphasizes the even greater importance of using diet and exercise to lower blood cholesterol levels.

A New Look at Vitamins

The Antioxidant Connection. Scientists have found that a common reaction that occurs in all body cells—oxidation—produces a by-product called oxygen free radicals. Capable of causing structural damage, these highly unstable molecules create more unstable molecules, which set in motion a chain reaction that plays an important role in atherosclerosis and perhaps in arthritis and aging itself. Free radicals alter LDL cholesterol in such a way that it can more easily clog artery walls.

The body has a number of mechanisms for soaking up harmful free radicals. Among these are the so-called antioxidant vitamins—vitamins C, E, and beta carotene (the vegetable form of vitamin A).

Vitamin E and Heart Disease—More Research Needed. In two studies in 1993 involving more than 120,000 women and men, Harvard researchers found evidence strongly suggesting that large doses of vitamin E reduced the risk of developing coronary heart disease. The greatest benefit came from taking supplements containing 100 International Units (IU), an amount impossible to get from diet alone and far in excess of the recommended daily allowance of 10 IUs a day.

Evidence also surfaced that vitamin E can interfere with the stickiness of platelets (blood cells that initiate blood clot formation), which is the final step leading to a heart attack. Before large amounts of vitamin E supplements can be recommended, more studies are needed to rule out any other factors that might account for the drop in heart disease risk, and to determine whether taking megadoses of vitamin E is safe long-term. In the meantime, you can find good sources of vitamin E in vegetable oils, wheat germ, seeds, whole grains, and nuts. And remember, no vitamin pill will compensate for eating too much fat and not exercising.

Beta Carotene and Vitamin C. Many studies detailing the effects of beta carotene and vitamin C on heart disease are positive. Some, but not all, find that beta carotene, the pigment that gives yellow and orange vegetables their color, reduces the risk of heart attack and stroke. The same can be said for the effects of vitamin C on heart disease risk.

Getting plenty of beta carotene and vitamin C in your diet may lower your risk of developing cancer, although the association hasn't been proven conclusively.

The bottom line, says the NCI, is this: Eat plenty of antioxidant-rich fruits and vegetables—at least five servings a day. In announcing the NCI's 5-A-Day-For-Better-Health program, the NIH director said, "What Americans need today...is an updated and simple message....that will stand the test of time and [be] something people can stick with all their lives."

Reducing fat, especially saturated fat, and eating plenty of fruits and vegetables is clearly this year's nutrition message. Harvard researchers found over a five-year period that people who ate more than two servings of fruits and vegetables a day were four times less likely to die from a heart attack than were those who ate less than one serving a day.

Folic Acid and Healthy Births. Women of childbearing age can reduce their risks of having a baby with a neural tube defect by consuming lots of foods rich in folic acid. These defects, which appear in 2,500 American newborns each year, include spina bifida (in which the casing of the spinal cord fails to close properly) and anencephaly (a condition in which much of the brain fails to form).

The U.S. Public Health Service recommends that women of childbearing age get 0.4 milligram (400 micrograms) of folic acid a day. Most American women, however, get only about half that amount. To get that much folic acid from food, you would need to eat more than 1 cup cooked broccoli, ⅔ cup cooked spinach, and 1 cup cooked turnip greens each day. Other foods high in folic acid, sometimes referred to as folate, are liver, nuts, and legumes such as chick peas, black-eyed peas, and lentils. An alternative to eating these foods would be taking an over-the-counter multivitamin supplement.

Mineral Mania

Iron May Not Be the Culprit. Iron got a bad rap recently when Finnish researchers said men who ate lots of iron-rich meats had an increased risk of heart disease. They suggested the excess iron promoted hardening of the arteries by making harmful free radicals more active. However, it might have been the extra saturated fat in the meat that increased the risk of heart disease. Rather than worrying about getting too much iron, the message for now should be to eat fewer foods high in saturated fats.

Calcium for Strong Bones. Calcium for children, adolescents, young adults, and older folks equals stronger, healthier bones. This, in turn,

would eliminate some of the almost 250,000 hip fractures that occur each year in the U.S. because of osteoporosis—a bone-thinning disease. Just a 20 percent drop in hip fractures would save up to $2 billion in health care a year. For bones to reach the maximum strength heredity will allow, it's important to consume enough low-fat milk and dairy products and to exercise during childhood, adolescence, and young adulthood.

Especially encouraging is the finding that even after bones reach their full length in adolescence, they continue to strengthen through the twenties, after which the normal age-related decline in bone strength begins. After menopause when the fall in estrogen production speeds the loss of bone substance, women can still benefit from getting enough calcium (at least 1,000 milligrams a day). More good news: Consuming the recommended amounts of calcium doesn't pose the kidney stone risk doctors once thought.

Milk's Benefits Outweigh Possible Concerns. Because milk contains calcium as well as other nutrients, ignore recent scares about the dangers of milk for children, say the American Dietetic Association, the American Academy of Pediatrics, and the American Medical Association. This advice comes in response to a claim by a group called the Physicians Committee for Responsible Medicine that people should avoid dairy and meat products because of their high fat and cholesterol content and because of the unproven possibility that milk might be causing diabetes in children. This isn't bad advice, especially in light of the high incidence of heart disease in this country. But there are lean alternatives to high-fat dairy products, namely skim milk, low-fat yogurt, and low-fat cheeses, that children can safely eat during bone-forming years.

A Drink a Day

In 1992, the MR FIT report showed that for men who were at high risk for coronary heart disease, two drinks a day lowered their risk of developing heart disease by 22 percent. A similar study of women showed the same benefit from one-half to one drink a day. (One drink equals 4 fluid ounces of wine, 12 fluid ounces of beer, or 1½ fluid ounces of 80-proof liquor.)

One study of almost 130,000 people over a 10-year period showed those who had one or two drinks a day were 30 percent less likely to die from heart disease than those who didn't drink at all. Alcohol appears to work because it raises the level of protective HDL by 10 to 15 percent and decreases the stickiness of platelets that form clots.

Does this mean you should start drinking? Certainly not if you have had any problem related to alcohol or if you don't drink now. Social problems with alcohol and its habit-forming potential are all too familiar. And drinking more than two or three drinks a day can cause a wide range of harmful effects, including high blood pressure, weight gain, and, in a few people, cirrhosis. Furthermore, calories from alcohol not only make you fat, according to a Swiss study, but they also add to fat around the waistline, contributing to the "beer belly" that increases the risk for heart disease.

Get Moving

The AHA now considers lack of regular exercise to be as significant in contributing to heart disease as high blood pressure, cigarette smoking, high blood cholesterol, and obesity. In fact, smoking and obesity affect fewer Americans than does lack of exercise, making inactivity the most common behavioral risk factor for heart disease.

The small percentage of Americans who are physically active has not increased since the mid-1980s—three out of five adults still lead sedentary lives. Almost 30 percent of all adults get no physical exercise whatsoever, which will make it almost impossible to reach the Public Health Service's goal of decreasing the percentage of those who don't exercise to less than 15 percent of the population by the year 2000. To help reach that goal, the Centers for Disease Control and Prevention and the AHA want you to know that "no pain, no gain" is an outmoded slogan. Their new emphasis is that any exercise is better than no exercise.

Encouraging Youths. The AHA recommendation comes at a time when increasing numbers of teens throughout the nation may be at risk for health problems later in life because they're not exercising enough, aren't eating enough fruits and vegetables, and are eating too much fat. Work with your children at home and with their schools to develop and encourage regular participation in nutrition and physical education classes. The payoff years later will be healthier adults who remain active longer and who will require less medical care and spend fewer health-care dollars.

Never Too Late To Start. Although it's clear that starting an exercise program and eating well early pay big dividends later, research confirms that it's never too late to start. Both middle-aged and older men and women can benefit from regular exercise. Improved bone density, less risk of heart attack, and a decreased chance of developing diabetes are clear benefits.

Benefits Are Many. Many studies have focused on men, but a three-year study of women clearly showed that those who exercised regularly were less likely to gain weight, to have a fall in their protective HDL levels, or to see a rise in blood pressure. They were less stressed and less anxious and reported feeling good more often than those who got the least exercise. All these changes led to less chance of heart disease and to a slowing of the aging process.

Regular exercise—a combination of strength training, aerobic activity, and stretching—also can prevent the slow decline of muscle mass and increase in body fat that happens as the decades pass. Authorities conclude that without exercise, you lose about 6½ pounds of muscle tissue each decade while adding fat. Much of the loss of muscle tissue and the accompanying decline in ability to do what you want can be offset by a regular exercise program that includes some muscle strengthening exercises.

Enjoy Life, Live Longer

Can regular exercise extend your life? The answer appears to be yes, anywhere from a few months to a few years. According to one study, even 75-year-olds who begin exercising live a bit longer.

Men who took up brisk walking, tennis, biking, jogging, or gardening between ages 45 and 54 lived an average of 10 months longer than those who remained sedentary. Middle-aged men who gave up cigarettes added 1½ years to their lives. Those who both stopped smoking and started exercising gained 2½ years of life. Exercise seemed to extend lives mostly by warding off heart attacks, but all causes of death declined somewhat.

Another point to remember is that regular exercise, even if it doesn't extend your life for long, can ensure that you are better able to enjoy the years you have.

The Food
& Fitness
Connection

PLEASE
STAY ON
THE PATH

To help Americans make nutritious food choices and plan healthful meals, the U.S. Department of Agriculture has developed the Food Guide Pyramid, which is a visual companion to the Dietary Guidelines.

The placement of food groups in the pyramid corresponds with the recommended number of servings that you should eat daily. For example, you should strive to eat the most servings from the group at the base of the pyramid—breads, cereal, rice, and pasta—and the fewest from the group at the top—fats, oils, and sweets. Although fats and sugar are obvious in foods such as butter and candy, they're found in other foods as well. This is illustrated by small circles (symbolizing fat) and triangles (symbolizing sugar) throughout the pyramid.

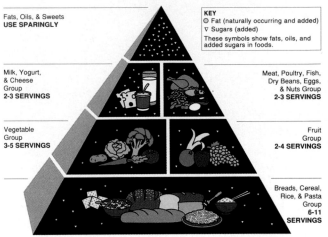

Food Guide Pyramid
A Guide to Daily Food Choices

Fats, Oils, & Sweets
USE SPARINGLY

KEY
◯ Fat (naturally occurring and added)
▽ Sugars (added)
These symbols show fats, oils, and added sugars in foods.

Milk, Yogurt, & Cheese Group
2-3 SERVINGS

Meat, Poultry, Fish, Dry Beans, Eggs, & Nuts Group
2-3 SERVINGS

Vegetable Group
3-5 SERVINGS

Fruit Group
2-4 SERVINGS

Breads, Cereal, Rice, & Pasta Group
6-11 SERVINGS

While you're building your diet according to the pyramid, don't forget the cornerstone—exercise. Pick an activity you like and do it on a regular basis. Or better yet, pick a few activities that are fun for you. The variety will help keep you motivated and interested. Walking is an excellent choice for beginners because it requires little skill, doesn't require elaborate equipment, and can be done almost anywhere. As you adapt to the exercise, you can make it more challenging by increasing your pace and level of intensity (pages 18–19).

Using exercise equipment is another fitness alternative that doesn't require a lot of skill yet offers a first-rate workout. Machines such as a treadmill, stationary bicycle, and stair stepper are convenient and easy to use (pages 20–21). They provide excellent cardiovascular benefits while toning muscle groups in the lower body, yet they don't place undue stress on joints. The level of intensity and length of the workout can be adjusted to a comfortable level so either a beginner or a bona fide athlete can receive a quality workout.

To guide you on your journey toward a healthier diet, turn to "The *Cooking Light* Kitchen" (pages 24–25) for tips on reducing calories, fat, and sodium in your favorite recipes without giving up good taste. And look to "What's New In the Marketplace" (pages 26–29) for a clear explanation of the new food labels you will be seeing on your grocer's shelves. The new labels are designed to standardize and clarify nutrition information, making it easier to comparison shop. You be the judge.

Within the pages of *Cooking Light* you'll find a wealth of nutrition and fitness information that will help you achieve your goals for a healthier lifestyle. Share these tips with family and friends so they too can reap the rewards. The tips are flagged with the following symbols:

NUTRITION   FITNESS

Overleaf: *For a revitalizing snack that won't slow you down after a workout, take along Lemon-Basil Tuna Pockets (page 201), Pimiento Cheese Apple Wedges (page 201), raw vegetables, and Citrus Spritzer (page 106).*

Nutrition Basics for *Cooking Light*

In ancient times, Egyptians revered the pyramid for its supposed mystical powers. Today, however, the pyramid serves a more practical use in helping Americans strip away the mystery of understanding good nutrition.

The Food Guide Pyramid from the U.S. Department of Agriculture gives visual punch to the government's guidelines that recommend eating lots of fruits, vegetables, grains, pastas, and breads. These foods supply vitamins, minerals, complex carbohydrates, and dietary fiber—important nutrition components that contribute to overall health. Furthermore, these nutrients may help prevent heart disease, cancer, and a host of other diseases.

The pyramid also illustrates the limited role that fats, oils, and sweets should play in your diet. Eating high-fat, high-calorie foods has been linked to an increased risk for heart disease, stroke, obesity, diabetes, and some types of cancer. The danger of eating too much of these foods is emphasized by the fact that diet is implicated in one-third of cancer deaths and in a large percentage of heart attacks.

BUILDING FROM THE BOTTOM

The Food Guide Pyramid is built on the foundation that eating right means eating a wide variety of foods in moderation every day. There are no bad foods, only bad eating habits. In fact, health experts agree that the more you know about nutrition, the better your eating habits will be and the greater your food choices, including an occasional hot fudge sundae or homemade chocolate chip cookie.

Within the pyramid, placement of some foods has caused controversy. For instance, legumes (dried beans and peas) are low in fat and high in complex carbohydrates, yet they are found near the top of the pyramid, indicating they should be eaten in limited amounts. Legumes are placed with the animal proteins not because they should be restricted but because the nutrient composition of legumes is similar to that of other proteins, making them a suitable substitute for meat, poultry, or fish. Keep this in mind when choosing a protein source, and include dried beans and peas often as a main part of the meal.

SIZING UP A SERVING

Savvy cooks know that to serve a balanced, nutritious diet from the specified food groups, you have to know how much of each food to serve. The serving sizes listed in the chart below are guidelines, but also keep in mind these caveats:
• Count your serving size as more than one serving if you eat a significantly larger portion than the suggested serving size.
• Use the same serving size for children age six or older as you would for an adult.
• Count two-thirds of the adult serving size as one serving for children ages two to five.
• Ask your physician or a registered dietition for advice on feeding children under two. Fat should not be restricted in their diets.

HOW MUCH IS A SERVING?

BREAD, CEREAL, RICE, AND PASTA
1 slice bread
1 ounce ready-to-eat cereal
½ cup cooked cereal, rice, or pasta

VEGETABLES
1 cup raw, leafy vegetables or
½ cup other vegetables (cooked or raw)
¾ cup vegetable juice

FRUIT
1 medium apple, banana, or orange
½ cup chopped cooked or canned fruit
¾ cup fruit juice

MILK, YOGURT, AND CHEESE
1 cup milk or yogurt
1½ ounces natural cheese
2 ounces process cheese

MEAT
2 to 3 ounces cooked lean meat, fish, or poultry
½ cup cooked dried beans, 1 egg, or
2 tablespoons peanut butter counts
as 1 ounce of lean meat

GETTING A FIX ON FATS

Reducing your fat intake to 30 percent or less of total daily calories can help lower your risk of heart disease and certain cancers. That's what the government's Dietary Guidelines advocate, and major health advisory groups such as the American Heart Association, the American Cancer Society, and the National Academy of Sciences concur.

Low-fat doesn't mean no fat, however. Our bodies need some fat to survive. Positive functions of fat include the following:

• carrying and storing the fat-soluble vitamins (A, D, E, and K) in the body
• helping maintain the function of cell membranes
• cushioning and protecting vital organs
• maintaining hormonal balance

Just remember that saturated fats like those found in red meat, whole milk dairy products, and palm and coconut oils are the main dietary culprits in raising blood cholesterol. Therefore, they should be eaten sparingly.

Monounsaturated fats such as olive oil, canola oil, and peanut oil and polyunsaturated fats such as corn oil, safflower oil, and sesame oils are the preferred choices. Keep in mind, however, that eating too much fat of any kind can be unhealthy. Saturated fats should constitute no more than 10 percent of daily calories or one-third of your total fat calories, and polyunsaturated fats also should not exceed 10 percent. The remainder of fat calories should come from monounsaturated sources.

Reducing total fat intake typically will lower saturated fat intake. Several studies have shown that even a modest low-fat diet—one that supplies 30 percent of calories from fat—can reduce blood cholesterol levels by about 10 percent. This translates into a 20 percent drop in heart disease risk.

Unfortunately, many people misinterpret the 30 percent fat guideline and try to apply it to every food eaten. One out of five people surveyed in a 1991 Gallup poll mistakenly believed that every single food eaten should be less than 30 percent in terms of fat calories. If this were true, many foods that fit into a well-balanced eating plan would be excluded, including oil and margarine (100 percent of calories from fat), regular and low-calorie salad dressings (75 to 100 percent of calories from fat), and salmon (36 percent of calories from fat). Faced with this misinterpretation, it's no wonder that more than half of American adults are doing less than they could to eat a well-balanced, nutritious low-fat diet.

ESTABLISHING A FAT BUDGET

Applying this numerical advice to actual foods isn't always easy. That's why establishing a fat budget is helpful. Your budget should focus on grams of fat instead of counting calories and calculating what percent of these calories comes from fat. *Cooking Light* recipes and commercial food products list grams of fat per serving, so you can consume your budget however you choose, staying within your daily allowance. This way, no one food has to have 30 percent or less of its calories from fat, but the day's fat intake will balance to 30 percent of the calories if you stay within your limits.

To determine your budget, refer to page 17 for calculating grams of fat or refer to the chart on page 82 for a simple listing of fat grams.

LOOKING TO A FAT-FREE FUTURE

Following the pyramid's recommendations isn't difficult. The advent of reduced-fat and fat-free foods means that heart-healthy grocery shopping has never been easier. From 1981 to 1992, the number of reduced-fat, low-fat, and fat-free products introduced into supermarkets rose from 38 to 1,257—an increase of 3,300 percent! Currently, two out of three adults eat reduced-fat or low-fat products, according to the Calorie Control Council. The best news is that manufacturers are responding to consumer demand by continuing to develop new products.

There's hope for the future, too. According to recent surveys, children recognize the importance of eating lots of fruits, vegetables, and whole grains. They also recognize that it's all right to eat foods such as cakes, cookies, and chips, but not in abundance. Conclusions based on these surveys indicate that children, even those as young as six years old, have a grasp of basic nutrition: Balance, variety, and moderation are the keys to a healthful diet.

Computing Nutrition

Your Daily Needs

To estimate your daily calorie requirement, multiply your current weight by 15. Remember that this is only a rough guide because calorie requirements vary according to age, body size, and level of activity. If a change of weight is desired, add or subtract 500 calories per day to allow for weight gain or loss of 1 pound a week. However, a diet of less than 1,200 calories a day is not recommended unless medically supervised. For more information concerning your requirements, consult a registered dietitian.

Implement the *Cooking Light* 50-20-30 guidelines (page 30) by calculating the amount of carbohydrate, protein, and fat needed for optimal health. Multiply your calorie requirement by the percentages 50, 20, and 30 for the number of calories to be provided by each nutrient. Divide the carbohydrate and protein calories by 4 (4 calories per gram) and the fat by 9 (9 calories per gram) to determine how many grams of each nutrient you need.

For example, here's how to calculate the distribution for a 2,000-calorie diet:

50% carbohydrate = 2,000 calories x .50 = 1,000 calories ÷ 4 = 250 grams carbohydrate

20% protein = 2,000 x .20 = 400 calories ÷ 4 = 100 grams protein

30% fat = 2,000 x .30 = 600 calories ÷ 9 = 67 grams fat

Therefore, for a person eating 2,000 calories a day, at least 1,000 calories should be from carbohydrate. No more than 400 calories should be from protein, and no more than 600 calories should be from fat.

Every Recipe Analyzed

Calories and a nutrient breakdown per serving accompany every recipe. The nutrients listed include grams of protein, fat, saturated fat, carbohydrate, and fiber, along with milligrams of cholesterol, iron, sodium, and calcium.

When planning meals, refer to the daily amounts of nutrients listed below to make the most of the values that follow *Cooking Light* recipes. The amounts listed for fiber, sodium, and cholesterol are suggested daily intakes; the amounts of iron and calcium are the Recommended Dietary Allowances (RDAs) for these nutrients:

Fiber	25 to 35 grams
Iron	15 milligrams
Calcium	800 milligrams
Sodium	3,300 milligrams or less
Cholesterol	300 milligrams or less

Determining Calorie Percentages

Use *Cooking Light* nutrient breakdowns to calculate the percentage of calories contributed by carbohydrate, protein, and fat. Let's say you are looking at the recipe for Tamale Pie (complete recipe on page 158), and you want to determine the percentage of fat in the recipe.

First, find in the analysis the number of grams of fat per serving which is 8.7 grams for this recipe. To find the percentage of calories from fat, multiply grams of fat by 9 (the number of calories per gram of fat) to get fat calories per serving. Then divide this number by the calories per serving. Fat contributes 23 percent of the calories.

Tamale Pie

Per Serving: PROTEIN 25.6g FAT 8.7g (Saturated Fat 3.0g)
CARBOHYDRATE 40.8g FIBER 4.9g CHOLESTEROL 48mg
IRON 4.7mg SODIUM 445mg CALCIUM 105mg

To calculate the calories contributed by carbohydrate and protein, multiply grams of carbohydrate or protein per serving by 4 (the number of calories per gram of carbohydrate or protein). Divide the quantity by total calories.

Meeting the 50-20-30 Guidelines

Not all recipes will fall so neatly within the guidelines. When this occurs, combine these foods with others to meet the recommended percentages: more than 50 percent carbohydrate, about 20 percent protein, and no more than 30 percent fat. Saturated fat is part of the total fat content and should be no more than one-third of the daily fat grams. The goal is to achieve the recommended balance of nutrients on a daily basis, taking into consideration three meals and a snack.

How the Recipes Are Analyzed

The recipes are developed for people interested in lowering their intake of calories, fat, saturated fat, cholesterol, and/or sodium to maintain healthy eating patterns. If you are following a medically prescribed diet, consult a registered dietitian to see how *Cooking Light* recipes can fit into your specific meal plan.

The calorie and nutrient breakdown of each recipe is derived from computer analysis, based primarily on information from the U.S. Department of Agriculture. The nutrient values are as accurate as possible and are based on these assumptions:

• All nutrient breakdowns are listed per serving.
• All meats are trimmed of fat and skin before cooking.
• When a range is given for an ingredient (for example, 3 to 3½ cups flour), the lesser amount is calculated.
• A percentage of alcohol calories evaporates when heated, and this reduction is reflected in the calculations.
• When a marinade is used, only the amount of marinade absorbed or used (not discarded) is calculated.
• Garnishes and optional ingredients are not calculated.
• Fruits and vegetables listed in the ingredients are not peeled unless specified.

Exercise—The Perfect Partner

By now, the benefits of exercise are well known. You can recite them without blinking an eye: It strengthens your heart and lungs, improves circulation, reduces your chance of heart attack and stroke, reduces obesity and blood pressure, boosts your metabolic rate, improves muscle tone, helps lower your cholesterol, and helps relieve stress and tension.

Exercise sounds great, and it is. So why do you find it hard to begin and even harder to stick with an exercise program? Perhaps because you believe, mistakenly, that it's all or nothing—run marathons at daybreak, cycle up Mount Everest, do aerobics until you drop, or do nothing.

The U.S. Public Health Service concludes that fewer than 20 percent of adults get enough regular exercise to have a positive impact on cardiovascular health. Forty percent exercise only occasionally; another 40 percent are sedentary. And, of the adults who do start an exercise program, more than half drop out in less than a year.

Armed with recent findings that even mild physical activity can significantly improve health, the Centers for Disease Control and Prevention, the American College of Sports Medicine, the American Heart Association, and other scientific groups now declare that any amount of exercise is better than none. This concept veers away from the traditional dictum that mandates continuous aerobic activity for at least 30 minutes three times a week at an intensity sufficient to make the heart beat at 50 to 75 percent of its maximum rate.

Although you must exercise at this level to attain peak fitness, numerous long-term studies show there's no absolute level of exercise that you must achieve to reduce health risks. Even moderate daily activities such as leisure walking, yard work, and taking the stairs instead of the elevator can improve your health and mental attitude.

The best news is that it's never too late to begin exercising. Even men and women as old as 90 who start a weight-training program increase both the size and strength of their muscles, allowing them to walk a little faster, take longer strides, and get in and out of chairs more easily.

A SURE WAY TO FITNESS

Debate continues on how much activity it takes to be healthy versus fit, but experts do agree on two things: You've got to get up to shape up, and you should choose an exercise you like—one that's fun for you. Walking is fast becoming the exercise of choice. In fact, it's estimated that more than 67 million men and women walk regularly.

Walking is easy, safe, inexpensive, and benefits everyone, regardless of age. It's also relaxing yet invigorating and requires little athletic skill. And you don't have to join a club, wear special exercise clothes, or buy equipment other than sturdy, comfortable shoes. You can walk with friends, take the dog for a stroll, or go it alone. In addition, the ever-increasing number of shopping malls has made walking easier than ever—it's safe, convenient, protected from the elements, and entertaining.

BEFORE YOU BEGIN

Before you get started, congratulate yourself on your commitment to walk. Tell yourself you're going to give it a good try and stick with the program. Keep in mind as you begin that you're in no hurry. You're walking for lifetime health, not overnight results. Forget the stopwatch, heart rate monitor, walking form, and comparisons to friends. Your goal is personal health and fitness.

If you're over age 40 and new to exercising, check with your physician first. No matter what your age, it's smart to get a checkup if you are noticeably overweight, have a history of heart disease, or if you smoke, have high blood pressure, or have high cholesterol levels.

READY, SET, WALK

Every exercise program should begin with warm-up exercises to increase respiration, circulation, and body temperature. A good warm-up also increases flexibility by stretching muscles, tendons, and connective tissues, thereby reducing your risk of injury.

Now you're ready to go! Aim for 30 uninterrupted minutes of walking at least three times a week. Depending on your age and how active you've been, you may want to start with a 10-minute walk. Walk at a comfortable but steady pace, brisk enough to make your heart beat faster. Slow down if you are breathing too hard. You should be able to easily carry on a conversation while exercising. If you can't, ease up and walk more slowly.

Walk with your head erect, back straight, and abdomen flat. Keep your knees slightly bent. Swing your arms freely at your sides. In the beginning, limit your walks to level areas, avoiding steep hills. You'll be able to increase your time and pace gradually as your body adapts to exercise.

As you walk, check your pulse rate periodically to see whether you are exercising within your target zone. See page 65 for instructions on how to check your heart rate.

After walking, allow your body a few minutes to cool down. Don't stand still or lie down; walk around to let your body readjust gradually as your heart rate and blood pressure return to normal.

KEEP MOVING

If you stop exercising on a regular basis, the beneficial health effects rapidly disappear. As with eating habits, exercise should be a lifetime commitment. Following are tips to stay motivated, increase your level of activity, and improve the quality of your life in years to come:

• Pick an activity you enjoy, one that is suited to your needs and can be done year-round.

• Consider varying your workouts as you increase your activity level. Walk one day and jog another, ride either a stationary or regular bicycle, swim, or use a stair-climber. By varying workouts, you won't get bored as quickly; therefore, you'll be more likely to stay with a program longer.

• Go slowly. If you've been inactive for 20 years, it may be several months before you can walk two miles briskly. Stay with it! You'll have the confidence of knowing you're getting healthier.

• Exercise regularly. Schedule an exercise appointment with yourself and keep it. Consider keeping a diary of the dates, times, distance, and duration of each exercise session. You'll be able to see at a glance the progress you've made.

• Set realistic goals. Don't expect dramatic changes overnight. If your long-term goal is to walk a mile, make your short-term goal to walk a quarter-mile.

Perhaps the best advice for staying motivated is to discuss your exercise program and goals with family and friends. Their encouragement, confidence, and involvement may be just what you need to keep going. In fact, family exercise is an excellent way to spend time together, and the mutual support helps everyone make a long-term commitment to fitness and health.

In short, you need to think fit to be fit. Get on your feet and move. Find something you like to do and do it often. Remember, it's never too late to take charge of your health. By exercising regularly, you'll be stepping into a healthier life.

BEGINNING A WALKING PROGRAM

If you're ready to start walking, you may want to begin with the walking program suggested below. Check your pulse periodically to see whether you are exercising within your target zone. As you get more in shape, try exercising within the upper range of your target heart zone. Remember that your goal is to continue getting the benefits you seek while enjoying your activity.

Week	Target Zone Exercising	Total Time in Minutes (warm up, target zone exercising, and cool down)
1	Walk briskly 5 minutes	15 minutes
2	Walk briskly 7 minutes	17 minutes
3	Walk briskly 9 minutes	19 minutes
4	Walk briskly 11 minutes	21 minutes
5	Walk briskly 13 minutes	23 minutes
6	Walk briskly 15 minutes	25 minutes
7	Walk briskly 18 minutes	28 minutes
8	Walk briskly 20 minutes	30 minutes
9	Walk briskly 23 minutes	33 minutes
10	Walk briskly 26 minutes	36 minutes
11	Walk briskly 28 minutes	38 minutes
12	Walk briskly 30 minutes	40 minutes

Let's Talk Technique

Exercise plays an integral part in maintaining good health. Regular exercise not only increases physical strength and stamina but also can improve one's overall sense of well-being. Luckily, exercise can be done indoors, eliminating the need to plan around inclement weather.

Exercising indoors on equipment such as a stationary bicycle, treadmill, or stair stepper can provide an excellent cardiovascular workout. It will also tone and strengthen calves, quadriceps, hamstrings, and buttocks. If used correctly, these machines place minimal stress on the ankle, knee, and hip joints, decreasing the risk of injury to these areas.

However, exercise equipment produces positive results only if used properly. Check the photographs on these two pages for warm-up ideas and proper techniques.

Before beginning a workout on one of the machines, spend at least 3 to 5 minutes warming up. The warm-up promotes a gradual increase in respiration, circulation, and body temperature as well as stretches the muscles, tendons, and connective tissue—all of which helps reduce the risk of injury.

Strive to use one of the machines for at least 20 minutes per session. If you are beginning an exercise program, start with a 5-minute session and gradually increase the length and intensity of your workout. If you feel overly tired, dizzy, or faint, stop and rest. Next time, lower the machine's level of intensity. After working out, cool down for at least 5 minutes to allow your body to adjust gradually to the decreased physical demands.

For a complete workout program, exercise at least four times a week. Alternate use of the machines described with two days spent on strength training, such as lifting weights, with an emphasis on the upper body.

STRETCHES

Back and shoulder stretch—Place hands on legs slightly above knees. Knees should be slightly bent. Keep the center of body weight over heels. Slowly press left shoulder toward right knee while slightly pulling back right shoulder until you feel a slight stretch. Hold for 20 seconds. Repeat with opposite shoulder.

Inner-thigh stretch—Stand with feet a comfortable distance apart. Slowly bend right knee until knee is over toes (do not extend knee beyond toes). Rest hands on leg just above bent knee for support. Keep left leg straight with left foot flexed upward. Hold for 20 seconds. Repeat with opposite leg.

Quadricep and hip flexor stretch—Bring left leg forward, bending knee until knee is directly over heel. Do not bounce. Keep back straight and head aligned with spine. Support right leg on toes, keeping right leg straight. Use hands for support by resting left hand on bent knee and right hand on the ground. Hold for 20 seconds. Repeat with opposite knee.

STATIONARY BICYCLE

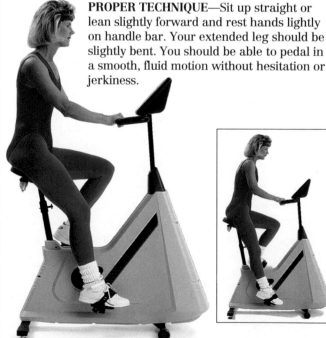

PROPER TECHNIQUE—Sit up straight or lean slightly forward and rest hands lightly on handle bar. Your extended leg should be slightly bent. You should be able to pedal in a smooth, fluid motion without hesitation or jerkiness.

Improper technique—If your extended leg is bent more than slightly, the seat position is too low. In this position, you cannot use your legs to their maximum efficiency. Your legs may also cramp more easily if they are bent too much.

Improper technique—If your extended leg is completely straightened, the seat position is too high. Check height of seat by rotating the pedals a few times. You should be able to pedal in a continuous, fluid motion without rocking from side to side. Riding with the seat too high increases strain on the knees and may cause saddle soreness.

TREADMILL

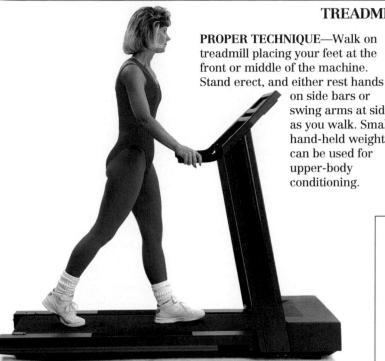

PROPER TECHNIQUE—Walk on treadmill placing your feet at the front or middle of the machine. Stand erect, and either rest hands on side bars or swing arms at sides as you walk. Small hand-held weights can be used for upper-body conditioning.

Improper technique—Do not place your feet at the end of the treadmill. You risk falling off and causing an injury. Also, you may not be able to reach the console to turn off the machine when you are finished with the workout.

Improper technique—If you are leaning too far forward and feel the need to clutch the side bars, the level of intensity is too high. You will tire easily this way and receive a poor workout. Decrease the level of intensity to one that is more comfortable.

STAIR STEPPER

Improper technique—Do not support your weight by bending over and resting arms on side bars. This decreases your cardiovascular benefit. If you feel the need to lean on the machine to keep going, the level of intensity is too high. Lower the level to one that is more comfortable.

PROPER TECHNIQUE—Place feet squarely on pedals. To prevent knee strain, make sure knees do not extend past toes. Stand up straight, and rest hands on side bars.

Improper technique—Do not lock arms to support your weight. This decreases your cardiovascular benefit. If you feel the need to support your weight, the level of intensity is too high. Lower the level to one that is more comfortable. Also, do not stand on balls of feet; this increases your risk of leg injury and may cause cramping of the calf muscles.

Set Yourself Up for Success

Whether you're striving to improve your diet, spend more time exercising, or boost your self-image, it's hard to make permanent lifestyle changes—unless you believe you can do it. Positive "self-talk" helps keep you motivated and helps you stay on course.

So beginning today, substitute "can" for "can't." Tell yourself, "I can do it!" Say it with enthusiasm, and say it often:

• "I *can* manage my weight without depriving myself."
• "I *can* make time for an exercise I enjoy."
• "I *can* learn to control my reaction to stress."
• "I *can* help reduce my chances of developing heart disease, diabetes, stroke, and cancer by adopting healthy eating and lifestyle habits."

Focus on what you can do—then do it. You can take charge of your life and health. Use the following information to motivate you to achieve your health and personal goals.

IT'S ALL IN YOUR MIND

Research shows that determination to make healthy lifestyle changes can help you achieve your goals. And a study of people with coronary artery disease helps confirm that being motivated to improve your health can have a significant, positive influence on your progress.

In the study, a group of people with coronary heart disease received low-fat diet and exercise instructions to slow the progression of plaque formation in their arteries. Some people were assigned regular exercise plans along with nutrition classes to encourage and reinforce lifestyle changes. Others were encouraged only once to join a local exercise group and to see their doctor regularly. The group that received ongoing instruction, encouragement, and reinforcement had slower narrowing of the coronary arteries than the group that did not. Those in the study who made considerable reductions in their fat intake, exercised regularly, and learned to handle stress actually reversed blockage in their coronary arteries. The bottom line: People with coronary artery disease can make a difference in their long-term health by losing weight, exercising regularly, and eliminating foods rich in saturated fats and cholesterol. But the key to success, researchers feel, is the motivation to begin and the determination to continue.

NOW'S THE TIME

Procrastination doesn't pay off. Start an exercise program today because the sooner you begin to exercise regularly, the sooner your health and quality of life will improve. Although scientists have recently reported that exercise doesn't add more than one and one-half years to life span, don't let this news discourage you from exercising. They're missing the point: It's not always how long you live, but *how you live* long.

Exercise does help you feel better, look better, and function better for longer. It provides vim and vigor, reduces your chances of living your elder years crippled by heart disease or stroke, and extends your active years by building self-esteem and self-reliance. And recent studies show that daily activities such as walking and yard work help reduce your risk of heart disease.

A FUNNY THING HAPPENED ON THE WAY TO GOOD HEALTH

Laugh your way to good health. Laughter, it appears, does more for us than ease our troubles, unclutter our minds, and boost our spirits. Humor, scientists say, is one reason why some people recover from illness faster than others and are healthier in general.

Experts in the field of gelotology, the study of humor and its effects on the body, say that a good laugh improves circulation and exercises the heart. At the same time, the respiratory and muscular systems get a mini-workout, which boosts the delivery of oxygen to body tissue. Laughing, experts say, enhances mental activity such as memory and stimulates the body's immune system, helping it fight infection.

In contrast, anger and hostility can damage your health. Researchers studying the correlation of Type A personalities and the risk of heart disease say that negative traits also raise your cholesterol level. But of all the traits the classic Type A personality possesses—hostility, impatience, immersion in work, and fierce competitiveness—it's the hostility that puts them most at risk for heart disease.

One way to counteract the negative health effects of anger and hostility, along with learning to deal more constructively with life's daily stressors, is to eat a diet low in fat. Researchers in Oregon compared the diets and mental health of more than 300 people in a five-year study known as the Family Heart Study. Their conclusion? People who eat a low-fat diet have "the blues" (depression) less often and feel less anger (aggressive hostility). Although more studies are needed, scientists speculate that eating a healthy diet (one low in fat and high in fruits and vegetables) helps people feel more in control of their lives, which leads to greater self-esteem and well-being. Learning to take control of your life enhances your ability to cope more effectively with life's daily stresses and strains.

To sum it up, the most important thing to remember is that you can take responsibility for your health. Act now. If you smoke, stop. Ask others not to smoke around you. If you need to lose a few pounds, cut back on sweets and fats and eat more fruits and vegetables. Drink alcohol moderately, if at all. Get enough sleep. De-stress your life. Become more sociable and extend your circle of friends. Get up and do something you enjoy. Find the humor in life. Smile. Laugh. Lighten up.

Continue to discover ways you can improve your health and your feeling of self-esteem, permanently. But be patient; change rarely occurs overnight. Try selecting just one lifestyle change and let it become a habit before adding another. Good health is up to you and you can achieve it!

TOBACCO TABOO

Cigarette smoking leads the pack when it comes to bad habits that can harm your health. With every puff, smokers increase their risk of developing heart disease, stroke, emphysema, and cancer. Smoking is responsible for one in every five deaths annually. Yet, amazingly, 50 million Americans continue to smoke.

And they're affecting others too. Close to 55,000 nonsmoking Americans die each year from the effects of passive smoking: close to 4,000 from lung cancer; up to 17,000 from other cancers; and 32,000 to 35,000 from heart disease.

But nonsmokers made headway when the U.S. Environmental Protection Agency (EPA) released results of a four-year study. The report states that secondhand smoke, or passive smoking, has a serious and substantial health impact on nonsmokers.

Technically known as environmental tobacco smoke, secondhand smoke has conclusively been branded a cancer-causing agent by the EPA. The only sure way to protect nonsmokers from secondhand smoke, says the American Heart Association, is to eliminate smoking from areas that smokers share with nonsmokers.

Although secondhand smoke endangers everyone, infants and children suffer the most. Children who live with a smoker are more likely to have colds, bronchitis, and pneumonia, especially during the first two years of life. They also tend to develop chronic coughs and experience more ear infections and allergic reactions than do children who live in a smoke-free home.

Protect yourself and your children from secondhand smoke:
• Let family, friends, coworkers, and others know that you mind if they smoke. Ask visitors not to smoke in your home.
• Request seating in the nonsmoking sections of restaurants and public transportation.
• Be certain your children's schools and child-care facilities are smoke-free.
• Support legislation to restrict smoking or to set up smoke-free areas in public places and at the workplace.
• Contact your local American Cancer Society, American Lung Association, or other health agencies and volunteer your efforts to reduce smoking in your community.

The *Cooking Light* Kitchen

Is your recipe file collecting dust because the recipes in it are not in keeping with today's lighter guidelines? Well, don't despair. With a few simple modifications, most of your favorite standbys can be dusted off and pared down to meet current nutrition standards without sacrificing good taste.

We've modified a scalloped corn recipe to show how easily substitutions can be made. (See page 215 for the complete recipe for Garden Scalloped Corn.) Using evaporated skimmed milk to replace the half-and-half provides the same rich flavor without adding any cholesterol and only minimal fat (1 gram) to the recipe.

To further reduce the fat and cholesterol, use egg substitute instead of whole eggs. Also, replace the regular Cheddar cheese with 50% less-fat Cheddar cheese, which melts nicely. The calorie, fat, and cholesterol savings for our light version of Garden Scalloped Corn are 79 calories, 5.9 grams of fat (3.2 grams of saturated fat), and 87 milligrams of cholesterol per serving.

The sodium is also reduced in the lightened version by using no-salt-added cream-style corn and unsalted crackers. Using these items as replacements for their traditional counterparts results in a savings of 226 milligrams of sodium per serving.

Try your hand at modifying some other family favorites. You may be surprised at how easy and tasty your changes can be.

GARDEN SCALLOPED CORN

Cooking Light

Calories per Serving: 126
Calories from Fat: 22%

2 (16½-ounce) cans no-salt-added cream-style corn
⅔ cup crushed unsalted crackers
⅔ cup chopped green pepper
⅔ cup finely shredded carrot
½ cup chopped celery
¼ cup plus 2 tablespoons sliced green onions
1 (4-ounce) jar diced pimiento, drained
1 cup frozen egg substitute, thawed
⅓ cup evaporated skimmed milk
2 tablespoons reduced-calorie margarine
1 teaspoon sugar
½ teaspoon salt
½ teaspoon hot sauce
Vegetable cooking spray
½ cup (2 ounces) shredded 50% less-fat Cheddar
   cheese
½ teaspoon paprika

Per Serving: PROTEIN 5.9g FAT 3.1g (Saturated Fat 0.8g)
CARBOHYDRATE 21.5g FIBER 1.6g CHOLESTEROL 3mg
IRON 1.2mg SODIUM 239mg CALCIUM 65mg

Traditional

Calories per Serving: 205
Calories from Fat: 40%

3½ cups frozen whole kernel corn, thawed
2 (17-ounce) cans cream-style corn
½ cup half-and-half
½ cup crushed round buttery crackers
½ cup chopped onion
4 eggs, beaten
1 (4-ounce) jar diced pimiento, drained
½ teaspoon salt
½ teaspoon pepper
¾ cup (3 ounces) Cheddar cheese
2 tablespoons butter or margarine

Per Serving: PROTEIN 7.0g FAT 9.0g (Saturated Fat 4.0g)
CARBOHYDRATE 27.6g FIBER 2.1g CHOLESTEROL 90mg
IRON 1.1mg SODIUM 465mg CALCIUM 83mg

KEEP IT LIGHT AND KEEP THE FLAVOR

Fat-Off Ladle—The raised rim, which has small slots around it, makes this ladle useful for removing fat from meat-, fish-, or poultry-based soups and stews. Lower the ladle into the broth and allow the fat that rises to the top to flow through the slots in the rim and into the bowl of the ladle. When the ladle is full, remove it from the broth and discard the fat that has collected. Repeat the procedure until all the visible fat is removed. A fat-off ladle can be used when preparing Chicken Posole (page 229).

Steaming Basket—There are several varieties of steaming baskets, ranging from elaborate stackable Chinese steaming baskets to folding baskets that fit into standard saucepans. A steaming basket suspends food over boiling water, allowing steam heat to circulate around the food. After placing food in the basket, cover tightly to retain the heat. Steaming minimizes vitamin and mineral loss and retains the flavor and texture of foods. Use a steamer when preparing Steamed Salmon with Caramelized Onions (page 124).

Grill—To cook on a grill, place the food on a rack over the heat source, which can be charcoal, gas, or an electric unit. The temperature is regulated by positioning the rack at different distances from the heat source. Grilling requires no fat; coating the grill rack with vegetable cooking spray keeps foods from sticking without adding many calories. Grilling meat, fish, or poultry allows the fat to drip away from the food. Marinating and basting lean cuts of meat while grilling helps keep them from drying out. Use a grill to prepare Easy Lamb Chops Jalapeño (page 164).

Wok—The bottom of this wide, bowl-shaped pan is either rounded for cooking over a gas flame or flat for use on an electric range. Electric woks with non-stick surfaces are also available. Woks emit intense, even heat that allows foods to be cooked quickly using minimal amounts of oil. Woks with non-stick surfaces often do not require any oil to be added. Foods to be cooked in a wok are usually cut into small pieces and are tossed gently during cooking to prevent sticking and promote even cooking. A wok can be used to cook Vegetable Stir-Fry (page 219).

Pressure Cooker—The airtight lid of this pot locks into place, trapping steam to build up pressure. A valve on the lid regulates the pressure. The steam heat and the pressure create high temperatures that often cook foods in half the time it takes conventionally. Pressure cooking retains flavor and nutrients and is useful for foods that require long, moist-heat cooking such as soups, stews, and less tender cuts of meat. Use a pressure cooker to cook lean cuts of meat for fork-tender results.

Yogurt Cheesemaker—The funnel shape of this piece of equipment results in thickened yogurt because it allows liquid to drain. To use, spoon yogurt into the funnel and place in a measuring cup. Cover with plastic wrap, and refrigerate overnight. After draining, the yogurt will be of a creamy consistency suitable for dips and spreads. Yogurt cheese is an excellent alternative for cream cheese or sour cream. A yogurt cheesemaker can be used for Chicken Curry in Phyllo Baskets (page 101).

What's New in the Marketplace?

More Functional Food Labeling

It took an act of Congress, but consumers have won the battle to make food labels more accurate, complete, and useful.

The Nutrition Labeling and Education Act (NLEA) passed by Congress in 1990 gave the legal okay for a new system of food labeling that had been proposed by the FDA. The mission was simple: to devise labels for processed foods that would help people follow more healthful diets and to encourage food companies to improve the nutritional qualities of their products.

Although complying with these new regulations may cost food manufacturers as much as $2.3 billion over the next 20 years, the savings in terms of public health should far exceed the costs. Potential health benefits include decreased rates of heart disease, cancer, osteoporosis, obesity, and high blood pressure.

COMPLIANCE MANDATORY

All manufacturers of processed foods must comply with the new labeling requirements by May 1994, but many have already made the change.

Some foods are exempt from the new labeling requirements, including unprocessed meat and poultry, coffee, tea, most spices, small packages (generally those no larger than a roll of LifeSavers®), restaurant food, and food produced by small businesses. However, manufacturers of these foods can include nutritional information on their product labels as long as the information complies with the new labeling regulations.

The USDA, which regulates meat and poultry labeling, has agreed to follow the FDA's labeling format as closely as possible for processed meat and poultry products. This is great news for consumers, who, for example, might have faced one label format for meat lasagna and another for cheese lasagna. Consumers will also benefit from voluntary point-of-purchase information, provided primarily by grocers, for the 20 most frequently eaten fresh fruits, vegetables, and fish.

LABEL MAKEOVER

The look and content of food labels have changed, beginning with the title. "Nutrition Facts" replaces "Nutrition Information Per Serving," signaling consumers that the label meets the new regulations.

Savvy shoppers will appreciate having more information to help them make wise food choices. Nutritional information will include standard serving sizes, nutrients, daily values, and health and nutrient claims. The ingredient panel has also been updated.

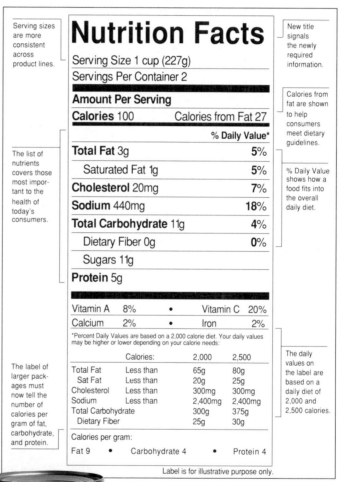

Nutrition Facts

Serving sizes are more consistent across product lines.

Serving Size 1 cup (227g)
Servings Per Container 2

Amount Per Serving

Calories 100   Calories from Fat 27

New title signals the newly required information.

Calories from fat are shown to help consumers meet dietary guidelines.

	% Daily Value*
Total Fat 3g	5%
Saturated Fat 1g	5%
Cholesterol 20mg	7%
Sodium 440mg	18%
Total Carbohydrate 11g	4%
Dietary Fiber 0g	0%
Sugars 11g	
Protein 5g	

The list of nutrients covers those most important to the health of today's consumers.

% Daily Value shows how a food fits into the overall daily diet.

Vitamin A	8%	•	Vitamin C	20%
Calcium	2%	•	Iron	2%

*Percent Daily Values are based on a 2,000 calorie diet. Your daily values may be higher or lower depending on your calorie needs:

	Calories:	2,000	2,500
Total Fat	Less than	65g	80g
Sat Fat	Less than	20g	25g
Cholesterol	Less than	300mg	300mg
Sodium	Less than	2,400mg	2,400mg
Total Carbohydrate		300g	375g
Dietary Fiber		25g	30g

The label of larger packages must now tell the number of calories per gram of fat, carbohydrate, and protein.

The daily values on the label are based on a daily diet of 2,000 and 2,500 calories.

Calories per gram:

Fat 9   •   Carbohydrate 4   •   Protein 4

Label is for illustrative purpose only.

Serving Sizes. To help consumers understand and compare nutrition listings, serving sizes will be consistent for all products and will reflect the amounts of food that most people actually eat. Previously, serving size was left to the discretion of the food manufacturer, and shoppers had to be alert to unrealistic portion sizes.

The NLEA defines serving size as the amount of food customarily eaten at one time by the average person over four years of age. This information will appear on the label in both common household measure and metric measure such as ½ cup (114 grams). The FDA has established a list of 139 food-product categories for manufacturers to use to specify the standard serving size for a given food.

Single-serving containers (packaged food intended to be eaten as one serving) will be analyzed as a single serving even if the amount in the container is greater than the reference amount for that food. For example, the standard serving size for a soft drink is 8 ounces (240 milliliters). However, a 12-ounce can (360 milliliters) is usually consumed as a single serving, so its nutrient content will be based on the contents of the entire can. Any nutrient claims such as "low sodium" also would be based on the contents of the entire can.

List of Nutrients. To reflect consumers' health concerns of the 1990s and the priority of current dietary recommendations, the following information per average serving must appear on updated food labels:
- calories
- calories derived from fat
- total fat
- saturated fat
- cholesterol
- sodium
- total carbohydrate
- dietary fiber
- sugars
- protein
- vitamins A and C
- calcium
- iron

The listing of niacin, riboflavin, and thiamine was previously required but is now optional because of the abundance of these B-vitamins in the modern American diet. Considering current health concerns, the inclusion of saturated fat and dietary fiber will be particularly useful to health-conscious shoppers.

Saturated fat. The breakdown of saturated fat ranks in the FDA's top 10 nutrient requirements because of the proven link between saturated fat and heart disease. Although up to 30 percent of daily calories consumed should come from fat, only one-third of that, or 10 percent of daily calories, should come from saturated fat.

To illustrate, let's say a product contains 13 grams of fat with 5 grams coming from saturated fat. For a 2,000-calorie diet, that's equivalent to 20 percent of the day's fat quota of 65 grams and 25 percent of the saturated fat allotment of 20 grams a day.

Dietary fiber. By increasing the amount of fiber in your diet, researchers say you may improve your odds of warding off some types of cancer and other diseases. However, Americans fail miserably at including enough roughage in their diets. On average, Americans eat only half the recommended amount of 25 to 35 grams of fiber per day. The new labels will aid consumers in selecting more fiber-rich foods and in meeting their daily fiber goals.

Daily Values. The new labels will contain a column called Percent Daily Value that will help determine how a product fits into your daily diet. (See label on page 26.)

This column of percentages gives an estimate of how much a given product supplies toward your daily goal for the nutrients listed. This column also indicates how close you are getting to your daily limit.

The daily values, which are listed at the bottom of the label, are calculated for a 2,000-calorie diet. For large men or vigorously active people, the figures for a 2,500-calorie diet are included. The calculations are based on:
- fat—30 percent of calories
- saturated fat—10 percent of calories
- carbohydrate—60 percent of calories
- protein— 10 percent of calories
- fiber—11.5 grams of fiber per 1,000 calories

The amounts for sodium (2,400 milligrams) and for cholesterol (300 grams) are the same no matter how many calories you eat. Daily values for vitamins and minerals are not based on a specific caloric intake either.

For those eating significantly less than or more than 2,000 calories, this information should be used as a guide to indicate foods rich in a certain nutrient or high in fat, for example, instead of as exact amounts to consume.

The daily values will also help you comparison shop. For instance, if a serving of Brand A's frozen chicken casserole has a Percent Daily Value of 32 for total fat, compared to Brand B's Percent Daily Value of 44, Brand A is the better choice for a low-fat diet.

Health Claims. To help consumers separate fact from fiction, only the following claims for nutrient-disease relationships may be made by food manufacturers:

- fat and cancer risk
- saturated fat and cholesterol and heart disease risk
- soluble fiber (found in fruits, vegetables, and grains) and heart disease risk
- fiber (found in fruits, vegetables, and grain products) and cancer risk
- foods containing vitamins A and C (fruits and vegetables) and cancer risk
- calcium and osteoporosis risk
- sodium and risk of high blood pressure

Manufacturers must follow rigid rules, however, before issuing health claims for any of their products. Just because a food is calcium-rich doesn't mean it can be advertised as reducing the risk of osteoporosis; the calcium must also be in a form that is easily absorbed. Also, food producers are permitted only to say a food "may" or "might" reduce the risk of disease, and they must state that other factors such as exercise may play a role in disease prevention.

NUTRIENT CLAIM DEFINITIONS

The NLEA has clarified manufacturers' advertising claims. To use various nutrient content statements, the product must meet exact standards. Here's a sampling of claims and their new definitions:

Free—can refer to a product containing only trivial amounts of a nutrient, which makes the product unlikely to have a physiological effect. For example, "calorie-free" means fewer than 5 calories per serving, and "sugar-free" and "fat-free" both mean less than 0.5 grams per serving.

Light—can describe a product containing one-third fewer calories or half the fat of a comparable food. It can also mean that the sodium content of a low-calorie, low-fat food has been reduced at least 50 percent.

"Light" can still be used to describe properties such as a food's color or texture as long as the label explains the intent—"light brown sugar" or "light and fluffy," for example.

Good Source—means that one serving of a food contains 10 to 19 percent of the Daily Value for a particular nutrient.

Low—may be used on foods that could be eaten frequently without exceeding dietary guidelines. Per serving and per 100 grams (a little less than ½ cup) of food, these amounts are defined as:

low fat—3 grams or less per serving.

low saturated fat—1 gram or less per serving.

low sodium—less than 140 milligrams per serving.

low cholesterol—less than 20 milligrams per serving.

low calorie—40 calories or less per serving.

Percent Fat Free—must refer to a low-fat or fat-free product. The

claim must accurately reflect the amount of fat present in 100 grams of the food. For a food containing 2.5 grams fat per 50 grams of the food, the claim must be "95 percent fat free."

Lean and Extra Lean—can be used to describe the fat content of meat, poultry, seafood, and game.

lean—less than 10 grams fat, less than 4 grams saturated fat, and less than 95 milligrams cholesterol per serving and per 100 grams.

extra lean—less than 5 grams fat, less than 2 grams saturated fat, and less than 95 milligrams cholesterol per serving and per 100 grams.

Fresh—can be used on raw food that has never been frozen or heated and has no preservatives.

Ingredients. Manufacturers will still be required to list ingredients in descending order by weight, but descriptions of ingredients will now be more specific. Here are a few examples: All color additives must be listed individually instead of being grouped under the term "colors"; caseinate must be identified as a milk derivative when used in foods that claim to be nondairy, such as coffee whiteners; and protein hydrolysates must be listed by name instead of merely being called "flavors" or "flavor enhancers." These specific listings will help people who may be allergic to these ingredients avoid foods that contain them.

Certain common foods such as mayonnaise and bread that are made following "standard" recipes previously were exempt from having to list all ingredients. However, most consumers don't know what these foods are made of, so the FDA is requiring a full ingredient listing on them.

Consumers also will be getting more information about the actual amount of juice in a juice beverage. Plus, when a product contains several types of juices and the predominantly named juice is present in only small amounts, the product's name must state that the beverage is flavored with that juice or state the amount of the juice within 5 percent; for example, "raspberry-flavored juice blend" or "juice blend, 2 to 7 percent raspberry juice."

Exercise Equipment— Gadgets to Gizmos

Americans love gadgets, and sporting goods manufacturers are satisfying the appetites of gizmo-hungry exercise enthusiasts. Following is a sampling of futuristic equipment that's available today:

• **Cross-country, video-interactive simulator.** Pop in a video of a cross-country skier on a scenic trail, and the ski machine will vary the workout intensity by the movements of the skier. As the video takes you up a hill, the lower-body resistance of the ski machine automatically increases to simulate uphill skiing. Conversely, the machine eases resistance when the video courses you downhill.

• **Exerlopers**™ are guaranteed to put a little spring in your step. Designed to absorb the shock of running or jogging, Exerlopers are skatelike boots that have arched springboards attached to the soles. Lace on a pair of these booties and experience the "gravity-defying" activity of loping. As your feet strike the ground, the springs collapse, bringing your feet close to the ground and then bouncing you up again. This action, claims the manufacturer, reduces skeletal shock, requires your muscles to work harder, and causes your body to burn more calories with every stride.

• And then there's the **ropeless jump rope** that helps you get the aerobic and upper-body toning and conditioning of the traditional method—without the inconvenience of a rope!

Similar in appearance to a short cane, these weighted handles (one for each hand) simulate the feel and motion of a jump rope. Workouts are tailored by adjusting the position of the weight on the handle.

Try nontraditional exercising with Exerlopers, Wave Webs, or a ropeless jump rope.

• **Wave Webs**™ make water workouts more challenging. The unusual design is what makes them work—these stretchy, nylon-blend gloves have fingers that are webbed to create greater water resistance for a more intense workout.

• The hula hoop craze that swept the country in the 1950s is recurring in the 90s as the **Twist 'N Ski**™. Combining the arm movements of skiing with twisting movements, this exercise machine is touted as a fun and easy way to trim and shape your waist, hips, and legs.

And what do experts say is the best piece of equipment you can buy? The one you're actually going to use—and keep using. When weighing cost versus benefits, remember that an exercise machine or piece of equipment you don't enjoy is likely to turn into an expensive coat rack or be tucked into a corner of the closet.

Healthy American Meals

The menu chapters reflect the growing interest in decreasing fat intake while maintaining flavor and freshness. Each menu has been carefully developed for your enjoyment, and each meets our guidelines for healthy eating: At least 50 percent of the total menu calories are derived from carbohydrate, about 20 percent are from protein, and less than 30 percent are contributed by fat. Each menu also has less than 10 percent of the calories coming from saturated fat.

Breakfast and Brunch. Wake up to a sunny start with recipes that will delight young and old alike. (Menus begin on page 34.)
- Treat your children to a special breakfast on the first day of school (page 34).
- On a leisurely weekend, please family and friends with a hearty Low-country brunch (page 40).
- When football season rolls around, fuel the home-team fans with a rib-sticking brunch before the big game (page 42).

Quick and Easy. There's no need to sacrifice flavor for convenience. These effortless menus get you in and out of the kitchen in a hurry, but they taste as though you had toiled over them all day. (Menus begin on page 46.)
- Use the make-ahead recipes in Lunch After the Workout (page 46) to keep your weekend free for rest and play.
- For a light summer meal, try Seafood Supper in a Snap (page 48).
- Make an evening special with Dinner for Your Sweetheart (page 55).

That's Entertaining. Entertaining is more than formal dining-room fare. Try your hand at entertaining in a variety of settings. (Menus begin on page 58.)
- Head outdoors for feasting and fun with Repast by the River (page 58).
- To combat the winter blues, create a midwinter paradise with Touch of the Tropics (page 63).
- Get out of the kitchen by centering a party around the grill using Satay Grill Party (page 66).

Holiday Celebrations. Celebrate throughout the year with holiday menus that satisfy the appetite but aren't laden with the excess fat and calories that often accompany holiday fare. (Menus begin on page 76.)
- New Year's Day Celebration packs in the flavor but remains true to your mealtime resolutions (page 76).
- Lightened favorites sparkle in Feast Before the Fireworks (page 83).
- Attractive, appetizing recipes won't leave guests overstuffed when you serve the Christmas open house menu (page 89).

Overleaf: *A menu of Roasted Mushroom and Fennel Salad, Crisp Rosemary-Pepper Breadsticks, Steamed Chicken Roulades with Chunky Tomato Sauce, steamed baby carrots, steamed green beans, and Sparkling Berry Cooler paints a vivid picture of the exciting menus in this section. (Menu begins on page 72.)*

Right: *Although Italian food is popular for lunch and dinner, the Italian touch can be just as appealing for breakfast. Start your day with Three-Pepper Frittata, Italian Sweet Bread, and Bountiful Fresh Fruit Cup. (Menu begins on page 38.)*

Breakfast
&
Brunch

The children will get a nutritious start to the school year with Warm Vanilla-Almond Milk, Frosty Fruit, Raisin-Bran Loaf, and Apple-Maple Spread.

First-Day-of-School Breakfast

Raisin-Bran Loaf
Apple-Maple Spread
Frosty Fruit
Warm Vanilla-Almond Milk

SERVES 4
TOTAL CALORIES PER SERVING: 412
(Calories from Fat: 19%)

Young scholars will be up to academic challenges when given a nourishing breakfast before heading off to school. That first day of classes can set the stage for good eating habits as well as good study habits.

Hearty Raisin-Bran Loaf will help tide youngsters over until lunchtime. Serve each person a slice of bread topped with 1 tablespoon of creamy Apple-Maple Spread—a tasty, reduced-fat alternative to butter or margarine. The bread can be made ahead. Just wrap the loaf tightly in plastic

wrap after it has cooled, and it will remain fresh up to 1 week.

Frosty Fruit is sure to perk up sleepyheads. Banana chunks and whole strawberries are frozen in a luscious coating of fruit-flavored yogurt, crunchy cereal, and pecans. Make these treats the night before, and freeze. Take them out of the freezer about 15 minutes before serving.

Complete this child-pleasing meal with Warm Vanilla-Almond Milk—a yummy change of pace for a breakfast beverage.

RAISIN-BRAN LOAF

2½ cups wheat bran flakes cereal, divided
½ cup hot water
3 tablespoons vegetable oil
1½ cups all-purpose flour
1 teaspoon baking powder
1 teaspoon baking soda
⅓ cup firmly packed brown sugar
½ teaspoon ground cinnamon
¼ teaspoon ground nutmeg
1 cup nonfat buttermilk
¼ cup frozen egg substitute, thawed
2 teaspoons grated orange rind
½ cup raisins
Vegetable cooking spray

Combine 1½ cups bran flakes, hot water, and oil in a small bowl; set aside.

Combine flour and next 5 ingredients in a large bowl; make a well in center of mixture. Combine buttermilk, egg substitute, and orange rind; add to dry ingredients, stirring just until dry ingredients are moistened. Stir in softened cereal mixture, remaining 1 cup bran flakes, and raisins.

Spoon batter into an 8½- x 4½- x 3-inch loafpan coated with cooking spray. Bake at 350° for 55 minutes or until a wooden pick inserted in center comes out clean. Let cool in pan on a wire rack 10 minutes; remove from pan, and let cool completely. Yield: 16 servings (136 calories per ½-inch slice).

Per Slice: PROTEIN 3.5g FAT 3.0g (Saturated Fat 0.6g)
CARBOHYDRATE 25.5g FIBER 1.9g CHOLESTEROL 1mg
IRON 3.4mg SODIUM 177mg CALCIUM 57mg

APPLE-MAPLE SPREAD

½ cup light process cream cheese product,
  softened
1 cup apple-cinnamon low-fat yogurt
2 tablespoons reduced-calorie maple syrup

Beat cream cheese in a small bowl at medium speed of an electric mixer until creamy.

Spoon yogurt onto several layers of heavy-duty paper towels, spreading to ½-inch thickness. Cover with additional paper towels; let stand 5 minutes.

Add to cream cheese, scraping from towels using a rubber spatula. Add syrup, stirring well. Cover and chill until ready to serve. Yield: 1 cup (30 calories per tablespoon).

Per Tablespoon: PROTEIN 1.3g FAT 1.3g (Saturated Fat 0.8g)
CARBOHYDRATE 3.3g FIBER 0g CHOLESTEROL 5mg
IRON 0mg SODIUM 48mg CALCIUM 29mg

FROSTY FRUIT

¼ cup nutlike cereal nuggets
3 tablespoons finely chopped pecans, toasted
12 fresh strawberries
1 medium banana, peeled and cut into 12 slices
24 wooden picks
⅓ cup strawberry-banana low-fat yogurt

Combine cereal nuggets and pecans; stir well, and set aside. Place strawberries and banana slices on wooden picks; dip in yogurt, coating halfway up sides of fruit.

Roll yogurt-coated portion of strawberries and bananas in cereal mixture. Place on a baking sheet lined with wax paper. Cover; freeze 45 minutes or until firm. Yield: 4 servings (125 calories per serving).

Per Serving: PROTEIN 2.6g FAT 4.2g (Saturated Fat 0.5g)
CARBOHYDRATE 21.5g FIBER 3.1g CHOLESTEROL 1mg
IRON 0.7mg SODIUM 60mg CALCIUM 40mg

WARM VANILLA-ALMOND MILK

3 cups skim milk
3 tablespoons honey
2 teaspoons vanilla extract
¼ teaspoon almond extract
Ground nutmeg (optional)
Cinnamon sticks (optional)

Combine first 4 ingredients in a small saucepan. Cook over medium-low heat just until thoroughly heated, stirring frequently. Pour into serving mugs. If desired, sprinkle with nutmeg, and garnish with cinnamon sticks. Yield: 4 servings (121 calories per ¾-cup serving).

Per Serving: PROTEIN 6.3g FAT 0.3g (Saturated Fat 0.2g)
CARBOHYDRATE 22.7g FIBER 0g CHOLESTEROL 4mg
IRON 0.1mg SODIUM 96mg CALCIUM 227mg

Down-Home Southern Breakfast

Country-Style Sausage Links
Sweet Potato Browns
Cornmeal Daisy Biscuits
Warm Apple Lemonade

SERVES 6
TOTAL CALORIES PER SERVING: 422
(Calories from Fat: 26%)

Traditional Southern breakfasts do not always comply with today's nutrition guidelines. However, this menu offers down-home goodness with updated recipes that are trimmed of calories and fat but not flavor.

Fat is reduced in the sausage links by using lean ground pork combined with flavor-enhancing herbs. Sweet Potato Browns offers a new twist to an old favorite by replacing all-purpose potatoes with sweet potatoes. These hash browns derive their delicate flavor from low-fat ingredients. The biscuits and warm spiced lemonade make this rib-sticking meal complete. (Menu calories allow 2 sausage links and 1 biscuit per person.)

Fresh-from-the-oven Cornmeal Daisy Biscuits and Warm Apple Lemonade will tempt everyone to the table.

COUNTRY-STYLE SAUSAGE LINKS

1 pound lean ground pork
1 egg white, lightly beaten
3 tablespoons minced onion
2 tablespoons chopped fresh parsley
1½ teaspoons rubbed sage
½ teaspoon dried whole thyme
½ teaspoon freshly ground
　　black pepper
½ teaspoon fennel seeds
1 clove garlic, minced

Combine all ingredients in a medium bowl; stir well. Shape mixture into 12 links.

Place a large nonstick skillet over medium heat until hot. Add half of sausage links, and cook 8 to 10 minutes or until browned, turning frequently. Drain well on paper towels. Repeat procedure with remaining links. Yield: 12 links (77 calories each).

Per Link: PROTEIN 8.3g FAT 4.4g (Saturated Fat 1.5g)
CARBOHYDRATE 0.6g FIBER 0.2g CHOLESTEROL 27mg
IRON 0.4mg SODIUM 26mg CALCIUM 8mg

SWEET POTATO BROWNS

Butter-flavored vegetable cooking spray
1½ teaspoons margarine
3 cups peeled, shredded sweet potato (about 2½ medium)
1½ cups peeled, diced Granny Smith apple
3 tablespoons minced onion
1 tablespoon brown sugar
¼ teaspoon ground allspice
3 tablespoons unsweetened apple juice

Coat a large nonstick skillet with cooking spray; add margarine. Place over medium-high heat until margarine melts. Add potato, apple, and onion; sauté 5 minutes. Add brown sugar, allspice, and apple juice; cook, stirring constantly, 5 minutes or until potato is tender. Serve immediately. Yield: 6 servings (104 calories per serving).

Per Serving: PROTEIN 1.1g FAT 1.4g (Saturated Fat 0.3g)
CARBOHYDRATE 22.6g FIBER 2.8g CHOLESTEROL 0mg
IRON 0.5mg SODIUM 20mg CALCIUM 18mg

CORNMEAL DAISY BISCUITS

1½ cups all-purpose flour
½ cup cornmeal
2 teaspoons baking powder
¼ teaspoon baking soda
¼ teaspoon salt
1 tablespoon sugar
3 tablespoons margarine
¾ cup nonfat buttermilk
1 tablespoon all-purpose flour
1½ tablespoons reduced-calorie strawberry preserves

Combine 1½ cups flour, cornmeal, baking powder, soda, salt, and sugar in a medium bowl; cut in margarine with a pastry blender until mixture resembles coarse meal. Add buttermilk, stirring just until dry ingredients are moistened.

Sprinkle 1 tablespoon flour over work surface. Turn dough out onto surface, and knead 3 or 4 times. Roll dough to ½-inch thickness; cut into rounds using a 2-inch biscuit cutter. Place rounds on an ungreased baking sheet. With a knife, cut six ½-inch slashes evenly around edge of each biscuit to form petals. Press thumb in center of each biscuit, leaving an indentation. Place ¼ teaspoon preserves in each indentation. Bake at 425° for 10 minutes or until lightly browned. Yield: 1½ dozen (78 calories each).

Per Biscuit: PROTEIN 1.8g FAT 2.1g (Saturated Fat 0.4g)
CARBOHYDRATE 12.8g FIBER 0.5g CHOLESTEROL 0mg
IRON 0.7mg SODIUM 111mg CALCIUM 39mg

WARM APPLE LEMONADE

2¾ cups water
1¼ cups unsweetened apple juice
¾ cup fresh lemon juice
¼ cup plus 1 tablespoon honey
¼ teaspoon ground nutmeg
3 whole allspice
3 whole cloves
1 (3-inch) stick cinnamon
Lemon slices studded with whole cloves (optional)

Combine first 8 ingredients in a medium saucepan; bring to a boil. Reduce heat, and simmer, uncovered, 10 minutes. Remove and discard whole spices. Pour into individual mugs; top with lemon slices, if desired. Yield: 4½ cups (86 calories per ¾-cup serving).

Per Serving: PROTEIN 0.2g FAT 0.1g (Saturated Fat 0g)
CARBOHYDRATE 23.3g FIBER 0.1g CHOLESTEROL 0mg
IRON 0.3mg SODIUM 3mg CALCIUM 7mg

Sunny Italian Breakfast

Three-Pepper Frittata
Italian Sweet Bread
Bountiful Fresh Fruit Cup
Espresso

SERVES 4
TOTAL CALORIES PER SERVING: 337
(Calories from Fat: 20%)

On a leisurely weekend morning, treat the family to a taste of Italy. The pepper frittata offers a blend of Italian herbs and two cheeses. Pair it with the sweet bread and lightly sweetened fresh fruit.

For early morning convenience, bake the bread the day before, and warm the slices before serving (1 slice per serving). Savor a rich cup of espresso before beginning the day's activities.

Italy is known for its outstanding cuisine, and Italian Sweet Bread and espresso provide a mouth-watering hint of this Mediterranean paradise.

THREE-PEPPER FRITTATA

Olive oil-flavored vegetable cooking spray
1 small onion, thinly sliced
½ cup sliced fresh mushrooms
¼ cup chopped green pepper
¼ cup chopped sweet red pepper
¼ cup chopped sweet yellow pepper
2 tablespoons chopped ripe olives
1 tablespoon chopped fresh parsley
½ teaspoon dried whole basil
¼ teaspoon dried whole oregano
¼ teaspoon pepper
⅛ teaspoon garlic powder
1½ cups frozen egg substitute, thawed
¼ cup skim milk
3 tablespoons (¾ ounce) shredded part-skim
   mozzarella cheese
1 (¼-inch-thick) green pepper ring
1 (¼-inch-thick) sweet red pepper ring
1 (¼-inch-thick) sweet yellow pepper ring
2 tablespoons freshly grated Romano cheese

Coat a 10-inch ovenproof skillet with cooking spray; place over medium-high heat until hot. Add onion, mushrooms, and chopped peppers; sauté until vegetables are tender. Stir in olives and next 5 ingredients. Set aside.

Combine egg substitute, milk, and mozzarella cheese in a small bowl, stirring well. Pour over vegetable mixture. Cook, uncovered, over medium heat 8 to 10 minutes or until egg substitute is set and a slight crust forms on bottom of frittata. Arrange pepper rings in center of frittata. Sprinkle with Romano cheese.

Broil frittata 5½ inches from heat (with electric oven door partially opened) 2 to 3 minutes or until golden. Cut frittata into 8 wedges, and serve immediately. Yield: 4 servings (104 calories per 2 wedges).

Per Serving: PROTEIN 12.7g FAT 2.8g (Saturated Fat 1.3g)
CARBOHYDRATE 6.9g FIBER 1.2g CHOLESTEROL 7mg
IRON 2.5mg SODIUM 259mg CALCIUM 138mg

ITALIAN SWEET BREAD

Vegetable cooking spray
½ cup skim milk
¼ cup margarine
2 packages active dry yeast
½ teaspoon sugar
¼ cup warm water (105° to 115°)
¼ cup sugar
2 eggs
1 teaspoon grated lemon rind
1 teaspoon vanilla extract
½ teaspoon salt
4 cups all-purpose flour, divided
2 tablespoons all-purpose flour
¼ cup chopped blanched almonds
¼ cup golden raisins
¼ cup chopped candied cherries

Cut a piece of aluminum foil long enough to fit around a 1½-quart soufflé dish, allowing a 1-inch overlap; fold lengthwise into thirds. Coat dish and one side of foil with cooking spray. Wrap foil around outside of dish, coated side against dish, allowing it to extend 3 inches above rim to form a collar. Secure with string.

Combine milk and margarine in a saucepan; cook over medium heat until margarine melts, stirring occasionally. Cool to 105° to 115°.

Combine yeast, ½ teaspoon sugar, and warm water in a 1-cup liquid measuring cup; let stand 5 minutes.

Combine milk mixture, yeast mixture, ¼ cup sugar, eggs, lemon rind, vanilla extract, and salt in a large bowl; beat at medium speed of an electric mixer until blended. Add 2 cups flour, and beat an additional 2 minutes at medium speed. Gradually stir in enough of the remaining 2 cups flour to make a soft dough.

Sprinkle 2 tablespoons all-purpose flour evenly over work surface. Turn dough out onto floured surface, and knead until dough is smooth and elastic (about 8 to 10 minutes). Place dough in a large bowl coated with cooking spray, turning to coat top. Cover dough, and let rise in a warm place (85°), free from drafts, 1 hour or until dough is doubled in bulk.

Punch down dough; cover and let rest 5 minutes. Turn dough out onto work surface; flatten slightly. Sprinkle dough with almonds, raisins, and cherries; knead 4 or 5 times or until nuts and fruit are incorporated. Shape dough into a ball, and place in prepared dish.

Cover and let rise in a warm place, free from drafts, 45 minutes or until dough is doubled in bulk. Bake at 350° for 50 minutes or until loaf sounds hollow when tapped. (Cover with aluminum foil the last 30 minutes of baking to prevent over-browning, if necessary.) Let loaf cool in dish 10 minutes.

Remove loaf from dish, and let cool on a wire rack. Cut loaf into wedges. Yield: 18 wedges (180 calories per wedge).

Per Wedge: PROTEIN 4.6g FAT 4.4g (Saturated Fat 0.8g) CARBOHYDRATE 30.4g FIBER 1.3g CHOLESTEROL 25mg IRON 1.7mg SODIUM 119mg CALCIUM 23mg

BOUNTIFUL FRESH FRUIT CUP

½ cup unsweetened orange juice
¼ cup Chablis or other dry white wine
1 teaspoon orange zest
¾ cup coarsely chopped fresh pear
¾ cup coarsely chopped Granny Smith apple
½ cup seedless red grapes, halved

Combine first 3 ingredients in a small saucepan; place mixture over medium heat. Bring mixture to a boil; reduce heat, and simmer, uncovered, 5 minutes. Let cool.

Combine pear, apple, and grapes in a medium bowl. Pour juice mixture over fruit, tossing gently. Cover and chill thoroughly. Yield: 4 servings (48 calories per ½-cup serving).

Per Serving: PROTEIN 0.5g FAT 0.2g (Saturated Fat 0g) CARBOHYDRATE 12.4g FIBER 1.3g CHOLESTEROL 0mg IRON 0.2mg SODIUM 2mg CALCIUM 11mg

Low-Country Brunch

Shrimp and Grits
Steamed green beans
Sweet Potato Muffins
Fresh Melon Ambrosia
Spiced Peach Tea

SERVES 6
TOTAL CALORIES PER SERVING: 567
(Calories from Fat: 16%)

For a brunch that's rich in flavor, color, and texture, plan a menu featuring South Carolina's Low-country cuisine. European, African, West Indian, and Mediterranean cultures influence this unique Southern fare.

This menu features a piquant shrimp mixture ladled over piping hot seared grits. Accompany the main dish with steamed green beans (½ cup per person), a delicately flavored sweet potato muffin for each person, and a glass of Spiced Peach Tea. Ambrosia provides a sweet ending to this Low-country feast.

Shrimp and Grits, steamed green beans, Sweet Potato Muffins, and Spiced Peach Tea take your taste buds on a delectable trip south.

SHRIMP AND GRITS

¼ cup plus 3 tablespoons all-purpose flour
1½ pounds unpeeled medium-size fresh shrimp
Vegetable cooking spray
1 teaspoon vegetable oil
½ cup chopped onion
½ cup chopped green pepper
¼ cup chopped sweet red pepper
¼ cup chopped fresh parsley
1½ teaspoons chopped fresh thyme
⅛ teaspoon ground red pepper
2 cups canned low-sodium chicken broth, undiluted
1 tablespoon lemon juice
¼ cup plus 3 tablespoons water
Seared Grits

Sprinkle flour in an 8-inch square pan. Bake at 350° for 12 to 15 minutes or until lightly browned, stirring occasionally. Set aside, and let cool.

Peel and devein shrimp; set aside.

Coat a Dutch oven with cooking spray; add oil, and place over medium-high heat until hot. Add onion and chopped peppers; sauté until tender. Add parsley and next 4 ingredients; bring to a boil. Reduce heat, and simmer, uncovered, 8 minutes.

Add shrimp to vegetable mixture, and stir well. Combine browned flour and water; stir well. Add to shrimp mixture, stirring well. Cook over medium heat, stirring constantly, 8 to 10 minutes until mixture is thickened. Serve over Seared Grits. Yield: 6 servings (253 calories per serving).

Seared Grits

¾ cup quick-cooking grits, uncooked
3 cups skim milk
⅛ teaspoon salt
Vegetable cooking spray

Combine first 3 ingredients in a saucepan; stir well. Cook, uncovered, over medium-low heat until thickened, stirring often. Spread in a 9-inch square pan coated with cooking spray. Cover; chill until firm. Cut into 6 rectangles. Coat a nonstick skillet with cooking spray; place over medium-high heat until hot. Add rectangles; cook 3 minutes on each side or until browned, turning gently. Yield: 6 servings.

Per Serving: PROTEIN 24.9g FAT 3.5g (Saturated Fat 0.7g) CARBOHYDRATE 29.6g FIBER 1.7g CHOLESTEROL 132mg IRON 3.8mg SODIUM 267mg CALCIUM 202mg

SWEET POTATO MUFFINS

1¾ cups all-purpose flour
2 teaspooons baking powder
¼ teaspoon salt
¼ cup firmly packed brown sugar
1 teaspoon ground cinnamon
½ teaspoon ground nutmeg
⅛ teaspoon ground cloves
¾ cup skim milk
½ cup mashed, cooked sweet potato
3 tablespoons vegetable oil
1 egg, lightly beaten
½ teaspoon vanilla extract
3 tablespoons currants
Vegetable cooking spray

Combine first 7 ingredients in a bowl. Combine milk and next 4 ingredients; add to dry ingredients, stirring just until moistened. Stir in currants. Spoon into muffin pans coated with cooking spray, filling half full. Bake at 400° for 25 minutes or until a wooden pick inserted in center comes out clean. Remove from pans immediately. Yield: 1 dozen (147 calories each).

Per Muffin: PROTEIN 3.2g FAT 4.4g (Saturated Fat 0.8g) CARBOHYDRATE 23.6g FIBER 0.9g CHOLESTEROL 19mg IRON 1.3mg SODIUM 116mg CALCIUM 67mg

FRESH MELON AMBROSIA

¼ cup unsweetened orange juice
¼ cup unsweetened pineapple juice
1 tablespoon light rum
1 tablespoon honey
1 teaspoon grated orange rind
1 cup honeydew melon balls
1 cup cantaloupe melon balls
1 cup watermelon balls
2 tablespoons unsweetened shredded coconut

Combine first 5 ingredients in a small saucepan. Bring to a boil; reduce heat, and simmer, uncovered, 1 minute.

Combine melon balls in a medium bowl; add orange juice mixture, and toss gently. Cover and chill.

To serve, spoon mixture evenly into individual dessert bowls, and sprinkle each serving with 1 teaspoon coconut. Yield: 6 servings (70 calories per ½-cup serving).

Per Serving: PROTEIN 0.9g FAT 1.8g (Saturated Fat 1.5g) CARBOHYDRATE 14.1g FIBER 1.0g CHOLESTEROL 0mg IRON 0.3mg SODIUM 8mg CALCIUM 12mg

SPICED PEACH TEA

6 orange spice-flavored tea bags
3 cups boiling water
2 cups peach juice blend
1 cup water
¼ cup sugar
2 tablespoons lemon juice
½ teaspoon almond extract

Combine tea bags and water; cover and steep 5 minutes. Remove and discard tea bags; set tea aside.

Combine peach juice and next 4 ingredients in a medium saucepan; stir well. Bring to a boil; reduce heat, and simmer, uncovered, 5 minutes. Combine tea and peach juice mixture; stir well. Cover and chill thoroughly. Serve over ice. Yield: 1½ quarts (75 calories per 1-cup serving).

Per Serving: PROTEIN 0.2g FAT 0.0g (Saturated Fat 0g) CARBOHYDRATE 18.9g FIBER 0g CHOLESTEROL 0mg IRON 0mg SODIUM 10mg CALCIUM 0mg

You'll be ready to cheer the team to victory after a brunch of Savory Turkey Hash, Sesame-Cheese Batter Bread (page 44), and refreshing Triple Fruit Sparkler (page 44).

Winning Football Brunch

Savory Turkey Hash
Carrot-Waldorf Salad
Sesame-Cheese Batter Bread
Triple Fruit Sparkler
Ginger Crinkles

SERVES 8
TOTAL CALORIES PER SERVING: 568
(Calories from Fat: 12%)

Instead of tailgating, invite home-team fans over to enjoy a line-up of hearty, healthy foods before the big game.

Kick off the event with Savory Turkey Hash. The all-star appeal of this dish comes from a subtle combination of four flavorful herbs. Sure to score from the sidelines is crunchy Carrot-Waldorf Salad—a tasty, low-fat variation of a traditional

favorite. Round out this touchdown menu with slices of fresh-baked Sesame-Cheese Batter Bread (1 slice per person), refreshing Triple Fruit Sparkler, and a light dessert of crisp gingersnaps (2 per person).

This brunch won't slow guests down with unnecessary fat and calories. Instead they will be full of energy to cheer the team to victory.

SAVORY TURKEY HASH

Vegetable cooking spray
1½ cups chopped onion
1 cup chopped green pepper
1 cup chopped sweet red pepper
4 cups chopped cooked turkey breast (skinned before cooking and cooked without salt)
2½ cups cooked, peeled, and diced potato
¼ cup chopped fresh parsley
1 teaspoon dried whole basil
½ teaspoon dried whole oregano
¼ teaspoon salt
¼ teaspoon pepper
¼ teaspoon dried whole marjoram
⅓ cup skim milk
⅓ cup canned no-salt-added chicken broth, undiluted
1 tablespoon all-purpose flour
1 egg white, lightly beaten
1 teaspoon vegetable oil

Coat a large nonstick skillet with cooking spray; place over medium-high heat until hot. Add onion and chopped peppers; sauté until tender. Transfer mixture to a large bowl. Stir in turkey and next 7 ingredients.

Combine milk, chicken broth, flour, and egg white; stir well with a wire whisk. Add to turkey mixture, and stir well.

Coat a large nonstick skillet with cooking spray; add oil. Place over medium-high heat until hot. Spoon turkey mixture evenly into skillet; press firmly with a spatula. Reduce heat to medium, and cook 10 to 12 minutes or until liquid has evaporated and bottom of mixture is browned. Yield: 8 servings (192 calories per serving).

Per Serving: PROTEIN 26.1g FAT 1.6g (Saturated Fat 0.4g)
CARBOHYDRATE 17.4g FIBER 2.1g CHOLESTEROL 65mg
IRON 2.2mg SODIUM 137mg CALCIUM 43mg

CARROT-WALDORF SALAD

2 cups shredded carrot
1½ cups chopped Red Delicious apple
1 cup thinly sliced celery
¼ cup pitted chopped dates
¼ cup plain nonfat yogurt
¼ cup nonfat mayonnaise
2 tablespoons unsweetened orange juice
1 teaspoon grated lemon rind
Spinach leaves (optional)

Combine first 4 ingredients in a medium bowl. Combine yogurt, mayonnaise, orange juice, and lemon rind; stir well. Pour over carrot mixture; toss gently. Cover and chill at least 1 hour. To serve, spoon mixture into a spinach-lined serving bowl, if desired. Yield: 8 servings (59 calories per ½-cup serving).

Per Serving: PROTEIN 1.0g FAT 0.2g (Saturated Fat 0.1g)
CARBOHYDRATE 14.7g FIBER 2.5g CHOLESTEROL 0mg
IRON 0.3mg SODIUM 122mg CALCIUM 32mg

 ## MAKING A FAT DIFFERENCE

A busy schedule leaves little time for worrying about reducing fat in your diet. Try these tried-and-true tips:
• Build meals around potatoes, rice, or pasta. Use meat and cheese as accompaniments.
• Select lean meats, fish, and poultry. Trim off visible fat before cooking, and remove skin from poultry.
• Serve a vegetarian dish for at least one meal each week. But don't rely on high-fat cheese as a meat substitute! Instead, serve legumes, which have only a trace of fat and are rich in complex carbohydrates.

• Cook foods by baking, steaming, roasting, boiling, or broiling. Instead of frying, sauté or stir-fry foods using just a teaspoon of fat or, better yet, vegetable cooking spray.
• Experiment with herbs, spices, and seasonings instead of butter to add flavor to your dishes.
• Drink skim milk. You can wean yourself gradually from whole milk to 2%, then to 1%, then to skim.
• Reach for fresh fruit, raw vegetables, air-popped popcorn, or rice cakes instead of chips, cookies, ice cream, or candy bars.

SESAME-CHEESE BATTER BREAD

2¼ cups all-purpose flour, divided
3 tablespoons sugar
1 tablespoon dried parsley flakes
¼ teaspoon salt
¼ teaspoon garlic powder
1 package active dry yeast
1 cup skim milk
2 tablespoons margarine
1 egg
½ cup (2 ounces) shredded part-skim mozzarella
   cheese
Vegetable cooking spray
2 teaspoons sesame seeds

Combine 1¼ cups flour and next 5 ingredients in a large bowl; stir well. Set aside.

Combine milk and margarine in a small saucepan; cook over medium heat until margarine melts. Cool to 120° to 130°.

Gradually add milk mixture to flour mixture, beating at low speed of an electric mixer until blended. Add egg, and beat at low speed until blended. Beat mixture an additional 3 minutes at medium speed. Gradually stir in remaining 1 cup flour and cheese.

Spoon batter into a 9- x 5- x 3-inch loafpan coated with cooking spray. Cover and let rise in a warm place (85°), free from drafts, 35 minutes or until batter is doubled in bulk.

Sprinkle loaf with sesame seeds. Bake at 350° for 35 to 40 minutes or until loaf is golden. Remove loaf from pan, and let cool on a wire rack. Yield: 18 servings (97 calories per ½-inch slice).

Per Slice: PROTEIN 3.4g FAT 2.4g (Saturated Fat 0.7g)
CARBOHYDRATE 15.1g FIBER 0.6g CHOLESTEROL 14mg
IRON 0.9mg SODIUM 74mg CALCIUM 45mg

TRIPLE FRUIT SPARKLER

2 cups apricot nectar
2 cups unsweetened orange juice
2 cups unsweetened pineapple juice
2 cups orange-flavored sparkling mineral water,
   chilled

Combine first 3 ingredients in a large pitcher, and stir well. Chill thoroughly.

Just before serving, stir in mineral water. Serve over ice. Yield: 2 quarts (98 calories per 1-cup serving).

Per Serving: PROTEIN 0.9g FAT 0.1g (Saturated Fat 0g)
CARBOHYDRATE 24.3g FIBER 0.6g CHOLESTEROL 0mg
IRON 0.5mg SODIUM 16mg CALCIUM 21mg

GINGER CRINKLES

¼ cup margarine, softened
¾ cup sugar
¼ cup molasses
1 tablespoon grated lemon rind
1 egg
2 cups all-purpose flour
2 teaspoons baking soda
¼ teaspoon salt
1 tablespoon ground ginger
½ teaspoon ground cinnamon
Vegetable cooking spray

Beat margarine at medium speed of an electric mixer until creamy; gradually add sugar, beating well. Add molasses, lemon rind, and egg; beat well.

Combine flour and next 4 ingredients; stir well. Gradually add flour mixture to margarine mixture, stirring well. Divide dough in half. Shape each half into a ball, and wrap in wax paper; chill 1 hour.

Shape each half into 18 (1-inch) balls. Place 2 inches apart on cookie sheets coated with cooking spray. Bake at 350° for 12 minutes or until golden. Remove from cookie sheets, and let cool completely on wire racks. Yield: 3 dozen (61 calories each).

Per Cookie: PROTEIN 0.9g FAT 1.5g (Saturated Fat 0.3g)
CARBOHYDRATE 11.0g FIBER 0.2g CHOLESTEROL 6mg
IRON 0.5mg SODIUM 80mg CALCIUM 19mg

Enhance old-fashioned flavors with updated cooking techniques. Oven-Barbecued Pork, Sautéed Kale and White Beans, and Cornmeal Drop Biscuits take advantage of Southern favorites. (Menu begins on page 53.)

Quick
&
Easy

Lunch After the Workout

Vichyssoise with Pesto
Fruity Yogurt Muffins
Spiced Cheese Spread
Strawberry-Spinach Salad
Crunchy Cereal Bars
Sparkling water

SERVES 4
TOTAL CALORIES PER SERVING: 545
(Calories from Fat: 21%)

Invite friends to join you for a workout and a revitalizing lunch. Prepare the recipes ahead, and serve them chilled or at room temperature.

Accompany the meal with muffins (1 per person), each topped with 1 tablespoon of spread. Complete the meal with high-energy cereal bars (1 per person). Don't forget to offer plenty of refreshing water with the meal.

Replenish your energy with Vichyssoise with Pesto, Strawberry-Spinach Salad, Fruity Yogurt Muffins, and Spiced Cheese Spread.

VICHYSSOISE WITH PESTO

3½ cups peeled and cubed potato
1 cup chopped leeks
½ cup chopped celery
1 teaspoon chicken-flavored bouillon granules
1 clove garlic, minced
1 bay leaf
1¾ cups water
2 cups 1% low-fat milk
⅓ cup grated Parmesan cheese, divided
Dash of salt
⅔ cup 1% low-fat cottage cheese
⅓ cup tightly packed fresh basil leaves, chopped

Combine first 7 ingredients in a large saucepan. Bring mixture to a boil. Cover, reduce heat, and simmer 20 minutes or until vegetables are tender.

Remove from heat, and let cool. Remove and discard bay leaf.

Place half of potato mixture in container of an electric blender; cover and process until smooth, stopping once to scrape down sides. Transfer to a large bowl. Repeat procedure with remaining mixture. Add milk, 3 tablespoons Parmesan cheese, and salt to puree; stir well. Cover and chill thoroughly.

Combine remaining Parmesan cheese, cottage cheese, and basil in blender; cover and process until smooth. Ladle potato mixture into bowls. Swirl in basil mixture with a knife. Yield: 1½ quarts (239 calories per 1½-cup serving).

Per Serving: PROTEIN 14.9g FAT 4.2g (Saturated Fat 2.4g)
CARBOHYDRATE 36.3g FIBER 2.7g CHOLESTEROL 12mg
IRON 1.7mg SODIUM 602mg CALCIUM 299mg

FRUITY YOGURT MUFFINS

1 cup chopped fresh rhubarb
2 cups all-purpose flour, divided
1 teaspoon baking powder
¼ teaspoon baking soda
¼ teaspoon salt
¼ cup sugar
1 (8-ounce) carton strawberry-banana low-fat
    yogurt
¼ cup unsweetened orange juice
2 tablespoons vegetable oil
1 teaspoon vanilla extract
1 egg, lightly beaten
Vegetable cooking spray
1 tablespoon sugar

Combine rhubarb and 2 tablespoons flour in a small bowl; toss well. Set aside.

Combine remaining flour, baking powder, soda, salt, and ¼ cup sugar in a large bowl; make a well in center of mixture. Combine yogurt and next 4 ingredients in a medium bowl. Stir in rhubarb. Add to dry ingredients, stirring just until dry ingredients are moistened.

Spoon batter into muffin pans coated with cooking spray, filling three-fourths full. Sprinkle evenly with 1 tablespoon sugar. Bake at 400° for 18 to 20 minutes or until golden. Remove from pans immediately. Yield: 14 muffins (128 calories each).

Per Muffin: PROTEIN 3.0g FAT 2.9g (Saturated Fat 0.6g) CARBOHYDRATE 22.1g FIBER 0.6g CHOLESTEROL 16mg IRON 0.9mg SODIUM 92mg CALCIUM 51mg

SPICED CHEESE SPREAD

1 (8-ounce) package Neufchâtel cheese,
    softened
2 tablespoons sifted powdered sugar
2 tablespoons plain nonfat yogurt
2 tablespoons amaretto
2 teaspoons apple pie spice

Combine all ingredients in a small mixing bowl; beat at medium speed of an electric mixer until mixture is smooth.

Cover and chill until ready to serve. Yield: 1¼ cups (39 calories per tablespoon).

Per Tablespoon: PROTEIN 1.2g FAT 2.7g (Saturated Fat 1.7g) CARBOHYDRATE 1.8g FIBER 0g CHOLESTEROL 9mg IRON 0.1mg SODIUM 46mg CALCIUM 13mg

STRAWBERRY-SPINACH SALAD

2 cups fresh strawberry halves
2 tablespoons sugar
2 tablespoons balsamic vinegar
3½ cups torn fresh spinach
¼ teaspoon freshly ground pepper

Combine strawberry halves, sugar, and vinegar in a small bowl; toss gently. Cover and chill at least 2 hours, stirring occasionally.

To serve, combine strawberry mixture, spinach, and pepper; toss well. Yield: 4 servings (50 calories per 1-cup serving).

Per Serving: PROTEIN 1.0g FAT 0.3g (Saturated Fat 0g) CARBOHYDRATE 12.0g FIBER 2.6g CHOLESTEROL 0mg IRON 0.9mg SODIUM 15mg CALCIUM 28mg

CRUNCHY CEREAL BARS

½ cup semisweet chocolate morsels
2 tablespoons margarine
4 cups miniature marshmallows
4 cups crisp rice cereal
2 cups toasted oat cereal
Vegetable cooking spray

Combine chocolate morsels and margarine in top of a double boiler; bring water to a boil. Reduce heat to low, and cook until chocolate melts, stirring frequently.

Add marshmallows, and cook, stirring constantly, until marshmallows melt. Stir in cereals.

Spread mixture evenly in a 13- x 9- x 2-inch pan coated with cooking spray. Let cool. Cut into bars. Yield: 20 bars (89 calories each).

Per Bar: PROTEIN 1.0g FAT 2.9g (Saturated Fat 1.1g) CARBOHYDRATE 15.7g FIBER 0.2g CHOLESTEROL 0mg IRON 0.7mg SODIUM 77mg CALCIUM 8mg

Seafood Supper in a Snap

Seasoned Fish and
Tomatoes
Spicy Yellow Rice
Quick Broccoli Vinaigrette
Commercial whole wheat
dinner rolls
Raspberry Cream Pie

SERVES 6
TOTAL CALORIES PER SERVING: 473
(Calories from Fat: 22%)

Dinner at the snap of a finger?
Although that's exaggerating,
there's no doubt this is a menu
that's easy to prepare—and the
key is timing.

Make the dessert the day before, so all you'll have to do is
slice and serve. Cut the plum tomatoes into slices to accompany
the amberjack fillets; then prepare the rice. As the rice cooks,
finish preparing and baking the
fish. Spend the last few minutes
steaming the broccoli and warming the dinner rolls (1 per person).

*It's smooth sailing with a menu of Seasoned Fish and Tomatoes,
Spicy Yellow Rice, Quick Broccoli Vinaigrette, and dinner rolls.*

SEASONED FISH AND TOMATOES

6 (4-ounce) amberjack fillets
1 teaspoon dried whole oregano
½ teaspoon cracked pepper
6 plum tomatoes, cut into ¼-inch-thick slices
Vegetable cooking spray
¾ cup Chablis or other dry white wine
2 tablespoons sliced ripe olives
Fresh cilantro sprigs (optional)
Whole peppercorns (optional)

Sprinkle fillets with oregano and cracked pepper.
Place fillets and tomato in a 13- x 9- x 2-inch
baking dish coated with cooking spray. Add wine.
Bake, uncovered, at 350° for 15 minutes or until fish
flakes easily when tested with a fork.

To serve, place tomato slices evenly on individual
serving plates, using a slotted spoon. Top each
serving with a fillet, and sprinkle evenly with olives.
If desired, garnish each serving with an oregano
sprig and whole peppercorns. Serve immediately.
Yield: 6 servings (142 calories per serving).

Per Serving: PROTEIN 24.6g FAT 3.2g (Saturated Fat 0.8g)
CARBOHYDRATE 3.4g FIBER 0.9g CHOLESTEROL 49mg
IRON 0.7mg SODIUM 95mg CALCIUM 20mg

SPICY YELLOW RICE

Vegetable cooking spray
1¼ cups chopped onion
¾ cup long-grain rice, uncooked
1¾ cups plus 2 tablespoons water
¾ teaspoon ground turmeric
½ teaspoon hot sauce
¼ teaspoon salt
¼ teaspoon garlic powder
¼ teaspoon pepper
1 bay leaf

Coat a large nonstick skillet with cooking spray; place over medium-high heat until hot. Add onion, and sauté until tender. Add rice, stirring gently.

Add water and remaining ingredients to rice mixture; bring to a boil. Cover, reduce heat, and simmer 22 minutes or until rice is tender and liquid is absorbed. Remove and discard bay leaf. Yield: 6 servings (104 calories per ½-cup serving).

Per Serving: PROTEIN 2.2g FAT 0.4g (Saturated Fat 0.1g)
CARBOHYDRATE 22.6g FIBER 0.8g CHOLESTEROL 0mg
IRON 1.3mg SODIUM 103mg CALCIUM 14mg

QUICK BROCCOLI VINAIGRETTE

1½ pounds fresh broccoli
2 tablespoons balsamic vinegar
1 teaspoon Dijon mustard
½ teaspoon olive oil
¼ teaspoon pepper
⅛ teaspoon salt

Trim off large leaves of broccoli, and remove tough ends of lower stalks. Wash broccoli; cut into spears. Arrange in a vegetable steamer over boiling water. Cover; steam 5 minutes or until crisp-tender. Drain; transfer to a serving platter, and keep warm.

Combine vinegar and remaining ingredients, stirring well with a wire whisk. Drizzle vinegar mixture over broccoli, and serve immediately. Yield: 6 servings (22 calories per serving).

Per Serving: PROTEIN 1.9g FAT 0.7g (Saturated Fat 0.1g)
CARBOHYDRATE 3.5g FIBER 2.0g CHOLESTEROL 0mg
IRON 0.6mg SODIUM 91mg CALCIUM 31mg

RASPBERRY CREAM PIE

½ cup graham cracker crumbs
¼ cup finely chopped pecans
3 tablespoons reduced-calorie margarine,
    melted
1 tablespoon sugar
1 (12-ounce) package frozen raspberries in
    light syrup, thawed
1 envelope unflavored gelatin
¼ cup cold water
¼ teaspoon grated lime rind
1 tablespoon fresh lime juice
1 (8-ounce) carton raspberry low-fat yogurt
1 cup lite whipped topping
Lime slices (optional)

Combine first 4 ingredients in a small bowl, stirring well. Press mixture into bottom and halfway up sides of a 9-inch pieplate. Bake at 350° for 8 to 10 minutes or until golden. Remove from oven, and let cool on a wire rack.

Place raspberries in container of an electric blender; cover and process until smooth. Pour raspberry puree through a wire-mesh strainer; press with the back of spoon against sides of the strainer to squeeze out juice. Discard pulp and seeds remaining in strainer.

Sprinkle gelatin over cold water in a small nonaluminum saucepan; let stand 1 minute. Cook over low heat, stirring constantly, until gelatin dissolves. Remove from heat, and stir in reserved raspberry puree, lime rind, and lime juice. Chill until the consistency of unbeaten egg white.

Add yogurt, and stir well. Gently fold in whipped topping. Spoon mixture into prepared pie crust. Cover and chill at least 2 hours. Garnish with lime slices, if desired. Yield: 10 servings (133 calories per serving).

Per Serving: PROTEIN 2.2g FAT 5.6g (Saturated Fat 1.3g)
CARBOHYDRATE 19.9g FIBER 0.4g CHOLESTEROL 1mg
IRON 0.5mg SODIUM 82mg CALCIUM 40mg

Dinner with International Flair

Pepperoncini-Cheese Dip
Commercial breadsticks
Mediterranean Pizza Loaf
Spicy Orange Salad
Frosty Cappuccino

SERVES 4
TOTAL CALORIES PER SERVING: 607
(Calories from Fat: 19%)

What could be more all-American—or easier—than pizza and ice cream for dinner? This menu expands that theme, borrowing from other cultures to flavor this typical supper fare.

Create an appetizer with an Italian accent by stirring pepperoncini peppers into a creamy cheese-based dip. Use crisp commercial breadsticks as dippers. (Menu calories reflect 2 tablespoons dip and 2 breadsticks per person.) Store the dip in the refrigerator for up to one week, and try it with fresh vegetables instead of breadsticks the second time around.

For the entrée, give pizza a Greek accent by topping the French bread base with lamb, eggplant, and oregano. A light sprinkling of feta cheese adds to the authenticity of the flavors.

Travel to Mexico to create a salad that boasts two south-of-the-border staples—oranges and cilantro. For a refreshing finale, combine dessert and a cocktail into one. The frozen coffee cubes for Frosty Cappuccino can be made ahead, so all you do at the end of the meal is blend and serve. It's easy to create an international dinner couched in the familiarity of American favorites!

PEPPERONCINI-CHEESE DIP

¼ cup 1% low-fat cottage cheese
¼ cup plus 2 tablespoons light process cream
    cheese product
¼ cup nonfat sour cream alternative
¼ cup canned finely chopped pepperoncini
    peppers, drained
1 tablespoon grated Parmesan cheese
⅛ teaspoon garlic powder
Pepperoncini pepper (optional)

Combine first 3 ingredients in container of an electric blender; cover and process until smooth. Transfer to a bowl; stir in chopped peppers, Parmesan cheese, and garlic powder. Garnish with a pepperoncini pepper, if desired. Serve with commercial breadsticks. Yield: 1 cup (19 calories per tablespoon).

Per Tablespoon: PROTEIN 1.4g FAT 1.0g (Saturated Fat 0.6g)
CARBOHYDRATE 0.8g FIBER 0.1g CHOLESTEROL 3mg
IRON 0.1mg SODIUM 85mg CALCIUM 14mg

From front: Mediterranean Pizza Loaf and Spicy Orange Salad (page 52) make an exciting cross-cultural blend of flavors. For starters, serve Pepperoncini-Cheese Dip and breadsticks.

MEDITERRANEAN PIZZA LOAF

6 ounces lean ground lamb
½ cup chopped onion
2 cloves garlic, minced
2½ cups peeled, cubed eggplant
1 cup sliced fresh mushrooms
¼ cup water
1 teaspoon dried whole oregano, divided
⅓ cup no-salt-added tomato paste
1 (1-pound) loaf French bread
½ cup frozen artichoke hearts, thawed and
   chopped
3 tablespoons crumbled feta cheese

Combine first 3 ingredients in a medium-size nonstick skillet; cook over medium heat until browned, stirring until meat crumbles. Drain and pat dry with paper towels. Wipe drippings from skillet with a paper towel.

Place skillet over medium-high heat until hot. Add eggplant and mushrooms; sauté 2 minutes. Stir in water and ¾ teaspoon oregano. Cover, reduce heat, and simmer 5 minutes or until vegetables are tender. Add lamb mixture and tomato paste, stirring well; cook 1 minute or until thoroughly heated.

Slice bread in half lengthwise. Place one half, cut side up, on a baking sheet. Reserve remaining half for another use. Broil 5½ inches from heat (with electric oven door partially opened) 1½ minutes or until lightly toasted. Spoon lamb mixture evenly over bread. Top with artichokes, cheese, and remaining ¼ teaspoon oregano. Broil 5½ inches from heat (with electric oven door partially opened) 3 minutes or until cheese softens. Cut into 4 equal pieces, and serve immediately. Yield: 4 servings (323 calories per serving).

Per Serving: PROTEIN 18.7g FAT 6.5g (Saturated Fat 2.4g)
CARBOHYDRATE 47.6g FIBER 3.4g CHOLESTEROL 37mg
IRON 3.2mg SODIUM 488mg CALCIUM 100mg

SPICY ORANGE SALAD

2 tablespoons unsweetened orange juice
2 tablespoons white vinegar
2 teaspoons olive oil
⅛ teaspoon ground coriander
⅛ teaspoon ground cumin
⅛ teaspoon ground red pepper
1 medium head Bibb lettuce, separated into leaves
1 cup watercress sprigs
1 tablespoon minced fresh cilantro
2 cups orange sections (about 6 oranges)

Combine first 6 ingredients; stir with a wire whisk. Arrange lettuce and watercress on salad plates; sprinkle with minced cilantro. Top evenly with orange sections. Drizzle vinegar mixture evenly over salads. Yield: 4 servings (79 calories per serving).

Per Serving: PROTEIN 1.5g FAT 2.5g (Saturated Fat 0.3g)
CARBOHYDRATE 14.4g FIBER 5.1g CHOLESTEROL 0mg
IRON 0.3mg SODIUM 5mg CALCIUM 54mg

FROSTY CAPPUCCINO

¼ cup ground coffee
2 teaspoons unsweetened cocoa
2 teaspoons grated orange rind
¼ teaspoon ground cinnamon
1¾ cups water
1 cup 1% low-fat milk
¼ cup plus 2 tablespoons firmly packed brown sugar
2 tablespoons Kahlúa or other coffee-flavored
   liqueur

Combine first 4 ingredients in coffee filter or filter basket of a drip coffee maker. Add water to coffee maker. Prepare coffee according to manufacturer's instructions. Transfer to a pitcher. Stir in milk and remaining ingredients. Pour into ice cube trays; freeze until firm.

Position knife blade in food processor bowl. Add coffee ice cubes; process 2 minutes. Serve immediately. Yield: 4 cups (133 calories per 1-cup serving).

Per Serving: PROTEIN 2.4g FAT 0.8g (Saturated Fat 0.5g)
CARBOHYDRATE 26.0g FIBER 0g CHOLESTEROL 2mg
IRON 1.4mg SODIUM 39mg CALCIUM 98mg

Dinner in the New South

Oven-Barbecued Pork
Sautéed Kale and White
Beans
Cornmeal Drop Biscuits
Pineapple Mint Julep
Sundaes
Orange Spice Tea

SERVES 6
TOTAL CALORIES PER SERVING: 579
(Calories from Fat: 17%)

This menu combines the flavors of the South with updated ingredients and cooking techniques.

The barbecue uses pork tenderloin—one of the leanest cuts of pork. In the side dish, the greens are enhanced with fiber-rich vegetables. Cornmeal adds flavor to the biscuits without adding a lot of fat. (Menu calories reflect 2 biscuits per person.) The dessert—a fruit sauce ladled over nonfat yogurt—is almost fat-free. Savor this guiltless fare on the porch as the sun slowly dips beyond the horizon.

The blending of pineapple and bourbon gives Pineapple Mint Julep Sundaes (page 54) flavor with a hint of Old South tradition.

OVEN-BARBECUED PORK

2 (¾-pound) pork tenderloins
Vegetable cooking spray
2½ tablespoons no-salt-added catsup
1½ tablespoons cider vinegar
1 tablespoon reduced-calorie maple syrup
2 teaspoons Dijon mustard
1 teaspoon low-sodium Worcestershire sauce
⅛ teaspoon ground red pepper
Fresh rosemary sprigs (optional)

Trim fat from tenderloins. Place tenderloins on a rack in a roasting pan coated with cooking spray.

Combine catsup and next 5 ingredients; brush lightly over tenderloins. Insert a meat thermometer into thickest part of tenderloin, if desired.

Bake, uncovered, at 400° for 30 minutes or until meat thermometer registers 160°, basting with remaining catsup mixture. Let stand 10 minutes; slice diagonally across grain into thin slices. Place on serving plates, and garnish with rosemary sprigs, if desired. Yield: 6 servings (152 calories per serving).

Per Serving: PROTEIN 24.5g FAT 4.3g (Saturated Fat 1.4g)
CARBOHYDRATE 2.5g FIBER 0g CHOLESTEROL 79mg
IRON 1.3mg SODIUM 113mg CALCIUM 9mg

SAUTÉED KALE AND WHITE BEANS

1 medium onion
Vegetable cooking spray
3½ cups chopped kale (about 5 ounces)
¼ cup water
1 cup canned cannellini beans, drained
½ cup chopped plum tomato
½ teaspoon dried whole rosemary, crushed
⅛ teaspoon salt

Slice onion, and separate into rings. Coat a large nonstick skillet with cooking spray; place over medium-high heat until hot. Add onion, and sauté 5 minutes or until tender. Add kale and water; cover, reduce heat, and simmer 8 minutes or until kale is wilted, stirring frequently. Stir in beans and remaining ingredients. Cook, uncovered, over medium heat until thoroughly heated. Yield: 6 servings (51 calories per ½-cup serving).

Per Serving: PROTEIN 2.6g FAT 0.5g (Saturated Fat 0g)
CARBOHYDRATE 9.5g FIBER 1.7g CHOLESTEROL 0mg
IRON 1.0mg SODIUM 113mg CALCIUM 38mg

CORNMEAL DROP BISCUITS

1¼ cups all-purpose flour
⅓ cup yellow cornmeal
1½ teaspoons baking powder
¼ teaspoon salt
¼ cup chopped green onions
¼ teaspoon garlic powder
⅛ teaspoon ground red pepper
¼ cup plus 2 tablespoons skim milk
2 tablespoons vegetable oil
1 tablespoon honey
1 egg, lightly beaten
Vegetable cooking spray

Combine first 7 ingredients in a large bowl; make a well in center of mixture. Combine milk, oil, honey, and egg; add to dry ingredients, stirring just until dry ingredients are moistened.
Drop dough by heaping tablespoonfuls, 2 inches apart, onto baking sheets coated with cooking spray.

Bake at 400° for 10 to 12 minutes or until lightly browned. Yield: 1 dozen (98 calories each).

Per Biscuit: PROTEIN 2.5g FAT 3.0g (Saturated Fat 0.6g)
CARBOHYDRATE 15.1g FIBER 0.6g CHOLESTEROL 19mg
IRON 0.9mg SODIUM 97mg CALCIUM 40mg

PINEAPPLE MINT JULEP SUNDAES

¾ cup unsweetened pineapple juice
1 tablespoon cornstarch
3 tablespoons bourbon
1 (8-ounce) can crushed pineapple in juice, drained
1 tablespoon minced fresh mint
3 cups vanilla nonfat frozen yogurt
Fresh mint sprigs (optional)

Combine pineapple juice and cornstarch in a small saucepan, stirring until smooth. Stir in bourbon, and cook over medium heat, stirring constantly, until mixture is thickened. Stir in crushed pineapple and minced mint; cook until thoroughly heated.
Scoop ½ cup frozen yogurt into each dessert dish; top evenly with pineapple mixture. Garnish with fresh mint sprigs, if desired. Serve immediately. Yield: 6 servings (121 calories per serving).

Per Serving: PROTEIN 3.6g FAT 0.1g (Saturated Fat 0g)
CARBOHYDRATE 27.9g FIBER 0.3g CHOLESTEROL 0mg
IRON 0.2mg SODIUM 59mg CALCIUM 135mg

ORANGE SPICE TEA

¾ cup unsweetened orange juice
⅓ cup sugar
8 orange spice-flavored tea bags
2 (3-inch) sticks cinnamon
5½ cups boiling water

Combine first 4 ingredients in a large pitcher. Add boiling water; cover and steep 10 minutes. Remove and discard tea bags and cinnamon sticks; let cool. Serve over ice. Yield: 1½ quarts (59 calories per 1-cup serving).

Per Serving: PROTEIN 0.2g FAT 0.0g (Saturated Fat 0g)
CARBOHYDRATE 14.9g FIBER 0.1g CHOLESTEROL 0mg
IRON 0.1mg SODIUM 7mg CALCIUM 3mg

Dinner for Your Sweetheart

Bruschetta with Basil
Vegetable-Cheese Linguine
Chocolate Meringue Hearts
Strawberry Sparkler

SERVES 2
TOTAL CALORIES PER SERVING: 700
(Calories from Fat: 11%)

When it's just you and your beloved for dinner, prepare this elegant yet easy meal that's simple enough to make after a day at work.

The romance of Italy inspired this colorful menu. Begin the evening with bruschetta, an Italian appetizer with simple elegance. Toss the pasta and serve for the main course.

For dessert, entice your sweetheart with Chocolate Meringue Hearts, a triple chocolate delight. Prepare meringues up to 2 days ahead and store in an airtight container for an effortless dessert on this special night. After the meal, pour Strawberry Sparkler for a memorable toast.

Settle in for a romantic evening of music and candlelight when you serve Vegetable-Cheese Linguine (page 56) and Bruschetta with Basil.

BRUSCHETTA WITH BASIL

2 (¾-ounce) slices Italian bread
½ teaspoon olive oil
1 tablespoon nonfat cream cheese product
½ ounce goat cheese
2 teaspoons grated Parmesan cheese
1 (7-ounce) jar roasted red pepper in water
2 small fresh basil sprigs

Place bread slices on an ungreased baking sheet; brush bread slices evenly with olive oil. Bake at 450° for 5 minutes or until lightly browned.

Combine cream cheese, goat cheese, and Parmesan cheese in a small bowl; stir well. Spread mixture evenly over bread slices.

Cut 1 piece of red pepper into 6 julienne strips. Reserve remaining red pepper for another use. Arrange 3 pepper strips over each bread slice; top each slice with a basil sprig. Yield: 2 appetizer servings (114 calories per serving).

Per Serving: PROTEIN 5.0g FAT 3.3g (Saturated Fat 1.5g)
CARBOHYDRATE 14.9g FIBER 0.7g CHOLESTEROL 9mg
IRON 0.6mg SODIUM 298mg CALCIUM 83mg

VEGETABLE-CHEESE LINGUINE

Vegetable cooking spray
4 ounces fresh shiitake mushrooms, sliced
¼ cup sliced green onions
1 cup torn fresh spinach
1 cup seeded, diced plum tomato
¼ cup minced fresh parsley
2 tablespoons canned low-sodium chicken broth, undiluted
3 ounces linguine, uncooked
3 tablespoons freshly grated Parmesan cheese

Coat a large nonstick skillet with cooking spray; place over medium-high heat until hot. Add mushrooms and green onions; sauté 3 minutes. Add spinach, tomato, parsley, and chicken broth; cook 1 minute. Set aside, and keep warm.

Cook pasta according to package directions, omitting salt and fat; drain. Place pasta in a large bowl; add cheese, tossing well. Add mushroom mixture, and toss gently. Serve immediately. Yield: 2 servings (240 calories per 2-cup serving).

Per Serving: PROTEIN 11.9g FAT 4.4g (Saturated Fat 1.9g)
CARBOHYDRATE 39.3g FIBER 3.8g CHOLESTEROL 7mg
IRON 3.7mg SODIUM 206mg CALCIUM 171mg

CHOCOLATE MERINGUE HEARTS

2 egg whites
¼ teaspoon cream of tartar
¼ cup sugar
1 tablespoon unsweetened cocoa
¼ teaspoon vanilla extract
⅔ cup chocolate nonfat frozen yogurt, softened
2 teaspoons chocolate syrup

Line a baking sheet with parchment or heavy brown paper. Draw 2 (4- x 3-inch) hearts on paper. Set aside.

Beat egg whites and cream of tartar at high speed of an electric mixer until mixture is foamy. Combine sugar and cocoa. Gradually add sugar mixture to egg whites, 1 tablespoon at a time, beating until stiff peaks form and sugar dissolves (2 to 4 minutes). Fold in vanilla.

Pipe egg white mixture onto hearts on paper, building up sides to form a shell. Bake at 250° for 1 hour. Turn oven off. Cool in oven 2 hours with oven door closed. Carefully remove from paper; let cool completely on wire racks.

Place meringue hearts on individual dessert plates. Scoop ⅓ cup frozen yogurt into each meringue heart, and drizzle evenly with chocolate syrup. Serve immediately. Yield: 2 servings (195 calories per serving).

Per Serving: PROTEIN 6.3g FAT 0.5g (Saturated Fat 0.2g)
CARBOHYDRATE 42.5g FIBER 0g CHOLESTEROL 0mg
IRON 0.6mg SODIUM 118mg CALCIUM 93mg

STRAWBERRY SPARKLER

1 cup sliced fresh strawberries
¼ cup frozen strawberry daiquiri fruit juice concentrate, thawed
¾ cup champagne, chilled
½ cup lemon-flavored sparkling water, chilled
2 fresh strawberries (optional)

Place sliced strawberries in container of an electric blender; cover and process until smooth. Pour strawberry puree into a pitcher; add strawberry juice concentrate, and stir well. Cover and chill.

Just before serving, stir in champagne and sparkling water. Pour into chilled champagne flutes. Garnish with fresh strawberries, if desired. Yield: 2 cups (151 calories per 1-cup serving).

Per Serving: PROTEIN 0.7g FAT 0.3g (Saturated Fat 0g)
CARBOHYDRATE 21.0g FIBER 2.0g CHOLESTEROL 0mg
IRON 0.7mg SODIUM 5mg CALCIUM 22mg

Flaky Pastry-Wrapped Pork, creamy Lemon Nutmeg Yams, and steamed asparagus will impress the most discriminating guests at your dinner party. (Menu begins on page 69.)

That's
Entertaining

Repast by the River

Chicken and Black-Eyed
Pea Salad
Gingered Melon Salad
Sweet Onion Focaccia
Cocoa Brownie Drops
Sparkling water

SERVES 6
TOTAL CALORIES PER SERVING: 544
(Calories from Fat: 21%)

After a day on the river, ravenous paddlers are ready to eat. Trail mix may have gotten them through the rapids, but this portable meal is the extra stroke needed to get the exhausted rafters home.

Keep the perishable foods fresh by packing them in a large cooler. Place the Chicken and Black-Eyed Pea Salad and Gingered Melon Salad in airtight containers and stack over ice in the cooler. Surround the salads with chilled bottles of sparkling water, and seal the focaccia and cookies in zip-top bags to take along. Tuck in some lettuce leaves to serve with the chicken salad. (Menu calories include 1 wedge of focaccia and 2 cookies per person.)

The next time you're "roughing it" outdoors, skip the usual sandwich and carry along Chicken and Black-Eyed Pea Salad, Gingered Melon Salad, Sweet Onion Focaccia, and sparkling water.

CHICKEN AND BLACK-EYED PEA SALAD

2 (15.8-ounce) cans black-eyed peas, drained
2 cups chopped cooked chicken breast (skinned
   before cooking and cooked without fat)
¾ cup minced celery
¾ cup minced sweet red pepper
½ cup minced green onions
⅓ cup minced fresh cilantro
3 tablespoons commercial oil-free Italian dressing
2 tablespoons country-style Dijon mustard
6 red leaf lettuce leaves

Combine peas, chicken, celery, red pepper, green onions, cilantro, Italian dressing, and mustard in a large bowl; stir well. Cover and chill.

To serve, place a lettuce leaf on each individual salad plate; spoon 1 cup black-eyed pea mixture onto each lettuce leaf. Yield: 6 servings (220 calories per 1-cup serving).

Per Serving: PROTEIN 24.2g FAT 3.1g (Saturated Fat 0.7g)
CARBOHYDRATE 23.8g FIBER 2.9g CHOLESTEROL 40mg
IRON 2.7mg SODIUM 471mg CALCIUM 57mg

GINGERED MELON SALAD

¾ cup water
¼ cup sugar
1 teaspoon peeled, grated gingerroot
1 cup cantaloupe balls
1 cup honeydew melon balls
1 cup watermelon balls

Combine water, sugar, and gingerroot in a medium saucepan. Bring to a boil; reduce heat, and simmer, uncovered, 14 minutes, stirring occasionally. Remove from heat, and let cool completely.

Combine melon balls in a medium bowl. Pour sugar mixture over melon balls, and toss gently. Cover and chill. Yield: 6 servings (62 calories per ½-cup serving).

Per Serving: PROTEIN 0.6g FAT 0.2g (Saturated Fat 0.1g)
CARBOHYDRATE 15.6g FIBER 0.8g CHOLESTEROL 0mg
IRON 0.1mg SODIUM 7mg CALCIUM 7mg

SWEET ONION FOCACCIA

1 tablespoon cumin seeds
1 tablespoon reduced-calorie margarine
1½ cups finely chopped onion
1 teaspoon sugar
2 cups plus 2 tablespoons bread flour, divided
½ cup whole wheat flour
½ teaspoon salt
1 package active dry yeast
1 cup warm skim milk (120° to 130°)
3 tablespoons olive oil
2 tablespoons bread flour
Vegetable cooking spray

Place cumin seeds in a large nonstick skillet; cook over medium-high heat until toasted, stirring frequently. Remove from skillet, and cool. Add margarine to skillet; place over medium heat until margarine melts. Add onion and sugar; sauté until onion is browned. Set aside.

Combine 1 cup bread flour and next 3 ingredients in a large mixing bowl; stir well. Gradually add milk and olive oil to flour mixture, beating well at low speed of an electric mixer. Beat an additional 2 minutes at medium speed. Gradually stir in enough of the remaining 1 cup plus 2 tablespoons bread flour to make a soft dough.

Sprinkle 2 tablespoons bread flour over work surface. Turn dough out onto surface; knead until smooth and elastic (about 8 to 10 minutes). Place in a large bowl coated with cooking spray, turning to coat top. Cover and let rise in a warm place (85°), free from drafts, 45 to 55 minutes or until doubled.

Punch dough down. Press onto a 15-inch round pizza pan coated with cooking spray. Poke holes in dough at 1-inch intervals with handle of a wooden spoon. Spread onion mixture over dough; press lightly. Sprinkle with toasted cumin seeds. Let rise, uncovered, in a warm place, free from drafts, 30 minutes. Bake at 375° for 20 minutes or until golden. Cut into wedges. Serve warm or at room temperature. Yield: 16 servings (124 calories per wedge).

Per Wedge: PROTEIN 3.7g FAT 3.6g (Saturated Fat 0.4g)
CARBOHYDRATE 19.3g FIBER 1.4g CHOLESTEROL 0mg
IRON 1.4mg SODIUM 90mg CALCIUM 31mg

COCOA BROWNIE DROPS

¾ cup reduced-calorie margarine, softened
⅔ cup sugar
½ cup firmly packed brown sugar
½ cup frozen egg substitute, thawed
1¾ cups all-purpose flour
1 teaspoon baking soda
½ teaspoon salt
½ cup unsweetened cocoa
¾ cup miniature chocolate chips

Beat softened margarine at medium speed of an electric mixer until creamy; gradually add sugars, beating well. Add egg substitute, ¼ cup at a time, beating well after each addition.

Combine flour, baking soda, salt, and cocoa. Add to margarine mixture, stirring just until blended. Stir in miniature chocolate chips. Drop cookie dough by level tablespoonfuls, 2 inches apart, onto ungreased cookie sheets. Bake at 375° for 6 minutes. Remove from cookie sheets, and let cool on wire racks. Yield: 4 dozen (69 calories each).

Per Cookie: PROTEIN 1.1g FAT 2.9g (Saturated Fat 0.8g)
CARBOHYDRATE 10.4g FIBER 0.1g CHOLESTEROL 0mg
IRON 0.6mg SODIUM 74mg CALCIUM 9mg

Invite the Neighbors

Pumpkin Bisque
Turkey Sandwiches on
Cornmeal Bread
Broccoli-Potato Caesar
Salad
Spiced Cranberry Tea

SERVES 10
TOTAL CALORIES PER SERVING: 592
Calories from Fat: 16%

Give a warm welcome to the new family on the block with this fall harvest supper. Keep it cozy—invite one other family. Before the meal, encourage the children to play outdoors. Relays in the brisk fall air are good ice-breakers and will fuel appetites.

When you're ready to eat, start with bowls of warm, inviting Pumpkin Bisque followed by hearty turkey sandwiches and Caesar salad. Top off the meal with fragrant mugs of Spiced Cranberry Tea.

Adorned with a mixture of sour cream and pumpkin pie spice, creamy Pumpkin Bisque is a warm way to signal the onset of the harvest season.

PUMPKIN BISQUE

3 cups sliced carrot
2 (13¾-ounce) cans no-salt-added chicken broth, undiluted and divided
3 cups canned pumpkin
1 (12-ounce) can evaporated skimmed milk
¼ cup water
1 tablespoon sugar
1½ teaspoons pumpkin pie spice
½ teaspoon chicken-flavored bouillon granules
¼ teaspoon salt
¼ teaspoon ground white pepper
¼ cup low-fat sour cream
2 teaspoons skim milk
⅛ teaspoon pumpkin pie spice

Combine carrot and 1 cup broth in a saucepan; bring to a boil. Cover, reduce heat, and simmer 15 to 20 minutes or until tender. Let cool slightly.

Transfer carrot and liquid to container of an electric blender; cover and process until smooth. Transfer to a 3-quart saucepan; add remaining broth, pumpkin, and next 7 ingredients. Cook over medium heat until hot, stirring frequently; ladle into bowls. Combine sour cream, 2 teaspoons milk, and ⅛ teaspoon pumpkin pie spice. Spoon dollops of sour cream mixture over bisque. Pull a wooden pick through dollops. Yield: 2½ quarts (85 calories per 1-cup serving).

Per Serving: PROTEIN 4.4g FAT 1.6g (Saturated Fat 0.7g)
CARBOHYDRATE 13.6g FIBER 2.0g CHOLESTEROL 4mg
IRON 0.8mg SODIUM 201mg CALCIUM 131mg

TURKEY SANDWICHES ON CORNMEAL BREAD

¼ cup reduced-calorie mayonnaise
¼ cup low-fat sour cream
4 ounces nonfat cream cheese product, softened
¼ cup apple chutney
½ teaspoon curry powder
¾ cup fresh cranberries
½ cup chopped tart cooking apple
1½ tablespoons sugar
⅛ teaspoon ground cinnamon
¼ cup unsweetened orange juice
1 teaspoon lemon juice
20 slices Cornmeal Bread, toasted
30 argula leaves
1¼ pounds thinly sliced cooked turkey breast
   (skinned before cooking and cooked without fat)

Combine first 3 ingredients in a medium bowl; beat at medium speed of an electric mixer until smooth. Add chutney and curry powder; stir well.

Combine cranberries and next 5 ingredients in a saucepan. Bring to a boil; reduce heat, and simmer, uncovered, 3 minutes or until thickened.

Spread chutney mixture evenly over 10 slices of Cornmeal Bread. Top each evenly with argula leaves and turkey. Spoon cranberry mixture evenly over turkey; top with remaining 10 bread slices. Yield: 10 servings (344 calories per serving).

Cornmeal Bread

¾ cup skim milk
¼ cup margarine
2 packages active dry yeast
½ cup warm water (105° to 115°)
⅓ cup sugar
1 teaspoon salt
1 egg
4¼ cups all-purpose flour, divided
¾ cup yellow cornmeal
2 teaspoons all-purpose flour, divided
Vegetable cooking spray

Combine milk and margarine in a saucepan; cook over medium heat until margarine melts. Cool to 105° to 115°.

Combine yeast and warm water in a 1-cup liquid measuring cup; let stand 5 minutes. Combine yeast mixture, milk mixture, sugar, and salt in a bowl; beat at low speed of an electric mixer until blended. Add egg, 1 cup flour, and cornmeal; beat at medium speed until well blended. Gradually stir in enough of the remaining 3¼ cups flour to make a soft dough.

Sprinkle 1 teaspoon flour over work surface. Turn dough out onto floured surface; knead until smooth and elastic (about 8 to 10 minutes). Place dough in a bowl coated with cooking spray; turn to coat top. Cover and let rise in a warm place (85°), free from drafts, 1 hour or until doubled in bulk.

Punch dough down; divide in half. Sprinkle ½ teaspoon flour over work surface. Roll 1 portion of dough into a 10- x 6-inch rectangle. Roll up jellyroll fashion, starting at short side, pressing firmly to eliminate air pockets. Pinch ends to seal. Place dough, seam side down, in an 8½- x 4½- x 3-inch loafpan coated with cooking spray. Repeat procedure with remaining ½ teaspoon flour and dough.

Cover and let rise in a warm place, free from drafts, 45 minutes or until doubled. Bake at 350° for 25 minutes or until loaves sound hollow when tapped. Remove from pans; let cool on wire racks. Use 20 slices for Turkey Sandwiches. Reserve remaining slices for another use. Yield: 32 (½-inch) slices.

Per Serving: PROTEIN 24.4g   FAT 6.4g   (Saturated Fat 1.4g)
CARBOHYDRATE 45.5g   FIBER 1.9g   CHOLESTEROL 67mg
IRON 3.0mg   SODIUM 351mg   CALCIUM 80mg

 HIGH HEAT, GOOD VOLUME
Bread baking requires a high oven temperature. Popovers and cream puffs bake at a setting of 400° to 450°. This intense heat causes the batter to create steam, which acts as the leavening agent. The leavening action increases the bread's volume before proteins coagulate and set the structure.

Most other breads bake best between 350° and 400°. This range is high enough to allow for expansion, but low enough to prevent the outside of a dense loaf from burning before the inside is done. Although higher oven temperatures usually mean better volume and quality, batters and doughs containing large amounts of sugar do best with temperatures in the range of 325° to 375°. That's because sugar caramelizes at high temperatures, and this could darken the crust.

BROCCOLI-POTATO CAESAR SALAD

½ cup nonfat sour cream alternative
1½ tablespoons olive oil
1 tablespoon Dijon mustard
1 tablespoon white wine vinegar
¼ teaspoon freshly ground pepper
1 clove garlic, minced
1 pound round red potatoes
3 cups broccoli flowerets
½ cup diced sweet red pepper
3 tablespoons freshly grated Parmesan cheese
3 tablespoons minced fresh parsley

Combine first 6 ingredients in a small bowl; stir well. Set aside.

Wash potatoes. Cook in boiling water to cover 18 to 20 minutes or until tender; drain and cool slightly. Cut potatoes into ¼-inch-thick slices, and place in a large bowl. Pour sour cream mixture over potatoes, and toss gently.

Arrange broccoli in a vegetable steamer over boiling water; cover and steam 4 to 5 minutes or until broccoli is tender. Drain. Add broccoli, red pepper, Parmesan cheese, and minced parsley to potato mixture; stir gently. Yield: 5 cups (79 calories per ½-cup serving).

Per Serving: PROTEIN 3.4g FAT 2.8g (Saturated Fat 0.7g)
CARBOHYDRATE 10.4g FIBER 1.7g CHOLESTEROL 1mg
IRON 1.0mg SODIUM 97mg CALCIUM 44mg

SPICED CRANBERRY TEA

6 cups water
10 cranberry herb tea bags
2¾ cups cranberry-raspberry drink
¼ cup sugar
4 (3-inch) strips orange rind
4 (3-inch) strips lemon rind
1⅔ cups unsweetened orange juice

Bring water to a boil in a large saucepan. Add tea bags; remove from heat. Cover and steep 5 minutes.

Remove and discard tea bags. Add cranberry-raspberry drink, sugar, and rind strips, stirring until sugar dissolves. Bring to a boil over medium heat. Cover, reduce heat, and simmer 10 minutes. Strain, discarding rind strips. Stir in orange juice. Serve immediately. Yield: 2½ quarts (84 calories per 1-cup serving).

Per Serving: PROTEIN 0.3g FAT 0.0g (Saturated Fat 0g)
CARBOHYDRATE 20.6g FIBER 0.1g CHOLESTEROL 0mg
IRON 0.1mg SODIUM 5mg CALCIUM 4mg

HEALTHY SHOPPING BEYOND THE SUPERMARKET

A recent consumer survey showed that nearly half of American shoppers believe healthy foods cost more. It's true that brown rice, fat-free chips, fat-free crackers, and nonfat and low-fat cheeses often command premium prices at the local supermarket. But a little creative shopping in other places can help the food budget and build up your supply of healthy groceries. Try some of these alternatives.

Farmers Markets. These are great places to buy seasonal produce at its peak, support local farmers, and try new varieties that don't always make it to stores. Prices are generally lower than or equal to those in supermarkets, and spur-of-the-moment markdowns are common.

Food Co-ops. Team up with neighbors to save money. Buying food as a group directly from wholesalers can eliminate "middleman" costs. If there's not a food co-op in your area, check local library or telephone listings to find out about co-ops in your state. They may allow outsiders to join, or they may be able to provide advice for starting one.

Health Food Stores. These stores are good places to stock up on bulk grains. Shoppers can scoop their own brown rice and whole wheat flours and pastas and save on costly packaging. The stores also have a variety of interesting grains and legumes that few supermarkets stock, such as quinoa and wheat berries. Look for whole wheat tortillas and different varieties of tofu in the refrigerator section.

Caribbean Pepperpot (page 64) is a blend of shrimp, scallops, and colorful peppers served atop barley rather than rice for a new taste twist. Cilantro, the leaves of the coriander plant, adds extra seasoning.

Touch of the Tropics

Caribbean Pepperpot
Mixed Greens with Strawberry-Mustard Dressing
Corn Popovers
Mango-Lime Ice
Spiked Jamaican Fruit Punch

SERVES 8
TOTAL CALORIES PER SERVING: 590
(Calories from Fat: 7%)

Shake off the winter blues with this Caribbean-inspired menu. Invite a few friends to join you on this culinary trip to the islands.

For the main course, accompany the pepperpot, a traditional Caribbean stew, with Mixed Greens with Strawberry-Mustard Dressing and Corn Popovers (1 per person). Keep temperatures rising with a Jamaican punch that's a blend of tropical fruit juices, rum, and a fruit-flavored liqueur.

Use a lush tropical fruit for dessert with Mango-Lime Ice. Although frosty snow drifts may be piled up outside the window, warm breezes and blue skies will come to mind with every mouthful of this island feast.

CARIBBEAN PEPPERPOT

1 pound fresh okra
1 medium-size sweet red pepper
1 medium-size sweet yellow pepper
1 medium-size green pepper
1 medium onion
Vegetable cooking spray
2 tablespoons minced jalapeño pepper
5 cloves garlic, minced
2 cups clam juice
2 cups canned no-salt-added chicken broth,
    undiluted
1 (14½-ounce) can no-salt-added whole tomatoes,
    undrained and coarsely chopped
1 tablespoon dried whole thyme
½ teaspoon freshly ground pepper
3 bay leaves
1½ pounds unpeeled medium-size fresh shrimp
1¼ pounds sea scallops
¼ cup minced fresh cilantro
2 teaspoons grated orange rind
3 cups hot cooked barley (cooked without salt
    or fat)

Trim okra, and cut diagonally into ½-inch pieces. Cut sweet peppers, green pepper, and onion into ½-inch pieces. Set aside.

Coat a Dutch oven with cooking spray; place over medium heat until hot. Add okra; sauté 5 minutes or until lightly browned. Add pepper pieces, onion pieces, jalapeño pepper, and garlic; sauté 10 minutes or until vegetables are tender. Stir in clam juice and next 5 ingredients. Bring to a boil; cover, reduce heat, and simmer 30 minutes.

Peel and devein shrimp. Add shrimp and scallops to mixture; stir well. Bring to a boil; reduce heat, and cook 5 minutes or until shrimp turns pink and scallops are opaque. Remove and discard bay leaves. Stir in cilantro and orange rind.

Place ½ cup cooked barley in each individual serving bowl. Spoon 1½ cups pepperpot over barley in each bowl. Yield: 6 servings (218 calories per serving).

Per Serving: PROTEIN 28.8g FAT 2.7g (Saturated Fat 0.5g)
CARBOHYDRATE 19.1g FIBER 3.1g CHOLESTEROL 123mg
IRON 3.6mg SODIUM 388mg CALCIUM 132mg

MIXED GREENS WITH STRAWBERRY-MUSTARD DRESSING

⅔ cup plain nonfat yogurt
½ cup sliced strawberries
1 tablespoon commercial honey mustard
1 clove garlic
2 cups torn romaine lettuce
2 cups torn red leaf lettuce
1 cup torn Boston lettuce
1 cup torn arugula
1 cup torn radicchio
½ medium-size purple onion, thinly sliced and
    separated into rings
1 cup julienne-cut canned hearts of palm

Combine first 4 ingredients in container of an electric blender; cover and process until smooth. Cover and chill.

Combine romaine lettuce and next 4 ingredients in a large bowl, tossing well. Arrange greens evenly on individual salad plates; top greens evenly with purple onion and hearts of palm. Drizzle yogurt mixture evenly over salads. Yield: 8 servings (51 calories per serving).

Per Serving: PROTEIN 2.5g FAT 0.3g (Saturated Fat 0.1g)
CARBOHYDRATE 10.9g FIBER 1.5g CHOLESTEROL 0mg
IRON 0.7mg SODIUM 71mg CALCIUM 68mg

CORN POPOVERS

1 cup bread flour
1 tablespoon yellow cornmeal
1 tablespoon minced fresh chives
1 teaspoon sugar
¼ teaspoon salt
¼ teaspoon ground red pepper
¾ cup skim milk
½ cup fresh corn cut from cob (about 1 ear)
3 egg whites
1 egg
2 teaspoons vegetable oil
Vegetable cooking spray

Combine first 6 ingredients in a large bowl; stir well. Combine milk, corn, egg whites, egg, and oil in container of an electric blender; cover and process 30 seconds, stopping once to scrape down sides.

Add milk mixture to dry ingredients; stir well with a wire whisk. Pour batter evenly into muffin pans coated with cooking spray, filling three-fourths full. Place in a cold oven. Turn oven on 450°, and bake 15 minutes. Reduce heat to 350°, and bake an additional 30 to 35 minutes or until popovers are crusty and brown. Serve immediately. Yield: 1 dozen popovers (77 calories each).

Per Popover: PROTEIN 3.6g FAT 1.7g (Saturated Fat 0.3g)
CARBOHYDRATE 11.7g FIBER 0.3g CHOLESTEROL 19mg
IRON 0.7mg SODIUM 77mg CALCIUM 24mg

MANGO-LIME ICE

½ cup sugar
2 cups water
1¾ cups pureed ripe mango (about 4 medium)
¼ cup fresh lime juice
¼ teaspoon ground ginger

Combine sugar and water in a small saucepan. Bring to a boil; cook, stirring constantly, over medium heat until sugar dissolves. Boil 3 minutes without stirring. Remove from heat, and let cool slightly.

Combine sugar mixture, mango, lime juice, and ginger, stirring well with a wire whisk. Spoon mango mixture into an 11- x 7- x 1½-inch baking dish. Cover and freeze until firm.

Remove from freezer, and let stand 15 minutes. Transfer mixture in batches to container of an electric blender or food processor; cover and process until smooth. Scoop ice into individual dessert bowls. Serve immediately. Yield: 4 cups (83 calories per ½-cup serving).

Per Serving: PROTEIN 0.3g FAT 0.1g (Saturated Fat 0g)
CARBOHYDRATE 21.7g FIBER 0.7g CHOLESTEROL 0mg
IRON 0.1mg SODIUM 1mg CALCIUM 6mg

SPIKED JAMAICAN FRUIT PUNCH

1 cup guava nectar
1 cup unsweetened pineapple juice
¾ cup fresh orange juice
¾ cup light rum
¼ cup fresh lime juice
¼ cup Midori
Orange slices (optional)
Lime slices (optional)

Combine first 6 ingredients in a large pitcher; stir well. Chill thoroughly. Serve over ice. If desired, garnish with orange and lime slices. Yield: 4 cups (161 calories per ½-cup serving).

Per Serving: PROTEIN 0.3g FAT 0.1g (Saturated Fat 0g)
CARBOHYDRATE 16.5g FIBER 0.1g CHOLESTEROL 0mg
IRON 0.2mg SODIUM 1mg CALCIUM 8mg

COUNTING THE BEATS

To determine your heart rate, locate your radial artery (on the thumb side of your wrist) and take your pulse during your exercise session. Take your pulse count for 10 seconds and then multiply that number by 6 to get your actual heart rate. If that number is above your target heart rate (THR) zone, slow the intensity of your workout. If the number is below the zone, step up the pace.

AGE	PREDICTED MAXIMUM HEART RATE (in minutes)	TARGET HEART RATE ZONE 60%	90%	NUMBER OF HEARTBEATS IN 10 SECONDS 60%	90%
20	200	120	180	20	30
25	195	117	176	20	29
30	190	114	171	19	29
35	185	111	167	19	28
40	180	108	162	18	27
45	175	105	158	18	26
50	170	102	153	17	26
55	165	99	149	17	25
60	160	96	144	16	24

MATHEMATICAL FORMULA
Maximum Heart Rate (MHR) = 220 minus age
MHR x 60% and 90% = THR in minutes

Satay Grill Party

Roasted Eggplant Spread
with Pita Chips
Satay Trio
Fragrant Basmati Rice
Minted Cucumber and
Tomato Salad
Grilled Honey Fruit
Skewers

SERVES 8
TOTAL CALORIES PER SERVING: 641
(Calories from Fat: 28%)

Satay, morsels of skewered
and grilled meat, is enjoyed
throughout Southeast Asia. Street
vendors typically sell the aro-
matic skewers with a spicy peanut sauce.

Satay is a perfect main course
for a barbecue. You can prepare
the meat ahead and grill it
quickly. Combine the hearty
satay with seasoned rice and a
cool, crisp salad for a complete
meal. Serve Grilled Honey Fruit
Skewers to close the meal with a
refreshing hint of sweetness.

A simple basting mixture of only four ingredients adds tremendous flavor to Grilled Honey Fruit Skewers (page 68).

ROASTED EGGPLANT SPREAD WITH PITA CHIPS

4 (6-inch) pita bread rounds
1 (1-pound) eggplant, peeled and cut into ½-inch
   cubes
2 cloves garlic, minced
Vegetable cooking spray
1 teaspoon dark sesame oil
⅓ cup finely chopped sweet red pepper
⅓ cup finely chopped onion
2 teaspoons peeled, minced gingerroot
½ teaspoon curry powder
3 tablespoons minced fresh cilantro
1½ tablespoons rice wine vinegar
1½ tablespoons water
¼ teaspoon salt

Separate each pita bread into 2 rounds; cut each round into 6 wedges, and place on ungreased baking sheets. Bake at 350° for 10 minutes or until lightly browned. Set aside.

Combine eggplant and garlic in a 15- x 10- x 1-inch jellyroll pan coated with cooking spray. Coat eggplant and garlic with cooking spray; toss well. Cover and bake at 400° for 10 minutes. Uncover and stir well. Bake, uncovered, an additional 15 minutes or until eggplant is tender. Transfer mixture to a medium bowl.

Coat a medium nonstick skillet with cooking spray; add oil. Heat over medium-high heat until hot. Add red pepper and next 3 ingredients; sauté 3 to 4 minutes or until vegetables are tender. Add to eggplant mixture. Stir in cilantro, vinegar, water, and salt. Let cool.

Position knife blade in food processor bowl; add eggplant mixture. Process until smooth, scraping sides of processor bowl occasionally. Transfer mixture to a serving bowl. Serve with toasted pita wedges. Yield: 8 appetizer servings (65 calories per 3 tablespoons dip and 6 pita chips).

Per Serving: PROTEIN 1.6g FAT 1.2g (Saturated Fat 0.1g)
CARBOHYDRATE 12.0g FIBER 2.5g CHOLESTEROL 0mg
IRON 1.0mg SODIUM 157mg CALCIUM 38mg

SATAY TRIO

¾ pound lean boneless pork
¾ pound lean boneless lamb
¾ pound skinned, boned chicken breasts
⅓ cup reduced-sodium teriyaki sauce
⅓ cup unsweetened pineapple juice
1 tablespoon curry powder
1 tablespoon chili powder
2 tablespoons honey
2 tablespoons lemon juice
1 teaspoon ground ginger
Vegetable cooking spray
Peanut Sauce

Cut pork, lamb, and chicken into ¼-inch-wide strips, and place in a large heavy-duty, zip-top plastic bag. Combine teriyaki sauce and next 6 ingredients; pour over meat. Seal bag, and shake until meat is well coated. Marinate in refrigerator 8 hours, turning bag occasionally.

Soak 24 (10-inch) bamboo skewers in water 30 minutes; set aside.

Drain meat; discard marinade. Thread pork, lamb, and chicken alternately onto soaked skewers. Coat grill rack with cooking spray; place on grill over medium-hot coals (350° to 400°). Place skewers on rack; grill, covered, 1 to 2 minutes on each side or until done. Serve with Peanut Sauce. Yield: 8 servings (300 calories per serving).

Peanut Sauce

Vegetable cooking spray
½ cup chopped onion
1 tablespoon peeled, minced gingerroot
1½ teaspoons sugar
2 cloves garlic, minced
⅔ cup 1% low-fat milk
⅓ cup creamy peanut butter
2 tablespoons reduced-sodium teriyaki sauce
1 tablespoon lemon juice
2 teaspoons hot sauce

Coat a large nonstick skillet with cooking spray; place over medium-high heat until hot. Add onion, gingerroot, sugar, and garlic; sauté until onion is tender.

Combine onion mixture, milk, and remaining ingredients in container of an electric blender; cover and process until smooth, stopping once to scrape down sides. Yield: 1⅓ cups.

Per Serving: PROTEIN 32.2g FAT 14.6g (Saturated Fat 4.0g)
CARBOHYDRATE 9.6g FIBER 1.1g CHOLESTEROL 87mg
IRON 1.8mg SODIUM 299mg CALCIUM 50mg

FRAGRANT BASMATI RICE

1¼ cups basmati rice
½ teaspoon salt
¼ teaspoon ground cardamom
¼ teaspoon ground turmeric
¼ teaspoon ground red pepper
⅛ teaspoon ground cinnamon
Dash of saffron
2½ cups water

Combine all ingredients in a medium saucepan. Bring to a boil, and stir. Cover, reduce heat, and simmer 20 minutes. Remove from heat, and let rice stand 5 minutes. Yield: 8 servings (117 calories per ½-cup serving).

Per Serving: PROTEIN 2.3g FAT 0.2g (Saturated Fat 0.1g)
CARBOHYDRATE 25.6g FIBER 0.4g CHOLESTEROL 0mg
IRON 1.4mg SODIUM 148mg CALCIUM 11mg

MINTED CUCUMBER AND TOMATO SALAD

1 tablespoon minced fresh mint
¼ teaspoon salt
1 clove garlic, minced
1 (8-ounce) carton plain nonfat
   yogurt
1 tablespoon lemon juice
2 cups thinly sliced English cucumber
2 cups thinly sliced plum tomato
½ cup fresh cilantro sprigs

Combine mint, salt, and garlic; crush, using a mortar and pestle. Combine mint mixture, yogurt, and lemon juice; stir well. Cover and chill.

Combine cucumber, tomato, and cilantro in a medium bowl. Add yogurt mixture, and toss well. Yield: 8 servings (32 calories per ½-cup serving).

Per Serving: PROTEIN 2.3g FAT 0.2g (Saturated Fat 0.1g)
CARBOHYDRATE 5.7g FIBER 0.8g CHOLESTEROL 1mg
IRON 0.5mg SODIUM 102mg CALCIUM 69mg

GRILLED HONEY FRUIT SKEWERS

4 medium-size ripe nectarines
2 medium bananas
32 (1-inch) chunks fresh pineapple
2 tablespoons lemon juice
3 tablespoons reduced-calorie margarine, melted
3 tablespoons honey
¾ teaspoon ground cinnamon
Vegetable cooking spray
Fresh mint sprig (optional)

Slice each nectarine into 8 wedges, and place wedges in a large bowl. Peel and slice each banana into 8 slices. Add banana and pineapple to nectarine wedges. Pour lemon juice over fruit mixture, and toss well. Cover and chill at least 1 hour.

Soak 16 (6-inch) wooden skewers in water for 30 minutes. Drain fruit mixture, reserving juice. Thread fruit alternately onto skewers. Combine reserved juice, margarine, honey, and ground cinnamon; stir well.

Coat grill rack with cooking spray; place on grill over medium-hot coals (300° to 350°). Brush kabobs lightly with honey mixture, and place on rack. Grill, uncovered, 2 minutes on each side, basting occasionally with remaining honey mixture. Garnish with a mint sprig, if desired. Yield: 8 servings (127 calories per serving).

Per Serving: PROTEIN 1.0g FAT 3.4g (Saturated Fat 0.5g)
CARBOHYDRATE 26.4g FIBER 2.5g CHOLESTEROL 0mg
IRON 0.5mg SODIUM 42mg CALCIUM 11mg

 ## THE IMPORTANCE OF FAMILY DINNERS

Your family may be so busy that it seems impossible to gather everyone around the dinner table each night. According to some researchers, though, it's worth the effort. They suggest that family rituals—from mealtimes to holidays—give security and stability to families, even in difficult circumstances.

One study in which grown children of alcoholic parents were interviewed found that children whose families ate together nightly were less likely to become alcoholics themselves in later life. Even children whose own family rituals were disrupted by alcoholism were strongly protected from an alcoholic future when they married into families that observed such traditions.

In another study, college students and their parents were interviewed about their family traditions. Those students who felt their family's rituals were important and meaningful had higher self-esteem and were better adjusted socially than those who didn't value family traditions. This suggests that whether it's dinner or an annual vacation, the way a family feels about its rituals is more important than the rituals themselves.

Supper Club Soirée

Tuna Niçoise Canapés
Pastry-Wrapped Pork
Lemon Nutmeg Yams
Steamed asparagus
Poached Pear Salad with
Cranberry-Port Vinaigrette
Spiced Ginger Biscotti

SERVES 8
TOTAL CALORIES PER SERVING: 729
(Calories from Fat: 24%)

Next time you host your supper club, wow members with this elegant menu. It may take extra time to prepare, but it's worth the effort. For an easy side dish, steam fresh asparagus (2 pounds) until crisp-tender. (Menu calories are calculated including 3 canapés and 1 biscotti per person.)

Potato slices are the base for a lively mixture of tuna, green beans, and tomatoes in Tuna Niçoise Canapés.

TUNA NIÇOISE CANAPÉS

24 (¼-inch-thick) slices baking potato (about 2 medium)
Vegetable cooking spray
2 tablespoons malt vinegar
1 teaspoon dried whole thyme, divided
¼ teaspoon garlic powder
⅛ teaspoon salt
¾ cup thinly sliced fresh green beans
½ teaspoon freshly ground pepper
1 (5-ounce) tuna steak (¾ inch thick)
2 teaspoons olive oil, divided
2½ tablespoons nonfat sour cream alternative
1 tablespoon Dijon mustard
2 teaspoons capers
12 cherry tomatoes

Arrange potato slices in a single layer on a baking sheet coated with cooking spray. Spray slices with cooking spray. Turn slices, and spray again; brush with vinegar. Combine ½ teaspoon thyme, garlic powder, and salt; sprinkle evenly over slices. Bake at 400° for 15 minutes or until tender; let cool.

Arrange beans in a vegetable steamer over boiling water. Cover; steam 10 minutes or until tender.

Press pepper into both sides of tuna. Coat a nonstick skillet with cooking spray; add 1 teaspoon oil. Place over medium-high heat until hot. Add tuna; cook 4 minutes on each side or until fish flakes easily when tested with a fork. Remove from heat; let cool completely. Flake tuna; place in a bowl. Add beans; toss well. Combine remaining ½ teaspoon thyme, remaining 1 teaspoon oil, sour cream, mustard, and capers; add to tuna mixture, and stir well.

Arrange potato slices on a serving platter. Cut each cherry tomato into 4 slices; arrange 2 tomato slices on top of each potato slice. Spoon tuna mixture over tomato slices. Yield: 24 appetizers (34 calories each).

Per Appetizer: PROTEIN 2.1g FAT 0.9g (Saturated Fat 0.2g)
CARBOHYDRATE 4.4g FIBER 0.6g CHOLESTEROL 2mg
IRON 0.5mg SODIUM 52mg CALCIUM 6mg

PASTRY-WRAPPED PORK

1 (1½-pound) lean boneless pork loin roast
½ cup cream sherry
3 heads garlic, unpeeled
Vegetable cooking spray
½ cup sun-dried tomato (without oil)
2 tablespoons fine, dry breadcrumbs, toasted
¼ teaspoon dried whole rosemary, crushed
½ teaspoon freshly ground pepper
¼ teaspoon salt
16 sheets commercial frozen phyllo pastry,
    thawed

Trim fat from roast; place roast in a large heavy-duty, zip-top plastic bag. Pour sherry over roast. Seal bag, and shake until roast is well coated. Marinate roast in refrigerator at least 4 hours, turning bag occasionally.

Gently peel outer skin from garlic; cut off top one-fourth of each head, and discard. Place garlic, cut side up, in center of a piece of heavy-duty aluminum foil; coat with cooking spray. Fold aluminum foil over garlic, sealing tightly. Bake at 350° for 1 hour or until garlic is soft. Remove from oven, and let cool completely. Remove and discard papery skin from garlic. Scoop out soft garlic with a small spoon; set garlic aside.

Pour boiling water over sun-dried tomato to cover; let stand 5 minutes or until tomato is softened. Drain and chop tomato. Combine chopped tomato and garlic in a small bowl; add breadcrumbs and rosemary, stirring well. Set aside.

Remove roast from bag; discard marinade. Cut roast into 8 slices. Cut a deep pocket in top of each pork slice. Fill pockets evenly with tomato mixture. Sprinkle both sides of slices with ground pepper and salt.

Coat a large nonstick skillet with vegetable cooking spray; place skillet over medium-high heat until hot. Add pork slices; cook 3 minutes on each side or until pork is browned. Drain and pat dry with paper towels.

Place 1 sheet of phyllo on wax paper (keep remaining phyllo covered). Coat phyllo with cooking spray. Fold phyllo in half lengthwise; place 1 pork slice 3 inches from one end. Fold narrow end of phyllo over top of slice. Fold sides of phyllo over pork slice, and roll up.

Place a second sheet of phyllo on wax paper; cut to a 12-inch square, and coat with cooking spray. Place wrapped pork slice in center of phyllo square. Bring points of phyllo square to middle, gently twisting points together in center; pull ends up and out to resemble a package. Coat bundle with cooking spray, and place on an ungreased baking sheet. Repeat procedure with remaining phyllo pastry and pork slices.

Bake, uncovered, at 350° for 30 to 35 minutes or until pork is done. Serve immediately. Yield: 8 servings (280 calories per serving).

Per Serving: PROTEIN 21.7g   FAT 9.0g   (Saturated Fat 2.6g)
CARBOHYDRATE 27.0g   FIBER 0.8g   CHOLESTEROL 51mg
IRON 2.5mg   SODIUM 407mg   CALCIUM 35mg

LEMON NUTMEG YAMS

6 medium-size sweet potatoes (about 3 pounds)
3 tablespoons brown sugar
2 tablespoons reduced-calorie margarine
2 teaspoons grated lemon rind
½ teaspoon ground nutmeg
¼ teaspoon salt

Scrub potatoes; prick several times with a fork. Bake at 375° for 1 hour or until done. Let potatoes cool slightly. Cut potatoes in half lengthwise, and scoop out pulp; discard skins. Place pulp in a medium bowl; add brown sugar and remaining ingredients. Beat at medium speed of an electric mixer until mixture is smooth. Yield: 8 servings (159 calories per ½-cup serving).

Per Serving: PROTEIN 2.0g   FAT 2.2g   (Saturated Fat 0.4g)
CARBOHYDRATE 33.6g   FIBER 3.7g   CHOLESTEROL 0mg
IRON 0.8mg   SODIUM 118mg   CALCIUM 31mg

POACHED PEAR SALAD WITH CRANBERRY-PORT VINAIGRETTE

3 small ripe pears
1¼ cups tawny port
⅓ cup thinly sliced shallots
¼ cup fresh cranberries
3 tablespoons raspberry vinegar
3 tablespoons cranberry juice cocktail
3 tablespoons water
2 teaspoons vegetable oil
¼ teaspoon chicken-flavored bouillon granules
4 cups torn red leaf lettuce
4 cups torn escarole
2 cups torn fresh watercress
½ cup crumbled blue cheese
Freshly ground pepper (optional)

Core pears; cut each into 8 slices. Combine port and shallots in a medium saucepan; bring to a boil. Add pear slices, and stir well. Cook over high heat 2 minutes or until pears are crisp-tender, stirring frequently. Remove pear slices and shallots from wine mixture, using a slotted spoon; set aside.

Combine 2 tablespoons wine mixture, cranberries and next 5 ingredients in a small saucepan; bring to a boil. Cook 2 minutes or until mixture begins to thicken slightly, stirring frequently. Remove from heat, and let cool.

Combine leaf lettuce, escarole, and watercress in a large bowl. Add cranberry mixture, and toss gently. Arrange lettuce mixture evenly on individual salad plates; spoon pear and shallot mixture evenly over salad greens. Sprinkle evenly with blue cheese and pepper, if desired. Serve immediately. Yield: 8 servings (85 calories per serving).

Per Serving: PROTEIN 2.2g FAT 3.5g (Saturated Fat 1.6g)
CARBOHYDRATE 12.5g FIBER 2.0g CHOLESTEROL 5mg
IRON 0.5mg SODIUM 130mg CALCIUM 64mg

SPICED GINGER BISCOTTI

½ cup frozen egg substitute, thawed
1½ teaspoons instant coffee granules
½ teaspoon almond extract
2 cups all-purpose flour
¾ teaspoon baking powder
¼ teaspoon salt
½ cup sugar
½ teaspoon ground cardamom
¼ cup margarine, cut into small pieces
¼ cup finely chopped crystallized ginger
Vegetable cooking spray

Combine egg substitute, coffee granules, and almond extract; stir well with a wire whisk. Set aside.

Position knife blade in food processor bowl; add flour and next 4 ingredients, and process until combined. Add margarine, and pulse 12 to 14 times or until mixture resembles coarse meal. Transfer mixture to a large bowl, and stir in ginger. Add egg substitute mixture, and stir until dry ingredients are moistened.

Divide dough in half. Shape each half into an 8-inch log. Transfer logs to a cookie sheet coated with cooking spray. Bake at 325° for 34 minutes. Let cool on wire rack 10 minutes. Cut each log diagonally into 12 slices. Place slices on cookie sheets, cut side down. Bake 12 minutes; turn cookies over, and bake 10 to 12 minutes or until dry. Let cool on wire racks. Yield: 2 dozen cookies (80 calories each).

Per Cookie: PROTEIN 1.6g FAT 2.0g (Saturated Fat 0.4g)
CARBOHYDRATE 13.8g FIBER 0.3g CHOLESTEROL 0mg
IRON 1.0mg SODIUM 65mg CALCIUM 14mg

Challenge your guests to identify the secret ingredient (vanilla) in Peaches with Fruit Sauce (page 74). Fresh blueberries and mint sprigs dress up this rich-tasting dessert.

After the Art Museum Opening

Steamed Chicken Roulades with Chunky Tomato Sauce
Steamed green beans
Steamed baby carrots
Roasted Mushroom and Fennel Salad
Crisp Rosemary-Pepper Breadsticks
Peaches with Fruit Sauce
Sparkling Berry Cooler

SERVES 6
TOTAL CALORIES PER SERVING: 657
(Calories from Fat: 16%)

After viewing the inspirational artistry that graces the halls of the new museum, preserve the mood at your dinner table. Seat guests around the table that you've decorated with a few favorite collectibles.

To assure time to visit with guests, prepare the breadsticks, beverage base, peaches, and dessert sauces ahead. Assemble the dessert just before serving. (Menu calories reflect ½ cup green beans, ½ cup carrots, and 2 breadsticks per person.)

STEAMED CHICKEN ROULADES WITH CHUNKY TOMATO SAUCE

6 (4-ounce) skinned, boned chicken breast halves
¼ teaspoon salt
¼ teaspoon pepper
18 large fresh spinach leaves
Vegetable cooking spray
2 teaspoons olive oil
2⅔ cups coarsely chopped sweet red pepper
¾ cup chopped onion
2 teaspoons minced garlic
1 (14½-ounce) can no-salt-added stewed tomatoes, undrained and chopped
½ cup Chablis or other dry white wine
1 tablespoon balsamic vinegar
¼ cup minced fresh basil
Fresh basil sprigs (optional)

Place chicken breasts between 2 sheets of heavy-duty plastic wrap, and flatten to ¼-inch thickness, using a meat mallet or rolling pin. Sprinkle evenly with salt and pepper; set aside.

Arrange spinach in a vegetable steamer over boiling water. Cover and steam 30 seconds. Arrange 3 spinach leaves on each chicken breast. Roll up chicken lengthwise, tucking ends under. Secure with wooden picks.

Coat a large nonstick skillet with cooking spray; add olive oil. Place over medium-high heat until hot. Add chicken; cook until browned on all sides. Remove from skillet, and set aside. Add chopped pepper and next 5 ingredients to skillet; bring to a boil. Return chicken to skillet. Cover, reduce heat, and simmer 15 to 20 minutes or until chicken is done. Remove chicken from skillet, and keep warm. Stir minced basil into tomato mixture; cook, uncovered, over medium heat 10 to 15 minutes or until most of liquid evaporates, stirring occasionally.

Remove wooden picks from chicken; cut each breast into 5 (½-inch-thick) slices. Arrange 5 slices on each serving plate. Spoon tomato mixture around slices. Garnish each serving with a basil sprig, if desired. Yield: 6 servings (182 calories per serving).

Per Serving: PROTEIN 28.0g FAT 3.3g (Saturated Fat 0.6g)
CARBOHYDRATE 9.8g FIBER 1.8g CHOLESTEROL 66mg
IRON 2.3mg SODIUM 193mg CALCIUM 54mg

ROASTED MUSHROOM AND FENNEL SALAD

3 cups torn romaine lettuce
2 cups torn curly endive
1 cup torn radicchio
¼ cup balsamic vinegar
¼ cup canned no-salt-added chicken broth, undiluted
2 tablespoons olive oil
2 teaspoons Dijon mustard
1 teaspoon crushed garlic
⅛ teaspoon salt
1 fennel bulb (about ½ pound)
2 (3½-ounce) packages fresh shiitake mushrooms, quartered
Vegetable cooking spray
⅛ teaspoon freshly ground pepper

Combine romaine lettuce, curly endive, and radicchio in a large bowl; set aside.

Combine vinegar and next 5 ingredients in a small jar; cover tightly, and shake vigorously.

Trim off tough outer stalks from fennel bulb. Cut bulb in half lengthwise; remove and discard core. Cut fennel into thin strips. Combine fennel strips, mushrooms, and ¼ cup vinegar mixture; toss well.

Spread fennel mixture in a single layer in a 15- x 10- x 1-inch jellyroll pan coated with cooking spray. Bake at 400° for 15 to 20 minutes or until mushrooms are crisp on edges and fennel is tender. Add warm vegetable mixture and remaining vinegar mixture to lettuce mixture; toss well. Place 1¼ cups mixture on each individual salad plate. Sprinkle evenly with pepper. Serve immediately. Yield: 6 servings (69 calories per 1¼-cup serving).

Per Serving: PROTEIN 2.3g FAT 5.2g (Saturated Fat 0.6g)
CARBOHYDRATE 4.8g FIBER 1.1g CHOLESTEROL 0mg
IRON 1.7mg SODIUM 114mg CALCIUM 50mg

CRISP ROSEMARY-PEPPER BREADSTICKS

3½ cups all-purpose flour, divided
1 tablespoon sugar
1 teaspoon salt
1 package rapid-rise yeast
1¼ cups very warm water (120° to 130°)
1 tablespoon olive oil
2 tablespoons minced fresh rosemary
1 teaspoon freshly ground pepper
2 tablespoons plus 2 teaspoons all-purpose flour, divided
Vegetable cooking spray

Combine 1 cup flour, sugar, salt, and yeast in a large mixing bowl; stir well. Gradually add hot water and olive oil, beating at low speed of an electric mixer until blended. Add rosemary and pepper; beat an additional 2 minutes at medium speed. Gradually stir in enough of the remaining 2½ cups flour to make a soft dough.

Sprinkle 2 tablespoons flour evenly over work surface. Turn dough out onto floured surface, and knead until dough is smooth and elastic (about 10 minutes). Shape dough into a ball; cover and let rest 10 minutes.

Divide dough in half. Sprinkle work surface with 1 teaspoon flour. Roll 1 portion of dough into a 12-inch square on floured surface. Cut dough into ½-inch-wide strips.

Place strips ¼ inch apart on a large baking sheet coated with cooking spray. Repeat procedure with remaining 1 teaspoon flour and remaining half of dough.

Cover breadsticks, and let stand 10 minutes. Brush breadsticks lightly with water. Bake at 400° for 12 to 15 minutes or until golden. Remove breadsticks from oven, and reduce temperature to 300°. Let breadsticks cool on baking sheets 15 minutes.

Return breadsticks to oven, and bake at 300° an additional 12 minutes or until crisp. Yield: 4 dozen (39 calories each).

Per Breadstick: PROTEIN 1.1g   FAT 0.4g   (Saturated Fat 0.1g)
CARBOHYDRATE 7.7g   FIBER 0.3g   CHOLESTEROL 0mg
IRON 0.5mg   SODIUM 49mg   CALCIUM 4mg

PEACHES WITH FRUIT SAUCE

1 cup frozen blueberries, thawed
⅓ cup low-sugar grape spread
1 cup chopped canned apricots in juice, drained
⅓ cup no-sugar-added apricot spread
1 cup peach nectar
1 cup water
2 vanilla beans, split lengthwise
3 large fresh peaches, peeled, pitted, and sliced
2 cups vanilla ice milk

Combine blueberries and grape spread in container of an electric blender; cover and process until smooth. Strain puree; discard skins. Cover and chill.

Combine apricots and apricot spread in container of electric blender; cover and process until smooth. Strain puree; discard pulp. Cover and chill.

Combine nectar, water, and vanilla beans in a nonstick skillet. Bring to a boil; add peaches. Cover, reduce heat, and simmer 10 minutes or until tender. Let cool; cover and chill. Remove peaches from liquid; arrange on serving plates. Top each with ⅓ cup ice milk. Spoon purees around ice milk. Serve immediately. Yield: 6 servings (179 calories per serving).

Per Serving: PROTEIN 2.7g   FAT 2.1g   (Saturated Fat 1.2g)
CARBOHYDRATE 40.0g   FIBER 2.1g   CHOLESTEROL 6mg
IRON 0.3mg   SODIUM 68mg   CALCIUM 74mg

SPARKLING BERRY COOLER

2½ cups raspberry nectar, chilled
1½ cups fresh blood orange juice, chilled
2 cups berry-flavored sparkling mineral water, chilled
18 fresh raspberries

Combine first 3 ingredients in a pitcher. Pour into glasses; add 3 raspberries to each. Serve immediately. Yield: 1½ quarts (94 calories per 1-cup serving).

Per Serving: PROTEIN 0.5g   FAT 0.1g   (Saturated Fat 0g)
CARBOHYDRATE 22.8g   FIBER 0.8g   CHOLESTEROL 0mg
IRON 0.5mg   SODIUM 17mg   CALCIUM 8mg

Harvest Stew and Overnight Whole Wheat Pan Rolls will delight all the goblins at your Halloween party. (Menu begins on page 86.)

Holiday Celebrations

New Year's Day Celebration

Smothered Ragoût
Basmati Rice Pilaf
Romaine Salad with
Avocado Dressing
Commercial French bread
Apple-Cherry Brown Betty

SERVES 8
TOTAL CALORIES PER SERVING: 674
(Calories from Fat: 24%)

Celebrate the New Year with this hearty menu. The Smothered Ragoût boasts tender beef and chicken in a rich tomato sauce. For a taste sensation, spoon the ragoût over seasoned basmati rice and serve French bread (1 slice per person) along with the crisp, fresh salad. Enjoy the dessert warm topped with nonfat frozen yogurt.

Make a resolution to get the year off to a great start by serving Smothered Ragoût and Basmati Rice Pilaf.

SMOTHERED RAGOÛT

1½ pounds lean boneless chuck roast
6 cups water
3 (5-ounce) chicken thighs, skinned
Vegetable cooking spray
2 medium onions, cut in half lengthwise and
    thinly sliced
½ cup sliced celery
½ cup chopped green pepper
2 cloves garlic, minced
2 cups peeled, seeded, and chopped tomato
½ cup Chablis or other dry white wine
1 (8-ounce) can no-salt-added tomato sauce
½ teaspoon salt
2 bay leaves

Trim fat from roast; cut roast into 2-inch pieces. Place in a Dutch oven; add water. Bring to a boil; cover, reduce heat, and simmer 1 hour. Add chicken; cook an additional hour. Remove beef and chicken from broth. Let cool. Bone chicken; shred beef and chicken. Skim fat from broth; set aside ¼ cup broth. Reserve remaining broth for another use.

Coat pan with cooking spray; place over medium-high heat until hot. Add onion, celery, green pepper, and garlic; sauté until vegetables are tender. Stir in reserved broth, chopped tomato, and remaining ingredients; cook, uncovered, over medium heat 15 minutes, stirring frequently. Stir in beef and chicken; cook an additional 10 minutes. Remove and discard bay leaves. Yield: 8 servings (203 calories per serving).

Per Serving: PROTEIN 23.6g FAT 8.0g (Saturated Fat 2.6g)
CARBOHYDRATE 8.3g FIBER 1.8g CHOLESTEROL 73mg
IRON 2.4mg SODIUM 222mg CALCIUM 25mg

BASMATI RICE PILAF

Vegetable cooking spray
1 teaspoon reduced-calorie margarine
1 tablespoon minced walnuts
2 tablespoons minced onion
1 clove garlic, minced
2 cups canned low-sodium chicken broth,
    undiluted
1 cup basmati rice, uncooked
¼ cup raisins

Coat a large saucepan with cooking spray; add margarine. Place over medium-high heat until hot. Add walnuts, and cook, stirring constantly, until walnuts are toasted. Remove from saucepan, and set aside.

Add onion and garlic to saucepan; sauté until tender. Add chicken broth. Bring to a boil; stir in rice and raisins. Cover, reduce heat, and simmer 15 minutes. Remove from heat, and let stand 10 minutes. Add toasted walnuts; toss gently with a fork. Serve immediately. Yield: 8 servings (120 calories per ½-cup serving).

Per Serving: PROTEIN 2.8g FAT 1.9g (Saturated Fat 0.3g)
CARBOHYDRATE 23.0g FIBER 0.6g CHOLESTEROL 0mg
IRON 1.4mg SODIUM 26mg CALCIUM 10mg

ROMAINE SALAD WITH AVOCADO DRESSING

⅓ cup unsweetened grapefruit juice
¼ cup water
1 tablespoon no-oil Italian dressing mix
2 teaspoons vegetable oil
¼ cup mashed ripe avocado
8 cups shredded Romaine lettuce
1 cup julienne-cut sweet red pepper (about 1
    medium size)
2 tablespoons grated Parmesan cheese

Combine first 4 ingredients in a small jar; cover tightly, and shake vigorously to blend. Add avocado; cover and shake well. Chill thoroughly.

Combine lettuce and pepper strips in a large bowl; drizzle avocado mixture over salad, and toss gently. Place 1 cup lettuce mixture on each individual salad plate, and sprinkle servings evenly with cheese. Yield: 8 servings (52 calories per 1-cup serving).

Per Serving: PROTEIN 1.7g FAT 2.8g (Saturated Fat 0.7g)
CARBOHYDRATE 5.0g FIBER 1.3g CHOLESTEROL 1mg
IRON 1.1mg SODIUM 254mg CALCIUM 39mg

APPLE-CHERRY BROWN BETTY

1 cup all-purpose flour
½ teaspoon baking powder
½ teaspoon baking soda
⅛ teaspoon salt
⅓ cup firmly packed brown sugar
½ cup vanilla low-fat yogurt
2 tablespoons vegetable oil
2 tablespoons unsweetened orange juice
Vegetable cooking spray
2 medium Granny Smith apples, peeled, cored, and
    thinly sliced
2 teaspoons lemon juice
1 cup frozen dark sweet cherries, thawed
¼ cup sugar
¼ cup all-purpose flour
2 tablespoons sugar
2 tablespoons margarine, softened
2 tablespoons fine, dry breadcrumbs
1 teaspoon ground cinnamon
4 cups vanilla nonfat frozen yogurt

Combine first 5 ingredients in a medium bowl; stir well. Combine low-fat yogurt, oil, and orange juice; stir well. Add yogurt mixture to flour mixture, and stir just until blended. Spoon into a 9-inch square baking dish coated with cooking spray; set aside.

Combine apple slices and lemon juice; toss gently. Arrange apple slices and cherries over batter in pan; sprinkle with ¼ cup sugar.

Combine ¼ cup flour, 2 tablespoons sugar, and margarine; stir until well blended. Stir in breadcrumbs and cinnamon; sprinkle over fruit. Bake at 350° for 45 minutes or until done. To serve, spoon warm dessert evenly into individual dessert bowls; top each serving with ⅓ cup frozen yogurt. Yield: 12 servings (226 calories per serving).

Per Serving: PROTEIN 4.5g FAT 4.7g (Saturated Fat 0.9g)
CARBOHYDRATE 43.2g FIBER 1.3g CHOLESTEROL 1mg
IRON 1.1mg SODIUM 151mg CALCIUM 133mg

St. Patrick's Day Feast

Corned Beef-Cabbage Pie
Tangy Vegetable Salad
Irish Soda Drop Biscuits
Lemon-Cheese Squares
Coffee

SERVES 8
TOTAL CALORIES PER SERVING: 553
(Calories from Fat: 25%)

Host a St. Patrick's Day party featuring this casual menu. The entrée highlights two Irish favorites—corned beef and cabbage. The colorful, crisp vegetable salad and slightly sweet drop biscuits (1 per person) are followed by refreshing Lemon-Cheese Squares (1 each) to conclude the feast.

Tangy Vegetable Salad, Corned Beef-Cabbage Pie, and Irish Soda Drop Biscuits will make Irish eyes smile with pleasure.

CORNED BEEF-CABBAGE PIE

1 (2-pound) corned beef brisket
1 medium cabbage (about 2 pounds)
2 (13¾-ounce) cans no-salt-added beef broth
½ cup (2 ounces) shredded 50% less-fat Swiss cheese
½ cup skim milk
2 tablespoons plus 1 teaspoon all-purpose flour
2 tablespoons water
1 tablespoon brown sugar
2 tablespoons coarse-grained mustard
¼ teaspoon pepper
8 sheets commercial frozen phyllo pastry, thawed
Butter-flavored vegetable cooking spray
Chopped parsley (optional)

Trim fat from brisket; place brisket in a Dutch oven. Cover with water to a depth of 2 inches above brisket. Bring to a boil; cover, reduce heat, and simmer 3 hours or until very tender. Drain; shred meat.

Separate cabbage into leaves. Place leaves and beef broth in a Dutch oven; bring to a boil. Cover, reduce heat, and simmer 30 minutes or until tender, stirring frequently. Drain; reserve ¾ cup cooking liquid. Arrange leaves in a 1½-quart oval gratin dish. Top leaves with corned beef and cheese.

Combine reserved ¾ cup liquid and milk in a saucepan. Combine flour and 2 tablespoons water, stirring well; add to milk mixture. Cook, stirring constantly, over medium heat until thickened. Remove from heat; stir in brown sugar, mustard, and pepper. Spoon over cheese.

Place 1 sheet of phyllo on a damp towel (keep remaining phyllo covered). Coat with cooking spray. Layer remaining 7 sheets phyllo on first sheet coating each with cooking spray. Place stack of phyllo over mixture in dish. Trim edges to within 1 inch of dish. Cut 1-inch slits in phyllo evenly around edge of dish. Gently press edges toward dish. Bake at 350° for 30 minutes or until lightly browned. Sprinkle with parsley, if desired. Yield: 8 servings (218 calories per serving).

Per Serving: PROTEIN 15.7g FAT 7.0g (Saturated Fat 2.3g) CARBOHYDRATE 19.2g FIBER 2.7g CHOLESTEROL 32mg IRON 2.3mg SODIUM 242mg CALCIUM 129mg

TANGY VEGETABLE SALAD

1¼ cups sliced leeks
½ cup water
2 cups julienne-cut carrot (about 3 carrots)
1 (10-ounce) package frozen whole green beans, thawed
⅓ cup white wine vinegar
¼ cup chopped fresh parsley
3 tablespoons lemon juice
1 tablespoon olive oil
1 tablespoon Dijon mustard
1 teaspoon sugar
¾ teaspoon dried whole tarragon
⅛ teaspoon freshly ground pepper
1 clove garlic, minced

Combine leeks and water in a small saucepan. Bring to a boil; cover, reduce heat, and simmer 10 minutes or until tender. Drain, reserving leeks and liquid. Set aside.

Arrange carrot in a vegetable steamer over boiling water. Cover and steam 8 minutes; drain. Plunge immediately into ice water; drain.

Combine leeks, carrot, and green beans in a large bowl; set aside. Combine reserved liquid, vinegar, and remaining ingredients; stir well with a wire whisk. Pour mixture over vegetables; toss gently. Cover and chill thoroughly. Serve with a slotted spoon. Yield: 8 servings (56 calories per ½-cup serving).

Per Serving: PROTEIN 1.2g FAT 2.0g (Saturated Fat 0.3g)
CARBOHYDRATE 9.0g FIBER 2.0g CHOLESTEROL 0mg
IRON 1.1mg SODIUM 74mg CALCIUM 35mg

IRISH SODA DROP BISCUITS

2 cups all-purpose flour
¾ teaspoon baking soda
½ teaspoon salt
⅓ cup sugar
3 tablespoons margarine
¾ cup nonfat buttermilk
1 egg, lightly beaten
Vegetable cooking spray

Combine first 4 ingredients in a medium bowl; cut in margarine with a pastry blender until mixture resembles coarse meal. Combine buttermilk and egg, stirring until blended. Add to flour mixture; stir just until dry ingredients are moistened.

Drop mixture by rounded tablespoonfuls, 2 inches apart, onto a baking sheet coated with cooking spray. Bake at 350° for 10 to 12 minutes or until biscuits are lightly browned. Yield: 16 biscuits (101 calories each).

Per Biscuit: PROTEIN 2.5g FAT 2.7g (Saturated Fat 0.6g)
CARBOHYDRATE 16.7g FIBER 0.4g CHOLESTEROL 14mg
IRON 0.8mg SODIUM 154mg CALCIUM 27mg

LEMON-CHEESE SQUARES

Vegetable cooking spray
15 vanilla wafers, finely crushed
2 (3-ounce) packages lemon-flavored gelatin
2 cups boiling water
4 ounces Neufchâtel cheese, softened and cut into small pieces
1 (12-ounce) can evaporated skimmed milk
½ cup sugar
1 cup peeled and coarsely chopped kiwifruit
1 cup coarsely chopped strawberries

Coat a 13- x 9- x 2-inch baking dish with cooking spray; sprinkle crushed wafers evenly over bottom and up sides of dish. Set aside.

Combine gelatin and water in a medium bowl, stirring 2 minutes or until gelatin dissolves. Add Neufchâtel cheese; stir with a wire whisk until cheese melts and mixture is smooth. Chill 55 minutes or until consistency of unbeaten egg white, stirring occasionally.

Pour milk into a large glass or stainless steel bowl; freeze 30 minutes or just until ice crystals form around edge of bowl.

Beat ice cold milk at high speed of an electric mixer until soft peaks form. Gradually add sugar, 1 tablespoon at a time, beating until stiff peaks form. Fold milk mixture into gelatin mixture. Spoon into prepared dish. Cover; chill at least 3 hours or until set.

Just before serving, top with chopped fruit. Yield: 12 servings (173 calories per serving).

Per Serving: PROTEIN 4.7g FAT 3.7g (Saturated Fat 1.7g)
CARBOHYDRATE 30.5g FIBER 1.0g CHOLESTEROL 12mg
IRON 0.4mg SODIUM 144mg CALCIUM 98mg

A Children's Easter Egg Party

Eggstra Special PB and J's
Garden Dip
Celery and carrot sticks
Spicy Nibbles
Sugar Bunnies
Jumbled Up Bubbly

SERVES 8
TOTAL CALORIES PER SERVING: 538
(Calories from Fat: 27%)

Here's an Easter party menu with super child appeal. Let the youngsters enjoy lunch before gallivanting to the yard to hunt for specially decorated eggs.

Prepare the dip the day before and refrigerate. The snack mix and cookies can also be made ahead. Assemble the sandwiches the morning of the party. Cover them with a damp paper towel and plastic wrap; refrigerate until serving time. Serve each person 2 tablespoons dip and carrot and celery sticks (3 of each per person). Later, let your little ones help transform the sandwiches into bright egg-shaped creations. They can also help cut out and decorate the cookies. (Menu calories include ¼ cup snack mix and 1 cookie per person.)

EGGSTRA SPECIAL PB AND J'S

½ cup plus 2 tablespoons creamy peanut butter
3 tablespoons currants
1 tablespoon honey
16 (¾-ounce) slices white bread
8 (¾-ounce) slices wheat bread
⅔ cup reduced-calorie strawberry preserves
2 chewy fruit rolls

Combine first 3 ingredients; set aside.

Trim crusts from bread. Cut each slice into an oval using a 3½-inch egg-shaped cookie cutter. Spread preserves evenly over one side of white bread ovals. Spread peanut butter mixture evenly over both sides of wheat bread ovals. Place each wheat bread oval over a white bread oval, preserve side up; top with a white bread oval, preserve side down.

Cut attractive designs from fruit rolls, and decorate sandwiches to resemble Easter eggs. Yield: 8 servings (266 calories per serving).

Per Serving: PROTEIN 9.9g FAT 11.9g (Saturated Fat 2.0g)
CARBOHYDRATE 36.0g FIBER 2.3g CHOLESTEROL 1mg
IRON 1.5mg SODIUM 323mg CALCIUM 45mg

GARDEN DIP

¼ cup plus 2 tablespoons 1% low-fat cottage cheese
¼ cup nonfat mayonnaise
3 tablespoons low-fat sour cream
2 tablespoons skim milk
2 tablespoons chopped fresh chives
2 tablespoons chopped fresh basil
2 teaspoons chopped fresh dillweed
½ teaspoon minced garlic
⅛ teaspoon hot sauce
⅛ teaspoon low-sodium Worcestershire sauce

Combine first 4 ingredients in container of an electric blender or food processor; cover and process until smooth. Add chives and remaining ingredients; cover and process until mixture is combined. Transfer to a bowl; cover and chill.

Serve with celery sticks and carrot sticks. Yield: 1 cup (12 calories per tablespoon).

Per Tablespoon: PROTEIN 0.9g FAT 0.4g (Saturated Fat 0.3g)
CARBOHYDRATE 1.3g FIBER 0g CHOLESTEROL 1mg
IRON 0.1mg SODIUM 72mg CALCIUM 14mg

Sugar Bunnies and Jumbled Up Bubbly (page 82) capture the spirit and warmth of the Easter season.

SPICY NIBBLES

2 cups small unsalted pretzels
2 cups crispy corn cereal squares
1 cup crispy multi-bran cereal squares
1 cup Cheddar cheese goldfish crackers
2 tablespoons reduced-calorie margarine
1 tablespoon low-sodium Worcestershire sauce
1 tablespoon commercial taco seasoning mix

Combine first 4 ingredients in a large bowl; toss well, and set aside.

Combine margarine, Worcestershire, and seasoning mix in a small saucepan. Cook over medium heat, stirring constantly, until margarine melts and mixture is smooth. Drizzle over cracker mixture, and toss well. Spread mixture in a 15- x 10- x 1-inch jellyroll pan. Bake at 275° for 45 minutes or until crisp, stirring twice. Cool completely, and store in an airtight container. Yield: 1½ quarts (49 calories per ¼-cup serving).

Per Serving: PROTEIN 1.1g FAT 1.4g (Saturated Fat 0.1g)
CARBOHYDRATE 8.6g FIBER 0.4g CHOLESTEROL 1mg
IRON 0.8mg SODIUM 101mg CALCIUM 4mg

SUGAR BUNNIES

⅓ cup margarine, softened
1½ ounces Neufchâtel cheese, softened
⅓ cup sugar
¼ cup frozen egg substitute, thawed
½ teaspoon grated lemon rind
2 teaspoons fresh lemon juice
¼ teaspoon vanilla extract
2¼ cups all-purpose flour
2 teaspoons baking powder
⅛ teaspoon salt
1 teaspoon all-purpose flour, divided
Vegetable cooking spray
30 semisweet chocolate miniature morsels
1 tablespoon sifted powdered sugar

Beat margarine and cheese at medium speed of an electric mixer until creamy; gradually add ⅓ cup sugar, beating well. Add egg substitute and next 3 ingredients; beat well.

Combine 2¼ cups flour, baking powder, and salt. Gradually add to margarine mixture, mixing well. Shape into a ball; cover and chill at least 1 hour.

Sprinkle ½ teaspoon flour evenly over work surface. Divide dough into 2 portions. Roll 1 portion of dough to ⅛-inch thickness on floured surface; cut with a 3-inch bunny-shaped cookie cutter. Place on a cookie sheet coated with cooking spray. Repeat procedure with remaining ½ teaspoon flour and dough. Place 1 chocolate morsel on each to make eyes. Bake at 375° for 13 minutes or until lightly browned. Remove from cookie sheets, and place on wire racks; sprinkle cookies evenly with powdered sugar. Let cool. Yield: 2½ dozen (68 calories each).

Per Cookie: PROTEIN 1.3g FAT 2.6g (Saturated Fat 0.6g)
CARBOHYDRATE 9.9g FIBER 0.3g CHOLESTEROL 1mg
IRON 0.5mg SODIUM 62mg CALCIUM 17mg

JUMBLED UP BUBBLY

3 cups unsweetened pineapple juice, chilled
3 cups unsweetened white grape juice, chilled
2 cups club soda, chilled

Combine juices in a pitcher. Add club soda just before serving. Serve immediately. Yield: 2 quarts (115 calories per 1-cup serving).

Per Serving: PROTEIN 0.3g FAT 0.1g (Saturated Fat 0g)
CARBOHYDRATE 29.0g FIBER 0.1g CHOLESTEROL 0mg
IRON 0.5mg SODIUM 17mg CALCIUM 31mg

 FIGURING THE FAT
Don't become confused when calculating percentage of fat in your diet. Instead, determine your fat budget according to your calorie level. Then keep track of the fat grams you consume, making sure you don't go over the budgeted amount.

DAILY FAT BUDGET		
Calories per Day	30 Percent of Calories	Grams of Fat
1,200	360	40
1,500	450	50
1,800	540	60
2,000	600	67
2,200	660	73

Feast Before the Fireworks

Herbed Grilled Catfish
Hearty Baked Beans
Zippy Deviled Eggs
Corn Relish Salad
Chocolate Squares with Peppermint Ice Milk
Iced tea

SERVES 10
TOTAL CALORIES PER SERVING: 679
(Calories from Fat: 18%)

The Fourth of July, the ever popular patriotic holiday, is usually celebrated outdoors with fireworks, parades, family reunions, and great food. Here's a menu lightened for your hot-weather gathering that still meets traditional expectations.

Our Herbed Grilled Catfish is terrific and is easier and more healthful than its deep-fried counterparts. Complement the fish with some lightened favorites—Hearty Baked Beans, Zippy Deviled Eggs, and Corn Relish Salad.

For dessert, offer each guest a rich-tasting chocolate square topped with a peppermint ice milk. Enjoy this sweet summer treat as the fireworks begin.

HERBED GRILLED CATFISH

1 tablespoon plus 1 teaspoon paprika
½ teaspoon garlic powder
½ teaspoon salt
½ teaspoon black pepper
½ teaspoon dried whole thyme
½ teaspoon dried whole oregano
⅛ teaspoon ground red pepper
10 (4-ounce) farm-raised catfish fillets
Vegetable cooking spray
Fresh oregano (optional)
Fresh thyme (optional)

Combine first 7 ingredients. Sprinkle mixture evenly on both sides of fillets. Place fillets in a grilling basket coated with cooking spray.

Coat grill rack with cooking spray; place on grill over medium-hot coals (350° to 400°). Place basket on rack; grill, covered, 4 minutes on each side or until fish flakes easily when tested with a fork. Transfer to a serving platter. If desired, garnish with fresh oregano and thyme. Yield: 10 servings (142 calories per serving).

Per Serving: PROTEIN 22.6g FAT 4.8g (Saturated Fat 1.3g)
CARBOHYDRATE 0.8g FIBER 0.3g CHOLESTEROL 44mg
IRON 1.3mg SODIUM 219mg CALCIUM 11mg

HEARTY BAKED BEANS

3 slices turkey bacon
1½ cups chopped onion
2 cloves garlic, minced
4½ cups canned pinto beans, drained
⅓ cup firmly packed brown sugar
⅓ cup molasses
⅓ cup reduced-calorie catsup
2½ tablespoons prepared mustard
¼ teaspoon salt
¼ teaspoon pepper
Vegetable cooking spray
1 small green pepper, cut into rings

Cut bacon crosswise into ¼-inch-wide strips; place in a nonstick skillet. Cook over medium heat 5 minutes or until crisp, stirring occasionally. Add onion and garlic; cook until tender, stirring frequently.

Combine onion mixture, beans, and next 6 ingredients; spoon into a 2-quart baking dish coated with cooking spray. Cover; bake at 325° for 1 hour. Top with pepper rings; bake, uncovered, 1 hour. Yield: 10 servings (186 calories per ½-cup serving).

Per Serving: PROTEIN 7.5g FAT 1.2g (Saturated Fat 0.3g)
CARBOHYDRATE 37.2g FIBER 3.5g CHOLESTEROL 3mg
IRON 2.8mg SODIUM 360mg CALCIUM 74mg

Celebrate Independence Day with Herbed Grilled Catfish (page 83), Zippy Deviled Eggs, Corn Relish Salad, and Hearty Baked Beans (page 83).

ZIPPY DEVILED EGGS

¼ cup 1% low-fat cottage cheese
5 hard-cooked eggs
2 tablespoons reduced-calorie mayonnaise
1 tablespoon nonfat sour cream alternative
1 teaspoon chopped fresh chives
1 teaspoon prepared mustard
½ teaspoon prepared horseradish
⅛ teaspoon onion powder
Paprika (optional)
Fresh parsley sprigs (optional)

Place cottage cheese in container of an electric blender; cover and process until smooth.

Slice eggs in half lengthwise; remove yolks. Mash 2 yolks; reserve remaining yolks for another use. Add cottage cheese, mayonnaise, and next 5 ingredients. Pipe into egg whites. If desired, garnish with paprika and parsley. Yield: 10 servings (34 calories per serving).

Per Serving: PROTEIN 3.1g FAT 1.9g (Saturated Fat 0.5g)
CARBOHYDRATE 0.7g FIBER 0g CHOLESTEROL 44mg
IRON 0.1mg SODIUM 81mg CALCIUM 10mg

CORN RELISH SALAD

Vegetable cooking spray
3 cups finely diced zucchini
¼ cup sliced green onions
3 cups frozen whole kernel corn, thawed
1 cup quartered cherry tomatoes
1 tablespoon minced fresh thyme
½ teaspoon grated lemon rind
¼ teaspoon salt
¼ teaspoon pepper
2 tablespoons fresh lemon juice
2 teaspoons vegetable oil

Coat a nonstick skillet with cooking spray; place over medium-high heat until hot. Add zucchini and onions; sauté until crisp-tender. Combine zucchini mixture, corn, and tomato in a bowl. Combine thyme and remaining ingredients. Pour over corn mixture; toss. Yield: 10 servings (54 calories per ½-cup serving).

Per Serving: PROTEIN 1.9g FAT 1.1g (Saturated Fat 0.2g)
CARBOHYDRATE 11.2g FIBER 1.6g CHOLESTEROL 0mg
IRON 0.4mg SODIUM 64mg CALCIUM 9mg

CHOCOLATE SQUARES WITH PEPPERMINT ICE MILK

1½ cups all-purpose flour
1 teaspoon baking soda
½ teaspoon salt
½ cup plus 1 tablespoon sugar
¼ cup unsweetened cocoa
¾ cup nonfat buttermilk
3½ tablespoons vegetable oil
1 tablespoon white vinegar
1 teaspoon vanilla extract
Vegetable cooking spray
Peppermint Ice Milk

Combine first 5 ingredients in a medium bowl; make a well in center of mixture. Combine buttermilk, oil, white vinegar, and vanilla; add to dry ingredients, stirring just until dry ingredients are moistened.

Spoon batter into a 9-inch square pan coated with cooking spray. Bake at 350° for 20 minutes or until a wooden pick inserted in center of cake comes out clean. Cool completely on a wire rack. Just before serving, cut into squares. Place 1 square on each individual dessert plate, and top each with ½ cup Peppermint Ice Milk. Yield: 12 servings (260 calories per serving).

Peppermint Ice Milk

⅔ cup sugar
2 cups skim milk
1½ cups evaporated skimmed milk
⅔ cup frozen egg substitute, thawed
¾ teaspoon vanilla extract
⅓ cup finely crushed peppermint candy

Combine first 5 ingredients in container of an electric blender; cover and process until sugar dissolves. Stir in peppermint candy.

Pour mixture into freezer can of a 2-quart hand-turned or electric freezer. Freeze according to manufacturer's instructions. Let ripen 1 hour, if desired. Yield: 1½ quarts.

Per Serving: PROTEIN 7.8g FAT 4.6g (Saturated Fat 1.0g)
CARBOHYDRATE 47.1g FIBER 0.4g CHOLESTEROL 3mg
IRON 1.4mg SODIUM 265mg CALCIUM 187mg

Jack-O'-Lantern Salad is a bewitching surprise for anxious trick-or-treaters.

Halloween Pumpkin-Carving Contest

Harvest Stew
Jack-O'-Lantern Salad
Overnight Whole Wheat Pan Rolls
Autumn Spice Squares

SERVES 6
TOTAL CALORIES PER SERVING: 542
(Calories from Fat: 19%)

Chilly autumn breezes, rustling leaves, and stores filled with costumes signal a favorite holiday for entertaining—Halloween! Several days before trick or treating, invite neighbors to compete in a pumpkin-carving contest. Ask them to bring their favorite stencils, markers, candles, and whatever else they may need to create a ghoulish masterpiece.

Once the artistry is complete, make the jack-o'-lanterns the centerpiece for a bountiful fall supper. Satisfy hungry sculptors with warming bowls of Harvest Stew, child-pleasing Jack-O'-Lantern Salad, and fresh-baked whole wheat rolls (1 per guest).

After crowning the pumpkin-carving winner, treat everyone to moist and tender Autumn Spice Squares. Menu calories reflect square 1 per person.

HARVEST STEW

1½ pounds top round steak
Vegetable cooking spray
¾ cup chopped onion
2 cloves garlic, minced
½ teaspoon freshly ground pepper
2 (13¾-ounce) cans no-salt-added beef
    broth
1 (14½-ounce) can no-salt-added whole
    tomatoes, undrained and chopped
2 bay leaves
1½ cups peeled, cubed pumpkin or sweet
    potato
1 cup peeled, cubed acorn squash or butternut
    squash
1 cup peeled, cubed red potato
2 teaspoons beef-flavored bouillon granules
½ teaspoon chili powder
¼ teaspoon ground allspice
¼ teaspoon ground cloves
¼ cup water
3 tablespoons all-purpose flour

Trim fat from steak. Cut steak into 1-inch pieces. Coat a Dutch oven with cooking spray; place over medium heat until hot. Add steak pieces, onion, garlic, and pepper. Cook until meat is browned on all sides, stirring frequently. Drain and pat dry with paper towels. Wipe drippings from pan with a paper towel.

Return meat mixture to pan. Add broth, tomato, and bay leaves. Bring to a boil; cover, reduce heat, and simmer 1 hour and 15 minutes or until meat is tender. Stir in pumpkin and next 6 ingredients. Bring to a boil; cover, reduce heat, and simmer 55 minutes or until vegetables are tender. Remove and discard bay leaves.

Combine water and flour, stirring well. Add to beef mixture; cook, stirring constantly, until mixture is thickened. Yield: 9 cups (259 calories per 1½-cup serving).

Per Serving: PROTEIN 29.2g   FAT 5.1g   (Saturated Fat 1.8g)
CARBOHYDRATE 22.0g   FIBER 1.7g   CHOLESTEROL 65mg
IRON 3.8mg   SODIUM 395mg   CALCIUM 73mg

JACK-O'-LANTERN SALAD

3 medium-size oranges
⅓ cup water
¼ cup unsweetened orange juice
2 tablespoons sugar
1 tablespoon fresh lemon juice
2 (3-inch) sticks cinnamon, broken
1 whole nutmeg, halved
3 whole cloves
1 (4-inch-long) strip lemon rind
1 (4-inch-long) strip orange rind
Green leaf lettuce leaves (optional)
2 (5-inch-long) thin strands black licorice
    (⅛ inch thick)
1 (5-inch-long) thick strand black licorice
    (½ inch thick)
18 currants

Peel oranges with a knife, removing membrane. Cut each in half lengthwise; set aside.

Combine water and next 8 ingredients in a small saucepan. Bring to a boil; cover, reduce heat, and simmer 15 minutes. Remove from heat, and let cool. Remove and discard cinnamon sticks, nutmeg, cloves, lemon rind, and orange rind. Add orange halves; cover and chill at least 4 hours, stirring occasionally.

Line individual salad plates with lettuce leaves, if desired. Remove orange halves from liquid, using a slotted spoon; discard liquid. Place an orange half on each plate.

Cut each thin licorice strand crosswise into 3 equal sections; place 1 strand on each orange half for a mouth. Cut thick licorice crosswise into 6 equal pieces. Place 1 piece at top of each orange half for a stem. Form eyes and noses with currants. Yield: 6 servings (63 calories per serving).

Per Serving: PROTEIN 0.9g   FAT 0.2g   (Saturated Fat 0g)
CARBOHYDRATE 15.6g   FIBER 3.3g   CHOLESTEROL 0mg
IRON 0.2mg   SODIUM 2mg   CALCIUM 32mg

OVERNIGHT WHOLE WHEAT PAN ROLLS

1 tablespoon sugar
1 package active dry yeast
1 cup warm water (105° to 115°)
2¼ cups unbleached all-purpose flour, divided
1 cup whole wheat flour
3 tablespoons sugar
¾ teaspoon salt
3 tablespoons vegetable oil
2 tablespoons unbleached all-purpose flour
Vegetable cooking spray

Combine 1 tablespoon sugar, yeast, and warm water in a 1-cup liquid measuring cup; let stand 5 minutes. Combine yeast mixture, 1½ cups unbleached flour, whole wheat flour, 3 tablespoons sugar, salt, and oil in a large bowl; beat at medium speed of an electric mixer until well blended. Gradually stir in enough of the remaining ¾ cup unbleached flour to make a soft dough.

Sprinkle 2 tablespoons unbleached flour evenly over work surface. Turn dough out onto floured surface, and knead until smooth and elastic (about 8 to 10 minutes). Place dough in a large bowl coated with cooking spray, turning to coat top. Cover and let rise in a warm place (85°), free from drafts, 1 hour or until doubled in bulk.

Punch down dough, and divide into 15 equal portions; shape each portion into a ball. Place balls in a 13- x 9- x 2-inch pan coated with cooking spray. Cover and refrigerate overnight.

Remove rolls from refrigerator. Let rise in a warm place, free from drafts, 30 minutes or until dough is doubled in bulk. Bake at 375° for 15 to 20 minutes or until rolls are golden. Yield: 15 rolls (130 calories each).

Per Roll: PROTEIN 3.2g FAT 3.1g (Saturated Fat 0.6g)
CARBOHYDRATE 23.0g FIBER 1.6g CHOLESTEROL 0mg
IRON 1.1mg SODIUM 119mg CALCIUM 4mg

AUTUMN SPICE SQUARES

1½ cups all-purpose flour
1 teaspoon baking powder
1 teaspoon baking soda
½ teaspoon salt
1 teaspoon ground cinnamon
¼ teaspoon ground ginger
⅛ teaspoon pepper
1 cup unsweetened applesauce
⅔ cup sugar
¼ cup vegetable oil
1 egg, lightly beaten
1 teaspoon vanilla extract
1 (8-ounce) can crushed pineapple in juice, drained
3 tablespoons semisweet chocolate mini-morsels
Vegetable cooking spray
2 teaspoons powdered sugar

Combine first 7 ingredients in a large mixing bowl; make a well in center of mixture.

Combine applesauce, sugar, oil, egg, and vanilla; add to dry ingredients, stirring just until dry ingredients are moistened. Stir in pineapple and chocolate morsels.

Spoon batter into a 13- x 9- x 2-inch pan coated with cooking spray. Bake at 350° for 20 minutes or until a wooden pick inserted in center comes out clean.

Cool completely on a wire rack. Sift powdered sugar over cooled cake. Yield: 2 dozen squares (90 calories each).

Per Square: PROTEIN 1.2g FAT 3.1g (Saturated Fat 0.8g)
CARBOHYDRATE 14.8g FIBER 0.5g CHOLESTEROL 9mg
IRON 0.5mg SODIUM 99mg CALCIUM 21mg

For an impressive opener at your holiday gathering, serve Smoked Turkey and Sun-Dried Tomato Pâté (page 90) accompanied by commercial French baguette rounds.

Host a Christmas Open House

Smoked Turkey and Sun-Dried Tomato Pâté
Commercial French baguette rounds
Sautéed Shrimp Cakes
Christmas Confetti
Lemon-Lime Marinated Fruit
Easy Coconut Macaroons
White wine

SERVES 12
TOTAL CALORIES PER SERVING: 538
(Calories from Fat: 14%)

When you want to entertain friends without a lot of fuss, host an open house. And there's no better time than December, when everyone is anticipating the most celebrated holiday of the year.

The recipes in this collection should appeal to everyone, including the cook. Guests will love the robust flavors of the pâté. Serve it with toasted French baguette slices (¼ cup pâté and 4 [¼-inch-thick] bread slices per person). Enjoy using left-over pâté as a sandwich spread the next day.

Sautéed Shrimp Cakes are equally easy. Prepare these delightful seafood patties a day before and refrigerate. Reheat them on a rack in a 375° oven moments before guests arrive.

Rich red and green vegetables in Christmas Confetti add a seasonal touch to this holiday menu. The marinated fruit and simple-to-prepare coconut macaroons should satisfy the crowd's craving for sweets. Considering the ease and appeal of these recipes, you may want to make this party an annual event.

SMOKED TURKEY AND SUN-DRIED TOMATO PÂTÉ

1¼ cups sun-dried tomato
1 cup hot water
1½ pounds smoked turkey breast, cubed
½ cup light process cream cheese product
¼ cup chopped onion
3 tablespoons Chablis or other dry white wine
2 tablespoons nonfat sour cream alternative
2 teaspoons Dijon mustard
1 teaspoon white wine Worcestershire sauce
¼ teaspoon paprika
¼ teaspoon ground white pepper
2 tablespoons chopped fresh parsley
Vegetable cooking spray
⅛ teaspoon paprika
Fresh parsley sprigs (optional)

Combine tomato and water in a small bowl; cover and let stand 15 minutes. Drain; set aside 1 tomato. Coarsely chop remaining tomato; set aside.

Position knife blade in food processor bowl. Add turkey and next 8 ingredients; process until smooth, scraping sides of processor bowl once. Transfer mixture to a medium bowl; stir in chopped tomato and chopped parsley. Spoon mixture into a 4-cup mold coated with cooking spray. Cover and chill 8 hours.

Unmold pâté onto serving platter. Sprinkle with paprika. Cut remaining softened sun-dried tomato into thin strips, and arrange over pâté. Garnish with parsley sprigs, if desired. Yield: 4 cups (19 calories per tablespoon).

Per Tablespoon: PROTEIN 2.4g FAT 0.6g (Saturated Fat 0.3g)
CARBOHYDRATES 1.0g FIBER 0.2g CHOLESTEROL 6mg
IRON 0.2mg SODIUM 107mg CALCIUM 5mg

SAUTÉED SHRIMP CAKES

Vegetable cooking spray
¼ cup plus 2 tablespoons finely chopped sweet red pepper
¼ cup plus 2 tablespoons finely chopped green onions
¾ pound unpeeled medium-size fresh shrimp
¼ cup plus 2 tablespoons Italian-seasoned breadcrumbs
3 tablespoons reduced-calorie mayonnaise
2 egg whites
¼ teaspoon salt
¼ teaspoon dried whole dillweed
⅛ teaspoon pepper
⅛ teaspoon ground red pepper
3 tablespoons minced water chestnuts
½ cup Italian-seasoned breadcrumbs
¼ cup reduced-calorie chili sauce

Coat a small nonstick skillet with cooking spray; place over medium-high heat until hot. Add sweet red pepper and green onions; sauté until vegetables are tender. Set aside.

Peel and devein shrimp; coarsely chop. Position knife blade in food processor bowl; add shrimp and next 7 ingredients. Pulse 10 times or until thoroughly combined. Spoon shrimp mixture into a large bowl; stir in sweet red pepper mixture and water chestnuts. Cover and chill 1 hour.

Shape mixture into 24 patties; dredge in ½ cup breadcrumbs. Coat a large nonstick skillet with cooking spray; place over medium-high heat until hot. Add half of patties; cook 3 minutes on each side or until golden. Remove from pan, and keep warm. Repeat procedure with remaining patties. Serve warm with reduced-calorie chili sauce. Yield: 12 appetizer servings (70 calories per 2 shrimp cakes and 1 teaspoon chili sauce).

Per Serving: PROTEIN 6.1g FAT 1.7g (Saturated Fat 0.4g)
CARBOHYDRATE 7.4g FIBER 0.2g CHOLESTEROL 34mg
IRON 0.9mg SODIUM 324mg CALCIUM 22mg

CHRISTMAS CONFETTI

3 (8-inch) pita bread rounds
Olive oil-flavored vegetable cooking spray
½ teaspoon garlic powder
1 teaspoon olive oil
⅔ cup chopped green pepper
½ cup chopped sweet red pepper
¼ cup chopped onion
1 clove garlic, minced
¾ cup canned red beans, drained
¾ cup canned navy beans, drained
¼ cup red wine vinegar
2 tablespoons water
2 teaspoons sugar
1 teaspoon chicken-flavored bouillon granules
2 teaspoons Dijon mustard
2 tablespoons chopped fresh parsley

Separate each pita into 2 rounds; cut each into 6 wedges. Place on ungreased baking sheets, and lightly coat wedges with cooking spray; sprinkle with garlic powder. Bake at 350° for 10 minutes or until lightly browned.

Coat a large nonstick skillet with cooking spray; add oil. Place over medium-high heat until hot. Add peppers, onion, and garlic; sauté 1 minute. Add red beans and next 6 ingredients. Bring to a boil, and cook 1 minute. Transfer to a serving bowl, and sprinkle with parsley. Serve with pita chips. Yield: 12 appetizer servings (91 calories per 3 tablespoons vegetable mixture and 3 pita chips).

Per Serving: PROTEIN 3.3g FAT 1.3g (Saturated Fat 0.2g)
CARBOHYDRATE 16.3g FIBER 2.8g CHOLESTEROL 0mg
IRON 1.4mg SODIUM 231mg CALCIUM 30mg

LEMON-LIME MARINATED FRUIT

2 medium Granny Smith apples, cored and sliced
2 medium-size red pears, cored and sliced
4 small naval oranges, peeled and sectioned
½ cup seedless red grapes, halved
½ cup honey
⅓ cup fresh lime juice
1 tablespoon lemon juice
¼ teaspoon grated lime rind

Combine first 4 ingredients in a medium bowl. Combine honey and remaining ingredients, stirring with a wire whisk; pour over fruit. Cover and chill at least 8 hours, stirring occasionally. Yield: 12 servings (93 calories per ½-cup serving).

Per Serving: PROTEIN 0.4g FAT 0.3g (Saturated Fat 0g)
CARBOHYDRATE 24.6g FIBER 3.5g CHOLESTEROL 0mg
IRON 0.2mg SODIUM 1mg CALCIUM 13mg

EASY COCONUT MACAROONS

⅓ cup sugar
2 tablespoons plus 2 teaspoons all-purpose flour
⅛ teaspoon salt
1 cup flaked coconut
2 egg whites
½ teaspoon vanilla extract
Vegetable cooking spray

Combine first 3 ingredients in a small bowl. Stir in coconut, egg whites, and vanilla.

Drop by tablespoonfuls, 2 inches apart, onto a cookie sheet coated with cooking spray. Bake at 350° for 20 minutes or until lightly browned. Remove from cookie sheet, and let cool on a wire rack. Yield: 1 dozen cookies (67 calories each).

Per Cookie: PROTEIN 0.9g FAT 2.6g (Saturated Fat 2.2g)
CARBOHYDRATE 10.3g FIBER 0.4g CHOLESTEROL 0mg
IRON 0.2mg SODIUM 52mg CALCIUM 2mg

 PARENTS SET THE EXAMPLE
A recent study examined ways to help obese children lose weight and keep it off. It came as no surprise that those who were most successful were the youngsters who got the most support from their parents or other family members.

The research also showed that children of active mothers were twice as likely to be active than were children of inactive mothers. When the fathers were active, the children were 3.5 times more likely to be active than were youngsters of inactive fathers. The big winners? Those children with two active parents.

Light
Recipes

There's no better way to create healthful and delicious meals than by including *Cooking Light* recipes. If you want to eat healthier foods but don't want to sacrifice taste, these recipes are for you. And you can feel confident as you use this book. Each recipe has been tested by our staff of home economists to meet *Cooking Light* standards for sound nutrition, excellent flavor, and striking visual appeal. The recipes foster good nutrition through use of whole grains, fresh fruits and vegetables, lean meats, and low-fat dairy products. To add to the visual appeal, many recipes include garnishing and serving suggestions.

Cooking Light recipes reflect the continuing interest in making meals as healthy as possible. The light touch in cooking results in foods that are higher in complex carbohydrates and fiber yet lower in fat, cholesterol, sugar, and sodium.

We've developed each recipe to meet our own strict standards for key nutrients such as fat, saturated fat, and sodium. We've also provided other nutrition information, including calories and fiber to help you create nutritionally sound meals.

Use the *Cooking Light* guidelines when mixing and matching these recipes to make healthy menus: Of the day's total calories remember these rules:

- At least 50 percent should come from carbohydrate
- About 20 percent should come from protein
- No more than 30 percent should come from fat

With just a pinch of planning and creativity, this 50-20-30 ratio can help you prepare satisfying and balanced meals. Imagine enjoying a hearty meal of Honey Pork Tenderloin (page 170), Winter Vegetable Sauté (page 219), and Triple Delight Cheesecake (page 246) and feeling great knowing the meal provides less than 30 percent of the calories from fat.

Whether you are preparing a quick breakfast, a last-minute lunch, or a wholesome dinner for family and friends, you'll find these recipes suitable for the occasion. A wide range of delicious entrées includes beef, pork, fish, poultry, and meatless main dishes. Along with these, side dishes, salads, and tasty desserts offer endless variety for creating exciting and nutritious meals.

The following chapters are full of tantalizing recipes that will not only make your mouth water but can also help keep you and your family healthy.

Overleaf: *Fruit adds a fresh touch to light recipes such as Tossed Greens with Strawberries (page 188), Chilled Apricot-Pear Soup (page 222), and Baked Fruit Compote (page 220).*

Right: *Inspiration comes from the ocean for (from top left) Tuna and Sun-Dried Tomato Crostini (page 98), Pickled Shrimp and Peppers (page 102), and Island Tea (page 106).*

Appetizers
&
Beverages

THREE-CHEESE SPREAD

1 (8-ounce) package nonfat cream cheese product, softened
1 cup (4 ounces) shredded reduced-fat Cheddar cheese
½ cup crumbled blue cheese
¼ cup chopped almonds, toasted
2 tablespoons skim milk
1 teaspoon low-sodium Worcestershire sauce

Combine all ingredients in a small bowl, stirring until smooth. Cover and refrigerate 8 hours.

Let cheese mixture stand at room temperature 30 minutes before serving. Serve with unsalted crackers, sliced apples, or sliced pears. Yield: 2 cups (32 calories per tablespoon).

Per Tablespoon: PROTEIN 2.8g   FAT 1.9g   (Saturated Fat 0.9g)
CARBOHYDRATE 0.7g   FIBER 0.1g   CHOLESTEROL 5mg
IRON 0.1mg   SODIUM 101mg   CALCIUM 64mg

ROASTED GARLIC AND PEPPER DIP

2 large heads garlic, unpeeled
1 teaspoon olive oil
1 cup plain nonfat yogurt
1 (7-ounce) jar diced sweet red pepper in water, drained
½ teaspoon freshly ground pepper
⅛ teaspoon salt
Dash of onion powder
1 (8-ounce) carton nonfat sour cream alternative

Gently peel outer skins from garlic; cut off top one-fourth of each head, and discard. Place garlic, cut side up, in center of a piece of heavy-duty aluminum foil; drizzle with olive oil. Fold aluminum foil over garlic, sealing tightly. Bake at 350° for 1 hour or until garlic is soft. Remove from oven; let cool completely. Remove and discard papery skin from garlic. Scoop out soft garlic with a spoon; set garlic aside.

Spoon yogurt onto several layers of heavy-duty paper towels; spread to ½-inch thickness. Cover with additional paper towels; let stand 5 minutes. Scrape yogurt into container of an electric blender, using a rubber spatula.

Add reserved garlic, red pepper, ground pepper, salt, and onion powder; cover and process on high speed 1 minute or until smooth, stopping once to scrape down sides. Spoon mixture into a serving bowl, and stir in sour cream. Serve with fresh raw vegetables or steamed shrimp. Yield: 2 cups (17 calories per tablespoon).

Per Tablespoon: PROTEIN 1.1g   FAT 0.2g   (Saturated Fat 0g)
CARBOHYDRATE 2.4g   FIBER 0.1g   CHOLESTEROL 0mg
IRON 0.1mg   SODIUM 20mg   CALCIUM 28mg

EGGPLANT CHUTNEY AND PITA CHIPS

1 (1½-pound) eggplant, cut into ½-inch-thick slices
¼ teaspoon salt
1½ cups diced onion
2 tablespoons minced garlic
2 tablespoons peeled, minced gingerroot
2 tablespoons balsamic vinegar
2 tablespoons honey
1 tablespoon no-salt-added tomato paste
½ teaspoon crushed red pepper
½ teaspoon curry powder
½ teaspoon ground cumin
Vegetable cooking spray
4 (6-inch) whole wheat pita bread rounds

Arrange eggplant slices in a single layer on a baking sheet; sprinkle with salt. Place a second baking sheet on eggplant, and place a heavy bowl on top baking sheet to weight it down. Let stand at room temperature 45 minutes. Transfer eggplant slices to a colander, and rinse well. Pat dry with paper towels; coarsely chop eggplant.

Combine chopped eggplant, onion, and next 8 ingredients in a large bowl; stir well. Spread eggplant mixture in a single layer in a 15- x 10- x 1-inch jellyroll pan coated with cooking spray. Bake, uncovered, at 375° for 30 to 35 minutes or until vegetables are tender, stirring once. Transfer eggplant mixture to a serving bowl.

Separate each pita bread into 2 rounds; reserve 1 round for another use. Cut each remaining round into 8 wedges. Place wedges on 2 ungreased baking sheets. Bake at 350° for 8 to 10 minutes or until lightly browned. Serve chutney warm or at room temperature with pita wedges. Yield: 3½ cups chutney and 56 chips (13 calories per 1 tablespoon chutney and 1 pita chip).

Per Serving: PROTEIN 0.3g FAT 0.1g (Saturated Fat 0g)
CARBOHYDRATE 3.0g FIBER 0.5g CHOLESTEROL 0mg
IRON 0.2mg SODIUM 23mg CALCIUM 8mg

TEX-MEX APPETIZER POPOVERS

1 cup (4 ounces) shredded reduced-fat Cheddar
  cheese
2 tablespoons minced fresh basil
1 tablespoon minced fresh chives
2 teaspoons minced fresh dillweed
2 teaspoons minced fresh marjoram
1 cup bread flour
2 teaspoons sugar
¼ teaspoon salt
1 cup skim milk
¾ cup frozen egg substitute, thawed
1 tablespoon reduced-calorie margarine,
  melted
Vegetable cooking spray

Combine first 5 ingredients in a small bowl, and set aside.

Combine flour, sugar, and salt in a bowl. Combine milk, egg substitute, and margarine in a medium bowl; stir well. Gradually add flour mixture to milk mixture, stirring with a wire whisk until smooth.

Coat miniature (1¾-inch) muffin pans with cooking spray; spoon 1½ tablespoons batter into each muffin cup. Place in a cold oven. Turn oven on 450°, and bake 5 minutes. Reduce heat to 350°, and bake an additional 25 to 30 minutes or until popovers are crusty and brown. Cut a small slit in the top of each popover; spoon cheese mixture evenly into popovers. Bake 5 minutes or until cheese melts. Serve immediately. Yield: 28 appetizers (40 calories each).

Per Appetizer: PROTEIN 2.7g FAT 1.2g (Saturated Fat 0.5g)
CARBOHYDRATE 4.5g FIBER 0.1g CHOLESTEROL 3mg
IRON 0.4mg SODIUM 69mg CALCIUM 47mg

CORN BISCOTTI APPETIZERS

1½ cups frozen whole kernel corn, thawed
1 (4-ounce) can chopped green chiles
2½ cups all-purpose flour
⅔ cup freshly grated Parmesan cheese
½ cup yellow cornmeal
⅓ cup sugar
1 teaspoon baking powder
½ teaspoon baking soda
½ teaspoon salt
½ cup frozen egg substitute, thawed
½ teaspoon ground red pepper
2 tablespoons all-purpose flour, divided
Vegetable cooking spray
1 (8-ounce) container nonfat cream cheese
  product, softened
½ cup hot jalapeño jelly

Position knife blade in food processor bowl; add corn. Process until corn is coarsely chopped, and set aside.

Drain chiles; press between paper towels until barely moist. Set aside.

Combine 2½ cups flour and next 6 ingredients in a medium bowl; stir well. Combine chopped corn, chiles, egg substitute, and red pepper in a small bowl; stir well. Add to flour mixture, stirring just until dry ingredients are moistened.

Sprinkle 1 tablespoon flour evenly over work surface. Turn half of dough out onto floured surface, and knead 10 to 12 times or until smooth. Place on a baking sheet coated with cooking spray, and shape into a 14-inch log. Repeat procedure with remaining 1 tablespoon flour and dough. Bake at 325° for 25 minutes. Transfer logs to a wire rack, and let cool 10 minutes.

Cut logs diagonally into ½-inch slices. Place slices on baking sheets, cut sides down. Bake at 325° for 20 minutes; turn slices over, and bake an additional 20 minutes or until dry. Remove from baking sheets, and cool completely on wire racks. To serve, spread cream cheese evenly over biscotti, and top with jelly. Yield: 52 appetizers (57 calories each).

Per Appetizer: PROTEIN 2.3g FAT 0.5g (Saturated Fat 0.3g)
CARBOHYDRATE 10.8g FIBER 0.4g CHOLESTEROL 2mg
IRON 0.5mg SODIUM 92mg CALCIUM 37mg

TUNA AND SUN-DRIED TOMATO CROSTINI

18 (⅓-inch-thick) slices French baguette
Olive oil-flavored vegetable cooking spray
3 tablespoons minced fresh basil
2 tablespoons nonfat mayonnaise
2 tablespoons plain nonfat yogurt
1 teaspoon crushed garlic
1 (6⅛-ounce) can 60% less-salt tuna in water,
    drained
⅓ cup minced green onions
2 tablespoons minced sun-dried tomato
1 tablespoon chopped ripe olives
18 large arugula leaves

Spray both sides of each bread slice with cooking spray; arrange in a single layer on a baking sheet. Bake at 300° for 15 minutes or until lightly browned.

Combine basil, mayonnaise, yogurt, and garlic; stir well. Add tuna and next 3 ingredients; stir well. To serve, place 1 arugula leaf on each bread slice; top each with 1 tablespoon tuna mixture. Yield: 1½ dozen appetizers (30 calories each).

Per Appetizer: PROTEIN 2.8g FAT 0.4g (Saturated Fat 0.1g)
CARBOHYDRATE 3.9g FIBER 0.2g CHOLESTEROL 3mg
IRON 0.3mg SODIUM 84mg CALCIUM 12mg

VEGETABLE SUSHI

1¼ cups short-grain rice, uncooked
2⅓ cups cold water
2 tablespoons rice wine vinegar
1 tablespoon sugar
1 tablespoon sake
¼ teaspoon salt
1 English cucumber
2 large carrots, scraped
1 tablespoon plus 1 teaspoon wasabi powder
2 teaspoons water

Rinse rice in 3 changes of water; drain on paper towels 30 minutes.

Combine rice and cold water in a medium saucepan. Cook, covered, over medium-high heat 10 to 12 minutes or until boiling. Increase heat to high,

and boil 2 minutes. Reduce heat to medium, and cook 5 minutes. Remove from heat, and let stand 15 minutes. Transfer rice to a large shallow dish.

Combine vinegar, sugar, sake, and salt in a saucepan; bring to a boil. Cook, stirring constantly, until sugar dissolves. Pour over rice; stir well. Cool slightly.

Cut cucumber crosswise into 5-inch pieces. Using a vegetable peeler and applying firm pressure, slice cucumber and carrot lengthwise into thin strips, cutting 20 strips from cucumber and 10 strips from each carrot. (Reserve center core of cucumber for another use.)

Cook cucumber and carrot strips in boiling water 30 seconds or until crisp-tender. Drain and rinse under cold water until cool. Drain and pat dry.

Combine wasabi powder and 2 teaspoons water, stirring well to form a paste. Shape 1 tablespoon rice mixture into an oval. Place on one end of a carrot strip. Spread a small amount of wasabi paste on rice mixture, and roll up, jellyroll fashion. Repeat procedure with remaining rice mixture, wasabi paste, carrot strips, and cucumber strips. (Dip your hands in water to prevent rice from sticking to hands, if necessary.) Arrange on a serving platter. Cover and chill. Yield: 40 appetizers (29 calories each).

Per Appetizer: PROTEIN 0.6g FAT 0.1g (Saturated Fat 0g)
CARBOHYDRATE 6.4g FIBER 0.4g CHOLESTEROL 0mg
IRON 0.3mg SODIUM 18mg CALCIUM 5mg

 ## FOR A SPLASH OF FLAVOR

Made from the white Trebbiano grape, balsamic vinegar used to carry a steep price tag and was available only in gourmet shops. This was partly because the vinegar was aged for many years in wooden casks, just like a fine wine. This aging process produced a dark color and sweet flavor; the longer the aging, the more mellow the flavor.

Fortunately, technology has shortened this process, making balsamic vinegar more affordable. Try sprinkling it on salad greens for a light dressing, drizzling it over fresh berries for a delicious dessert, or using it as an ingredient in low-fat sauces for meats and vegetables. If kept tightly capped at room temperature, balsamic vinegar, like other vinegars, will remain flavorful for about one year.

A variety of zesty seasonings enhances Grilled Bread and Wild Mushrooms.

GRILLED BREAD AND WILD MUSHROOMS

18 medium-size shiitake mushrooms
4 (1-inch-thick) slices Italian bread, cut into 1-inch
   cubes
Olive oil-flavored vegetable cooking spray
1 tablespoon olive oil
1 tablespoon minced fresh rosemary
1 tablespoon minced fresh dillweed
½ teaspoon freshly ground pepper
¼ teaspoon garlic powder
2 cups torn fresh arugula
1 tablespoon balsamic vinegar

Remove and discard mushroom stems. Combine mushrooms and bread cubes in a large bowl; coat with cooking spray, and toss well. Combine olive oil, rosemary, dillweed, pepper, and garlic powder; drizzle mixture over mushrooms and bread cubes, and toss well.

Alternately thread mushrooms and bread cubes onto 6 (10-inch) skewers; lightly coat with cooking spray.

Coat grill rack with cooking spray, and place on grill over medium-hot coals (350° to 400°). Place skewers on rack; grill, covered, 3 to 5 minutes, turning frequently, until browned on all sides.

Combine arugula and vinegar; toss well. Arrange arugula on individual serving plates. Top each with a skewer. Yield: 6 appetizer servings (108 calories per serving).

Per Serving: PROTEIN 3.2g FAT 3.1g (Saturated Fat 0.3g)
CARBOHYDRATE 17.1g FIBER 1.1g CHOLESTEROL 0mg
IRON 1.0mg SODIUM 166mg CALCIUM 27mg

HERBED SPINACH-RICOTTA STRUDEL

1 (10-ounce) package frozen chopped spinach,
   thawed
1½ cups lite ricotta cheese
¼ cup grated Parmesan cheese, divided
2 tablespoons cornstarch
½ cup minced green onions
¼ cup minced fresh basil
3 tablespoons minced fresh oregano
1 tablespoon minced fresh thyme
¼ teaspoon salt
2 egg whites
6 sheets commercial frozen phyllo pastry, thawed
Vegetable cooking spray

Drain spinach, and press between paper towels to remove excess moisture.

Place ricotta cheese in a cheesecloth-lined colander, and let drain 2 hours. Combine drained ricotta cheese, 2 tablespoons Parmesan cheese, and cornstarch in a medium bowl; stir well. Add drained spinach, green onions, basil, oregano, thyme, and salt; stir well.

Beat egg whites at high speed of an electric mixer until stiff peaks form. Fold one-fourth of beaten egg white into spinach mixture; gently fold in remaining egg white.

Place 1 sheet of phyllo on a damp towel (keep remaining phyllo covered); lightly coat phyllo with cooking spray. Repeat layers twice. Spoon half of spinach mixture along short side of phyllo, leaving 1-inch borders on outer edges and a 2-inch border at short end. Fold short edge of phyllo over filling; fold lengthwise edges in 1 inch, and roll up, jelly-roll fashion.

Lightly coat phyllo roll with cooking spray. Place, seam side down, on a baking sheet coated with cooking spray; pierce top several times with tip of a sharp knife, and sprinkle with 1 tablespoon Parmesan cheese.

Repeat procedure with remaining phyllo, spinach mixture, and Parmesan cheese. Bake at 375° for 35 to 40 minutes or until crisp and golden. Cut each strudel into 10 slices. Serve warm or at room temperature. Yield: 20 appetizer servings (47 calories per serving).

Per Serving: PROTEIN 3.7g FAT 1.2g (Saturated Fat 0.6g)
CARBOHYDRATE 6.4g FIBER 0.6g CHOLESTEROL 3mg
IRON 0.6mg SODIUM 76mg CALCIUM 57mg

PASTRY BEEF ROLLS

¼ cup nonfat mayonnaise
1½ teaspoons prepared horseradish
1 teaspoon balsamic vinegar
6 sheets commercial frozen phyllo pastry, thawed
Vegetable cooking spray
1 tablespoon sesame seeds, toasted and divided
6 very thin slices lean roast beef
6 green onions, cut into 7-inch pieces

Combine first 3 ingredients in a small bowl, stirring well. Set aside.

Place 1 sheet of phyllo on a damp towel (keep remaining phyllo covered). Lightly coat phyllo with cooking spray. Fold phyllo in half crosswise, bringing short ends together. Lightly coat with cooking spray. Fold in half again crosswise, bringing short ends together. Lightly coat with cooking spray.

Spread 2 teaspoons mayonnaise mixture over phyllo to within ½ inch of edges. Sprinkle ½ teaspoon sesame seeds over mayonnaise mixture. Top with 1 beef slice. Place 1 green onion in center, parallel with long edge. Roll up phyllo, jellyroll fashion, starting with long side; tuck ends under.

Place, seam side down, on a baking sheet coated with cooking spray. Lightly coat top of pastry with cooking spray. Repeat procedure with remaining phyllo, mayonnaise mixture, sesame seeds, beef slices, and green onions. Bake at 400° for 15 minutes or until crisp and golden. Cut each roll into thirds. Serve immediately. Yield: 1½ dozen appetizers (41 calories each).

Per Appetizer: PROTEIN 2.3g FAT 1.2g (Saturated Fat 0.3g)
CARBOHYDRATE 5.4g FIBER 0.1g CHOLESTEROL 6mg
IRON 0.5mg SODIUM 89mg CALCIUM 6mg

CHICKEN CURRY IN PHYLLO BASKETS

Vegetable cooking spray
5 sheets commercial frozen phyllo pastry,
    thawed
1 (8-ounce) carton plain nonfat yogurt
1½ cups finely diced, skinned smoked chicken
    breast
½ cup minced sweet red pepper
2 tablespoons finely chopped pecans, toasted
2 tablespoons minced green onions
2 teaspoons curry powder
⅛ teaspoon salt

Place 1 sheet phyllo on a damp towel (keep remaining phyllo covered). Lightly coat phyllo with cooking spray. Layer remaining 4 sheets phyllo on first sheet, lightly coating each sheet with cooking spray. Cut phyllo stack into 28 rounds, using a 2½-inch biscuit cutter; discard remaining phyllo. Place a phyllo round into each of 28 miniature (1¾-inch) muffin cups coated with cooking spray. Press phyllo rounds against the bottom and up the sides of each cup. Bake at 350° for 8 minutes or until golden; let cool completely in pans. Transfer to a serving platter.

Use a yogurt cheesemaker or line a colander with 4 layers of cheesecloth, allowing cheesecloth to extend over edge of colander; place in a glass bowl. Spoon yogurt into cheesemaker or colander; cover with plastic wrap. Refrigerate at least 8 hours. Spoon yogurt into a bowl; discard liquid. Add chicken and remaining ingredients; stir well. Cover and refrigerate up to 3 hours. Just before serving, spoon chicken mixture evenly into phyllo cups. Yield: 28 appetizers (37 calories each).

Per Appetizer: PROTEIN 3.4g FAT 1.2g (Saturated Fat 0.2g)
CARBOHYDRATE 3.4g FIBER 0.1g CHOLESTEROL 6mg
IRON 0.5mg SODIUM 86mg CALCIUM 19mg

CHICKEN PANCAKES WITH FRUIT SALSA

2 (6-ounce) skinned chicken breast halves
1 medium baking potato, peeled and grated
½ cup peeled, grated firm ripe pear
¼ cup grated onion
2 tablespoons all-purpose flour
½ teaspoon dried whole rosemary, crushed
½ cup frozen egg substitute, thawed
Vegetable cooking spray
2 teaspoons vegetable oil, divided
Fruit Salsa

Place chicken in a large nonstick skillet; add water to cover. Bring to a boil over medium-high heat; cover, reduce heat, and simmer 25 minutes or until tender. Remove chicken from broth, and let cool slightly. Bone and shred chicken; set aside. Skim and discard fat from broth; reserve broth for another use.

Combine chicken, potato, pear, and onion in a large bowl. Drain and press dry between paper towels. Return mixture to bowl. Add flour and rosemary, tossing well. Add egg substitute, and stir well.

Coat a large nonstick skillet with cooking spray; add 1 teaspoon oil, and place over medium heat until hot. Spoon half of chicken mixture, by rounded tablespoonfuls, into skillet, spreading into 12 (1-inch) pancakes. Cook 4 to 5 minutes or until browned on bottom. Turn and cook an additional 3 to 4 minutes or until browned.

Transfer pancakes to a serving platter, and keep warm. Repeat procedure with remaining 1 teaspoon oil and chicken mixture. Top pancakes evenly with Fruit Salsa. Yield: 2 dozen appetizers (41 calories each).

Fruit Salsa

2 cups diced firm ripe pear
1 cup diced fresh strawberries
1 tablespoon seeded, minced jalapeño pepper
1 tablespoon balsamic vinegar
1 teaspoon honey

Combine all ingredients in a small bowl; stir well. Let stand 1 hour. Yield: 2½ cups.

Per Appetizer: PROTEIN 3.1g FAT 0.8g (Saturated Fat 0.2g)
CARBOHYDRATE 5.6g FIBER 0.8g CHOLESTEROL 6mg
IRON 0.3mg SODIUM 14mg CALCIUM 7mg

PICKLED SHRIMP AND PEPPERS

25 unpeeled medium-size fresh shrimp (about
   1 pound)
2½ tablespoons brown sugar
2 teaspoons English-style dry mustard
½ teaspoon ground ginger
½ cup balsamic vinegar
3 tablespoons water
1½ tablespoons low-sodium Worcestershire sauce
1 tablespoon olive oil
1 teaspoon hot sauce
½ cup julienne-cut sweet red pepper
½ cup julienne-cut sweet yellow pepper
½ cup julienne-cut green pepper
25 medium-size fresh spinach leaves

Peel and devein shrimp, leaving tails intact.

Combine brown sugar and next 7 ingredients in
a medium saucepan; bring to a boil, stirring constantly until brown sugar dissolves. Reduce heat, and
simmer, uncovered, 5 minutes. Add shrimp, and
cook 3 to 5 minutes or until shrimp turn pink. Transfer shrimp mixture to a bowl; add peppers, and toss
well. Cover and marinate in refrigerator 3 hours.

Drain shrimp mixture, discarding liquid. Arrange
spinach leaves on a large serving platter; divide pepper strips evenly among spinach leaves. Top each
with 1 shrimp. Yield: 25 appetizers (17 calories each).

Per Appetizer: PROTEIN 2.4g FAT 0.4g (Saturated Fat 0.1g)
CARBOHYDRATE 0.9g FIBER 0.2g CHOLESTEROL 17mg
IRON 0.5mg SODIUM 20mg CALCIUM 9mg

SCANDINAVIAN SALMON TORTE

¾ cup frozen egg substitute, thawed
1 tablespoon water
Dash of salt
Vegetable cooking spray
5 ounces nonfat cream cheese product, softened
¼ cup plus 2 tablespoons diced smoked salmon
⅓ cup minced green onions
2 tablespoons diced pimiento, drained
2 teaspoons minced fresh dillweed
2 teaspoons capers, drained and minced
Fresh dillweed sprigs (optional)

Combine egg substitute, water, and salt in a small
bowl; stir well.

Coat a small nonstick skillet with cooking spray;
place over medium heat just until hot, not smoking.
Pour ¼ cup egg substitute mixture into skillet. As
mixture begins to cook, gently lift edges of mixture
with a spatula, and tilt pan to allow uncooked portions to flow underneath. When mixture is set, remove omelet from skillet, and place on wax paper.
Repeat procedure with remaining egg substitute
mixture.

Combine cream cheese and next 5 ingredients in
a small bowl; stir well. Place 1 omelet on a serving
platter. Spread half of salmon mixture evenly over
omelet. Top with second omelet. Repeat procedure
with remaining salmon mixture and omelet. Cover
tightly with plastic wrap, and chill thoroughly. Cut
into 8 wedges. Garnish with fresh dillweed sprigs,
if desired. Yield: 8 appetizer servings (39 calories
per serving).

Per Serving: PROTEIN 6.4g FAT 0.5g (Saturated Fat 0.1g)
CARBOHYDRATE 1.6g FIBER 0.1g CHOLESTEROL 5mg
IRON 0.7mg SODIUM 278mg CALCIUM 64mg

SCALLOP PUFFS IN ZUCCHINI

4 medium zucchini (about 1¾ pounds)
¾ cup water
½ pound bay scallops
¼ cup reduced-calorie mayonnaise
¼ cup (1 ounce) shredded reduced-fat Jarlsberg
   cheese
1 tablespoon minced fresh dillweed
1 teaspoon all-purpose flour
1 teaspoon lemon juice
½ teaspoon Dijon mustard
¼ teaspoon ground red pepper
1 egg white

Cut each zucchini into 6 pieces; scoop out pulp,
leaving ¼-inch-thick shells. Reserve pulp for another
use. Cook shells in boiling water 30 seconds or
until crisp-tender. Drain; rinse well. Drain again,
and set aside.

Bring ¾ cup water to a boil in a small saucepan.
Add scallops; reduce heat, and simmer 4 to 5

minutes or until scallops are opaque. Drain well, and set aside.

Combine mayonnaise and next 6 ingredients in a medium bowl. Add scallops, and stir gently.

Beat egg white at high speed of an electric mixer until stiff peaks form. Fold into scallop mixture. Spoon scallop mixture into reserved zucchini shells. Place on a large baking sheet. Bake at 425° for 10 minutes or until puffed and golden. Serve immediately. Yield: 2 dozen appetizers (23 calories each).

Per Appetizer: PROTEIN 2.4g   FAT 1.0g   (Saturated Fat 0.2g)
CARBOHYDRATE 1.3g   FIBER 0.1g   CHOLESTEROL 5mg
IRON 0.2mg   SODIUM 44mg   CALCIUM 14mg

MARINATED SEAFOOD FONDUE

1 cup sherry vinegar
¼ cup dry sherry
3 tablespoons sugar
2 tablespoons crushed garlic
2 teaspoons whole allspice
1 teaspoon black peppercorns
¼ teaspoon salt
3 bay leaves
24 medium-size fresh mushrooms
12 sun-dried tomatoes (without oil)
12 unpeeled medium-size fresh shrimp
    (about ½ pound)
½ pound swordfish steaks, cut into
    1-inch cubes
3 (10½-ounce) cans low-sodium chicken
    broth, undiluted
⅔ cup dry sherry

Combine first 8 ingredients in a medium saucepan; stir well. Bring to a boil; reduce heat, and simmer 1 minute. Place mushrooms and tomatoes in a shallow dish; pour half of hot vinegar mixture over mushroom mixture. Cover and let stand 1 hour, stirring occasionally. Let remaining marinade stand at room temperature 30 minutes.

Peel and devein shrimp, leaving tails intact. Combine shrimp and swordfish in a large heavy-duty, zip-top plastic bag; pour reserved marinade over seafood, and seal bag. Shake bag until seafood is well coated. Marinate in refrigerator 30 minutes.

Combine chicken broth and ⅔ cup sherry in a large saucepan. Bring to a boil; reduce heat, and simmer 1 minute. Transfer chicken broth mixture to a fondue pot, and continue to simmer over medium heat. Remove vegetables and seafood from marinade, and discard marinade. Thread vegetables and seafood onto fondue forks or wooden skewers. Place in simmering broth mixture, and cook 3 to 4 minutes or until seafood is done and vegetables are tender. Yield: 6 appetizer servings (118 calories per serving).

Per Serving: PROTEIN 14.8g   FAT 2.4g   (Saturated Fat 0.6g)
CARBOHYDRATE 9.2g   FIBER 0.8g   CHOLESTEROL 54mg
IRON 1.8mg   SODIUM 228mg   CALCIUM 24mg

CHINESE TURKEY DUMPLINGS

½ pound freshly ground raw turkey
1 (8-ounce) can sliced water chestnuts, drained
    and finely chopped
⅓ cup finely chopped green onions
¼ cup low-sodium teriyaki sauce, divided
1 egg white, lightly beaten
2 teaspoons peeled, grated gingerroot
40 fresh or frozen wonton skins, thawed
Vegetable cooking spray
⅓ cup dry sherry
1 teaspoon chili oil
½ teaspoon chili powder

Combine first 6 ingredients in a medium bowl; stir well. Place 1 heaping teaspoon turkey mixture in center of each wonton skin. Bring sides of wonton up around filling, and pinch together to form individual bundles.

Arrange bundles in a single layer in a steaming basket coated with cooking spray. Place over boiling water; cover and steam 20 minutes. Transfer dumplings to a serving platter.

Combine sherry, chili oil, and chili powder in a small saucepan; stir well. Bring to a boil; cook 1 minute. Serve with dumplings. Yield: 40 appetizers (21 calories each).

Per Appetizer: PROTEIN 1.7g   FAT 0.4g   (Saturated Fat 0.1g)
CARBOHYDRATE 2.3g   FIBER 0.1g   CHOLESTEROL 9mg
IRON 0.2mg   SODIUM 49mg   CALCIUM 3mg

PEANUTTY BANANA SHAKE

1 cup peeled, sliced banana (about 1 large banana)
2 cups skim milk
1 tablespoon creamy peanut butter
1 tablespoon honey

Place banana slices in a single layer on a baking sheet. Cover and freeze until firm. Place milk in a shallow container; cover and freeze 45 minutes or until milk is slushy.

Combine frozen banana, milk, peanut butter, and honey in container of an electric blender; cover and process until smooth. Serve immediately. Yield: 3 cups (160 calories per 1-cup serving).

Per Serving: PROTEIN 7.6g FAT 3.3g (Saturated Fat 0.8g)
CARBOHYDRATE 27.3g FIBER 1.9g CHOLESTEROL 3mg
IRON 0.3mg SODIUM 112mg CALCIUM 206mg

RASPBERRY BUTTERMILK SIPPER

2 cups fresh or frozen unsweetened raspberries
2½ cups nonfat buttermilk
⅓ cup sugar
1 teaspoon vanilla extract
½ teaspoon freshly grated nutmeg

Position knife blade in food processor bowl; add raspberries, and process until smooth. Place raspberry puree in a wire-mesh strainer; press with back of spoon against sides of the strainer to squeeze out juice. Discard pulp and seeds remaining in strainer.

Combine raspberry puree, buttermilk, and remaining ingredients in container of an electric blender; cover and process until smooth, stopping twice to scrape down sides. Cover and chill thoroughly. Yield: 4 cups (145 calories per 1-cup serving).

Per Serving: PROTEIN 5.9g FAT 0.8g (Saturated Fat 0.5g)
CARBOHYDRATE 29.4g FIBER 3.1g CHOLESTEROL 5mg
IRON 0.3mg SODIUM 160mg CALCIUM 190mg

Refreshing fruit juices create a tidal wave of taste sensations in Tropical Mimosas (top). Pink Elephants capture the essence of the islands with the help of guava nectar.

PINK ELEPHANTS

2¾ cups guava nectar, chilled
2 cups lemon-flavored sparkling mineral water, chilled
1 tablespoon plus 1 teaspoon superfine sugar
1 tablespoon plus 1 teaspoon lime juice
1 tablespoon plus 1 teaspoon grenadine
1 teaspoon bitters

Combine first 6 ingredients in a large pitcher; stir well. Serve immediately over crushed ice. Yield: 5 cups (104 calories per 1-cup serving).

Per Serving: PROTEIN 0.0g FAT 0.0g (Saturated Fat 0g)
CARBOHYDRATE 25.5g FIBER 0g CHOLESTEROL 0mg
IRON 0.3mg SODIUM 20mg CALCIUM 0mg

TROPICAL MIMOSAS

1½ cups unsweetened peach juice blend, divided
1½ cups unsweetened tangerine juice blend, divided
½ cup water
15 fresh mint leaves
1 cup orange-flavored sparkling mineral water, chilled
1½ cups frozen unsweetened sliced peaches
1 cup champagne, chilled
Fresh mint sprigs (optional)

Combine 1 cup peach juice, 1 cup tangerine juice, and ½ cup water; stir well. Pour juice mixture into an ice cube tray; place 1 fresh mint leaf in each compartment of ice cube tray. Freeze until firm.

Combine remaining ½ cup peach juice, ½ cup tangerine juice, sparkling water, and frozen peaches in container of an electric blender; cover and process until smooth, stopping once to scrape down sides. Add champagne, and stir well. Place frozen juice cubes in glasses; pour champagne mixture over frozen juice cubes. Garnish with fresh mint sprigs, if desired. Serve immediately. Yield: 5 cups (135 calories per 1-cup serving).

Per Serving: PROTEIN 0.5g FAT 0.0g (Saturated Fat 0g)
CARBOHYDRATE 25.2g FIBER 0.7g CHOLESTEROL 0mg
IRON 0.3mg SODIUM 19mg CALCIUM 4mg

CITRUS SPRITZER

3 (3- x ½-inch) strips orange rind
3 (3- x ½-inch) strips grapefruit rind
4 cups pineapple-orange juice
2 cups fresh pink grapefruit juice
2 cups sparkling mineral water, chilled
Orange curls (optional)
Grapefruit curls (optional)

Place citrus strips in a glass pitcher; crush slightly by gently pressing against pitcher with back of a spoon. Add juices; stir well. Cover and chill thoroughly. Just before serving, stir in sparkling water. Serve over ice. If desired, garnish with orange and grapefruit curls. Yield: 2 quarts (91 calories per 1-cup serving).

Per Serving: PROTEIN 0.6g FAT 0.2g (Saturated Fat 0g) CARBOHYDRATE 22.4g FIBER 0g CHOLESTEROL 0mg IRON 1.5mg SODIUM 13mg CALCIUM 11mg

ISLAND TEA

1 medium orange
2¼ cups water
1¾ cups pineapple-orange-banana juice
2 tablespoons chopped crystallized ginger
4 regular-size tea bags

Using a citrus zester or a paring knife, cut strips of rind from orange. Reserve ¼ cup strips, discarding remaining rind. Set aside.

Cut orange in half; squeeze juice from halves, reserving ¼ cup juice. Save remaining juice for another use.

Combine ¼ cup orange strips, ¼ cup orange juice, water, pineapple-orange-banana juice, and ginger in a large saucepan. Bring mixture to a boil; remove from heat.

Add tea bags; cover and steep 5 minutes. Remove and discard tea bags. Strain tea mixture, discarding ginger. Cover and chill. Serve over ice. Yield: 4 cups (98 calories per 1-cup serving).

Per Serving: PROTEIN 0.4g FAT 0.1g (Saturated Fat 0g) CARBOHYDRATE 24.5g FIBER 0g CHOLESTEROL 0mg IRON 2.1mg SODIUM 9mg CALCIUM 27mg

HOT SPICED CIDER

7½ cups unsweetened apple cider
1 cup water
1 cup chopped dried apple
½ cup golden raisins
4 whole allspice
2 (3-inch) sticks cinnamon
2 whole nutmeg, halved

Combine first 4 ingredients in a large saucepan; stir well. Tie allspice, cinnamon sticks, and nutmeg in a cheesecloth bag; add spice bag to cider mixture. Let stand at room temperature at least 1 hour.

Bring mixture to a simmer; remove and discard spice bag. Spoon chopped apple and raisins evenly into serving mugs. Pour cider mixture evenly over fruit. Serve warm. Yield: 9 cups (159 calories per 1-cup serving).

Per Serving: PROTEIN 0.6g FAT 0.3g (Saturated Fat 0.1g) CARBOHYDRATE 40.7g FIBER 1.3g CHOLESTEROL 0mg IRON 1.1mg SODIUM 18mg CALCIUM 22mg

CAFE MEXICANA

1 cup water
½ cup Kahlúa or other coffee-flavored liqueur
¼ cup firmly packed dark brown sugar
3 (3-inch) sticks cinnamon
6 whole cloves
7½ cups warm strong brewed coffee

Combine first 5 ingredients in a saucepan; bring to a boil. Cook, stirring constantly, until sugar dissolves. Strain mixture; discard cinnamon sticks and cloves. Combine sugar mixture and coffee; stir well. Serve warm. Yield: 9 cups (52 calories per 1-cup serving).

Per Serving: PROTEIN 0.2g FAT 0.0g (Saturated Fat 0g) CARBOHYDRATE 13.2g FIBER 0g CHOLESTEROL 0mg IRON 1.0mg SODIUM 7mg CALCIUM 9mg

Clockwise from top left: Overnight Molasses Pan Rolls (page 114), Whole Wheat Dinner Rolls (page 115), Bacon-Cornmeal Biscuits (page 109), and Kaiser Rolls (page 114) offer a choice of home-baked quick and yeast breads.

Breads

ANIMAL GRAHAMS

2 cups whole wheat flour
1 tablespoon all-purpose flour
½ teaspoon baking powder
½ teaspoon baking soda
⅛ teaspoon salt
⅓ cup maple syrup
¼ cup vanilla low-fat yogurt
3 tablespoons vegetable oil
Vegetable cooking spray

Combine first 5 ingredients in a large bowl; make a well in center of mixture. Combine maple syrup, yogurt, and oil in a small bowl; stir with a wire whisk until well blended. Add syrup mixture to dry ingredients, stirring just until dry ingredients are moistened. Shape into a ball. Knead 4 or 5 minutes or until dough is smooth.

Roll dough to ⅛-inch thickness; cut dough into desired shapes using 1-inch animal-shaped cookie cutters. Place on baking sheets coated with cooking spray. Bake at 350° for 10 minutes or until lightly browned. Remove crackers from sheets, and let cool on wire racks. Yield: 15 dozen (8 calories each).

Per Cracker: PROTEIN 0.2g FAT 0.3g (Saturated Fat 0.1g) CARBOHYDRATE 1.4g FIBER 0.2g CHOLESTEROL 0mg IRON 0.1mg SODIUM 5mg CALCIUM 3mg

WHOLE WHEAT BATTER CRACKERS

1 cup all-purpose flour
½ cup whole wheat flour
½ cup shreds of wheat bran cereal
2 teaspoons baking powder
½ teaspoon baking soda
1 tablespoon sugar
2 tablespoons margarine, melted
4 cloves garlic, chopped
1 cup 1% low-fat milk
¾ cup water
2 eggs
Vegetable cooking spray
¼ cup grated Parmesan cheese, divided

Combine first 11 ingredients in container of an electric blender; cover and process on high speed 2 minutes or until smooth, stopping twice to scrape down sides.

Pour ½ cup batter into a 13- x 9- x 2-inch pan coated with cooking spray; tilt pan to evenly cover bottom. Bake at 325° for 5 minutes. Remove from oven; coat with cooking spray, and sprinkle with 2 teaspoons cheese. Cut into 24 rectangles. Return to oven, and bake an additional 20 to 25 minutes or until golden. Remove from pan, and let cool on a wire rack. Repeat procedure 5 times with remaining batter and cheese. Yield: 12 dozen (10 calories each).

Per Cracker: PROTEIN 0.4g FAT 0.3g (Saturated Fat 0.1g) CARBOHYDRATE 1.4g FIBER 0.2g CHOLESTEROL 3mg IRON 0.1mg SODIUM 16mg CALCIUM 8mg

AMARETTO TEA SCONES

½ cup currants
¼ cup amaretto
1½ cups regular oats, uncooked
1 cup all-purpose flour
1½ teaspoons baking powder
¼ teaspoon salt
¼ cup sugar
¼ cup margarine, cut into pieces
¼ cup skim milk
1 egg, lightly beaten
2 drops almond extract
1 tablespoon all-purpose flour
Vegetable cooking spray
1 tablespoon sugar

Draw a 6-inch circle on parchment paper; turn paper over, and set aside.

Combine currants and amaretto in a small saucepan; bring to a boil. Cover; remove from heat, and let stand until completely cool. Drain well.

Position knife blade in food processor bowl; add oats. Process until finely ground. Combine processed oats, 1 cup flour, and next 3 ingredients in a large bowl. Cut in margarine with a pastry blender until mixture resembles coarse meal. Stir in drained currants. Combine milk, egg, and almond extract; add to flour mixture, and stir just until dry ingredients are moistened.

Sprinkle 1 tablespoon flour evenly over work surface. Turn dough out onto floured surface, and knead 4 or 5 times. (Dough may be slightly sticky.)

Divide dough into 4 equal portions. Pat 1 portion to a 6-inch circle on prepared parchment paper. Using a large metal spatula, transfer circle to a large baking sheet coated with cooking spray. Repeat procedure with remaining dough. Cut each circle into 6 wedges. Separate wedges slightly, and lightly coat with cooking spray. Sprinkle wedges evenly with 1 tablespoon sugar. Bake at 400° for 12 minutes or until golden. Yield: 2 dozen scones (84 calories each).

Per Scone: PROTEIN 1.9g FAT 2.9g (Saturated Fat 0.7g)
CARBOHYDRATE 12.8g FIBER 0.7g CHOLESTEROL 9mg
IRON 0.6mg SODIUM 72mg CALCIUM 23mg

BACON-CORNMEAL BISCUITS

1¼ cups self-rising flour
1 cup self-rising cornmeal
1 tablespoon brown sugar
⅛ teaspoon ground red pepper
3 tablespoons margarine
3 slices turkey bacon, cooked and crumbled
½ cup plus 2½ tablespoons nonfat buttermilk
2 teaspoons self-rising flour
Vegetable cooking spray

Combine first 4 ingredients in a medium bowl; cut in margarine with a pastry blender until mixture resembles coarse meal. Stir in turkey bacon. Add buttermilk, stirring with a fork just until dry ingredients are moistened.

Sprinkle 2 teaspoons flour evenly over work surface. Turn dough out onto floured surface, and knead 8 to 10 times. Roll dough to ½-inch thickness; cut into rounds with a 2-inch biscuit cutter. Place rounds on a baking sheet coated with cooking spray. Bake at 400° for 14 minutes or until biscuits are golden. Serve warm. Yield: 15 biscuits (98 calories each).

Per Biscuit: PROTEIN 2.5g FAT 3.1g (Saturated Fat 0.6g)
CARBOHYDRATE 14.8g FIBER 0.4g CHOLESTEROL 2mg
IRON 1.0mg SODIUM 316mg CALCIUM 80mg

HOT PEPPER CORN STICKS

½ cup plus 2 tablespoons yellow cornmeal
½ cup all-purpose flour
1 teaspoon baking powder
¼ teaspoon salt
2 tablespoons sugar
½ teaspoon crushed red pepper
½ cup nonfat buttermilk
¼ cup no-salt-added cream-style corn
2 tablespoons vegetable oil
1 egg, lightly beaten
Vegetable cooking spray

Combine first 6 ingredients in a medium bowl; make a well in center of mixture. Combine buttermilk, corn, oil, and egg; add to dry ingredients, stirring just until dry ingredients are moistened.

Place a cast-iron corn stick pan coated with cooking spray in a 425° oven for 3 minutes or until hot. Remove pan from oven; spoon batter into pan, filling two-thirds full. Bake at 425° for 14 minutes or until golden. Remove from pan, and serve warm. Yield: 10 corn sticks (106 calories each).

Per Corn Stick: PROTEIN 2.6g FAT 3.6g (Saturated Fat 0.7g)
CARBOHYDRATE 15.9g FIBER 0.7g CHOLESTEROL 22mg
IRON 0.8mg SODIUM 109mg CALCIUM 38mg

 ### BREAKFAST HELPS DIETERS
A study from Vanderbilt University suggests that eating breakfast can actually help dieters shed pounds more easily. When researchers placed a group of moderately overweight women on a 1,200-calorie diet either with two meals per day (no breakfast) or three meals per day (with breakfast), the number of pounds lost by those in the two regimens differed little.

But the big news from this report was not the amount of weight lost during the diets. More important were two other findings: The women who ate breakfast ended up consuming less total fat during the day. And the breakfast eaters had fewer impulses to snack than the breakfast skippers. Those two changes alone can help set the stage for long-term dieting success.

CORNMEAL-ZUCCHINI MUFFINS

1¼ cups all-purpose flour
¾ cup yellow cornmeal
1 teaspoon baking powder
1 teaspoon baking soda
¼ teaspoon salt
3 tablespoons brown sugar
¾ cup nonfat buttermilk
2½ tablespoons vegetable oil
1 egg, lightly beaten
1 cup shredded zucchini
Vegetable cooking spray
2 teaspoons yellow cornmeal
2 teaspoons brown sugar

Combine first 6 ingredients in a medium bowl; make a well in center of mixture. Combine buttermilk, oil, and egg; add to dry ingredients, stirring just until dry ingredients are moistened. Fold in zucchini.

Spoon batter into muffin pans coated with cooking spray, filling two-thirds full. Combine 2 teaspoons cornmeal and 2 teaspoons brown sugar; sprinkle evenly over batter. Bake at 400° for 15 minutes or until golden. Remove from pans immediately. Yield: 1 dozen (131 calories each).

Per Muffin: PROTEIN 3.3g   FAT 3.7g   (Saturated Fat 0.7g)
CARBOHYDRATE 20.9g   FIBER 0.9g   CHOLESTEROL 19mg
IRON 1.2mg   SODIUM 165mg   CALCIUM 57mg

FRESH APPLE MUFFINS

2 cups all-purpose flour
1 teaspoon baking powder
1 teaspoon baking soda
¼ teaspoon salt
⅓ cup sugar
¾ cup vanilla low-fat yogurt
¼ cup unsweetened apple juice
2 tablespoons vegetable oil
1 egg, lightly beaten
½ teaspoon vanilla extract
1¼ cups peeled, grated Granny Smith apple
Vegetable cooking spray
1½ teaspoons sugar

Combine first 5 ingredients in a medium bowl; make a well in center of mixture. Combine yogurt, apple juice, oil, egg, and vanilla; add to dry ingredients, stirring just until dry ingredients are moistened. Gently fold in apple.

Spoon batter into muffin pans coated with cooking spray, filling two-thirds full. Sprinkle 1½ teaspoons sugar evenly over batter. Bake at 400° for 20 to 22 minutes or until golden. Yield: 1 dozen (156 calories each).

Per Muffin: PROTEIN 3.4g   FAT 3.4g   (Saturated Fat 0.7g)
CARBOHYDRATE 28.0g   FIBER 1.2g   CHOLESTEROL 19mg
IRON 1.1mg   SODIUM 158mg   CALCIUM 61mg

BARELY SWEET POPOVERS

1⅓ cups bread flour
3 tablespoons sugar
¼ teaspoon salt
1¼ cups skim milk
2 eggs
2 egg whites
¼ teaspoon vanilla extract
Vegetable cooking spray

Combine first 3 ingredients in a bowl; stir well. Combine milk, eggs, egg whites, and vanilla in a mixing bowl; stir with a wire whisk until blended. Gradually add flour mixture to liquid mixture, stirring with a wire whisk until smooth.

Place popover pans in a 450° oven for 3 minutes or until hot. Remove pans from oven, and coat with cooking spray. Spoon batter into pans, filling half full. Bake at 450° for 45 to 50 minutes or until crusty and browned. Remove from pans immediately, and cut a slit in the top of each popover. Serve warm. Yield: 8 popovers (140 calories each).

Per Popover: PROTEIN 6.5g   FAT 2.0g   (Saturated Fat 0.5g)
CARBOHYDRATE 23.3g   FIBER 0.6g   CHOLESTEROL 56mg
IRON 1.2mg   SODIUM 123mg   CALCIUM 58mg

Add a little spice to your morning with nourishing Gingerbread Pancakes. For a treat, top with apple butter.

GINGERBREAD PANCAKES

2 teaspoons instant coffee granules
¼ cup boiling water
¾ cup whole wheat flour
¼ cup all-purpose flour
1 teaspoon baking powder
¼ teaspoon salt
3 tablespoons brown sugar
½ teaspoon ground ginger
¼ teaspoon ground cinnamon
⅛ teaspoon ground cloves
⅔ cup skim milk
1 egg, lightly beaten
1 tablespoon vegetable oil
Apple butter (optional)

Combine coffee granules and boiling water, stirring until granules dissolve. Cool completely.

Combine whole wheat flour, all-purpose flour, baking powder, salt, brown sugar, ginger, cinnamon, and cloves in a medium bowl; make a well in center of mixture.

Combine coffee mixture, milk, egg, and oil; add mixture to dry ingredients, stirring just until dry ingredients are moistened.

Preheat nonstick griddle to 325°. For each pancake, pour ¼ cup batter onto hot griddle; spread batter to a 5-inch circle. Cook pancakes until tops are covered with bubbles and edges look cooked; turn pancakes, and cook other side. Serve with apple butter, if desired. Yield: 7 (5-inch) pancakes (113 calories each).

Per Pancake: PROTEIN 4.0g FAT 3.0g (Saturated Fat 0.7g)
CARBOHYDRATE 18.0g FIBER 1.8g CHOLESTEROL 32mg
IRON 1.0mg SODIUM 150mg CALCIUM 70mg

BANANA PANCAKES

1 cup all-purpose flour
1 tablespoon sugar
⅛ teaspoon salt
1 cup nonfat buttermilk
1 teaspoon baking soda
½ cup mashed ripe banana
½ cup frozen egg substitute, thawed
1 tablespoon vegetable oil
Vegetable cooking spray

Combine first 3 ingredients in a large bowl; make a well in center of mixture. Combine buttermilk and soda, stirring well. Add banana, egg substitute, and oil; stir well. Add buttermilk mixture to dry ingredients, stirring just until dry ingredients are moistened.

Coat a nonstick griddle with cooking spray; preheat to 350°. For each pancake, pour ¼ cup batter onto hot griddle. Cook pancakes until tops are covered with bubbles and edges look cooked; turn and cook other side. Yield: 12 (4-inch) pancakes (75 calories each).

Per Pancake: PROTEIN 2.9g FAT 1.4g (Saturated Fat 0.3g) CARBOHYDRATE 12.6g FIBER 0.6g CHOLESTEROL 1mg IRON 0.7mg SODIUM 130mg CALCIUM 44mg

SOUTHERN SPOONBREAD

⅔ cup cornmeal
1 tablespoon plus 2 teaspoons sugar, divided
¼ teaspoon ground red pepper
2 cups skim milk
1 tablespoon margarine, melted
1 egg yolk, lightly beaten
3 egg whites
Vegetable cooking spray

Combine cornmeal, 1 tablespoon sugar, and red pepper in a saucepan. Add milk and margarine; cook over medium heat, stirring constantly with a wire whisk, until mixture is thickened and bubbly. Remove from heat; let cool 10 minutes. Add egg yolk; stir.

Beat egg whites at high speed of an electric mixer until foamy. Gradually add remaining 2 teaspoons sugar, beating until stiff peaks form. Fold one-third of egg whites into cornmeal mixture; fold in remaining egg whites. Pour mixture into a 1½-quart soufflé dish coated with cooking spray. Bake at 375° for 35 to 40 minutes or until puffed and golden. Serve warm. Yield: 8 servings (101 calories per serving).

Per Serving: PROTEIN 4.7g FAT 2.5g (Saturated Fat 0.6g) CARBOHYDRATE 14.7g FIBER 0.6g CHOLESTEROL 28mg IRON 0.6mg SODIUM 70mg CALCIUM 80mg

RAISIN-PEAR COFFEE CAKE

¼ cup margarine, softened
½ cup sugar
½ cup frozen egg substitute, thawed
1½ cups sifted cake flour
1 teaspoon baking powder
⅛ teaspoon salt
¼ cup plain low-fat yogurt
1¼ teaspoons vanilla extract
1½ cups finely chopped pear
⅓ cup chopped raisins
1 tablespoon lemon juice
¾ teaspoon ground cinnamon
½ teaspoon dried lemon rind
Vegetable cooking spray
⅓ cup sifted powdered sugar
1½ teaspoons lemon juice

Beat margarine at medium speed of an electric mixer until creamy; gradually add ½ cup sugar, beating well. Add egg substitute, and beat well.

Combine flour, baking powder, and salt; add to margarine mixture alternately with yogurt, beginning and ending with flour mixture. Mix after each addition. Stir in vanilla.

Combine pear and next 4 ingredients. Pour half of batter into an 8-inch square pan coated with cooking spray; top with half of pear mixture. Pour remaining batter into pan; top with remaining pear mixture. Bake at 350° for 30 minutes or until cake springs back when lightly touched. Combine powdered sugar and 1½ teaspoons lemon juice; stir. Drizzle over warm cake. Yield: 12 servings (163 calories per serving).

Per Serving: PROTEIN 2.6g FAT 4.1g (Saturated Fat 0.8g) CARBOHYDRATE 29.6g FIBER 1.1g CHOLESTEROL 0mg IRON 1.4mg SODIUM 113mg CALCIUM 37mg

CARAWAY BAGELS

3¼ cups all-purpose flour, divided
½ cup medium rye flour
1½ tablespoons caraway seeds
1 tablespoon sugar
¼ teaspoon salt
1 package active dry yeast
¾ cup water
½ cup skim milk
1 tablespoon vegetable oil
1 tablespoon all-purpose flour
Vegetable cooking spray
1 egg white
1 teaspoon water
2 teaspoons caraway seeds

Combine 1 cup all-purpose flour and next 5 in-gredients in a large bowl; stir well. Combine ¾ cup water, milk, and oil in a small saucepan; cook over medium heat until very warm (120° to 130°).

Gradually add liquid mixture to flour mixture, beating at low speed of an electric mixer until blended. Beat an additional 2 minutes at medium speed. Gradually stir in enough of the remaining 2¼ cups flour to make a soft dough.

Sprinkle 1 tablespoon all-purpose flour over work surface. Turn dough out onto surface; knead until smooth and elastic (about 8 minutes). Place in a large bowl coated with cooking spray, turning to coat top. Cover and let rise in a warm place (85°), free from drafts, 45 minutes or until doubled in bulk.

Punch dough down, and divide into 18 equal por-tions. Roll each portion into an 8-inch rope. Form each rope into a circle, overlapping ends; press ends together to seal. Place circles 2 inches apart on baking sheets coated with cooking spray.

Cover and let rise in a warm place, free from drafts, 15 minutes or until doubled. Combine egg white and 1 teaspoon water; brush over bagels, and sprinkle with 2 teaspoons caraway seeds. Place a pan of boiling water on lower rack of oven; place ba-gels on middle rack, and bake at 375° for 20 minutes or until golden. Yield: 1½ dozen (112 calories each).

Per Bagel: PROTEIN 3.4g   FAT 1.2g   (Saturated Fat 0.2g)
CARBOHYDRATE 21.5g   FIBER 1.3g   CHOLESTEROL 0mg
IRON 1.3mg   SODIUM 40mg   CALCIUM 19mg

EASY MUSTARD BREADSTICKS

1 (11-ounce) package refrigerated cracked wheat
  and honey twists
1 tablespoon reduced-calorie margarine
1 tablespoon coarse-grained mustard
1 tablespoon beer
1 tablespoon plus 2 teaspoons grated Parmesan
  cheese

Unroll and twist dough according to package di-rections. Place twists on an ungreased baking sheet.

Combine margarine, mustard, and beer in a small saucepan; cook over low heat, stirring frequently, until margarine melts and mixture is smooth. Brush mustard mixture over twists; sprinkle each with ½ teaspoon Parmesan cheese. Bake at 375° for 12 to 13 minutes or until golden. Yield: 10 breadsticks (90 calories each).

Per Breadstick: PROTEIN 2.3g   FAT 3.0g   (Saturated Fat 0.2g)
CARBOHYDRATE 14.2g   FIBER 1.0g   CHOLESTEROL 0mg
IRON 0mg   SODIUM 181mg   CALCIUM 9mg

 ### FACTS ON FIBER

As scientists study fiber in foods, it remains obvious that the two types of fiber com-pounds play major roles in health. Insoluble fiber, which is found in wheat bran, helps keep the intes-tines functioning properly. Because insoluble fiber helps speed the transit of foods through the lower part of the digestive tract, nutritionists recommend this fiber as a hedge against constipation. Prelimi-nary reports suggest it may also help prevent colon cancer.

Soluble fiber, the main fiber compound in foods such as oats, apples, and dried beans, tends to delay stomach emptying. Its main health role lies in its ability to lower blood cholesterol levels. And re-search suggests that soluble fiber may also help control blood sugar levels.

But rather than promote one type of fiber over another, health experts encourage Americans to aim for a total fiber intake of 20 to 35 grams per day.

You can achieve this goal and get plenty of both types of fiber by eating generous amounts of fruits, vegetables, and whole grains.

KAISER ROLLS

½ cup skim milk
2 tablespoons margarine
2 teaspoons sugar
1 package active dry yeast
1 teaspoon sugar
½ cup warm water (105° to 115°)
3 cups bread flour
½ teaspoon salt
Vegetable cooking spray
1 tablespoon plus 1 teaspoon cornmeal
2 teaspoons water
2 teaspoons poppy seeds

Combine first 3 ingredients in a small saucepan; heat until margarine melts, stirring occasionally. Cool to 105° to 115°.

Combine yeast, 1 teaspoon sugar, and warm water in a 1-cup liquid measuring cup; let stand 5 minutes.

Position knife blade in food processor bowl; add flour and salt. Add milk mixture and yeast mixture through food chute with processor running. Once the dough forms a ball, process 1 minute. Place dough in a large bowl coated with cooking spray, turning to coat top. Cover and let rise in a warm place (85°), free from drafts, 45 minutes or until doubled in bulk.

Coat a large baking sheet with cooking spray; sprinkle with cornmeal. Punch dough down, and shape into 14 equal portions. Shape each portion into a smooth ball, and place on prepared baking sheet. Cover and let rise in a warm place, free from drafts, 45 minutes or until doubled in bulk.

Using a sharp knife, score 6 (¼-inch-deep) slits in top of each roll, in a pinwheel pattern. Brush rolls lightly with water, and sprinkle evenly with poppy seeds. Bake at 425° for 10 minutes or until lightly browned. Yield: 14 rolls (134 calories each).

Per Roll: PROTEIN 4.2g FAT 2.4g (Saturated Fat 0.4g)
CARBOHYDRATE 23.6g FIBER 1.0g CHOLESTEROL 0mg
IRON 1.5mg SODIUM 108mg CALCIUM 23mg

OVERNIGHT MOLASSES PAN ROLLS

4 cups unbleached flour
3 tablespoons brown sugar
½ teaspoon salt
2 packages active dry yeast
2 cups water
½ cup molasses
3 tablespoons vegetable oil
2¼ cups plus 1 tablespoon whole wheat flour, divided
Butter-flavored vegetable cooking spray

Combine first 4 ingredients in a large mixing bowl; stir well. Set aside.

Combine water, molasses, and oil a small saucepan; cook over medium heat until very warm (120° to 130°).

Gradually add liquid mixture to flour mixture, beating at low speed of an electric mixer until well blended. Beat an additional 2 minutes at medium speed. Gradually stir in 2¼ cups whole wheat flour to make a soft dough.

Sprinkle remaining 1 tablespoon whole wheat flour evenly over work surface. Turn dough out onto floured surface, and knead until dough is smooth and elastic (about 8 to 10 minutes). Place dough in a large bowl coated with cooking spray, turning to coat top. Cover dough, and refrigerate at least 8 hours.

Punch dough down, and let rest at room temperature 15 minutes. Divide dough into 40 equal portions, and shape each portion into a ball. Place balls in two 9-inch square pans coated with cooking spray. Cover and let rise in a warm place (85°), free from drafts, 40 minutes or until dough is doubled in bulk.

Bake at 375° for 15 minutes or until lightly browned. Coat rolls lightly with cooking spray. Yield: 40 rolls (126 calories each).

Per Roll: PROTEIN 3.5g FAT 1.3g (Saturated Fat 0.3g)
CARBOHYDRATE 25.5g FIBER 1.5g CHOLESTEROL 0mg
IRON 1.5mg SODIUM 32mg CALCIUM 15mg

POPPY SEED FAN TANS

1 package active dry yeast
1 teaspoon sugar
½ cup warm water (105° to 115°)
1½ cups skim milk
3 tablespoons margarine
¼ cup plus 1 tablespoon sugar
½ teaspoon salt
5½ cups bread flour, divided
1 egg
3 tablespoons bread flour, divided
Butter-flavored vegetable cooking spray
1 tablespoon plus 1 teaspoon poppy seeds, divided

Combine first 3 ingredients in a 1-cup liquid measuring cup; let stand 5 minutes. Combine milk, margarine, ¼ cup plus 1 tablespoon sugar, and salt in a saucepan; cook over medium heat, stirring constantly, until margarine melts. Cool to 105° to 115°.

Combine yeast mixture, milk mixture, 2 cups flour, and egg; beat at medium speed of an electric mixer until well blended. Gradually stir in enough of the remaining 3½ cups flour to make a soft dough.

Sprinkle 1 tablespoon plus 2 teaspoons flour over work surface. Turn dough out onto surface, and knead until smooth and elastic (about 8 minutes). Place in a large bowl coated with cooking spray, turning to coat top. Cover and let rise in a warm place (85°), free from drafts, 1½ hours or until doubled in bulk.

Punch dough down; cover and let rest 5 minutes. Sprinkle 1 teaspoon flour over work surface. Divide dough into 4 portions. Roll 1 portion to an 18- x 11-inch rectangle. Coat rectangle with cooking spray; sprinkle with 1 teaspoon poppy seeds. Using a sharp knife, cut rectangle into 12 crosswise strips. Stack strips. Repeat with remaining flour, dough, and poppy seeds, creating 4 stacks of strips. Using a sharp knife, cut each stack crosswise into 9 equal pieces. Place, cut side up, in muffin pans coated with cooking spray. Cover and let rise in a warm place, free from drafts, 1 hour or until doubled in bulk. Bake at 375° for 14 to 15 minutes or until lightly browned. Yield: 3 dozen (102 calories each).

Per Roll: PROTEIN 3.3g FAT 1.6g (Saturated Fat 0.3g)
CARBOHYDRATE 18.2g FIBER 0.6g CHOLESTEROL 6mg
IRON 1.0mg SODIUM 51mg CALCIUM 22mg

WHOLE WHEAT DINNER ROLLS

3¼ cups all-purpose flour, divided
3 cups whole wheat flour, divided
¼ cup sugar
½ teaspoon salt
2 packages active dry yeast
1¾ cups water
⅓ cup margarine
2 tablespoons molasses
½ cup frozen egg substitute, thawed
1 tablespoon all-purpose flour
Vegetable cooking spray

Combine 2 cups all-purpose flour, 1 cup whole wheat flour, sugar, salt, and yeast in a large mixing bowl; stir well. Set aside.

Combine water, margarine, and molasses in a small saucepan; cook over medium heat until margarine melts, stirring occasionally. Cool mixture to 120° to 130°.

Gradually add liquid mixture to flour mixture, beating at low speed of an electric mixer until blended. Beat mixture an additional 4 minutes at medium speed. Add egg substitute, and beat well. Gradually stir in enough of the remaining 1¼ cups all-purpose flour and 2 cups whole wheat flour to make a soft dough.

Sprinkle 1 tablespoon flour evenly over work surface. Turn dough out onto floured surface, and knead until smooth and elastic (about 8 to 10 minutes). Place dough in a large bowl coated with cooking spray, turning to coat top. Cover and let rise in a warm place (85°), free from drafts, 30 minutes or until doubled in bulk.

Punch dough down, and divide into 36 equal portions. Roll each portion into a 10-inch rope. Tie each rope in a loose knot, leaving two long ends. Place on large baking sheets coated with cooking spray. Cover and let rise in a warm place, free from drafts, 20 minutes or until doubled in bulk. Bake at 375° for 12 minutes or until golden. Remove from baking sheets, and let cool on wire racks. Yield: 3 dozen (102 calories each).

Per Roll: PROTEIN 3.1g FAT 2.0g (Saturated Fat 0.4g)
CARBOHYDRATE 18.3g FIBER 1.7g CHOLESTEROL 0mg
IRON 1.1mg SODIUM 58mg CALCIUM 11mg

CHARACTER BREAD

2 packages active dry yeast
1 tablespoon sugar, divided
1 cup warm water (105° to 115°), divided
1 cup warm skim milk (105° to 115°)
3 tablespoons vegetable oil
1 teaspoon salt
5 cups unbleached flour, divided
2 tablespoons unbleached flour
Vegetable cooking spray
1 egg white
1 tablespoon water
4 raisins

Combine yeast, 1½ teaspoons sugar, and ½ cup warm water in a 1-cup liquid measuring cup; let stand 5 minutes.

Combine yeast mixture, remaining 1½ teaspoons sugar, remaining ½ cup warm water, milk, oil, salt, and 2 cups flour in a large mixing bowl; beat at medium speed of an electric mixer until blended. Gradually stir in enough of the remaining 3 cups flour to make a soft dough.

Sprinkle 2 tablespoons flour evenly over work surface. Turn dough out onto floured surface, and knead until smooth and elastic (about 8 to 10 minutes). Place dough in a large bowl coated with cooking spray, turning to coat top. Cover and let rise in a warm place (85°), free from drafts, 40 minutes or until doubled in bulk.

Punch dough down; divide in half. Set 1 portion aside. Form two-thirds of 1 portion of the dough into a ball for the body of a turtle. Place on a large baking sheet coated with cooking spray. Divide remaining one-third of portion into 6 equal pieces. Shape pieces into balls for head, legs, and tail; attach to body. With remaining half, form two-thirds of the dough into an oblong shape, tapering ends for the body of an alligator. Place on baking sheet. Divide remaining one-third of portion into 4 equal pieces. Shape pieces into balls for legs, and attach to body.

Cover and let rise in a warm place, free from drafts, 15 minutes. Combine egg white and 1 tablespoon water; brush over loaves. Using scissors, snip bodies of each loaf, if desired. Gently push raisins into dough for eyes. Bake at 350° for 40 minutes or until loaves sound hollow when tapped. Yield: 24 servings (109 calories per slice).

Per Slice: PROTEIN 3.3g   FAT 2.0g   (Saturated Fat 0.3g)
CARBOHYDRATE 19.8g   FIBER 0.7g   CHOLESTEROL 0mg
IRON 1.1mg   SODIUM 107mg   CALCIUM 14mg

PARMESAN RIBBON BREAD

1 package active dry yeast
1 teaspoon sugar
1¼ cups warm water (105° to 115°), divided
3½ cups bread flour, divided
½ teaspoon salt
1 tablespoon olive oil
2 teaspoons bread flour
Vegetable cooking spray
1 egg white, lightly beaten
1 tablespoon water
½ cup plus 1 tablespoon grated Parmesan cheese,
   divided
1½ teaspoons dried Italian seasoning, divided
1½ teaspoons coarsely ground pepper, divided

Combine yeast, sugar, and ¼ cup warm water in a 1-cup liquid measuring cup; let stand 5 minutes.

Combine 2 cups flour and salt in a large mixing bowl, and stir well. Add yeast mixture, remaining 1 cup warm water, and oil; beat at medium speed of an electric mixer until blended. Beat an additional 2 minutes at medium speed. Gradually stir in enough of the remaining 1½ cups flour to make a soft dough.

Sprinkle 2 teaspoons flour evenly over work surface. Turn dough out onto floured surface, and knead until smooth and elastic (about 8 to 10 minutes). Place dough in a large bowl coated with cooking spray, turning to coat top. Cover and let rise in a warm place (85°), free from drafts, 45 minutes or until doubled in bulk.

Punch down dough; set aside one-fourth of dough. Divide remaining dough into 2 equal portions. Roll each portion to a 12- x 9-inch rectangle. Combine egg white and 1 tablespoon water; brush over rectangles. Sprinkle each rectangle with 3 tablespoons Parmesan cheese, ½ teaspoon Italian seasoning, and

Enhance an elegant dinner with Parmesan Ribbon Bread. The rich aroma and flavor encased in the golden folds will elicit rave reviews from your guests. Carry out the stylish theme with cheese and a bottle of fine wine.

½ teaspoon pepper. Gently press cheese and herbs into dough, using a rolling pin. Fold each rectangle lengthwise into thirds. Pinch seam and ends to seal.

Roll reserved one-fourth of dough to a 20- x 6-inch rectangle; brush with egg white mixture. Sprinkle with remaining 3 tablespoons Parmesan cheese, ½ teaspoon Italian seasoning, and ½ teaspoon pepper. Gently press cheese and herbs into dough, using a rolling pin. Cut rectangle into 4 equal lengthwise strips.

With cheese side facing down, attach 1 strip of dough at one end of 1 loaf; wrap dough strip clockwise around loaf. Attach second strip where first strip

began; wrap strip counter-clockwise to form a criss-cross pattern around loaf. Pinch strip at ends to fasten securely. Repeat procedure with remaining loaf and strips.

Cover and let rise in a warm place, free from drafts, 50 minutes or until doubled in bulk. Brush loaves lightly with egg white mixture. Bake at 375° for 25 to 30 minutes or until loaves sound hollow when tapped. Yield: 24 servings (90 calories per 1-inch slice).

Per Slice: PROTEIN: 3.5g   FAT 1.5g   (Saturated Fat 0.5g)
CARBOHYDRATE 15.2g   FIBER 0.7g   CHOLESTEROL 1mg
IRON 1.1mg   SODIUM 87mg   CALCIUM 33mg

GOLDEN ALMOND TURBAN BREAD

½ cup golden raisins
½ cup chopped dried apricots
1½ cups water
1 package active dry yeast
½ cup warm skim milk (105° to 115°)
2 tablespoons honey
½ teaspoon salt
½ teaspoon grated lemon rind
¼ teaspoon ground coriander
2½ cups all-purpose flour, divided
1 tablespoon all-purpose flour
Vegetable cooking spray
3 tablespoons almond paste
2 teaspoons water, divided
1 egg white, lightly beaten

Combine raisins and apricots in a small saucepan; add 1½ cups water. Bring to a boil; cover and remove from heat. Let stand 10 minutes; drain, reserving ¼ cup liquid. Set fruit aside.

Heat reserved liquid until warm (105° to 115°), if necessary. Combine yeast and warm liquid in a 1-cup liquid measuring cup; let stand 5 minutes. Combine yeast mixture, milk, honey, salt, lemon rind, coriander, and 1½ cups flour; beat at medium speed of an electric mixer until well blended. Gradually stir in enough of the remaining 1 cup flour to make a soft dough.

Sprinkle 1 tablespoon flour evenly over work surface. Turn dough out onto floured surface, and knead until smooth and elastic (about 8 to 10 minutes). Place dough in a large bowl coated with cooking spray, turning to coat top. Cover and let rise in a warm place (85°), free from drafts, 1 hour or until doubled in bulk.

Punch dough down; cover and let rest 10 minutes. Roll dough into a 36- x 6-inch strip. Sprinkle soaked fruit evenly over dough; crumble almond paste evenly over fruit. Brush long edges of dough with 1 teaspoon water. Carefully roll up dough, jellyroll fashion, starting with long side; pinch ends and seam to seal.

Shape one end of dough into a 6½-inch circle, turning seam to inside of circle. Coil remaining dough onto the circle, gradually making a turban-like shape.

Place on a baking sheet coated with cooking spray; let rise in a warm place, free from drafts, 20 minutes (do not let double in size). Combine egg white and remaining 1 teaspoon water; brush over loaf. Bake at 350° for 30 minutes or until golden. Remove from baking sheet, and let cool completely on a wire rack. Yield: 12 servings (163 calories per wedge).

Per Wedge: PROTEIN 4.5g FAT 1.4g (Saturated Fat 0.2g)
CARBOHYDRATE 33.9g FIBER 1.9g CHOLESTEROL 0mg
IRON 1.8mg SODIUM 110mg CALCIUM 32mg

Turn your kitchen into a gourmet galley by preparing Salmon with Cranberry-Leek Sauce (page 124). Your efforts will be rewarded with compliments when you present this colorful dish at the dinner table.

Fish & Shellfish

GRILLED AMBERJACK WITH PEPPER-CORN SALSA

2 small sweet red peppers
1 cup fresh corn cut from cob (about 2 ears)
½ cup peeled, diced ripe papaya
¼ cup minced fresh cilantro
1 teaspoon olive oil
½ teaspoon freshly ground pepper
4 (4-ounce) amberjack steaks (¾ inch thick)
1 tablespoon low-sodium soy sauce
Vegetable cooking spray

Cut peppers in half lengthwise; remove and discard seeds and membrane. Place peppers, skin side up, on a baking sheet; flatten peppers with palm of hand. Broil 5½ inches from heat (with electric oven door partially opened) 15 to 20 minutes or until charred. Place peppers in ice water until cool. Remove from water; peel and discard skins. Dice roasted pepper, and place in a bowl. Set aside.

Place corn on a baking sheet; bake at 450° for 12 minutes, stirring occasionally. Add corn, papaya, cilantro, olive oil, and ground pepper to diced pepper.

Brush amberjack steaks with soy sauce. Coat grill rack with cooking spray; place on grill over hot coals (400° to 500°). Place steaks on rack; grill, covered, 4 to 5 minutes on each side or until fish flakes easily when tested with a fork. Serve with pepper mixture. Yield: 4 servings (247 calories per serving).

Per Serving: PROTEIN 28.6g FAT 7.6g (Saturated Fat 1.7g) CARBOHYDRATE 16.8g FIBER 3.2g CHOLESTEROL 43mg IRON 2.5mg SODIUM 153mg CALCIUM 14mg

BAKED SEA BASS AND VEGETABLES

Vegetable cooking spray
2 tablespoons reduced-calorie margarine
2 cups finely chopped red potato
1 cup chopped onion
¾ cup chopped carrot
2 teaspoons minced garlic
2 cups thinly sliced sweet red pepper
2 cups peeled, seeded, and chopped tomato
1 cup canned low-sodium chicken broth, undiluted
3 tablespoons sliced ripe olives
2 teaspoons capers, drained
½ teaspoon dried whole thyme
6 (4-ounce) sea bass fillets (1 inch thick)
2 tablespoons fresh lemon juice

Coat a large nonstick skillet with cooking spray; add margarine. Place over medium heat until margarine melts. Add potato, onion, carrot, and garlic; cover and cook 3 minutes. Add pepper and next 5 ingredients; cover and cook an additional 15 minutes or until vegetables are crisp-tender.

Place fillets over vegetable mixture; cover and cook 10 minutes or until fish flakes easily when tested with a fork. Transfer fillets and vegetable mixture to a serving platter, using a slotted spoon. Drizzle lemon juice evenly over fillets and vegetable mixture. Yield: 6 servings (245 calories per serving).

Per Serving: PROTEIN 24.4g FAT 8.2g (Saturated Fat 1.5g) CARBOHYDRATE 19.2g FIBER 3.6g CHOLESTEROL 77mg IRON 3.8mg SODIUM 282mg CALCIUM 123mg

BONE UP ON FISH

Fish is a delicious part of a low-fat diet—and it's quick and easy to prepare. No matter what the dish, best results come from selecting the freshest fish possible. Here are some tips:
• Sniff before buying. Ocean fish should smell like the sea, and freshwater varieties sometime smell like cucumbers. Any strong, fishy odor indicates spoilage, so don't buy that fish.
• When buying fish fillets and fish steaks, avoid those that look dried out. The pieces should be moist with a translucent sheen. If there are gaps between the fibers of the flesh, the fish is starting to deteriorate.
• Previously frozen, thawed fish often isn't marked as such, so only select fish labeled "fresh." Thawed fish is fine as long as it isn't put in the freezer again; twice-frozen fish loses flavor and texture.
• Pay attention to how fish is displayed and stored. Whole fish should be buried in ice, and fillets should be displayed in separate pans surrounded by ice. Stay away from markets where fish are piled high, mixed together, or placed under bright lights.

CRABMEAT-STUFFED FLOUNDER

Vegetable cooking spray
1 teaspoon reduced-calorie margarine
¼ cup chopped green onions
¼ pound fresh lump crabmeat, drained
½ cup soft French bread crumbs
¼ cup chopped fresh parsley
¼ cup plain nonfat yogurt
1 teaspoon dried whole oregano
1 teaspoon lemon juice
4 (3-ounce) flounder fillets
2 teaspoons reduced-calorie margarine, melted
1 ounce grated Romano cheese

Coat a small nonstick skillet with cooking spray; add 1 teaspoon margarine. Place over medium-high heat until margarine melts. Add green onions, and sauté 1 minute. Add crabmeat and next 5 ingredients; stir well.

Spoon ¼ cup crabmeat mixture in center of each fillet; roll up each fillet, jellyroll fashion, beginning at narrow end. Secure with wooden picks. Place rolls, seam side down, in an 8-inch square baking dish coated with cooking spray. Brush evenly with 2 teaspoons melted margarine. Bake, uncovered, at 350° for 10 minutes. Sprinkle cheese evenly over flounder; bake an additional 10 minutes or until fish flakes easily when tested with a fork. Transfer to a serving platter, and remove wooden picks. Serve immediately. Yield: 4 servings (184 calories per serving).

Per Serving: PROTEIN 25.7g FAT 5.7g (Saturated Fat 1.8g)
CARBOHYDRATE 6.4g FIBER 0.5g CHOLESTEROL 77mg
IRON 1.2mg SODIUM 316mg CALCIUM 167mg

PINEAPPLE-GOAT CHEESE GROUPER

4 (4-ounce) grouper fillets
1 (15¼-ounce) can pineapple slices in juice, undrained
2 tablespoons balsamic vinegar
1 tablespoon olive oil
2 ounces goat cheese, crumbled
¼ cup minced green onions
1 tablespoon minced fresh rosemary
2 teaspoons minced fresh garlic

Place fillets in a heavy-duty, zip-top plastic bag. Drain pineapple, reserving juice. Combine reserved juice, vinegar, and olive oil; stir well. Pour over fillets; seal bag, and shake gently until fillets are well coated. Marinate in refrigerator 30 minutes.

Arrange 4 pineapple slices in an 11- x 7- x 1½-inch baking dish. Remove fillets from marinade; discard marinade. Arrange fillets over pineapple. Sprinkle with cheese, green onions, rosemary, and garlic. Top with remaining pineapple. Bake at 375° for 25 minutes or until fish flakes easily when tested with a fork. Yield: 4 servings (218 calories per serving).

Per Serving: PROTEIN 24.5g FAT 7.7g (Saturated Fat 2.8g)
CARBOHYDRATE 12.4g FIBER 0.5g CHOLESTEROL 55mg
IRON 1.7mg SODIUM 221mg CALCIUM 124mg

HADDOCK WITH TROPICAL CHUTNEY

1 (8-ounce) can crushed pineapple in juice, undrained
2 medium-size oranges, peeled, sectioned, and diced
2 tablespoons minced unsalted cashews
2 tablespoons minced dried apricots
1 teaspoon peeled, grated gingerroot
½ teaspoon curry powder
4 (4-ounce) haddock steaks (¾ inch thick)
Vegetable cooking spray
1 tablespoon low-sodium soy sauce
2 teaspoons honey

Drain pineapple, reserving ¼ cup juice. Combine pineapple, 3 tablespoons reserved juice, orange, and next 4 ingredients; stir well. Let stand 1 hour at room temperature.

Place haddock steaks in an 11- x 7- x 1½-inch baking dish coated with cooking spray. Combine remaining 1 tablespoon pineapple juice, soy sauce, and honey; brush over steaks. Bake, uncovered, at 450° for 15 minutes or until fish flakes easily when tested with a fork. Transfer to individual serving plates. Serve with pineapple mixture. Yield: 4 servings (190 calories per serving).

Per Serving: PROTEIN 22.7g FAT 2.8g (Saturated Fat 0.5g)
CARBOHYDRATE 18.7g FIBER 2.1g CHOLESTEROL 65mg
IRON 2.0mg SODIUM 181mg CALCIUM 62mg

Enjoy a festive mixture of fish and vegetables in Grouper with Roasted Ratatouille.

GROUPER WITH ROASTED RATATOUILLE

1 (1-pound) eggplant
1 medium-size sweet red pepper
1 medium-size sweet yellow pepper
1 medium zucchini
2 small yellow squash
1 cup chopped sweet onion
2 cloves garlic, minced
Olive oil-flavored vegetable cooking
    spray
2 teaspoons minced fresh rosemary
¼ teaspoon salt
2 (8-ounce) grouper fillets, cut into
    1½-inch pieces
½ cup seeded, diced plum tomato
1 tablespoon balsamic vinegar
½ teaspoon freshly ground pepper
¼ pound fresh spinach leaves
Fresh rosemary sprigs (optional)

Peel eggplant; cut eggplant and peppers into 1-inch pieces. Cut zucchini and squash lengthwise in quarters; cut into 1-inch pieces. Combine eggplant, peppers, zucchini, squash, onion, and garlic in a 15- x 10- x 1-inch jellyroll pan, and coat with cooking spray; toss gently. Sprinkle rosemary and salt over vegetable mixture; toss gently. Bake at 400° for 25 minutes or until tender, stirring occasionally. Add grouper; bake an additional 12 minutes or until fish flakes easily when tested with a fork. Drain well.

Combine tomato, vinegar, and ground pepper. Add to fish mixture; toss gently. Arrange spinach leaves on individual serving plates; spoon fish mixture over spinach. Garnish with rosemary sprigs, if desired. Yield: 6 servings (132 calories per serving).

Per Serving: PROTEIN 17.6g FAT 1.7g (Saturated Fat 0.3g)
CARBOHYDRATE 12.9g FIBER 4.0g CHOLESTEROL 28mg
IRON 2.8mg SODIUM 161mg CALCIUM 88mg

BAKED MAHIMAHI WITH TOMATILLO SALSA

½ cup husked, finely chopped tomatillos
½ cup seeded, finely chopped yellow tomato
¼ cup minced green onions
3 tablespoons minced fresh cilantro
1 tablespoon seeded, minced jalapeño pepper
½ teaspoon ground cumin
¼ teaspoon salt
¼ teaspoon pepper
1½ tablespoons lemon juice
1 teaspoon dark sesame oil
4 (4-ounce) mahimahi fillets
Olive oil-flavored vegetable cooking spray

Combine first 8 ingredients in a small bowl; stir well. Cover and chill thoroughly.

Combine lemon juice and sesame oil; brush mixture evenly over both sides of each fillet. Place fillets in an 11- x 7- x 1½-inch baking dish coated with cooking spray. Bake, uncovered, at 450° for 15 minutes or until fish flakes easily when tested with a fork. Transfer to a serving platter. Spoon tomatillo mixture evenly over fillets. Serve immediately. Yield: 4 servings (124 calories per serving).

Per Serving: PROTEIN 21.7g FAT 2.4g (Saturated Fat 0.4g)
CARBOHYDRATE 3.5g FIBER 0.8g CHOLESTEROL 84mg
IRON 1.9mg SODIUM 254mg CALCIUM 14mg

THREE-PEPPERCORN MARLIN

½ cup raspberry vinegar
1 teaspoon red peppercorns, crushed
1 teaspoon green peppercorns, crushed
1 teaspoon black peppercorns, crushed
½ cup canned low-sodium chicken broth, undiluted
2 tablespoons no-sugar-added raspberry spread
1 teaspoon Dijon mustard
1 teaspoon cornstarch
1 tablespoon water
Vegetable cooking spray
4 (4-ounce) marlin fillets
2 teaspoons olive oil

Combine first 4 ingredients in a small saucepan. Bring to a boil; reduce heat, and simmer, uncovered, until mixture is reduced to ¼ cup. Add chicken broth, raspberry spread, and mustard; simmer, uncovered, 20 minutes, stirring occasionally.

Combine cornstarch and water, stirring until smooth. Add to broth mixture, stirring constantly until mixture comes to a boil; cook 1 minute. Set aside, and keep warm.

Coat grill rack with cooking spray; place on grill over medium-hot coals (350° to 400°). Brush both sides of each fillet with olive oil. Place fillets on rack; grill, covered, 6 minutes on each side or until fish flakes easily when tested with a fork. Transfer fillets to a serving platter, and spoon peppercorn mixture evenly over fillets. Yield: 4 servings (178 calories per serving).

Per Serving: PROTEIN 22.7g FAT 7.2g (Saturated Fat 1.6g)
CARBOHYDRATE 4.3g FIBER 0.4g CHOLESTEROL 44mg
IRON 1.6mg SODIUM 141mg CALCIUM 13mg

GRILLED GINGER SALMON FILLETS

3 tablespoons lime juice
2 tablespoons reduced-calorie margarine, melted
1 tablespoon peeled, minced gingeroot
⅛ teaspoon curry powder
Vegetable cooking spray
4 (4-ounce) salmon fillets (½ inch thick)
2 teaspoons chopped fresh parsley
Lime wedges (optional)

Combine first 4 ingredients in a small bowl; stir well. Set aside.

Coat a large piece of heavy-duty aluminum foil with cooking spray. Place foil on grill rack over medium-hot coals (350° to 400°). Puncture foil several times for ventilation. Place fillets on foil; grill, covered, 6 minutes on each side or until fish flakes easily when tested with a fork, basting frequently with lime mixture. Transfer to a serving platter, and sprinkle with parsley. Garnish with lime wedges, if desired. Yield: 4 servings (229 calories per serving).

Per Serving: PROTEIN 24.4g FAT 13.5g (Saturated Fat 2.2g)
CARBOHYDRATE 1.7g FIBER 0.1g CHOLESTEROL 77mg
IRON 0.6mg SODIUM 115mg CALCIUM 11mg

SALMON WITH CRANBERRY-LEEK SAUCE

Vegetable cooking spray
1 tablespoon reduced-calorie margarine, divided
1 cup chopped leeks
1 cup fresh or frozen cranberries, thawed
¾ cup unsweetened orange juice
¼ teaspoon dried whole thyme
¾ cup water
1 tablespoon raspberry vinegar
2 teaspoons honey
¼ teaspoon salt
¼ teaspoon pepper
1 small leek
4 (4-ounce) salmon steaks (½ inch thick)

Coat a large nonstick skillet with cooking spray; add 2 teaspoons margarine. Place over medium-high heat until margarine melts; add chopped leeks, and sauté until tender. Add cranberries, orange juice, and thyme. Cook, uncovered, 3 minutes or until cranberries are slightly tender. Remove 20 cranberries from mixture, using a slotted spoon; set aside. Add water to leek mixture. Bring to a boil; cover, reduce heat, and simmer 5 minutes.

Place leek mixture in a wire-mesh strainer; press with back of spoon against the sides of strainer to squeeze out liquid. Discard leek and cranberry pulp remaining in strainer. Bring strained mixture to a boil in a small saucepan; cook 1 minute or until mixture is reduced to ¾ cup. Stir in vinegar, honey, salt, and pepper. Set aside, and keep warm.

Remove and discard root, tough outer leaves, and top from small leek; cut leek into julienne strips. Coat skillet with cooking spray; add remaining 1 teaspoon margarine. Place over medium heat until margarine melts; add leek strips, and sauté until tender. Set aside, and keep warm.

Place salmon steaks on rack of a broiler pan coated with cooking spray. Broil 5½ inches from heat (with electric oven door partially opened) 3 minutes. Turn steaks, and broil an additional 2 minutes or until fish flakes easily when tested with a fork. Spoon reserved cranberry mixture evenly onto individual serving plates. Place steaks on cranberry mixture. Top evenly with sautéed leek and reserved whole cranberries. Serve immediately. Yield: 4 servings (275 calories per serving).

Per Serving: PROTEIN 25.1g FAT 12.2g (Saturated Fat 2.0g) CARBOHYDRATE 16.0g FIBER 0.8g CHOLESTEROL 77mg IRON 1.4mg SODIUM 240mg CALCIUM 34mg

STEAMED SALMON WITH CARAMELIZED ONIONS

Vegetable cooking spray
2 teaspoons reduced-calorie margarine
4 large onions (about 2 pounds), thinly sliced and separated into rings
2 tablespoons finely chopped pecans
1 tablespoon balsamic vinegar
½ teaspoon freshly ground pepper
6 (4-ounce) salmon steaks (½ inch thick)

Coat a nonstick skillet with cooking spray; add margarine. Place over medium-high heat until margarine melts. Add onion; sauté 5 minutes. Reduce heat to medium; cook 20 minutes or until onion is golden, stirring frequently. Remove from heat; stir in pecans, vinegar, and pepper. Set aside, and keep warm.

Arrange 3 salmon steaks in a vegetable steamer over boiling water. Cover; steam 5 minutes or until fish flakes easily when tested with a fork. Remove from steamer; keep warm. Repeat procedure with remaining steaks. To serve, place steaks on individual serving plates. Top steaks with caramelized onions. Yield: 6 servings (253 calories per serving).

Per Serving: PROTEIN 25.5g FAT 12.4g (Saturated Fat 2.0g) CARBOHYDRATE 9.3g FIBER 2.1g CHOLESTEROL 77mg IRON 0.8mg SODIUM 74mg CALCIUM 28mg

ORIENTAL RED SNAPPER

½ cup thinly sliced green onions
1 to 1½ tablespoons peeled, minced gingerroot
1 teaspoon sugar
¼ teaspoon salt
¼ to ½ teaspoon dried crushed red pepper
2 cloves garlic, crushed
2 tablespoons low-sodium soy sauce
2 tablespoons unsweetened pineapple juice
1 teaspoon dark sesame oil
4 (4-ounce) red snapper fillets

Combine first 9 ingredients; stir well. Place fillets in a shallow dish; spread green onion mixture evenly over fillets. Cover and marinate in refrigerator 30 minutes.

Line a steaming basket with a plate at least 1 inch smaller in diameter than the basket. Transfer fillets to plate, using a slotted spoon; discard marinade. Place steaming basket over boiling water. Cover and steam 10 minutes or until fish flakes easily when tested with a fork. Yield: 4 servings (143 calories per serving).

Per Serving: PROTEIN 23.7g FAT 2.7g (Saturated Fat 0.5g)
CARBOHYDRATE 4.1g FIBER 0.4g CHOLESTEROL 42mg
IRON 0.5mg SODIUM 395mg CALCIUM 49mg

BAKED SNAPPER VERACRUZANA

Vegetable cooking spray
1½ cups thinly sliced onion
2 tablespoons minced fresh garlic
1 cup thinly sliced sweet red pepper
½ cup thinly sliced celery
¼ cup sliced pimiento-stuffed olives
2 tablespoons seeded, minced jalapeño
    pepper
1 tablespoon capers, drained
2 (14½-ounce) cans no-salt-added stewed
    tomatoes, drained
¼ teaspoon fennel seeds
6 (4-ounce) red snapper fillets

Coat a large nonstick skillet with cooking spray; place over medium-high heat until hot. Add onion and garlic; sauté 5 minutes or just until tender. Add red pepper, celery, pimiento-stuffed olives, jalapeño pepper, and capers; cook 10 minutes, stirring frequently. Add tomatoes and fennel seeds; cook, uncovered, 15 minutes.

Place fillets in a 13- x 9- x 2-inch baking dish coated with cooking spray. Spoon vegetable mixture evenly over fillets. Bake at 400° for 15 minutes or until fish flakes easily when tested with a fork. Transfer to a serving platter. Yield: 6 servings (186 calories per serving).

Per Serving: PROTEIN 25.9g FAT 2.3g (Saturated Fat 0.4g)
CARBOHYDRATE 15.7g FIBER 1.5g CHOLESTEROL 42mg
IRON 1.8mg SODIUM 287mg CALCIUM 101mg

SOLE WITH ROASTED GARLIC-POTATO PUREE

2 small heads garlic, unpeeled
Olive oil-flavored vegetable cooking spray
1¼ cups peeled, diced red potato
¼ cup plus 3 tablespoons skim milk
¼ teaspoon salt
¼ teaspoon freshly ground pepper
4 (4-ounce) sole fillets
3 tablespoons freshly grated Parmesan cheese
2 tablespoons fine, dry breadcrumbs
Paprika (optional)
Fresh watercress (optional)

Gently peel outer skin from garlic; cut off top one-fourth of each head, and discard. Place garlic, cut side up, in center of a piece of heavy-duty aluminum foil; coat garlic with cooking spray. Fold aluminum foil over garlic, sealing tightly. Bake at 350° for 1 hour or until garlic is soft. Remove from oven, and let cool.

Remove and discard papery skin from garlic. Scoop out soft garlic, using a small spoon. Set aside soft garlic; discard remaining garlic.

Cook potato in boiling water to cover 15 to 20 minutes or until tender. Drain potato, and mash. Stir in roasted garlic, milk, salt, and pepper. Set aside, and keep warm.

Place fillets in an 11- x 7- x 1½-inch baking dish coated with cooking spray. Combine cheese and breadcrumbs; sprinkle over fillets. Bake, uncovered, at 425° for 12 to 15 minutes or until fish flakes easily when tested with a fork.

Transfer fillets to individual serving plates. Pipe or spoon potato puree evenly onto plates. If desired, sprinkle with paprika, and garnish with fresh watercress. Serve immediately. Yield: 4 servings (220 calories per serving).

Per Serving: PROTEIN 26.7g FAT 3.4g (Saturated Fat 1.3g)
CARBOHYDRATE 19.9g FIBER 1.3g CHOLESTEROL 64mg
IRON 1.2mg SODIUM 367mg CALCIUM 153mg

Enliven a nautical meal with the taste of oranges. Orange Julep Swordfish combines the best from land and sea.

ORANGE JULEP SWORDFISH

¼ cup unsweetened orange juice
3 tablespoons minced fresh mint
1 tablespoon peeled, grated gingerroot
1 tablespoon grated orange rind
2 tablespoons bourbon
2 (8-ounce) swordfish steaks (¾ inch thick)
4 (¼-inch-thick) orange slices
Vegetable cooking spray
Fresh mint sprigs (optional)

Combine first 5 ingredients in a large shallow dish. Place swordfish steaks and orange slices in a single layer in dish, turning to coat. Cover and marinate in refrigerator 30 minutes, turning once.

Coat grill rack with cooking spray; place on grill over medium-hot coals (350° to 400°). Place steaks on rack; grill, covered, 5 to 6 minutes on each side or until fish flakes easily when tested with a fork. Transfer steaks to a serving platter, and cut each steak in half.

Place orange slices on grill rack; grill, covered, 2 minutes on each side. Cut each slice into thirds, and arrange on serving platter. Garnish with fresh mint sprigs, if desired. Yield: 4 servings (169 calories per serving).

Per Serving: PROTEIN 23.1g   FAT 4.7g   (Saturated Fat 1.3g)
CARBOHYDRATE 7.9g   FIBER 2.2g   CHOLESTEROL 44mg
IRON 1.0mg   SODIUM 102mg   CALCIUM 29mg

SEARED TUNA PROVENÇAL

Olive oil-flavored vegetable cooking spray
2 teaspoons minced garlic
1 cup thinly sliced sweet red pepper
1 cup thinly sliced sweet yellow pepper
¾ cup thinly sliced purple onion
1½ cups peeled, seeded, and chopped tomato
¼ cup Burgundy or other dry red wine
½ teaspoon dried whole rosemary
½ teaspoon freshly ground pepper
¼ teaspoon salt
4 (4-ounce) tuna steaks (1 inch thick)
1 teaspoon olive oil

Coat a large nonstick skillet with cooking spray; place over medium-high heat until hot. Add garlic, and sauté 1 minute. Add sweet peppers and onion; sauté until tender. Add tomato, wine, and rosemary; bring to a boil. Reduce heat, and simmer, uncovered, 10 minutes or until vegetables are tender, stirring occasionally. Stir in ground pepper and salt. Set aside, and keep warm.

Brush both sides of each steak with olive oil. Coat a large cast-iron skillet with cooking spray. Place over high heat until almost smoking. Add tuna steaks, and sear 45 seconds to 1 minute on each side or until browned. Immediately place skillet in oven, and bake at 400° for 8 to 10 minutes or until fish flakes easily when tested with a fork. Transfer steaks to a serving platter. Spoon vegetable mixture evenly over steaks. Yield: 4 servings (219 calories per serving).

Per Serving: PROTEIN 28.1g FAT 7.4g (Saturated Fat 1.7g) CARBOHYDRATE 10.0g FIBER 2.6g CHOLESTEROL 43mg IRON 2.6mg SODIUM 202mg CALCIUM 20mg

CRABMEAT TIMBALES

3 cups loosely packed torn fresh spinach
Vegetable cooking spray
¼ cup diced plum tomato
3 tablespoons minced shallots
3 tablespoons minced celery
½ pound fresh lump crabmeat, drained
¼ cup plus 2 tablespoons frozen egg substitute, thawed
¼ cup reduced-calorie mayonnaise
Roasted Pepper Sauce

Remove stems from spinach. Wash leaves; arrange in a vegetable steamer over boiling water. Cover; steam 1 minute. Coat 4 (6-ounce) custard cups with cooking spray; line with spinach.

Coat a nonstick skillet with cooking spray; place over medium-high heat until hot. Add tomato, shallots, and celery; sauté 2 minutes. Remove from heat; stir in crabmeat. Spoon crabmeat mixture into spinach-lined cups. Combine egg substitute and mayonnaise; stir. Pour over crabmeat mixture. Bake, uncovered, at 325° for 25 minutes. Let cool 5 minutes; invert onto serving plates. Serve with Roasted Pepper Sauce. Yield: 4 servings (145 calories per serving).

Roasted Pepper Sauce

1 large sweet red pepper
1 small shallot, quartered
½ teaspoon Hungarian sweet paprika
½ teaspoon lemon juice
2 tablespoons plain nonfat yogurt
1½ teaspoons capers, drained

Cut pepper in half lengthwise; remove and discard seeds and membrane. Place pepper, skin side up, on a baking sheet; flatten with palm of hand. Broil 5½ inches from heat (with electric oven door partially opened) 15 to 20 minutes or until charred. Place pepper in ice water until cool. Remove from water; peel and discard skin. Coarsely chop pepper.

Combine pepper and next 3 ingredients in container of an electric blender; cover and process on medium speed 1 minute or until smooth, stopping once to scrape down sides. Transfer to a small bowl; stir in yogurt and capers. Yield: ¾ cup plus 2 tablespoons.

Per Serving: PROTEIN 15.9g FAT 5.8g (Saturated Fat 0.8g) CARBOHYDRATE 7.7g FIBER 2.3g CHOLESTEROL 62mg IRON 2.5mg SODIUM 449mg CALCIUM 116mg

HONEY-MUSTARD LOBSTER WITH ASPARAGUS

4 (8-ounce) fresh or frozen lobster tails, thawed
1 pound fresh asparagus
2 tablespoons reduced-calorie margarine
1½ tablespoons all-purpose flour
⅔ cup 1% low-fat milk
1½ tablespoons Dijon mustard
2 teaspoons honey
2 tablespoons minced fresh chives

Cook lobster tails in boiling water 8 minutes or until done; drain. Rinse tails thoroughly with cold water. Split and clean tails. Cut lobster meat into ⅜-inch slices. Set aside.

Snap off tough ends of asparagus. Remove scales from spears with a knife or vegetable peeler, if desired. Arrange asparagus in a vegetable steamer over boiling water. Cover and steam 8 minutes or until crisp-tender. Set aside, and keep warm.

Melt margarine in a small saucepan over low heat; add flour, stirring until smooth. Cook 1 minute, stirring constantly. Gradually add milk, mustard, and honey; cook over medium heat, stirring constantly, until mixture is thickened and bubbly. Stir in chives.

Arrange asparagus spears and lobster slices on individual serving plates; spoon mustard sauce evenly over asparagus and lobster. Serve immediately. Yield: 4 servings (203 calories per serving).

Per Serving: PROTEIN 28.4g FAT 3.7g (Saturated Fat 0.6g)
CARBOHYDRATE 13.4g FIBER 1.9g CHOLESTEROL 91mg
IRON 1.4mg SODIUM 569mg CALCIUM 143mg

STIR-FRIED SCALLOPS AND VEGETABLES

½ cup water
1 tablespoon cornstarch
2 tablespoons dry sherry
2 tablespoons low-sodium teriyaki sauce
½ teaspoon chicken-flavored bouillon granules
½ teaspoon ground cumin
½ teaspoon ground ginger
4 ounces fresh snow pea pods
Vegetable cooking spray
1 teaspoon vegetable oil
¾ cup fresh corn cut from cob (about 2 ears)
6 green onions, cut into 1½-inch pieces
1 tablespoon minced garlic
1 pound sea scallops, cut in half
3 tablespoons chopped walnuts, toasted

Combine first 7 ingredients in a small bowl; stir well. Set aside.

Wash snow peas; trim ends, and remove strings. Cut lengthwise into julienne strips. Set aside.

Coat a wok or large nonstick skillet with cooking spray; add oil. Heat at medium (350°) until hot. Add corn; stir-fry 2 minutes. Increase heat to medium-high (375°). Add snow peas, green onions, and garlic; stir-fry 3 minutes. Remove vegetables from wok; set aside. Wipe wok dry with a paper towel.

Coat wok with cooking spray; heat at medium-high heat until hot. Add scallops, and stir-fry 3 minutes or until scallops are opaque. Remove from wok; set aside.

Add reserved teriyaki mixture to wok; cook, stirring constantly, 1 minute or until mixture is thickened. Return vegetables and scallops to wok. Cook, stirring constantly, until mixture is thoroughly heated. Transfer to a serving platter, and sprinkle with walnuts. Serve immediately. Yield: 4 servings (213 calories per serving).

Per Serving: PROTEIN 23.1g FAT 6.3g (Saturated Fat 0.6g)
CARBOHYDRATE 16.7g FIBER 2.4g CHOLESTEROL 37mg
IRON 1.8mg SODIUM 445mg CALCIUM 63mg

You won't have to fish for compliments when you present steaming Grilled Scallops with Black Beans.

GRILLED SCALLOPS WITH BLACK BEANS

1 pound sea scallops
1 teaspoon olive oil
½ teaspoon ground cumin
¼ teaspoon ground red pepper
Vegetable cooking spray
1 cup diced onion
2 teaspoons minced garlic
½ cup minced sweet red pepper
2 cups canned black beans, drained
½ teaspoon ground cumin
1 teaspoon balsamic vinegar

Place scallops in a shallow dish. Combine olive oil, ½ teaspoon cumin, and ground red pepper; drizzle over scallops, and toss gently. Cover; marinate in refrigerator 30 minutes, stirring occasionally.

Coat a large nonstick skillet with cooking spray; place over medium-high heat until hot. Add onion and garlic; sauté until tender. Add sweet red pepper, and sauté until tender. Stir in black beans and ½ teaspoon cumin; sauté 3 minutes or until thoroughly heated. Remove from heat; stir in vinegar, and keep warm.

Remove scallops from marinade; discarding marinade, thread scallops onto 4 (8-inch) skewers. Coat grill rack with cooking spray; place on grill over medium coals (300° to 350°). Place skewers on rack; grill, uncovered, 3 minutes on each side or until scallops are opaque. Spoon black bean mixture evenly onto individual serving plates. Arrange grilled scallops evenly over black bean mixture. Serve immediately. Yield: 4 servings (266 calories per serving).

Per Serving: PROTEIN 28.7g FAT 3.1g (Saturated Fat 0.4g)
CARBOHYDRATE 31.4g FIBER 5.3g CHOLESTEROL 37mg
IRON 3.2mg SODIUM 460mg CALCIUM 72mg

PAPAYA SHRIMP WITH COCONUT RICE

1½ pounds unpeeled medium-size fresh shrimp
Vegetable cooking spray
1 teaspoon reduced-calorie margarine
¼ teaspoon ground red pepper
4 ounces fresh snow pea pods, trimmed
3 tablespoons low-sodium soy sauce
2 tablespoons dry sherry
2 teaspoons honey
¼ teaspoon ground cinnamon
2 teaspoons cornstarch
3 tablespoons canned low-sodium chicken broth, undiluted
⅔ cup peeled, cubed ripe papaya
2 cups cooked long-grain rice (cooked without salt or fat)
1½ tablespoons unsweetened flaked coconut
1¼ teaspoons curry powder

Peel and devein shrimp. Coat a wok or large non-stick skillet with cooking spray; add margarine and red pepper. Heat at medium-high (375°) until margarine melts. Add shrimp, and stir-fry 3 minutes. Remove shrimp from wok; set aside. Wipe wok dry with a paper towel.

Coat wok with cooking spray; heat at medium-high until hot. Add snow peas, and stir-fry 2 minutes or until crisp-tender. Remove from wok. Combine soy sauce, sherry, honey, and cinnamon, stirring well. Place soy sauce mixture in wok; bring to a boil and cook 1 minute. Combine cornstarch and chicken broth, stirring well; add to soy sauce mixture, stirring well. Add shrimp, snow peas, and papaya; cook just until thickened. Combine cooked rice, coconut, and curry powder; stir well. Place ½ cup rice mixture on each individual serving plate; spoon shrimp mixture evenly over rice. Yield: 4 servings (287 calories per serving).

Per Serving: PROTEIN 27.0g FAT 3.6g (Saturated Fat 1.5g)
CARBOHYDRATE 34.2g FIBER 2.1g CHOLESTEROL 221mg
IRON 5.4mg SODIUM 563mg CALCIUM 79mg

SHRIMP AND MUSSELS MEDLEY

1½ pounds unpeeled medium-size fresh shrimp
1 pound fresh mussels
Vegetable cooking spray
1 teaspoon olive oil
¾ cup chopped onion
⅔ cup chopped green pepper
⅔ cup chopped sweet red pepper
⅔ cup chopped sweet yellow pepper
5 cloves garlic, minced
2 cups peeled, chopped tomato
1½ cups Chablis or other dry white wine
⅓ cup chopped fresh cilantro
¼ teaspoon salt
4 cups cooked long-grain rice (cooked without salt or fat)

Peel and devein shrimp. Set aside. Remove beards on mussels, and scrub shells with a brush. Discard opened, cracked, or heavy mussels (they're filled with sand). Set aside.

Coat a Dutch oven with cooking spray; add olive oil. Place over medium-high heat until hot. Add onion and next 4 ingredients; sauté 3 minutes or until vegetables are tender. Add tomato, wine, cilantro, and salt; bring to a boil. Add shrimp and mussels. Cover and cook 8 minutes or until mussels are open and shrimp are done.

Place ½ cup cooked rice in each individual serving bowl; spoon shrimp mixture evenly over rice. Serve immediately. Yield: 8 servings (224 calories per serving).

Per Serving: PROTEIN 17.8g FAT 2.6g (Saturated Fat 0.4g)
CARBOHYDRATE 31.8g FIBER 2.1g CHOLESTEROL 101mg
IRON 4.0mg SODIUM 219mg CALCIUM 64mg

Artichoke and Spinach Stuffed Shells (page 143) contains a tantalizing blend of pasta and vegetables surrounded by a robust homemade sauce.

Grains
&
Pastas

BARLEY WITH TOMATOES

2 teaspoons reduced-calorie margarine
1 cup pearl barley, uncooked
1 cup sliced celery
1 cup chopped onion
1 (14½-ounce) can no-salt-added whole tomatoes,
    undrained and chopped
1 (13¾-ounce) can no-salt-added beef broth,
    undiluted
1 cup water
½ teaspoon sugar
½ teaspoon caraway seeds
¼ teaspoon salt
⅛ teaspoon pepper

Heat margarine in a large nonstick skillet over medium-high heat until margarine melts. Add barley, celery, and onion; sauté 5 minutes or until barley is lightly browned. Stir in tomato and remaining ingredients. Bring to a boil; cover, reduce heat, and simmer 1 hour and 15 minutes or until barley is tender and liquid is absorbed. Yield: 10 servings (103 calories per ½-cup serving).

Per Serving: PROTEIN 2.9g FAT 0.8g (Saturated Fat 0.1g)
CARBOHYDRATE 21.7g FIBER 4.3g CHOLESTEROL 0mg
IRON 0.8mg SODIUM 86mg CALCIUM 29mg

SPICY BULGUR

Vegetable cooking spray
1 teaspoon vegetable oil
1 cup bulgur (cracked wheat), uncooked
½ cup chopped green pepper
½ cup chopped green onions
½ cup sliced fresh mushrooms
2 (14½-ounce) cans no-salt-added whole
    tomatoes, undrained and chopped
1 (15-ounce) can black beans, drained
1 (4-ounce) can chopped green chiles, drained
1 teaspoon ground cumin
1 teaspoon chili powder
½ teaspoon pepper
¼ teaspoon salt

Coat a large nonstick skillet with cooking spray; add oil. Place over medium-high heat until hot. Add

bulgur and next 3 ingredients; sauté 5 minutes. Add tomato and remaining ingredients; bring to a boil. Cover, reduce heat, and simmer 15 minutes or until bulgur is tender and liquid is absorbed. Yield: 11 servings (100 calories per ½-cup serving).

Per Serving: PROTEIN 4.6g FAT 0.9g (Saturated Fat 0.2g)
CARBOHYDRATE 20.2g FIBER 3.8g CHOLESTEROL 0mg
IRON 1.5mg SODIUM 143mg CALCIUM 43mg

TABBOULEH SKILLET

1 tablespoon olive oil
1 cup bulgur (cracked wheat), uncooked
½ cup chopped green pepper
½ cup sliced green onions
1 clove garlic, minced
2 cups water
2 teaspoons lemon juice
¼ teaspoon salt
¼ teaspoon dried whole marjoram
⅛ teaspoon pepper
Dash of sugar
1 cup chopped yellow squash
1 cup chopped tomato

Heat oil in a nonstick skillet over medium-high heat. Add bulgur and next 3 ingredients; sauté 3 minutes. Add water and next 5 ingredients; bring to a boil. Cover, reduce heat, and simmer 15 minutes or until bulgur is tender and liquid is absorbed. Stir in squash and tomato. Cover; cook 5 minutes. Serve immediately. Yield: 10 servings (71 calories per ½-cup serving).

Per Serving: PROTEIN 2.2g FAT 1.7g (Saturated Fat 0.2g)
CARBOHYDRATE 13.1g FIBER 3.3g CHOLESTEROL 0mg
IRON 0.7mg SODIUM 64mg CALCIUM 13mg

ORIENTAL COUSCOUS

Vegetable cooking spray
½ cup sliced green onions
1½ cups water
2 tablespoons low-sodium soy sauce
½ teaspoon sugar
¼ teaspoon ground ginger
¼ teaspoon garlic powder
¼ teaspoon ground red pepper
1 cup couscous, uncooked

Coat a medium saucepan with cooking spray; place over medium-high heat until hot. Add green onions, and sauté until tender.

Add water and next 5 ingredients; bring to a boil. Remove from heat. Add couscous; cover and let stand 5 minutes or until couscous is tender and liquid is absorbed. Fluff couscous with a fork, and transfer to a serving bowl. Yield: 6 servings (131 calories per ½-cup serving).

Per Serving: PROTEIN 4.5g FAT 0.1g (Saturated Fat 0g)
CARBOHYDRATE 26.9g FIBER 0.7g CHOLESTEROL 0mg
IRON 0.8mg SODIUM 132mg CALCIUM 19mg

TRIPLE GRAIN SKILLET

Vegetable cooking spray
½ cup chopped celery
½ cup chopped carrot
½ cup chopped onion
1¾ cups canned low-sodium chicken broth, undiluted
1¼ cups water
⅓ cup long-grain brown rice, uncooked
⅓ cup bulgur (cracked wheat), uncooked
⅓ cup long-grain rice, uncooked
½ teaspoon dried whole sage
¼ teaspoon dried whole rosemary, crushed
¼ teaspoon salt
⅛ teaspoon pepper

Coat a large nonstick skillet with cooking spray; place over medium-high heat until hot. Add celery, carrot, and onion; sauté 3 minutes or until tender. Add chicken broth, water, and brown rice; bring to a boil. Cover, reduce heat, and simmer 30 minutes. Stir in bulgur and remaining ingredients. Cover and simmer an additional 25 to 30 minutes or until rice is tender and liquid is absorbed. Yield: 8 servings (95 calories per ½-cup serving).

Per Serving: PROTEIN 2.7g FAT 0.8g (Saturated Fat 0.2g)
CARBOHYDRATE 19.4g FIBER 2.0g CHOLESTEROL 0mg
IRON 1.0mg SODIUM 104mg CALCIUM 16mg

SOUTHWESTERN BROWN RICE

Vegetable cooking spray
½ cup chopped onion
1 (13¾-ounce) can no-salt-added chicken broth
¾ cup water
½ teaspoon sugar
½ teaspoon chili powder
¼ teaspoon salt
¼ teaspoon ground cumin
¼ teaspoon dried whole oregano
⅛ teaspoon ground red pepper
1 cup long-grain brown rice, uncooked
2 (4-ounce) cans chopped green chiles, drained
1 cup frozen whole kernel corn, thawed

Coat a large saucepan with cooking spray; place over medium-high heat until hot. Add onion, and sauté until tender. Add chicken broth and next 7 ingredients; bring to a boil. Stir in rice. Cover, reduce heat, and simmer 40 minutes. Stir in green chiles and corn. Cover and simmer an additional 15 minutes or until rice is tender and liquid is absorbed. Yield: 9 servings (107 calories per ½-cup serving).

Per Serving: PROTEIN 2.8g FAT 1.2g (Saturated Fat 0.2g)
CARBOHYDRATE 21.8g FIBER 1.6g CHOLESTEROL 0mg
IRON 0.6mg SODIUM 116mg CALCIUM 10mg

 ANATOMY OF A GRAIN
Refining processes destroy some or all of a grain's bran and germ, the most nutrient-dense portions. Although most grain products come enriched with some of those lost nutrients, not all of the nutrients are replaced.

If you were to peel off the husk or outer coating of a grain, you would find:
• Germ—the small region at one end of a grain kernel containing nutrients that support sprouting. The germ is rich in protein, vitamins, and minerals.
• Endosperm—the soft, inner portion of a grain. The endosperm is rich in starch and it contains a small amount of gluten, which helps keep bread light.
• Bran—the dark, protective shell of a grain. The bran is rich in fiber. A whole grain such as brown rice, for example, contains nearly three times as much fiber as refined white rice.

A simple recipe transforms an ordinary dish into a fiesta for the mouth with Easy Spanish Rice.

EASY SPANISH RICE

Vegetable cooking spray
½ cup chopped green pepper
½ cup chopped onion
2 (8-ounce) cans no-salt-added tomato sauce
1 (14½-ounce) can no-salt-added stewed tomatoes, undrained and chopped
1 cup long-grain rice, uncooked
¼ cup water
1 teaspoon chili powder
½ teaspoon dried whole oregano
¼ teaspoon salt
¼ teaspoon ground red pepper
¼ teaspoon ground cumin

Coat a large nonstick skillet with cooking spray, and place over medium-high heat until hot. Add green pepper and onion; sauté 5 minutes or until vegetables are tender.

Add tomato sauce and remaining ingredients to vegetables in skillet. Bring mixture to a boil; cover, reduce heat, and simmer 25 to 30 minutes or until rice is tender and liquid is absorbed. Spoon into a serving bowl. Yield: 8 servings (125 calories per ½-cup serving).

Per Serving: PROTEIN 3.0g FAT 0.3g (Saturated Fat 0.1g)
CARBOHYDRATE 27.7g FIBER 0.7g CHOLESTEROL 0mg
IRON 1.6mg SODIUM 99mg CALCIUM 27mg

BLACK-EYED PEAS AND RICE

2 teaspoons reduced-calorie margarine
1 cup long-grain rice, uncooked
½ cup chopped onion
½ cup chopped green pepper
3 cups canned low-sodium chicken broth,
    undiluted
1 (10-ounce) package frozen black-eyed peas,
    thawed
1 cup frozen whole kernel corn, thawed
½ teaspoon sugar
½ teaspoon dried whole thyme
¼ teaspoon salt
¼ teaspoon garlic powder
¼ teaspoon ground red pepper

Heat margarine in a saucepan over medium-high heat until margarine melts. Add rice, onion, and green pepper; sauté 3 minutes or until rice is lightly browned. Stir in broth and remaining ingredients. Bring to a boil; cover, reduce heat, and simmer 25 minutes or until rice is tender and liquid is absorbed. Yield: 11 servings (123 calories per ½-cup serving).

Per Serving: PROTEIN 4.6g FAT 1.3g (Saturated Fat 0.3g)
CARBOHYDRATE 23.7g FIBER 1.1g CHOLESTEROL 0mg
IRON 1.9mg SODIUM 84mg CALCIUM 15mg

HERBED RISOTTO

3 cups canned low-sodium chicken broth,
    undiluted
1 cup water
Vegetable cooking spray
½ cup sliced green onions
2 cloves garlic, minced
1 cup Arborio rice, uncooked
¾ cup Chablis or other dry white wine
2 teaspoons minced fresh oregano
¼ teaspoon salt
⅛ teaspoon ground white pepper
2 tablespoons freshly grated Parmesan cheese

Combine broth and water in a saucepan; place over medium heat. Cover and bring to a simmer; reduce heat to low, and keep warm.

Coat a large nonstick skillet with cooking spray; place over medium-high heat until hot. Add green onions and garlic; sauté until tender. Add rice and next 4 ingredients. Reduce heat to medium, and cook, stirring constantly, 4 minutes or until most of wine is absorbed. Add ½ cup simmering broth mixture to rice, stirring constantly until most of liquid is absorbed. Add remaining broth, ½ cup at a time, cooking and stirring constantly until each ½ cup is absorbed, about 40 minutes. (Rice will be tender and have a creamy consistency.) Sprinkle with Parmesan cheese, and serve immediately. Yield: 6 servings (151 calories per ½-cup serving).

Per Serving: PROTEIN 4.5g FAT 1.7g (Saturated Fat 0.6g)
CARBOHYDRATE 29.0g FIBER 0.7g CHOLESTEROL 2mg
IRON 2.3mg SODIUM 178mg CALCIUM 42mg

GARDEN WILD RICE

⅔ cup wild rice, uncooked
2½ cups water
1 teaspoon chicken-flavored bouillon granules
Vegetable cooking spray
1 teaspoon vegetable oil
1 cup thinly sliced celery
1 cup thinly sliced fresh mushrooms
¾ cup finely chopped onion
½ cup frozen English peas, thawed
½ teaspoon dried whole thyme
½ cup freshly grated Parmesan cheese

Rinse wild rice in 3 changes of hot water; drain. Combine rice, 2½ cups water, and bouillon granules in a medium saucepan. Bring to a boil; cover, reduce heat, and simmer 50 minutes or until rice is tender, stirring occasionally. Drain; set aside.

Coat a large nonstick skillet with cooking spray; add oil. Place over medium-high heat until hot. Add celery, mushrooms, and onion; sauté until vegetables are tender. Stir in reserved wild rice, peas, and thyme. Reduce heat, and cook until thoroughly heated, stirring frequently. Add cheese, and stir well. Yield: 8 servings (103 calories per ½-cup serving).

Per Serving: PROTEIN 5.7g FAT 2.9g (Saturated Fat 1.3g)
CARBOHYDRATE 14.2g FIBER 1.8g CHOLESTEROL 5mg
IRON 0.8mg SODIUM 247mg CALCIUM 101mg

GRILLED VEGETABLES AND CAPELLINI

2 tablespoons minced garlic
2 tablespoons chopped fresh basil
2 tablespoons chopped fresh rosemary
2 tablespoons Chablis or other dry white wine
2 tablespoons water
1½ tablespoons olive oil
16 fresh green beans
3 medium carrots, scraped
12 fresh asparagus spears
2 medium zucchini
4 plum tomatoes
1 medium-size sweet red pepper, seeded and cut
    into 4 pieces
Vegetable cooking spray
8 ounces capellini (angel hair pasta), uncooked
2 tablespoons fresh lemon juice

Combine first 6 ingredients in a small bowl; let stand at room temperature 1 hour.

Cook green beans and carrots in boiling water 5 to 6 minutes or until crisp-tender; drain. Rinse under cold water until cool; drain well.

Snap off tough ends of asparagus. Remove scales from stalks with a knife or vegetable peeler, if desired.

Arrange green beans, carrots, asparagus, zucchini, tomatoes, and red pepper pieces in grilling basket coated with cooking spray. Brush wine mixture over vegetables.

Place grill rack on grill over medium-hot coals (350° to 400°). Place grilling basket on rack; grill, uncovered, 10 to 14 minutes or until vegetables are tender, turning occasionally. Remove vegetables from basket, and slice diagonally. Set vegetables aside, and keep warm.

Cook pasta according to package directions, omitting salt and fat; drain well. Place pasta in a large serving bowl. Add vegetable mixture, remaining wine mixture, and lemon juice; toss gently. Serve immediately. Yield: 8 servings (169 calories per 1-cup serving).

Per Serving: PROTEIN 5.5g FAT 3.4g (Saturated Fat 0.5g)
CARBOHYDRATE 30.2g FIBER 3.1g CHOLESTEROL 0mg
IRON 2.1mg SODIUM 19mg CALCIUM 35mg

EGGPLANT AND DITALINI PASTA

2½ cups peeled, cubed eggplant
¼ teaspoon salt
Olive oil-flavored vegetable cooking spray
1 teaspoon olive oil
⅓ cup chopped onion
2 teaspoons minced garlic
1 (14½-ounce) can no-salt-added whole tomatoes,
    undrained and chopped
¼ cup water
6 ounces ditalini pasta, uncooked
¼ cup grated Romano cheese
1 tablespoon chopped fresh parsley

Place eggplant in a colander; sprinkle with salt. Let stand 1 hour. Rinse; pat dry with paper towels.

Coat a large nonstick skillet with cooking spray; add olive oil. Place over medium heat until hot. Add eggplant; cook 6 minutes, stirring frequently. Add onion; cook 3 minutes. Add garlic, and cook, stirring constantly, 1 minute. Stir in tomato and water. Reduce heat; cook, uncovered, 20 minutes.

Cook pasta according to package directions, omitting salt and fat; drain. Place pasta in a serving bowl. Add eggplant mixture, and toss gently. Sprinkle with cheese and parsley. Serve immediately. Yield: 5 servings (193 calories per 1-cup serving).

Per Serving: PROTEIN 7.6g FAT 3.2g (Saturated Fat 1.2g)
CARBOHYDRATE 34.0g FIBER 2.4g CHOLESTEROL 6mg
IRON 2.1mg SODIUM 202mg CALCIUM 120mg

LINGUINE WITH ASPARAGUS AND SHIITAKE MUSHROOMS

1 pound fresh asparagus
Olive oil-flavored vegetable cooking spray
1 teaspoon olive oil
3½ ounces fresh shiitake mushrooms, sliced
2 teaspoons minced garlic
½ cup chopped fresh parsley
¼ cup Chablis or other dry white wine
1½ tablespoons lemon juice
¼ teaspoon salt
¼ teaspoon crushed red pepper
6 ounces linguine, uncooked
2 tablespoons grated Parmesan cheese

Snap off tough ends of asparagus. Remove scales from stalks with a knife or vegetable peeler, if desired. Cut asparagus diagonally into ¾-inch pieces.

Coat a nonstick skillet with cooking spray. Add olive oil; place over medium-high heat until hot. Add asparagus, and sauté 1 minute. Add mushrooms and garlic; reduce heat to medium, and cook 3 minutes. Add parsley and next 4 ingredients; cook 2 minutes.

Cook linguine according to package directions, omitting salt and fat; drain well. Place linguine in a serving bowl. Add asparagus mixture and Parmesan cheese; toss gently. Serve immediately. Yield: 5 servings (171 calories per 1-cup serving).

Per Serving: PROTEIN 7.4g FAT 2.4g (Saturated Fat 0.7g)
CARBOHYDRATE 30.8g FIBER 2.7g CHOLESTEROL 2mg
IRON 2.4mg SODIUM 162mg CALCIUM 58mg

PENNE PASTA PRIMAVERA

2¾ cups fresh broccoli flowerets
Vegetable cooking spray
1 teaspoon olive oil
¾ cup chopped onion
2 teaspoons chopped garlic
1 (14½-ounce) can no-salt-added whole tomatoes, drained and chopped
¾ cup canned garbanzo beans, drained
¼ cup Chablis or other dry white wine
5 ounces penne pasta, uncooked
1½ tablespoons coarsely chopped fresh basil

Arrange broccoli in a vegetable steamer over boiling water. Cover and steam 4 minutes or until crisp-tender. Set aside, and keep warm.

Coat a medium nonstick skillet with cooking spray; add olive oil. Place over medium-high heat until hot. Add onion and garlic; sauté 3 minutes or until tender. Add tomato, garbanzo beans, and wine; cook 5 minutes over medium heat, stirring frequently.

Cook pasta according to package directions, omitting salt and fat; drain. Place pasta in a serving bowl. Add broccoli, tomato mixture, and basil; toss gently. Serve immediately. Yield: 6 servings (173 calories per 1-cup serving).

Per Serving: PROTEIN 7.5g FAT 2.1g (Saturated Fat 0.2g)
CARBOHYDRATE 31.8g FIBER 3.8g CHOLESTEROL 0mg
IRON 1.5mg SODIUM 76mg CALCIUM 66mg

CHEESE TORTELLINI WITH RED AND YELLOW TOMATO

2 cups peeled, seeded, and chopped tomato
1½ cups peeled, seeded, and chopped yellow tomato
½ cup chopped green onions
¼ cup chopped fresh cilantro
¼ cup chopped fresh flat-leaf parsley
1 tablespoon seeded, minced jalapeño pepper
2 tablespoons fresh lime juice
1 tablespoon sherry wine vinegar
¼ teaspoon salt
6 ounces fresh cheese tortellini

Combine first 9 ingredients in a large bowl; tossing gently. Set aside.

Cook tortellini according to package directions, omitting salt and fat; drain well.

Place pasta in a serving bowl. Add tomato mixture, and toss gently. Serve immediately. Yield: 6 servings (121 calories per 1-cup serving).

Per Serving: PROTEIN 5.5g FAT 2.4g (Saturated Fat 0.2g)
CARBOHYDRATE 19.6g FIBER 1.8g CHOLESTEROL 13mg
IRON 1.6mg SODIUM 228mg CALCIUM 46mg

 DO-ANYWHERE MUSCLE TONERS
When a tight schedule leaves no time for exercise class, sneak in a few muscle toners right where you are. Practice them at home or the office. Not all exercises require you to suit up and sweat it out.

• **Stomach Shaper.** Firmly pull in your stomach and hold for 6 seconds; release and then repeat as many times as possible. Do this while sitting or standing. With enough repetitions, it can be nearly as effective as doing 20 sit-ups.

• **Shoulder Shrugs.** Sit in a chair and grasp the chair bottom along the sides. Shrug your shoulders without letting go of the chair, as if you were trying to lift the chair. Hold for 6 seconds; relax.

• **Arm Pull.** Grasp a phone receiver, a rolling pin, or other object with hands placed at ends. Attempt to pull the object apart, resisting for 6 seconds. Hold the object in different positions (overhead, in front) to tone different muscles.

CAPELLINI WITH CILANTRO PESTO

1½ cups firmly packed fresh cilantro
1½ cups firmly packed fresh flat-leaf parsley
2 tablespoons water
1½ tablespoons fresh lime juice
1 tablespoon olive oil
¼ teaspoon salt
3 cloves garlic, halved
8 ounces capellini (angel hair pasta), uncooked
½ cup freshly grated Romano cheese
3 tablespoons chopped walnuts, lightly toasted

Position knife blade in food processor bowl; add first 7 ingredients. Process until smooth, scraping sides of processor bowl occasionally.

Cook pasta according to package directions, omitting salt and fat; drain. Place pasta in a serving bowl. Add cilantro mixture, Romano cheese, and walnuts; toss gently. Serve immediately. Yield: 4 servings (337 calories per 1-cup serving).

Per Serving: PROTEIN 13.7g FAT 11.0g (Saturated Fat 3.2g)
CARBOHYDRATE 46.1g FIBER 2.6g CHOLESTEROL 15mg
IRON 3.7mg SODIUM 334mg CALCIUM 200mg

ADOBE SHRIMP AND CAPELLINI

4 large dried New Mexico chile pods
1½ cups warm water
1 cup chopped onion
1 tablespoon chopped garlic
1 teaspoon dried whole oregano
Olive oil-flavored vegetable cooking spray
1 tablespoon olive oil
½ cup canned low-sodium chicken broth,
    undiluted
½ cup Chablis or other dry white wine
¼ cup white vinegar
1 teaspoon sugar
1½ pounds large fresh shrimp, peeled and
    deveined
8 ounces capellini (angel hair pasta), uncooked

Remove and discard seeds and membrane from chiles; cut chiles into small pieces. Combine chiles and water in a small bowl; let stand 30 minutes, stirring occasionally. Drain chiles, reserving ¼ cup liquid.

Position knife blade in food processor bowl; add chiles, ¼ cup reserved liquid, onion, garlic, and oregano. Process until smooth.

Coat a large nonstick skillet with cooking spray; add olive oil. Place over medium-high heat until hot. Add chile mixture; cook 5 minutes, stirring frequently. Add chicken broth, wine, vinegar, and sugar. Bring to a boil; reduce heat, and simmer 5 minutes, stirring occasionally. Add shrimp; simmer 3 to 5 minutes or until shrimp are done, stirring occasionally. Remove mixture from heat; keep warm.

Cook pasta according to package directions, omitting salt and fat; drain well. Place pasta in a serving bowl. Add shrimp mixture, and toss well. Serve immediately. Yield: 6 servings (280 calories per 1-cup serving).

Per Serving: PROTEIN 23.9g FAT 4.8g (Saturated Fat 0.7g)
CARBOHYDRATE 34.1g FIBER 1.8g CHOLESTEROL 136mg
IRON 4.1mg SODIUM 152mg CALCIUM 68mg

KEEPING OILS FRESH
Using cooking oil sparingly will help reduce your fat intake, but the oil will also be in the pantry longer, increasing its chances of becoming rancid. Always smell an oil before using. If there is an uncharacteristic odor, the oil should be discarded. Rancid oils contain peroxides and other substances that, along with tasting bad, can damage cells and raise the risk of hardened arteries. To help keep oils fresh longer, try these simple suggestions:
• Buy small bottles that will be empty within 6 months. A large bottle isn't a better buy if most of it has to be thrown away.
• Since oxygen causes rancidity, try to keep oils away from air. Always store them tightly capped, and when a bottle is half empty, decant it to a smaller bottle.
• Light and heat also cause oils to oxidize more rapidly. Tc prevent this, oil should be stored in opaque containers in a cool, dark place—not in the cabinet by the stove. Keeping oils in the refrigerator will double their shelf life but may make some oils thicken or turn cloudy. Such oils are safe to use, and usually will become clear again at room temperature.

Capellini with Lobster unites delicate angel hair pasta with tender morsels of lobster meat and is smothered in a creamy cheese sauce.

CAPELLINI WITH LOBSTER

2 (8-ounce) fresh or frozen lobster tails, thawed
Butter-flavored vegetable cooking spray
¼ cup minced green onions
2 teaspoons minced garlic
½ cup Chablis or other dry white wine
½ teaspoon ground green peppercorns
¼ cup all-purpose flour
1½ cups skim milk
¾ cup (3 ounces) shredded reduced-fat Monterey Jack cheese
2 tablespoons freshly grated Parmesan cheese
6 ounces capellini (angel hair pasta), uncooked
¼ cup chopped fresh flat-leaf parsley
Lemon slices (optional)
Green peppercorns (optional)

Cook lobster tails in boiling water 6 to 8 minutes or until done; drain. Rinse with cold water. Split and clean tails. Reserve shells for garnish, if desired. Coarsely chop lobster meat, and set aside.

Coat a nonstick skillet with cooking spray; place over medium-high heat until hot. Add green onions and garlic; sauté 1 minute or until tender. Add wine and ground peppercorns; cook 2 minutes or until wine evaporates. Combine flour and milk, stirring until smooth. Add to green onion mixture in skillet; cook over medium heat, stirring constantly with a wire whisk, until thickened and bubbly. Add lobster and cheeses; cook, stirring constantly, 2 minutes or until cheeses melt and lobster is heated.

Cook pasta according to package directions, omitting salt and fat; drain. Combine pasta and lobster mixture in a serving bowl; toss gently. Spoon onto individual serving plates, and sprinkle with parsley. If desired, garnish with lemon slices, lobster tails, and green peppercorns. Serve immediately. Yield: 5 servings (299 calories per 1-cup serving).

Per Serving: PROTEIN 25.5g FAT 5.2g (Saturated Fat 2.6g)
CARBOHYDRATE 36.2g FIBER 1.3g CHOLESTEROL 55mg
IRON 2.3mg SODIUM 414mg CALCIUM 314mg

CREAMY SPINACH FETTUCCINI

Butter-flavored vegetable cooking spray
1 tablespoon reduced-calorie margarine
3 tablespoons chopped onion
2 cups julienne-cut zucchini
1 cup julienne-cut carrot
4 ounces fresh crimini mushrooms, sliced
½ cup nonfat sour cream alternative
⅓ cup canned low-sodium chicken broth,
    undiluted
¾ to 1 teaspoon freshly ground pepper
6 ounces spinach fettuccini, uncooked
2 ounces reduced-fat, low-salt ham, cut into
    julienne strips

Coat a nonstick skillet with cooking spray; add margarine. Place over medium-high heat until margarine melts. Add onion; sauté 1 minute. Add zucchini and carrot; sauté 3 minutes. Stir in mushrooms; sauté 3 minutes. Remove from heat, and keep warm.

Combine sour cream, chicken broth, and pepper in a small bowl; stir well. Set aside.

Cook pasta according to package directions, omitting salt and fat; drain. Place pasta in a serving bowl. Add zucchini mixture, sour cream mixture, and ham; toss gently. Serve immediately. Yield: 5 servings (199 calories per 1-cup serving).

Per Serving: PROTEIN 10.1g FAT 4.0g (Saturated Fat 0.8g)
CARBOHYDRATE 31.1g FIBER 7.3g CHOLESTEROL 38mg
IRON 2.2mg SODIUM 164mg CALCIUM 36mg

GREEK FETTUCCINI

1 (7-ounce) jar sun-dried tomatoes in olive oil,
    undrained
Olive oil-flavored vegetable cooking spray
¼ cup chopped onion
2 tablespoons chopped green pepper
1 cup peeled, seeded, and finely chopped tomato
½ cup Chablis or other dry white wine
1 cup diced cooked chicken breast (skinned before
    cooking and cooked without salt)
1½ teaspoons chopped fresh oregano
3 tablespoons pitted, chopped Greek olives
8 ounces fettuccini, uncooked
2 ounces feta cheese, crumbled

Drain sun-dried tomatoes, reserving 1 teaspoon olive oil. Coarsely chop 2 tablespoons tomato. Reserve remaining olive oil and tomatoes for other uses. Coat a large nonstick skillet with cooking spray; add reserved 1 teaspoon olive oil. Place skillet over medium-high heat until hot. Add onion and green pepper; sauté 4 minutes. Add reserved 2 tablespoons sun-dried tomato, 1 cup tomato, and wine; cook, uncovered, over medium heat 10 minutes, stirring frequently. Add chicken and oregano; cook 2 minutes or until thoroughly heated. Stir in olives. Remove from heat, and keep warm.

Cook pasta according to package directions, omitting salt and fat; drain. Place pasta in a large bowl. Add chicken mixture and feta cheese; toss gently. Serve immediately. Yield: 6 servings (237 calories per 1-cup serving).

Per Serving: PROTEIN 16.3g FAT 5.3g (Saturated Fat 2.0g)
CARBOHYDRATE 33.8g FIBER 5.3g CHOLESTEROL 32mg
IRON 2.4mg SODIUM 259mg CALCIUM 85mg

ASPARAGUS LASAGNA

2 pounds fresh asparagus
3 cups peeled, chopped tomato
2 tablespoons chopped fresh basil
Olive oil-flavored vegetable cooking spray
1 teaspoon olive oil
¼ cup chopped fresh parsley
1 tablespoon minced garlic
¼ cup canned low-sodium chicken broth,
    undiluted
1 (15-ounce) carton lite ricotta cheese
½ (8-ounce) container nonfat cream cheese
    product, softened
2 tablespoons lemon juice
¼ cup grated Romano cheese
⅛ teaspoon ground nutmeg
6 lasagna noodles, uncooked

Snap off tough ends of asparagus. Remove scales from stalks with a knife or vegetable peeler, if desired. Coarsely chop asparagus. Arrange asparagus in a vegetable steamer over boiling water. Cover and steam 4 to 5 minutes or until crisp-tender. Set aside.

Combine tomato and basil in a medium saucepan. Cook over medium heat 20 minutes; remove from heat, and cool slightly. Position knife blade in food processor bowl; add tomato mixture. Process 20 seconds; set aside.

Coat a large nonstick skillet with cooking spray; add olive oil. Place over medium-high heat until hot. Add parsley and garlic; sauté 1 minute. Add chopped asparagus and chicken broth; simmer, uncovered, 5 minutes. Add ricotta cheese, cream cheese product, and lemon juice; stir well. Cook over medium heat, stirring constantly, until cheeses melt. Stir in Romano cheese and nutmeg. Remove from heat; keep warm.

Cook lasagna noodles according to package directions, omitting salt and fat; drain.

Coat an 11- x 7- x 1½-inch baking dish with cooking spray. Place 2 lasagna noodles in bottom of dish; top with half of asparagus mixture. Place 2 lasagna noodles over asparagus mixture; top with half of tomato mixture. Repeat procedure with remaining noodles and asparagus mixture. Top with remaining tomato mixture. Cover and bake 10 minutes at 375°. Uncover and bake an additional 15 minutes or until thoroughly heated. Yield: 8 servings (180 calories per serving).

Per Serving: PROTEIN 15.5g FAT 4.3g (Saturated Fat 1.9g)
CARBOHYDRATE 23.1g FIBER 3.2g CHOLESTEROL 16mg
IRON 1.8mg SODIUM 264mg CALCIUM 210mg

LINGUINE WITH ASPARAGUS AND GOAT CHEESE

½ pound fresh asparagus
½ cup canned no-salt-added chicken broth, undiluted
¼ cup Chablis or other dry white wine
¼ cup chopped shallots
¼ teaspoon pepper
½ (8-ounce) package Neufchâtel cheese, softened
2 ounces goat cheese, crumbled
2 tablespoons fresh lemon juice
8 ounces linguine, uncooked
½ cup thinly sliced sweet red pepper

Snap off tough ends of asparagus. Remove scales from stalks with a knife or vegetable peeler, if desired. Cut asparagus into 1-inch pieces. Set aside.

Combine chicken broth, white wine, chopped shallots, and pepper in a saucepan. Bring to a boil; add asparagus. Reduce heat, and simmer 5 minutes. Add cheeses and lemon juice; cook over low heat, stirring constantly, until cheeses melt. Set aside, and keep warm.

Cook pasta according to package directions, omitting salt and fat; drain. Place pasta in a serving bowl. Add asparagus mixture and sweet red pepper; toss gently. Serve immediately. Yield: 5 servings (284 calories per 1-cup serving).

Per Serving: PROTEIN 11.5g FAT 8.8g (Saturated Fat 5.2g)
CARBOHYDRATE 40.2g FIBER 2.5g CHOLESTEROL 27mg
IRON 2.7mg SODIUM 237mg CALCIUM 98mg

CHINESE CURLY NOODLES WITH CRABMEAT

Vegetable cooking spray
1 teaspoon dark sesame oil
⅓ pound fresh snow pea pods, trimmed
1 (7-ounce) package crimini mushrooms, sliced
1 cup canned low-sodium chicken broth, undiluted
1 tablespoon low-sodium soy sauce
2 teaspoons minced garlic
1 teaspoon peeled, minced gingerroot
2 cups shredded fresh spinach
1 pound fresh lump crabmeat, drained
8 ounces Chinese curly noodles, uncooked

Coat a large nonstick with cooking spray; add oil. Place over medium-high heat until hot. Add snow peas and mushrooms; sauté 2 minutes. Add chicken broth, soy sauce, garlic, and gingerroot; sauté 1 minute. Add spinach and crabmeat; sauté 3 minutes. Remove from heat, and keep warm.

Cook noodles according to package directions, omitting salt and fat; drain. Place noodles in a serving bowl, and add crabmeat mixture; toss well. Serve immediately. Yield: 8 servings (206 calories per 1-cup serving).

Per Serving: PROTEIN 17.5g FAT 2.8g (Saturated Fat 0.3g)
CARBOHYDRATE 24.8g FIBER 1.9g CHOLESTEROL 57mg
IRON 2.8mg SODIUM 247mg CALCIUM 80mg

Combine the subtle flavor of crabmeat with a spirited mixture of vegetables and spices to create Crabmeat Ravioli with Parslied Tomato Sauce.

CRABMEAT RAVIOLI WITH PARSLIED TOMATO SAUCE

Olive oil-flavored vegetable cooking spray
2 teaspoons olive oil, divided
1¼ cups finely chopped fresh mushrooms
¼ cup minced green onions
6 ounces fresh lump crabmeat, drained
2 tablespoons chopped fresh parsley
2½ ounces goat cheese, softened
2 ounces Neufchâtel cheese, softened
2 tablespoons water
1 teaspoon minced fresh thyme
48 fresh or frozen wonton skins, thawed
3 quarts water
3 cups finely chopped tomato
1½ teaspoons minced garlic
1 tablespoon chopped fresh parsley (optional)
Fresh thyme sprigs (optional)

Coat a large nonstick skillet with cooking spray; add 1 teaspoon olive oil. Place over medium-high heat until hot. Add mushrooms and green onions; sauté 1 minute. Add crabmeat, and cook 1 minute. Stir in 2 tablespoons parsley, cheeses, 2 tablespoons water, and thyme. Reduce heat to low; cook until cheeses melt, stirring frequently. Remove from heat; let cool slightly.

Place 1 tablespoon cheese mixture in center of each of 24 wonton skins. Brush edges of wonton skins with water; top with remaining 24 wonton skins. Press wonton edges together to seal, pushing out air. Trim wonton edges with scissors.

Bring 3 quarts water to a boil in a Dutch oven. Add one-third of ravioli; return water to a boil. Reduce heat; simmer, uncovered, 4 minutes or until ravioli are tender. Remove with a slotted spoon. Set aside, and keep warm. Repeat procedure with remaining ravioli.

Coat a large nonstick skillet with cooking spray; add remaining 1 teaspoon oil. Place over medium-high heat until hot. Add tomato and garlic; stir well. Reduce heat, and cook, uncovered, 10 minutes.

Position knife blade in food processor bowl; add tomato mixture. Pulse 5 times or until mixture is almost smooth.

Place 4 ravioli on each individual serving plate. Top with tomato mixture. If desired, garnish with 1 tablespoon parsley and thyme sprigs. Serve immediately. Yield: 6 servings (186 calories per serving).

Per Serving: PROTEIN 12.1g FAT 8.5g (Saturated Fat 3.8g)
CARBOHYDRATE 16.3g FIBER 2.2g CHOLESTEROL 96mg
IRON 1.9mg SODIUM 382mg CALCIUM 117mg

ARTICHOKE AND SPINACH STUFFED SHELLS

1 (10-ounce) package frozen chopped spinach, thawed
1 cup frozen artichoke hearts, thawed
12 jumbo pasta shells, uncooked
1 cup lite ricotta cheese
2 tablespoons chopped fresh basil
1 tablespoon chopped fresh parsley
¼ teaspoon salt
2 tablespoons lemon juice
⅓ cup nonfat sour cream alternative
2 (14½-ounce) cans no-salt-added stewed tomatoes, undrained and chopped
2 tablespoons cornstarch
1½ tablespoons chopped fresh basil
Vegetable cooking spray
Fresh basil sprigs (optional)

Cook spinach and artichoke hearts according to package directions, omitting salt; drain well. Chop artichoke hearts, and set aside.

Cook pasta shells according to package directions, omitting salt and fat; drain and set aside.

Position knife blade in food processor bowl; add spinach, ricotta cheese, and next 4 ingredients. Process 30 seconds or until smooth. Transfer to a bowl; stir in chopped artichokes and sour cream.

Combine tomato, cornstarch, and 1½ tablespoons basil in a saucepan; stir well. Cook over medium heat until thickened, stirring frequently. Spoon 1 cup tomato mixture in bottom of an 11- x 7- x 1½-inch baking dish coated with cooking spray.

Spoon spinach mixture evenly into shells. Arrange shells in baking dish. Pour remaining tomato mixture over shells. Bake, uncovered, at 350° for 30 minutes or until bubbly. Garnish with basil sprigs, if desired. Yield: 6 servings (185 calories per serving).

Per Serving: PROTEIN 11.2g FAT 2.1g (Saturated Fat 0.9g)
CARBOHYDRATE 32.9g FIBER 2.7g CHOLESTEROL 5mg
IRON 1.5mg SODIUM 206mg CALCIUM 169mg

OYSTERS AND PASTA SHELLS

Butter-flavored vegetable cooking spray
1 tablespoon reduced-calorie margarine
1½ cups chopped fresh mushrooms
¼ cup chopped green onions
1 (10-ounce) container fresh oysters, drained
½ cup canned low-sodium chicken broth, undiluted
2 tablespoons Chablis or other dry white wine
2 teaspoons chopped fresh oregano
¼ teaspoon hot sauce
¼ cup chopped fresh parsley
1 tablespoon fresh lemon juice
8 ounces small pasta shells, uncooked
⅔ cup grated fresh Parmesan cheese

Coat a large nonstick skillet with cooking spray; add margarine. Place over medium-high heat until margarine melts. Add mushrooms and green onions; sauté 1 minute. Add oysters, and sauté 2 minutes. Add chicken broth, wine, oregano, and hot sauce; cook 2 minutes. Add parsley and lemon juice; stir well. Remove from heat, and keep warm.

Cook pasta according to package directions, omitting salt and fat; drain. Place pasta in a serving bowl, and add oyster mixture; toss gently. Sprinkle with cheese. Serve immediately. Yield: 5 servings (284 calories per 1-cup serving).

Per Serving: PROTEIN 15.1g FAT 7.6g (Saturated Fat 3.3g)
CARBOHYDRATE 37.4g FIBER 1.8g CHOLESTEROL 35mg
IRON 4.1mg SODIUM 324mg CALCIUM 212mg

GRILLED CHICKEN SPAGHETTINI

5 (4-ounce) skinned, boned chicken breast halves
¼ cup lime juice, divided
1 (9-ounce) package frozen artichoke hearts,
    thawed
Olive oil-flavored vegetable cooking spray
1 teaspoon olive oil
¼ cup chopped shallots
⅓ cup canned low-sodium chicken broth,
    undiluted
¼ cup Chablis or other dry white wine
¾ teaspoon dried whole rosemary
1 teaspoon freshly ground pepper
12 ounces spaghettini, uncooked
3 tablespoons chopped oil-packed sun-dried
    tomato, rinsed and patted dry
2 tablespoons chopped fresh oregano

Place chicken and 2 tablespoons lime juice in a heavy-duty, zip-top plastic bag; seal bag, and shake until chicken is well coated. Marinate in refrigerator 2 hours, turning bag occasionally.

Cook artichoke hearts according to package directions, omitting salt; drain and set aside.

Coat a large nonstick skillet with cooking spray; add olive oil. Place over medium-high heat until hot. Add shallots, and sauté 2 minutes. Add chicken broth, wine, and rosemary. Cover, reduce heat, and simmer 5 minutes. Add artichoke hearts and pepper; cover and simmer 2 minutes. Stir in remaining 2 tablespoons lime juice; remove from heat, and keep warm.

Coat grill rack with cooking spray, and place on grill over medium-hot coals (350° to 400°). Place chicken on rack; grill, uncovered, 6 minutes on each side or until chicken is tender. Cut chicken into thin strips.

Cook spaghettini according to package directions, omitting salt and fat; drain. Place spaghettini in a serving bowl. Add sun-dried tomato, artichoke mixture, chicken strips, and oregano; toss gently. Serve immediately. Yield: 8 servings (293 calories per 1-cup serving).

Per Serving: PROTEIN 24.2g FAT 3.9g (Saturated Fat 0.9g)
CARBOHYDRATE 40.8g FIBER 1.7g CHOLESTEROL 45mg
IRON 3.5mg SODIUM 184mg CALCIUM 68mg

TURKEY TETRAZZINI TOSS

Vegetable cooking spray
1 (8-ounce) package presliced fresh mushrooms
¼ cup chopped onion
3 tablespoons all-purpose flour
1 cup canned no-salt-added chicken broth,
    undiluted
1 cup evaporated skimmed milk
1 cup frozen English peas, thawed
3 tablespoons dry sherry
¼ teaspoon salt
⅛ teaspoon pepper
8 ounces vermicelli, uncooked
2 cups shredded cooked turkey breast (skinned
    before cooking and cooked without salt)
2 tablespoons diced pimiento, drained
3 tablespoons freshly grated Parmesan cheese

Coat a large nonstick skillet with cooking spray; place over medium-high heat until hot. Add mushrooms and onion; sauté 3 minutes or until tender.

Combine flour and chicken broth, stirring with a wire whisk until smooth. Gradually add broth mixture to mushroom mixture, stirring constantly. Cook over medium heat, stirring constantly, 2 minutes or until thickened and bubbly. Gradually stir in milk and next 4 ingredients; cook over low heat 2 minutes or until thoroughly heated, stirring frequently.

Cook pasta according to package directions, omitting salt and fat; drain. Place pasta in a serving bowl. Add mushroom mixture, turkey, and pimiento; toss well. Sprinkle with cheese. Serve immediately. Yield: 7 servings (269 calories per 1-cup serving).

Per Serving: PROTEIN 23.7g FAT 2.3g (Saturated Fat 0.8g)
CARBOHYDRATE 37.0g FIBER 2.5g CHOLESTEROL 40mg
IRON 3.1mg SODIUM 242mg CALCIUM 164mg

Legumes and vegetables combine to create colorful Black and White Beans with Orzo Primavera (page 147), a satisfying meatless meal.

Meatless
Main
Dishes

BLACK BEANS AND RICE WITH
BAKED PLANTAINS

2 medium-size ripe plantains
Vegetable cooking spray
½ cup finely chopped onion
½ cup finely chopped green pepper
1 tablespoon minced garlic
3 cups canned black beans, drained
3 cups cooked brown rice (cooked without salt or fat)
1 cup minced fresh cilantro
1 tablespoon low-sodium Worcestershire sauce
½ teaspoon ground red pepper
¼ cup water
3 tablespoons firmly packed brown sugar
1 tablespoon lime juice
¼ teaspoon ground cinnamon

Rinse plantains, and pat dry; trim ends. Cut a lengthwise slit just through the skin of each plantain; place on a baking sheet lined with aluminum foil. Bake at 375° for 35 minutes or until plantains are tender. Remove from oven, and let cool. Peel and cut diagonally into ½-inch-thick slices. Set aside.

Coat a large nonstick skillet with cooking spray. Place over medium-high heat until hot. Add onion, green pepper, and garlic; sauté 5 minutes or until tender. Stir in beans and next 4 ingredients; cook 2 minutes or until thoroughly heated, stirring frequently. Transfer black bean mixture to a serving platter, and keep warm.

Combine water, brown sugar, lime juice, and cinnamon in a medium nonstick skillet. Bring to a boil; reduce heat, and simmer until sugar dissolves, stirring frequently. Add plantain slices, turning to coat. Cook 2 minutes or until thoroughly heated, stirring gently. Spoon plantain slices and sugar mixture over black bean mixture. Serve immediately. Yield: 6 servings (345 calories per serving).

Per Serving: PROTEIN 12.0g FAT 2.0g (Saturated Fat 0.3g)
CARBOHYDRATE 73.9g FIBER 6.7g CHOLESTEROL 0mg
IRON 3.7mg SODIUM 274mg CALCIUM 60mg

CARAMELIZED ONION, BLACK BEAN, AND
ORANGE BURRITOS

2 large oranges
1 tablespoon seeded, minced jalapeño pepper
2 teaspoons balsamic vinegar
Vegetable cooking spray
1 tablespoon frozen orange juice concentrate, thawed and undiluted
3 cups thinly sliced purple onion
¼ teaspoon dried whole thyme
1 cup canned black beans, drained and mashed
2 tablespoons water
½ teaspoon ground cumin
4 (8-inch) flour tortillas
½ cup (2 ounces) shredded 40% less-fat Cheddar cheese
¼ cup minced fresh cilantro

Peel and section oranges; chop sections, and drain well. Combine chopped orange sections, jalapeño pepper, and vinegar in a small bowl; let stand 1 hour.

Coat a large nonstick skillet with cooking spray; add orange juice concentrate. Place over medium-high heat until hot. Add onion; sauté 5 minutes or until tender. Reduce heat to medium-low; cook 15 to 20 minutes or until onion is golden, stirring occasionally. Remove from heat, and stir in thyme.

Combine beans, water, and cumin; stir well. Spoon bean mixture evenly down center of each tortilla. Top evenly with onion mixture; sprinkle with cheese and cilantro. Roll up tortillas, and secure with wooden picks. Place rolls, seam side up, on a baking sheet coated with cooking spray. Cover and bake at 350° for 12 to 15 minutes or until cheese melts. Place on individual serving plates, and top evenly with chopped orange mixture. Serve immediately. Yield: 4 servings (286 calories per serving).

Per Serving: PROTEIN 10.8g FAT 5.4g (Saturated Fat 1.9g)
CARBOHYDRATE 53.9g FIBER 7.1g CHOLESTEROL 7mg
IRON 2.6mg SODIUM 219mg CALCIUM 188mg

BLACK AND WHITE BEANS WITH ORZO PRIMAVERA

Vegetable cooking spray
1 teaspoon cumin seeds, crushed
¾ cup chopped onion
2 teaspoons minced garlic
2 teaspoons olive oil
1 (15-ounce) can black beans, drained
1 (16-ounce) can navy beans, drained
3½ cups canned low-sodium chicken broth,
    undiluted and divided
1 cup orzo, uncooked
2 teaspoons ground coriander
½ teaspoon ground turmeric
½ teaspoon ground red pepper
1 cup diced zucchini
1 cup cauliflower flowerets
1 cup diced fresh green beans
¾ cup seeded, chopped plum tomato

Coat a large heavy skillet with cooking spray; place over medium-high heat until hot. Add cumin seeds, and cook, stirring constantly, until seeds are fragrant and lightly browned. Add onion, garlic, and olive oil; sauté 3 to 5 minutes or until onion is tender. Stir in beans and 1 cup chicken broth. Bring to a boil; reduce heat, and simmer, uncovered, 15 to 20 minutes or until liquid is absorbed, stirring frequently. Set aside, and keep warm.

Place remaining 2½ cups chicken broth in a medium saucepan; bring to a boil. Add orzo, coriander, turmeric, and red pepper. Cover, reduce heat, and simmer 25 to 30 minutes or until liquid is absorbed and orzo is tender, stirring occasionally. Set aside, and keep warm.

Arrange zucchini, cauliflower, and green beans in a vegetable steamer over boiling water. Cover and steam 2 to 3 minutes or until vegetables are crisp-tender. Combine orzo mixture and steamed vegetables; toss gently. Spoon orzo mixture onto a serving platter; top with black bean mixture, and sprinkle with chopped tomato. Yield: 6 servings (286 calories per serving).

Per Serving: PROTEIN 14.5g FAT 3.8g (Saturated Fat 0.7g)
CARBOHYDRATE 50.4g FIBER 5.6g CHOLESTEROL 0mg
IRON 4.7mg SODIUM 298mg CALCIUM 75mg

BEAN-GOAT CHEESE TOSTADAS

Vegetable cooking spray
1 teaspoon olive oil
1 cup chopped purple onion
1 teaspoon chili powder
½ teaspoon ground cumin
2 (16-ounce) cans white kidney beans, drained
1 (4-ounce) can chopped green chiles, drained
2 tablespoons lime juice
8 (6-inch) corn tortillas
5 ounces goat cheese, crumbled
3½ cups shredded arugula
½ cup chopped fresh cilantro
½ cup nonfat sour cream alternative
Tomato-Mango Salsa

Coat a medium saucepan with cooking spray; add olive oil. Place over medium-high heat until hot. Add onion, chili powder, and cumin; sauté 3 minutes or until onion is tender. Add beans, chiles, and lime juice; stir well. Reduce heat to low, and cook until mixture is heated, mashing beans slightly with a potato masher or wooden spoon. Set aside, and keep warm.

Place tortillas on a baking sheet coated with cooking spray. Bake at 350° for 6 minutes; turn tortillas over, and bake an additional 6 minutes or until crisp.

Place 1 tortilla on each individual serving plate. Spoon bean mixture over tortillas; top with cheese. Combine arugula and cilantro; sprinkle over cheese. Top each tostada with 1 tablespoon sour cream. Serve with Tomato-Mango Salsa. Yield: 8 servings (234 calories per serving).

Tomato-Mango Salsa

¾ cup seeded, diced tomato
½ cup peeled, diced ripe mango
¼ cup diced purple onion
¼ cup chopped fresh cilantro
2 tablespoons lime juice
1½ teaspoons seeded, minced jalapeño pepper

Combine all ingredients in a small bowl; stir well. Cover and chill at least 2 hours. Yield: 1½ cups.

Per Serving: PROTEIN 12.3g FAT 5.9g (Saturated Fat 2.9g)
CARBOHYDRATE 34.6g FIBER 4.9g CHOLESTEROL 16mg
IRON 3.8mg SODIUM 407mg CALCIUM 182mg

GREEK WHITE BEAN RISOTTO

4½ cups canned low-sodium chicken broth,
    undiluted
Vegetable cooking spray
1 tablespoon minced garlic
8 ounces Arborio rice, uncooked
1 teaspoon dried whole oregano
¾ cup canned Great Northern beans, drained
¼ cup diced sun-dried tomato
¼ cup sliced ripe olives
1 (4-ounce) package feta cheese with basil and
    tomato, finely crumbled
¼ cup freshly grated Parmesan cheese

Pour broth into a medium saucepan; place over medium heat. Cover and bring to a simmer; reduce heat to low, and keep warm. (Do not boil.)

Coat a large saucepan with cooking spray; place over medium-high heat until hot. Add garlic; sauté 1 minute. Add rice and oregano; reduce heat to medium-low. Add 1 cup simmering broth, stirring constantly until most of broth is absorbed. Repeat procedure, adding ½ cup broth at a time. After 15 minutes, stir in beans, tomato, and olives. Continue to add broth, ½ cup at a time, stirring constantly until broth is absorbed, about 25 minutes. (Rice will be tender and have a creamy consistency.) Add cheeses; stir until melted. Yield: 5 servings (342 calories per serving).

Per Serving: PROTEIN 14.0g FAT 9.2g (Saturated Fat 5.0g)
CARBOHYDRATE 51.1g FIBER 2.6g CHOLESTEROL 24mg
IRON 4.4mg SODIUM 680mg CALCIUM 220mg

WHITE BEAN AND RADICCHIO GRATIN

Vegetable cooking spray
2 teaspoons olive oil
2 teaspoons minced garlic
1½ cups thinly sliced radicchio
1 cup sliced green onions
2 (16-ounce) cans Great Northern beans, drained
    and divided
¾ cup canned low-sodium chicken broth,
    undiluted
1 cup (4 ounces) shredded nonfat Swiss cheese
¾ cup soft breadcrumbs

Coat a large nonstick skillet with cooking spray; add olive oil. Place over medium-high heat until hot. Add garlic, and sauté until lightly browned. Add radicchio and green onions; sauté just until radicchio is wilted. Remove from heat, and stir in 3 cups beans; set aside.

Combine remaining 1 cup beans and chicken broth in container of an electric blender; cover and process until smooth. Add to radicchio mixture; stir. Spoon into a 1½-quart casserole coated with cooking spray. Combine cheese and breadcrumbs; sprinkle over bean mixture. Bake at 425° for 15 minutes or until golden. Yield: 6 servings (192 calories per serving).

Per Serving: PROTEIN 16.3g FAT 2.4g (Saturated Fat 0.5g)
CARBOHYDRATE 28.0g FIBER 4.2g CHOLESTEROL 4mg
IRON 2.7mg SODIUM 467mg CALCIUM 221mg

BROCCOLI-FETA PHYLLO STACKS

Butter-flavored vegetable cooking spray
1 cup chopped onion
2 cloves garlic, minced
1 (10-ounce) package frozen chopped broccoli,
    thawed and drained
1¼ cups nonfat ricotta cheese
8 ounces feta cheese, crumbled
½ teaspoon dried whole rosemary
½ teaspoon dried whole thyme
8 sheets commercial frozen phyllo pastry, thawed

Coat a large nonstick skillet with cooking spray; place over medium-high heat until hot. Add onion and garlic; sauté until onion is tender. Remove from heat. Add broccoli and next 4 ingredients, stirring well.

Coat a 13- x 9- x 2-inch baking dish with cooking spray. Cut phyllo in half crosswise; cut each half to fit dish. Discard trimmings. Place 1 sheet of phyllo in dish (keep remaining phyllo covered). Lightly coat phyllo with cooking spray. Layer 7 more sheets of phyllo on first sheet, lightly coating each with cooking spray. Spoon broccoli mixture over layered phyllo. Top with remaining 8 sheets of phyllo, lightly coating each with cooking spray. Cut into 8 rectangles. Bake, uncovered, at 400° for 30 minutes or until golden. Yield: 8 servings (195 calories per serving).

Per Serving: PROTEIN 13.6g FAT 6.7g (Saturated Fat 4.7g)
CARBOHYDRATE 22.4g FIBER 1.3g CHOLESTEROL 30mg
IRON 1.2mg SODIUM 349mg CALCIUM 239mg

Corn, Zucchini, and Black-Eyed Pea Quesadillas offers a garden-harvest version of a Mexican favorite.

CORN, ZUCCHINI, AND BLACK-EYED PEA QUESADILLAS

1 cup frozen black-eyed peas
1 cup water, divided
1 cup seeded, diced tomato
¼ cup peeled, diced avocado
2½ tablespoons minced fresh cilantro
2 tablespoons minced purple onion
1 tablespoon seeded, minced jalapeño pepper
2 tablespoons fresh lime juice
¼ teaspoon ground cumin
⅛ teaspoon garlic powder
Vegetable cooking spray
1 cup julienne-cut zucchini
1 cup frozen whole kernel corn, thawed
4 (8-inch) flour tortillas
¾ cup (3 ounces) shredded reduced-fat Cheddar cheese
¾ cup (3 ounces) shredded reduced-fat Monterey Jack cheese
Fresh cilantro sprigs (optional)

Combine peas and ½ cup water in a small saucepan; bring to a boil. Cover, reduce heat, and simmer 35 to 40 minutes or until tender; drain well.

Combine remaining ½ cup water, tomato, and next 7 ingredients in a medium bowl; stir well. Set aside.

Coat a large nonstick skillet with cooking spray; place over medium-high heat until hot. Add zucchini; sauté 3 minutes or until tender. Add corn; sauté 2 minutes. Remove from heat; stir in peas.

Place 2 tortillas on a baking sheet coated with cooking spray; top tortillas with cheeses and zucchini mixture. Top with remaining tortillas. Bake at 400° for 8 minutes or just until tortillas are crisp and cheese melts. Cut each into thirds. Place on individual serving plates; top with tomato mixture. Garnish with cilantro sprigs, if desired. Yield: 6 servings (258 calories per serving).

Per Serving: PROTEIN 14.4g FAT 8.8g (Saturated Fat 3.9g)
CARBOHYDRATE 33.9g FIBER 2.6g CHOLESTEROL 18mg
IRON 1.9mg SODIUM 203mg CALCIUM 264mg

HEARTY MUSHROOM HOMINY

4 cups canned no-salt-added beef broth, undiluted
   and divided
2 ounces dried shiitake mushrooms
4 (15½-ounce) cans yellow hominy, drained
1 (16½-ounce) can no-salt-added cream-style corn
2 (4-ounce) cans chopped green chiles, drained
½ pound small fresh mushrooms, halved
1 cup chopped green onions
2 tablespoons chili powder
½ teaspoon garlic powder
½ teaspoon dried whole oregano
½ teaspoon ground red pepper
¾ cup nonfat sour cream alternative
¼ cup freshly grated Parmesan cheese

Place 1 cup beef broth in a Dutch oven; bring to a boil. Add dried mushrooms, and remove from heat. Cover and let stand 30 minutes. Drain mushrooms, reserving liquid; chop mushrooms. Pour reserved liquid through a fine sieve into a bowl.

Return liquid and chopped mushrooms to pan. Stir in remaining 3 cups beef broth, hominy, and next 8 ingredients. Bring to a boil; cover, reduce heat, and simmer 30 minutes, stirring occasionally.

Spoon mixture evenly into individual bowls, and top each serving evenly with sour cream and Parmesan cheese. Yield: 6 servings (305 calories per serving).

Per Serving: PROTEIN 10.3g FAT 3.0g (Saturated Fat 1.0g)
CARBOHYDRATE 58.3g FIBER 10.0g CHOLESTEROL 3mg
IRON 2.7mg SODIUM 473mg CALCIUM 88mg

MACARONI WITH EGGPLANT, OLIVES, AND THYME

1 (1-pound) eggplant
¼ teaspoon salt
Vegetable cooking spray
2 teaspoons olive oil
5 plum tomatoes, seeded and cut into thin strips
2 tablespoons chopped fresh thyme
12 ounces small elbow macaroni, uncooked
3 ounces smoked fresh mozzarella cheese, diced
3 ounces part-skim mozzarella cheese, diced
¼ cup sliced pimiento-stuffed olives
3 tablespoons grated Parmesan cheese

Peel eggplant; cut into ½-inch-thick slices. Cut slices into ¼-inch-wide strips. Place in a colander; sprinkle with salt. Let stand 1 hour. Pat dry with paper towels.

Coat a large nonstick skillet with cooking spray; add olive oil. Place over medium-high heat until hot. Add eggplant, and sauté until eggplant is tender and lightly browned. Add tomato and thyme; sauté 2 minutes.

Cook macaroni according to package directions, omitting salt and fat; drain. Combine macaroni and eggplant mixture; stir in mozzarella cheeses. Spoon mixture into a 3-quart casserole; sprinkle with olives and Parmesan cheese. Bake at 350° for 20 to 25 minutes or until thoroughly heated. Yield: 8 servings (256 calories per serving).

Per Serving: PROTEIN 11.7g FAT 6.9g (Saturated Fat 3.1g)
CARBOHYDRATE 36.8g FIBER 2.1g CHOLESTEROL 16mg
IRON 2.1mg SODIUM 459mg CALCIUM 175mg

 COMPLEMENTING YOUR PROTEINS

Although vegetables do not contain a complete array of amino acids such as those found in animal foods, meals without meat and dairy products can still provide high-quality protein. That's because the different types of protein in vegetables, grains, and seeds can complement one another. The protein substances that red beans, for example, lack, are abundant in grains, nuts, and seeds. So if you mix red beans with a grain such as rice, the net result is a dish that mimics the protein found in meat. Although scientists say it is not necessary to mix beans and rice at the same meal, try to eat complementary protein foods over the course of the same day.

A quick review: To complement proteins found in legumes such as red beans, garbanzo beans, chick peas, peas, lentils, and peanuts, include cereal grains such as whole wheat, rice, oats, or pasta in your diet. For instance, match peanut butter with whole wheat bread and you will have a high-quality protein. Or match a legume with nuts or seeds. Keep in mind that if a meatless dish includes cheese or milk, there is no need to worry about complementing proteins. Dairy foods, as does meat, contain the full complement of protein compounds.

SPICY PEANUT NOODLES
AND VEGETABLES

⅔ cup water

3 tablespoons dry sherry

2 tablespoons low-sodium soy sauce

1 teaspoon sugar

2 teaspoons balsamic vinegar

½ teaspoon chicken-flavored bouillon granules

2½ tablespoons creamy peanut butter

2 (5-ounce) packages Chinese noodles

2½ cups fresh bean sprouts

Vegetable cooking spray

2 cups julienne-cut carrot (about 4 medium)

1 cup julienne-cut sweet red pepper (about 1 large)

5 green onions, cut into julienne strips

4 ounces firm tofu, drained and cut into ½-inch cubes

2 tablespoons sesame seeds, toasted

Combine first 6 ingredients in a small saucepan; bring to a boil, stirring constantly. Boil 1 minute. Add peanut butter, and cook, stirring constantly, until peanut butter melts. Remove from heat.

Cook noodles according to package directions, omitting salt and fat; drain well. Combine noodles and peanut butter mixture in a large bowl; toss well. Set aside.

Cook bean sprouts in boiling water 30 seconds; drain well.

Coat a large nonstick skillet with cooking spray; place skillet over medium-high heat until hot. Add carrot, red pepper, and green onions; sauté until crisp-tender. Add tofu, and cook until thoroughly heated, stirring gently. Combine noodle mixture and vegetable mixture; toss well. Sprinkle with sesame seeds. Serve immediately. Yield: 8 servings (234 calories per serving).

Per Serving: PROTEIN 10.1g FAT 5.8g (Saturated Fat 0.8g)
CARBOHYDRATE 33.6g FIBER 2.7g CHOLESTEROL 0mg
IRON 3.2mg SODIUM 212mg CALCIUM 37mg

MEXICAN POTATO RAGOÛT

1 pound round red potatoes, quartered

1 tablespoon olive oil, divided

2 cups diced onion

3 tablespoons chopped garlic

Vegetable cooking spray

2 cups cubed eggplant

2 cups cubed zucchini

1 cup coarsely chopped green pepper

1 (15-ounce) can garbanzo beans, drained

4 plum tomatoes, cut into thin wedges

½ cup minced fresh cilantro

2 teaspoons dried whole oregano

1 teaspoon grated lemon rind

½ teaspoon ground cumin

¼ teaspoon salt

1½ cups (6 ounces) shredded nonfat Monterey Jack cheese

Cook potato in boiling water to cover 10 to 15 minutes or just until tender. Drain and set aside.

Heat 1 teaspoon olive oil in a large nonstick skillet over medium-high heat. Add onion and garlic; sauté 5 minutes. Transfer to a 13- x 9- x 2-inch baking dish coated with cooking spray.

Add remaining 2 teaspoons olive oil to skillet; add eggplant, zucchini, and pepper; cook over medium heat 5 minutes, stirring frequently. Transfer to baking dish; add beans and next 6 ingredients, stirring well. Cover and bake at 350° for 30 minutes. Stir in reserved potato; sprinkle with cheese. Bake, uncovered, an additional 15 minutes or until thoroughly heated. Yield: 6 servings (245 calories per serving).

Per Serving: PROTEIN 14.0g FAT 4.1g (Saturated Fat 0.5g)
CARBOHYDRATE 38.2g FIBER 5.8g CHOLESTEROL 5mg
IRON 3.9mg SODIUM 401mg CALCIUM 288mg

Pinch edges of the potato mixture to create the unusual shape of Stuffed Potato Puffs. Add grilled baby vegetables to the menu for a perfect accent to this casual meal.

STUFFED POTATO PUFFS

3 large baking potatoes (about 2¼ pounds), scrubbed
½ pound fresh shiitake mushrooms
Vegetable cooking spray
1 teaspoon olive oil
1½ cups finely chopped green onions
1 tablespoon minced garlic
2 tablespoons Chablis or other dry white wine
½ teaspoon freshly ground pepper
½ cup plus 2 tablespoons grated Asiago cheese, divided
2 tablespoons minced fresh chives
¼ teaspoon salt
Fresh chives (optional)

Cook potatoes in a large saucepan in boiling water to cover 50 minutes or until tender. Drain; let cool.

Remove and discard stems from mushrooms; chop caps, and set aside.

Coat a large nonstick skillet with cooking spray; add olive oil, and place over medium-high heat until hot. Add green onions and garlic; sauté 3 minutes. Stir in chopped mushrooms. Cover, reduce heat, and cook 6 minutes or until mushrooms are tender, stirring occasionally. Stir in wine and pepper; cook, uncovered, until wine evaporates. Remove from heat; let cool completely. Add ½ cup cheese, and stir gently.

Peel potatoes and mash. Stir in minced chives and salt. Line a baking sheet with wax paper. Spoon

¼ cup potato mixture in a 3-inch circle on prepared baking sheet. Repeat with remaining potato to form 16 circles.

Spoon mushroom mixture evenly onto the centers of 8 circles. Top with remaining circles, and press gently around edges to seal. Pinch edges of each side to form a star shape. Sprinkle tops evenly with remaining 2 tablespoons cheese. Place stuffed potato patties on a baking sheet coated with cooking spray. Bake at 400° for 25 minutes or until golden. To serve, place 2 potato puffs on each individual serving plate. Garnish with chives, if desired. Yield: 4 servings (282 calories per serving).

Per Serving: PROTEIN 10.9g FAT 4.7g (Saturated Fat 2.7g)
CARBOHYDRATE 51.6g FIBER 5.7g CHOLESTEROL 7mg
IRON 3.2mg SODIUM 340mg CALCIUM 179mg

TUSCAN POTATO TART

4¾ cups diced sweet red pepper
1 (14½-ounce) can no-salt-added whole tomatoes, drained, seeded, and chopped
½ cup minced fresh basil
2 tablespoons plus 2 teaspoons minced garlic, divided
2 teaspoons olive oil, divided
1 (15-ounce) can garbanzo beans, drained
½ cup minced green onions
3 tablespoons sliced ripe olives
2 tablespoons balsamic vinegar
1 cup thinly sliced onion
1½ pounds red potatoes, thinly sliced
1 egg white, lightly beaten
½ teaspoon freshly ground pepper
¼ teaspoon salt
Vegetable cooking spray
¼ cup plus 2 tablespoons freshly grated Parmesan cheese

Combine red pepper, tomato, basil, 2 tablespoons garlic, and 1 teaspoon olive oil in a large bowl; stir well. Spread mixture in a 15- x 10- x 1-inch jellyroll pan. Broil 5½ inches from heat (with electric oven door partially opened) 15 minutes or until pepper is tender, stirring occasionally. Combine pepper mixture, garbanzo beans, and next 3 ingredients in a large bowl; stir well, and set aside.

Cut onion slices in half. Combine remaining 2 teaspoons garlic, remaining 1 teaspoon olive oil, onion, potato, egg white, ground pepper, and salt in a large bowl; toss well. Press evenly into a 14-inch pizza pan coated with cooking spray. Bake at 500° for 15 minutes. Spoon red pepper mixture over potato mixture. Bake an additional 10 minutes or until potato is tender. Sprinkle with Parmesan cheese, and cut into wedges. Yield: 6 servings (258 calories per serving).

Per Serving: PROTEIN 11.0g FAT 5.8g (Saturated Fat 1.7g)
CARBOHYDRATE 43.4g FIBER 5.9g CHOLESTEROL 5mg
IRON 4.1mg SODIUM 369mg CALCIUM 163mg

CHUNKY VEGETABLE RAGOÛT

Vegetable cooking spray
1 teaspoon olive oil
1 cup coarsely chopped onion
1 tablespoon minced fresh garlic
1½ cups thickly sliced small zucchini
2 (15½-ounce) cans yellow hominy, drained
1 (17-ounce) can no-salt-added corn, drained
1 (15-ounce) can no-salt-added pinto beans, drained
1 (14½-ounce) can no-salt-added whole tomatoes, undrained and chopped
1 teaspoon chicken-flavored bouillon granules
1 teaspoon chili powder
½ teaspoon ground cumin
½ teaspoon dried whole oregano
2 cups water
3 cups cooked couscous (cooked without salt or fat)
¼ cup plus 2 tablespoons nonfat sour cream alternative

Coat a Dutch oven with cooking spray; add olive oil. Place over medium-high heat until hot. Add onion and garlic; sauté 3 minutes. Add zucchini and next 9 ingredients; stir. Bring to a boil; cover, reduce heat, and simmer 20 minutes or until zucchini is tender.

Spoon ½ cup couscous into each individual serving bowl; spoon vegetable mixture evenly over couscous. Top each serving with 1 tablespoon sour cream. Yield: 6 servings (274 calories per serving).

Per Serving: PROTEIN 10.9g FAT 2.2g (Saturated Fat 0.4g)
CARBOHYDRATE 55.9g FIBER 4.2g CHOLESTEROL 0mg
IRON 2.5mg SODIUM 357mg CALCIUM 77mg

BAKED VEGETABLE HASH

Vegetable cooking spray
2 teaspoons olive oil, divided
3 cups sliced leeks
1 tablespoon minced garlic
½ teaspoon dried whole rosemary
1½ cups diced parsnips
1 cup diced carrot
1 cup peeled, diced potato
1 cup peeled, diced sweet potato
1 (10½-ounce) can low-sodium chicken broth
1 cup diced sweet red pepper
1 cup sliced fresh mushrooms
2 egg whites
¼ cup plain nonfat yogurt
¼ cup chopped fresh parsley
½ teaspoon freshly ground pepper
¼ teaspoon salt
1 cup (4 ounces) shredded reduced-fat Jarlsberg cheese

Coat a 12-inch ovenproof nonstick skillet with cooking spray; add 1 teaspoon olive oil. Place over medium-high heat until hot. Add leeks, garlic, and rosemary; sauté 5 minutes or until leeks are tender. Add parsnips and next 4 ingredients; stir well. Bring to a boil; cover, reduce heat, and simmer 8 to 10 minutes or until vegetables are tender, stirring occasionally. Remove 1 cup vegetable mixture, using a slotted spoon; set aside. Add red pepper and mushrooms to skillet; cook, uncovered, 4 minutes, stirring frequently.

Position knife blade in food processor bowl; add reserved 1 cup vegetable mixture, egg whites, and yogurt. Process until smooth, stopping once to scrape down sides. Transfer to a large bowl; stir in mushroom mixture, parsley, ground pepper, and salt.

Wipe skillet dry with a paper towel. Add remaining 1 teaspoon olive oil to skillet; place over medium-high heat until hot. Spread mixture evenly in skillet; cook 2 minutes. Place skillet in a 450° oven; bake, uncovered, 15 minutes. Sprinkle with cheese; bake an additional 5 minutes or until cheese melts. Serve immediately. Yield: 6 servings (197 calories per serving).

Per Serving: PROTEIN 11.9g FAT 2.6g (Saturated Fat 0.4g)
CARBOHYDRATE 33.5g FIBER 4.4g CHOLESTEROL 4mg
IRON 4.0mg SODIUM 273mg CALCIUM 236mg

VEGETABLE PAELLA

½ cup boiling water
¼ teaspoon saffron threads
Vegetable cooking spray
1 teaspoon olive oil
2 tablespoons minced garlic
¾ cup sliced green onions
¾ cup diced sweet red pepper
1 (9-ounce) package frozen artichoke hearts, thawed and quartered
3 cups canned low-sodium chicken broth, undiluted
1½ cups long-grain brown rice, uncooked
1 cup no-salt-added whole tomatoes, drained and chopped
2 teaspoons Hungarian sweet paprika
1 (15-ounce) can cannellini beans, drained
1 cup thinly sliced arugula
¾ cup frozen English peas, thawed
½ cup freshly grated Parmesan cheese
½ teaspoon freshly ground pepper

Combine boiling water and saffron; cover and let stand 10 minutes.

Coat a large saucepan with cooking spray; add olive oil. Place over medium-high heat until hot. Add garlic, and sauté 1 minute. Add green onions, red pepper, and artichoke hearts; sauté 5 minutes.

Stir in saffron water, chicken broth, brown rice, chopped tomato, and paprika. Bring to a boil; cover, reduce heat, and simmer 15 minutes. Stir in cannellini beans, arugula, and peas; cover and cook 15 to 20 minutes or until liquid is absorbed and rice is tender. Remove from heat, and let stand 5 minutes. Spoon into a serving bowl; sprinkle with Parmesan cheese and ground pepper. Yield: 6 servings (347 calories per serving).

Per Serving: PROTEIN 15.4g FAT 6.2g (Saturated Fat 2.3g)
CARBOHYDRATE 59.4g FIBER 5.2g CHOLESTEROL 6mg
IRON 4.0mg SODIUM 399mg CALCIUM 185mg

Let Jalapeño Brunch Scramble ignite your taste buds with southwestern flavor. Fan the flames with delicious Hot Pepper Corn Sticks (page 109).

JALAPEÑO BRUNCH SCRAMBLE

4 (6-inch) corn tortillas
Vegetable cooking spray
¾ cup sliced green onions
½ cup diced sweet red pepper
¼ cup sliced jalapeño pepper
¼ cup minced fresh cilantro
1 teaspoon ground cumin
2 cups frozen egg substitute, thawed
¼ cup plus 1½ tablespoons skim milk
¼ teaspoon ground red pepper
⅛ teaspoon salt
2 ounces feta cheese, crumbled

Fill a shallow baking dish with water. Dip tortillas, one at a time, into water for 2 seconds. Drain; place on an ungreased baking sheet. Bake at 500° for 4 minutes. Turn; bake 2 minutes or until crisp. Set aside.

Coat a large nonstick skillet with cooking spray; place over medium-high heat until hot. Add green onions, sweet red pepper, and jalapeño pepper; sauté until tender. Transfer to a bowl; stir in cilantro and cumin. Wipe skillet dry with a paper towel.

Combine egg substitute, milk, ground red pepper, and salt; stir well. Crumble tortillas into egg mixture; let stand 5 minutes.

Coat skillet with cooking spray; place over medium heat until hot enough to sizzle a drop of water. Pour egg substitute mixture into skillet. As mixture begins to cook, gently lift edges with a spatula and tilt pan to allow uncooked portions to flow underneath. When egg mixture is set, spoon vegetable mixture over top, and sprinkle with cheese. Broil 5½ inches from heat (with electric oven door partially opened) 1 minute or until cheese softens. Yield: 4 servings (191 calories per serving).

Per Serving: PROTEIN 17.5g FAT 4.8g (Saturated Fat 2.3g)
CARBOHYDRATE 19.8g FIBER 2.7g CHOLESTEROL 13mg
IRON 4.9mg SODIUM 480mg CALCIUM 197mg

RICE QUICHE IN PEPPER CUPS

4 medium-size green peppers
Vegetable cooking spray
1 teaspoon olive oil
1 teaspoon minced garlic
½ cup chopped banana pepper
½ cup sliced green onions
1½ cups cooked long-grain rice (cooked without salt or fat)
1 (2-ounce) jar diced pimiento, drained
½ teaspoon dried whole marjoram
2 (3¾ ounce) cartons frozen egg substitute with cheese, thawed
½ cup evaporated skimmed milk
⅛ teaspoon ground nutmeg
¼ cup (1 ounce) shredded reduced-fat Monterey Jack cheese

Cut tops off green peppers, and remove seeds. Blanch pepper shells and tops in boiling water 3 minutes or until crisp-tender. Drain and rinse under cold water until cool. Invert shells on paper towels to drain. Set tops aside.

Coat a medium nonstick skillet with cooking spray; add olive oil. Place over medium-high heat until hot. Add garlic, and sauté until tender. Add banana pepper and green onions; sauté until tender. Stir in rice, pimiento, and marjoram. Spoon rice mixture evenly into pepper shells; place shells in an 8-inch square baking dish coated with cooking spray.

Combine egg substitute, milk, and nutmeg, stirring well with a wire whisk. Pour mixture evenly over rice mixture in peppers. Top each pepper with 1 tablespoon cheese; place reserved tops on peppers. Bake, uncovered, at 350° for 30 to 35 minutes or until knife inserted in center comes out clean. Yield: 4 servings (263 calories per serving).

Per Serving: PROTEIN 14.7g FAT 6.8g (Saturated Fat 1.6g)
CARBOHYDRATE 36.4g FIBER 3.8g CHOLESTEROL 8mg
IRON 3.5mg SODIUM 298mg CALCIUM 183mg

TOFU PIZZA CASSEROLE

2 (14½-ounce) cans no-salt-added whole tomatoes, drained and chopped
2 (8-ounce) cans no-salt-added tomato sauce
2 teaspoons sugar
1 teaspoon dried Italian seasoning
2 teaspoons lemon juice
½ teaspoon freshly ground pepper
1 cup coarsely chopped sweet red pepper
1 cup coarsely chopped green pepper
1 cup thinly sliced onion
4 ounces firm tofu, drained and cut into ½-inch cubes
¼ cup sliced ripe olives
Vegetable cooking spray
1½ cups (6 ounces) shredded nonfat mozzarella cheese
1 cup skim milk
½ cup frozen egg substitute, thawed
1 tablespoon vegetable oil
1 cup all-purpose flour
¼ teaspoon salt
¼ cup grated Parmesan cheese

Combine first 6 ingredients in a large saucepan, stirring well; bring to a boil, stirring frequently. Add chopped peppers and onion; cook, uncovered, over medium heat until peppers and onion are tender, stirring frequently. Stir in tofu and olives. Spread mixture in a 13- x 9- x 2-inch baking dish coated with cooking spray; sprinkle with mozzarella cheese.

Beat milk, egg substitute, and oil in a mixing bowl at medium speed of an electric mixer until foamy. Add flour and salt; beat until smooth. Pour over mozzarella cheese, spreading to cover completely. Sprinkle with Parmesan cheese; bake, uncovered, at 400° for 30 minutes or until puffed and browned. Cut into rectangles. Yield: 8 servings (198 calories per serving).

Per Serving: PROTEIN 14.7g FAT 4.2g (Saturated Fat 1.1g)
CARBOHYDRATE 26.4g FIBER 1.6g CHOLESTEROL 6mg
IRON 2.9mg SODIUM 378mg CALCIUM 132mg

Ribbed Pork Roast with Herbed Cannellini Beans (page 169) serves up beautifully for either a formal dinner or an everyday meal. The spicy beans are a bold accompaniment to the mouth-watering roast.

Meats

TAMALE PIE

1 pound ground round
1 cup chopped onion
2 cups seeded, chopped tomato
1½ cups water
1 (16-ounce) can kidney beans, drained
½ cup no-salt-added tomato paste
2½ tablespoons chili seasoning mix
1 teaspoon chili powder
½ ounce unsweetened chocolate, grated
Cornbread Wedges
Fresh cilantro sprigs (optional)

Combine ground round and onion in a large non-stick skillet; cook over medium-high heat until beef is browned, stirring until it crumbles. Drain and pat dry with paper towels. Wipe drippings from skillet with a paper towel.

Return beef mixture to skillet. Add tomato and next 6 ingredients; bring mixture to a boil. Reduce heat, and simmer, uncovered, 10 minutes, stirring frequently.

Place 1 Cornbread Wedge on each individual serving plate. Spoon beef mixture evenly over wedges. Garnish with cilantro sprigs, if desired. Serve immediately. Yield: 6 servings (340 calories per serving).

Cornbread Wedges

⅔ cup yellow cornmeal
⅓ cup all-purpose flour
¾ teaspoon baking powder
¼ teaspoon baking soda
1 teaspoon sugar
¼ teaspoon dried crushed red pepper
Dash of salt
¾ cup nonfat buttermilk
2 tablespoons frozen egg substitute, thawed
1 tablespoon margarine, melted
Vegetable cooking spray

Combine first 7 ingredients in a bowl; make a well in center of mixture. Combine buttermilk, egg substitute, and margarine; add to dry ingredients, stirring just until dry ingredients are moistened.

Pour batter into a 9-inch pieplate coated with cooking spray. Bake at 400° for 14 minutes; remove from oven, and cool slightly on a wire rack. Cut cornbread into 6 wedges, and serve warm. Yield: 6 wedges.

Per Serving: PROTEIN 25.6g FAT 8.7g (Saturated Fat 3.0g)
CARBOHYDRATE 40.8g FIBER 4.9g CHOLESTEROL 48mg
IRON 4.7mg SODIUM 445mg CALCIUM 105mg

PIZZA-STYLE STUFFED PEPPERS

5 medium-size green peppers
¾ pound ground round
1 cup fresh mushrooms, chopped
¾ cup chopped onion
1 cup no-salt-added meatless spaghetti sauce
2 tablespoons water
1 teaspoon dried Italian seasoning
¼ teaspoon salt
¼ teaspoon pepper
2 cups cooked long-grain rice (cooked without salt or fat)
½ cup (2 ounces) shredded part-skim mozzarella cheese

Cut tops off green peppers, and remove seeds. Trim stem from tops, and discard. Chop remaining green pepper tops; set aside. Arrange pepper shells in a vegetable steamer over boiling water. Cover and steam 5 minutes. Drain shells, and set aside.

Combine ground round, mushrooms, onion, and reserved chopped green pepper in a large nonstick skillet; cook over medium heat until beef is browned, stirring until it crumbles. Drain and pat dry with paper towels. Wipe drippings from skillet with a paper towel.

Return meat mixture to skillet; add spaghetti sauce and next 4 ingredients. Bring to a boil; reduce heat, and simmer 5 minutes. Stir in rice. Spoon beef mixture evenly into shells; place shells in an 8-inch square baking dish. Pour hot water into baking dish to a depth of 1 inch. Bake at 350° for 15 minutes; sprinkle evenly with cheese, and bake an additional 5 minutes or until cheese melts. Yield: 5 servings (324 calories per serving).

Per Serving: PROTEIN 22.5g FAT 8.4g (Saturated Fat 2.8g)
CARBOHYDRATE 41.5g FIBER 4.4g CHOLESTEROL 48mg
IRON 5.4mg SODIUM 223mg CALCIUM 111mg

GOLDEN SHEPHERD'S PIE

1½ pounds ground round
1 cup chopped onion
1 cup shredded carrot
¾ cup chopped green pepper
1 cup frozen English peas, thawed
1 (14½-ounce) can no-salt-added whole tomatoes,
     undrained and chopped
½ cup no-salt-added tomato sauce
¼ cup water
1 tablespoon low-sodium Worcestershire sauce
1 teaspoon dried Italian seasoning
¼ teaspoon garlic powder
¼ teaspoon salt
¼ teaspoon pepper
Butter-flavored vegetable cooking spray
Potato Topping

Combine ground round, onion, carrot, and green pepper in a large nonstick skillet; cook over medium-high heat until beef is browned, stirring until it crumbles. Drain and pat dry with paper towels. Wipe drippings from skillet with a paper towel.

Return beef mixture to skillet; add peas and next 8 ingredients, stirring well. Bring to a boil; reduce heat, and simmer, uncovered, 25 minutes, stirring occasionally.

Spoon beef mixture into an 11- x 7- x 1½-inch baking dish coated with cooking spray. Spread Potato Topping over beef mixture; lightly coat top with cooking spray. Bake, uncovered, at 425° for 15 minutes. Broil 5½ inches from heat (with electric oven door partially opened) 1 to 2 minutes or until golden. Remove from oven; let stand 5 minutes before serving. Yield: 6 servings (296 calories per serving).

Potato Topping

2 cups peeled, cubed baking potato
1 teaspoon minced garlic
¼ cup plus 2 tablespoons skim milk
1 tablespoon minced fresh chives
1 tablespoon reduced-calorie margarine, melted
¼ teaspoon salt

Cook potato and garlic in boiling water to cover until tender. Drain potato; mash. Add milk, and beat at medium speed of an electric mixer until mixture is smooth. Stir in chives, margarine, and salt. Yield: 2 cups.

Per Serving: PROTEIN 28.7g FAT 8.7g (Saturated Fat 2.7g)
CARBOHYDRATE 25.6g FIBER 3.5g CHOLESTEROL 70mg
IRON 4.1mg SODIUM 332mg CALCIUM 77mg

TANGY BEEF STIR-FRY

1 pound lean boneless beef sirloin steak
2 teaspoons peeled, minced gingerroot
½ teaspoon grated tangerine rind
½ cup fresh tangerine juice
2 tablespoons dry sherry
2 tablespoons low-sodium soy sauce
2 teaspoons cornstarch
½ pound fresh snow pea pods
Vegetable cooking spray
1 teaspoon dark sesame oil
1 cup fresh bean sprouts
¾ cup diagonally sliced celery
3 cups cooked long-grain rice (cooked without salt
     or fat)

Partially freeze steak; trim fat from steak. Slice steak diagonally across grain into ¼-inch-wide strips; place strips in a bowl.

Combine gingerroot and next 4 ingredients; stir well. Pour over steak strips; toss to coat. Cover and marinate in refrigerator at least 30 minutes.

Drain steak strips, reserving marinade. Combine reserved marinade and cornstarch; stir well, and set aside. Wash snow peas; trim ends, remove strings, and set aside.

Coat a wok or large nonstick skillet with cooking spray; drizzle oil around top of wok, coating sides. Heat at medium-high (375°) until hot. Add steak strips, and stir-fry 5 minutes. Remove from wok.

Add snow peas, bean sprouts, and celery to wok; stir-fry 3 minutes. Add steak strips and marinade mixture; stir-fry 2 to 3 minutes or until mixture is slightly thickened. Serve over rice. Yield: 6 servings (253 calories per serving).

Per Serving: PROTEIN 19.3g FAT 4.9g (Saturated Fat 1.5g)
CARBOHYDRATE 31.0g FIBER 1.9g CHOLESTEROL 45mg
IRON 3.8mg SODIUM 189mg CALCIUM 42mg

Lasso an untamed mixture of hearty beef and onions in Broiled Flank Steak with Onion Marmalade.

BROILED FLANK STEAK WITH ONION MARMALADE

1 (1½-pound) lean flank steak
1 cup Burgundy or other dry red wine
3 tablespoons red wine vinegar
2 tablespoons coarse-grained mustard
4 cloves garlic, halved
Vegetable cooking spray
2 teaspoons vegetable oil
⅓ cup sugar
3 cups coarsely chopped purple onion
¼ teaspoon salt
⅛ teaspoon pepper
⅓ cup red wine vinegar
1 tablespoon coarse-grained mustard
Red mustard greens (optional)
Fresh chives (optional)

Trim fat from steak. Combine wine and next 3 ingredients in a heavy-duty, zip-top plastic bag. Add steak; seal bag, and shake until steak is well coated. Marinate steak in refrigerator 8 hours, turning bag occasionally.

Coat a large nonstick skillet with cooking spray; add oil. Sprinkle sugar over oil. Cook over medium heat 5 minutes or until sugar dissolves and turns caramel-colored, stirring frequently. Add onion, salt, and pepper; cook 15 to 20 minutes or until mixture thickens and onion is tender, stirring frequently. Add ⅓ cup vinegar and 1 tablespoon mustard, stirring well; remove from heat, and keep warm.

Remove steak from bag, and discard marinade. Place steak on rack of a broiler pan coated with cooking spray. Broil 5½ inches from heat (with electric oven door partially opened) 7 minutes on each side or to desired degree of doneness. Let stand 10 minutes.

Slice steak diagonally across grain into ¼-inch-thick slices. Serve with onion mixture. If desired, garnish with red mustard greens and fresh chives. Yield: 6 servings (300 calories per serving).

Per Serving: PROTEIN 23.2g FAT 15.2g (Saturated Fat 5.9g)
CARBOHYDRATE 17.1g FIBER 1.1g CHOLESTEROL 61mg
IRON 2.5mg SODIUM 242mg CALCIUM 27mg

SMOTHERED BEEF AND MUSHROOMS

1 (⅞-ounce) package dried porcini mushrooms
1 cup hot water
1 pound lean boneless top round steak
Vegetable cooking spray
1 pound small fresh mushrooms, halved
½ teaspoon dried whole marjoram
3 cloves garlic, minced
1 cup dry Marsala
1 tablespoon no-salt-added tomato paste
¼ teaspoon salt
¼ teaspoon pepper
2 teaspoons all-purpose flour
2 tablespoons water
8 (½-inch-thick) slices French bread, toasted

Combine porcini mushrooms and hot water in a small bowl; let stand 15 minutes. Drain, reserving liquid; coarsely chop porcini mushrooms. Set aside.

Partially freeze steak; trim fat from steak. Slice steak diagonally across grain into ¼-inch-wide strips; cut strips into 2-inch pieces. Coat a large nonstick skillet with cooking spray; place over medium-high heat until hot. Add steak, and cook 5 minutes or until browned on all sides. Remove steak from skillet. Drain and pat dry with paper towels. Wipe drippings from skillet with a paper towel.

Coat skillet with cooking spray. Add porcini mushrooms, halved mushrooms, marjoram, and garlic; sauté until tender. Return steak to skillet. Add reserved mushroom liquid, Marsala, and next 3 ingredients; stir well. Bring to a boil; cover, reduce heat, and simmer 30 minutes or until steak is tender.

Combine flour and 2 tablespoons water, stirring until smooth. Add to steak mixture, and stir well. Cook over medium heat, stirring constantly, until mixture is thickened.

To serve, place 2 slices French bread on each individual serving plate; spoon beef mixture evenly over bread. Serve immediately. Yield: 4 servings (337 calories per serving).

Per Serving: PROTEIN 33.4g FAT 7.1g (Saturated Fat 2.1g)
CARBOHYDRATE 33.0g FIBER 2.8g CHOLESTEROL 73mg
IRON 5.1mg SODIUM 402mg CALCIUM 38mg

COGNAC-MARINATED BEEF TENDERLOIN

Vegetable cooking spray
⅓ cup minced shallots
3 cloves garlic, minced
1 teaspoon dried whole thyme
1 teaspoon dried whole savory
1 teaspoon pepper
¼ teaspoon salt
¾ cup Cognac
1 (3-pound) beef tenderloin

Coat a saucepan with cooking spray; place over medium-high heat until hot. Add shallots and garlic; sauté until tender. Add thyme and next 4 ingredients; bring to a boil. Remove from heat; let cool.

Trim fat from tenderloin. Place tenderloin in a large heavy-duty, zip-top plastic bag. Pour Cognac mixture over tenderloin. Seal bag, and shake until tenderloin is well coated. Marinate in refrigerator 8 hours, turning bag occasionally.

Remove tenderloin from bag, discarding marinade. Place tenderloin on a rack in a roasting pan coated with cooking spray. Insert meat thermometer into thickest part of tenderloin, if desired.

Heat oven to 500°; place tenderloin in oven. Reduce heat to 350°, and bake for 50 to 55 minutes or until meat thermometer registers 140° (rare) or 160° (medium). Remove from oven, and let stand 10 minutes before slicing. Yield: 12 servings (176 calories per serving).

Per Serving: PROTEIN 24.1g FAT 8.0g (Saturated Fat 3.1g)
CARBOHYDRATE 0.3g FIBER 0g CHOLESTEROL 71mg
IRON 3.1mg SODIUM 66mg CALCIUM 7mg

BAVARIAN VEAL

1 pound veal cutlets (¼ inch thick)
2 tablespoons all-purpose flour
Vegetable cooking spray
1 teaspoon reduced-calorie margarine
1⅓ cups sliced fresh mushrooms
½ cup chopped green onions
¾ cup light beer
1 tablespoon Dijon mustard
½ teaspoon dried whole thyme
⅛ teaspoon pepper
¼ cup (1 ounce) shredded reduced-fat Swiss
   cheese
Green onion fans (optional)

Trim fat from cutlets. Place cutlets between 2 sheets of heavy-duty plastic wrap; flatten to ⅛-inch thickness, using a meat mallet or rolling pin. Sprinkle cutlets evenly with flour.

Coat a large nonstick skillet with cooking spray; add margarine. Place over medium-high heat until margarine melts. Add veal, and cook 3 minutes on each side or until browned. Remove veal from skillet. Drain and pat dry with paper towels. Wipe drippings from skillet with a paper towel.

Coat skillet with cooking spray. Add mushrooms and chopped green onions; sauté until tender. Add beer and next 3 ingredients; stir well. Return veal to skillet. Bring to a boil; cover, reduce heat, and simmer 15 minutes or until veal is tender.

Transfer veal to an ovenproof platter. Cook sauce over high heat 2½ minutes or until liquid is reduced by half; spoon over veal. Sprinkle evenly with cheese. Broil 5½ inches from heat (with electric oven door partially opened) 2 minutes or until cheese melts. Garnish with green onion fans; if desired. Yield: 4 servings (193 calories per serving).

Per Serving: PROTEIN 26.6g   FAT 5.9g   (Saturated Fat 1.8g)
CARBOHYDRATE 7.2g   FIBER 0.8g   CHOLESTEROL 99mg
IRON 1.9mg   SODIUM 235mg   CALCIUM 116mg

EASY VEAL MILANO

1 pound veal cutlets (¼ inch thick)
3 tablespoons all-purpose flour
¼ teaspoon salt
¼ teaspoon pepper
Vegetable cooking spray
1 teaspoon olive oil
1 cup sliced fresh mushrooms
2 cloves garlic, minced
1 (14½-ounce) can no-salt-added whole tomatoes,
   undrained and crushed
3 tablespoons sliced ripe olives
¼ teaspoon dried whole basil
2 cups cooked linguine (cooked without salt or fat)

Trim fat from cutlets; cut cutlets into 2-inch pieces. Combine flour, salt, and pepper; dredge veal pieces in flour mixture.

Coat a nonstick skillet with cooking spray; add olive oil. Place over medium-high heat until hot. Add veal, and cook 2 minutes on each side or until browned. Remove from skillet; set aside, and keep warm.

Coat skillet with cooking spray, and place over medium-high heat until hot. Add mushrooms and garlic; sauté until tender. Stir in tomato, olives, and basil; cook over high heat 3 minutes. Return veal to skillet; cover, reduce heat, and simmer 5 minutes. Serve over pasta. Yield: 4 servings (299 calories per serving).

Per Serving: PROTEIN 28.5g   FAT 6.3g   (Saturated Fat 1.4g)
CARBOHYDRATE 31.4g   FIBER 2.0g   CHOLESTEROL 94mg
IRON 3.4mg   SODIUM 337mg   CALCIUM 72mg

ROASTED VEAL WITH ROOT VEGETABLES

1 (3½-pound) boneless rolled veal rump roast
Buttermilk Marinade
1 teaspoon dried whole thyme
½ teaspoon pepper
Vegetable cooking spray
28 small round red potatoes
28 small boiling onions
6 large carrots, cut into thick strips
2 teaspoons vegetable oil
Fresh parsley sprigs (optional)
Fresh thyme sprigs (optional)

Roasted Veal with Root Vegetables, bathed in creamy Buttermilk Marinade, makes an impressive main course.

Unroll roast; trim fat from roast. Roll roast; tie securely at 2-inch intervals with string. Place in a large heavy-duty, zip-top plastic bag. Add half of Buttermilk Marinade. Seal bag; shake well. Marinate in refrigerator 8 hours, turning bag occasionally. Cover and refrigerate remaining Buttermilk Marinade.

Remove roast from marinade, and discard marinade. Pat roast dry with paper towels, and sprinkle with dried thyme and pepper. Place roast in a shallow roasting pan coated with cooking spray. Insert meat thermometer into thickest portion of roast, if desired.

Cook potatoes in boiling water to cover in a large Dutch oven 5 minutes; add onions and carrot. Cook an additional 3 minutes; drain. Place vegetables in a large bowl; add oil, and toss gently.

Arrange vegetables around roast in pan. Bake, uncovered, at 450° for 20 minutes. Reduce heat to 325°; cover and bake an additional 45 to 50 minutes or until meat thermometer registers 160° (medium), stirring vegetables once. Transfer roast and vegetables to a large serving platter, discarding pan drippings. Remove string from roast before slicing. If desired, garnish with fresh parsley and thyme sprigs. Serve with reserved Buttermilk Marinade. Yield: 14 servings (245 calories per serving).

Buttermilk Marinade

2 cups nonfat buttermilk
1 (8-ounce) carton low-fat sour cream
½ cup nonfat mayonnaise
3 tablespoons chopped fresh parsley
2 tablespoons grated Parmesan cheese
½ teaspoon garlic powder
½ teaspoon onion powder
⅛ teaspoon dry mustard

Combine all ingredients in a medium bowl; stir well. Yield: 3¾ cups.

Per Serving: PROTEIN 27.8g FAT 4.0g (Saturated Fat 1.5g)
CARBOHYDRATE 23.8g FIBER 3.1g CHOLESTEROL 92mg
IRON 2.6mg SODIUM 177mg CALCIUM 73mg

BRAISED VEAL CACCIATORE

4 (5-ounce) veal shanks
Vegetable cooking spray
1 (14½-ounce) can no-salt-added whole tomatoes,
    undrained and chopped
1½ cups sliced fresh mushrooms
1 cup chopped onion
½ cup shredded carrot
¼ cup chopped celery
⅓ cup Burgundy or other dry red wine
1 teaspoon dried whole rosemary
¼ teaspoon dried whole oregano
¼ teaspoon dried whole basil
¼ teaspoon salt
¼ teaspoon pepper
2 cloves garlic, minced
1 small lemon, quartered

Trim fat from veal shanks; place shanks in an 11- x 7- x 1½-inch baking dish coated with cooking spray. Bake, uncovered, at 425° for 30 minutes or until browned. Reduce heat to 400°.

Combine tomato and remaining ingredients in a large bowl; stir well. Pour tomato mixture over shanks. Cover and bake 1½ hours or until veal is tender. Remove and discard lemon. Yield: 4 servings (179 calories per serving).

Per Serving: PROTEIN 25.1g FAT 3.7g (Saturated Fat 1.0g)
CARBOHYDRATE 11.5g FIBER 1.7g CHOLESTEROL 94mg
IRON 2.2mg SODIUM 275mg CALCIUM 79mg

CHILI-STYLE LAMB CHOPS

6 (5-ounce) lean lamb loin chops (¾ inch thick)
Vegetable cooking spray
¾ cup reduced-calorie chili sauce
¼ cup low-sugar orange marmalade
2 teaspoons dark brown sugar
½ teaspoon coarse-grained mustard
¼ teaspoon salt
¼ teaspoon chili powder
⅛ teaspoon pepper

Trim fat from chops; place chops in an 11- x 7- x 1½-inch baking dish coated with cooking spray.

Combine chili sauce and remaining ingredients in a small saucepan; cook over medium heat, stirring constantly, until marmalade melts and brown sugar dissolves.

Pour chili sauce mixture evenly over chops. Bake, uncovered, at 350° for 50 minutes or to desired degree of doneness. Yield: 6 servings (188 calories per serving).

Per Serving: PROTEIN 23.8g FAT 6.8g (Saturated Fat 2.4g)
CARBOHYDRATE 6.4g FIBER 0.1g CHOLESTEROL 75mg
IRON 2.2mg SODIUM 207mg CALCIUM 20mg

EASY LAMB CHOPS JALAPEÑO

⅓ cup hot jalapeño jelly
2 teaspoons lemon juice
2 teaspoons margarine
4 (5-ounce) lean lamb loin chops (¾ inch thick)
½ teaspoon cracked pepper
¼ teaspoon salt
Vegetable cooking spray
Jalapeño pepper slices (optional)
Fresh cilantro sprigs (optional)

Combine first 3 ingredients in a small saucepan; cook over medium heat until jelly melts, stirring occasionally. Remove from heat, and keep warm.

Trim fat from chops; sprinkle chops with cracked pepper and salt.

Coat grill rack with cooking spray, and place on grill over medium-hot coals (350° to 400°). Place chops on rack; grill, uncovered, 15 minutes on each side or to desired degree of doneness, basting frequently with jalapeño jelly mixture.

Transfer to a small serving platter. If desired, garnish with jalapeño pepper slices and fresh cilantro sprigs. Yield: 4 servings (270 calories per serving).

Per Serving: PROTEIN 25.6g FAT 10.3g (Saturated Fat 3.3g)
CARBOHYDRATE 17.9g FIBER 0.1g CHOLESTEROL 81mg
IRON 2.2mg SODIUM 244mg CALCIUM 24mg

The mildly seasoned flavor of Classic Rack of Lamb emerges with pizzazz when joined by Green Beans in Sweet Vinaigrette (page 212).

CLASSIC RACK OF LAMB

1 (2-pound) rack of lamb (8 chops)
1 tablespoon coarse-grained mustard
¼ cup fine, dry breadcrumbs
2 tablespoons minced fresh parsley
½ teaspoon dried whole rosemary,
   crushed
⅛ teaspoon salt
⅛ teaspoon pepper
Vegetable cooking spray
Fresh rosemary sprigs (optional)

Trim fat from rack, leaving only small eye of ribs. Strip rib tips of all meat and fat. Spread mustard evenly over meat portion of rack.

Combine breadcrumbs and next 4 ingredients; stir well. Pat breadcrumb mixture evenly over meat portion of rack. Place rack, bone side down, on a rack in a roasting pan coated with cooking spray. Insert meat thermometer, if desired, making sure it does not touch bone.

Bake at 375° for 1 hour and 15 minutes or until meat thermometer registers 160° (medium). Remove from oven, and let stand 10 minutes before slicing. Garnish with fresh rosemary sprigs, if desired. Yield: 4 servings (246 calories per serving).

Per Serving: PROTEIN 26.6g FAT 12.5g (Saturated Fat 4.3g)
CARBOHYDRATE 5.0g FIBER 0.4g CHOLESTEROL 85mg
IRON 2.6mg SODIUM 263mg CALCIUM 33mg

HAM STEAKS WITH ORANGE-CARROT TOPPING

2 large carrots, scraped
Vegetable cooking spray
1 tablespoon honey
2 teaspoons reduced-calorie margarine
⅛ teaspoon paprika
Dash of ground cardamom
1 medium onion, thinly sliced and separated into
    rings
2 tablespoons Cointreau or other orange-flavored
    liqueur
4 (4-ounce) slices reduced-fat, low-salt ham
    (½ inch thick)
Orange slices (optional)

Using a vegetable peeler and applying firm pressure, slice carrots lengthwise into thin strips; set aside 1 cup. Reserve remaining strips for another use.

Coat a large nonstick skillet with cooking spray. Place over medium-high heat until hot. Add honey and next 3 ingredients; cook until margarine melts. Add onion, and sauté until tender. Add carrot strips and liqueur; cook, stirring until liquid evaporates. Transfer to a bowl; set aside, and keep warm.

Coat skillet with cooking spray, and place over medium-high heat until hot. Add ham slices, and cook 4 to 5 minutes on each side or until lightly browned. Transfer ham to serving plates, and top with carrot mixture. Garnish with orange slices, if desired. Yield: 4 servings (208 calories per serving).

Per Serving: PROTEIN 21.2g   FAT 7.3g   (Saturated Fat 1.9g)
CARBOHYDRATE 16.3g   FIBER 1.6g   CHOLESTEROL 56mg
IRON 0.3mg   SODIUM 907mg   CALCIUM 15mg

CAJUN PATTIES

1½ pounds lean ground pork
1 teaspoon cracked pepper
Vegetable cooking spray
¼ cup frozen unsweetened apple juice concentrate,
    thawed and undiluted
3 tablespoons pineapple preserves
1 tablespoon prepared horseradish
2¼ teaspoons dry mustard
3 ounces Neufchâtel cheese, softened

Combine pork and pepper in a medium bowl; stir well. Shape mixture into 6 (¾-inch-thick) patties.

Coat a large nonstick skillet with cooking spray; place over medium-high heat until hot. Add pork patties, and cook 7 minutes on each side. Drain and pat dry with paper towels. Wipe drippings from skillet with a paper towel.

Combine apple juice concentrate and next 3 ingredients in skillet, stirring well. Return patties to skillet; cook over low heat until thoroughly heated. Transfer patties to a serving platter; keep warm.

Beat Neufchâtel cheese in a small bowl at medium speed of an electric mixer until smooth; spread evenly over pork patties. Spoon apple juice concentrate mixture evenly over patties, and serve immediately. Yield: 6 servings (298 calories per serving).

Per Serving: PROTEIN 24.5g   FAT 16.1g   (Saturated Fat 6.4g)
CARBOHYDRATE 12.8g   FIBER 0.2g   CHOLESTEROL 88mg
IRON 1.1mg   SODIUM 125mg   CALCIUM 27mg

SESAME PORK BROCHETTES

1½ pounds lean boneless pork loin (½ inch thick)
¼ cup honey
3 tablespoons lemon juice
2 tablespoons sesame seeds, toasted and divided
1 tablespoon low-sodium soy sauce
¾ teaspoon ground cumin
½ teaspoon ground cinnamon
Vegetable cooking spray
3 cups cooked couscous (cooked without
    salt or fat)

Trim fat from pork; cut pork into ¼-inch-wide strips. Place pork in a large shallow dish.

Combine honey, lemon juice, 1 tablespoon plus 1 teaspoon sesame seeds, soy sauce, cumin, and cinnamon in container of an electric blender; cover and process until smooth. Pour over pork. Cover and marinate in refrigerator 2 hours.

Remove pork from marinade, reserving marinade. Thread pork onto 12 (10-inch) skewers. Place skewers on rack of a broiler pan coated with cooking spray. Broil 5½ inches from heat (with electric oven door partially opened) 4 minutes. Turn and baste with reserved marinade; broil an additional 4 minutes or until done.

Place couscous on a large serving platter. Arrange skewers over couscous, and sprinkle evenly with remaining 2 teaspoons toasted sesame seeds. Serve immediately. Yield: 6 servings (357 calories per serving).

Per Serving: PROTEIN 31.4g FAT 10.4g (Saturated Fat 3.3g)
CARBOHYDRATE 33.4g FIBER 0.5g CHOLESTEROL 83mg
IRON 1.7mg SODIUM 134mg CALCIUM 23mg

TEQUILA SUNRISE PORK

1 (1¼-pound) lean boneless pork shoulder
3 tablespoons tequila, divided
1 teaspoon dried whole oregano
½ teaspoon ground cumin
¼ teaspoon garlic powder
¼ teaspoon ground red pepper
Vegetable cooking spray
1 teaspoon vegetable oil
½ cup unsweetened orange juice
¼ cup water
1 large onion, thinly sliced
¾ teaspoon cornstarch
2 cups cooked orzo (cooked without salt or fat)
2 tablespoons chopped fresh parsley

Trim fat from pork; cut pork into ½-inch cubes. Combine 2 tablespoons tequila and next 4 ingredients in a large heavy-duty, zip-top plastic bag; add pork. Seal bag, and shake until pork is well coated. Marinate pork in refrigerator 1 hour, turning bag occasionally.

Remove pork from bag; discard marinade. Coat a large nonstick skillet with cooking spray; add oil. Place over medium-high heat until hot. Add pork, and cook until browned on all sides, turning occasionally. Drain and pat dry with paper towels. Wipe drippings from skillet with a paper towel.

Return pork to skillet. Add orange juice, water, and onion; stir well. Bring mixture to a boil; cover, reduce heat, and simmer 30 minutes or until pork is tender.

Combine cornstarch and remaining 1 tablespoon tequila, stirring until smooth; add to pork mixture. Bring to a boil; cook over medium heat, stirring constantly, until thickened. Remove from heat; stir in orzo and parsley. Serve immediately. Yield: 6 servings (316 calories per serving).

Per Serving: PROTEIN 22.1g FAT 11.9g (Saturated Fat 3.8g)
CARBOHYDRATE 28.7g FIBER 1.6g CHOLESTEROL 67mg
IRON 2.6mg SODIUM 57mg CALCIUM 28mg

PORK CHOP AND CABBAGE CASSEROLE

6 (6-ounce) lean center-cut loin pork chops (½ inch thick)
½ teaspoon pepper
Vegetable cooking spray
6 cups finely shredded cabbage (about 1 pound)
2 cups finely shredded red cabbage
½ cup finely chopped onion
1 clove garlic, minced
1 cup finely shredded carrot
¼ cup evaporated skimmed milk
2 tablespoons frozen apple juice concentrate, thawed and undiluted
2 tablespoons water
1 tablespoon Dijon mustard
1 tablespoon cider vinegar

Trim fat from chops. Rub chops with pepper. Coat a large nonstick skillet with cooking spray; place over medium-high heat until hot. Add chops, and cook 3 minutes on each side or until browned. Remove chops from skillet. Drain; pat dry with paper towels. Wipe drippings from skillet with a paper towel.

Cook cabbages in boiling water 5 minutes. Drain; transfer to a large bowl, and set aside.

Coat skillet with cooking spray; place skillet over medium-high heat until hot. Add onion and garlic; sauté until tender. Add carrot, and sauté 3 minutes. Add carrot mixture to reserved cabbage; toss well.

Spoon half of cabbage mixture into a 13- x 9- x 2-inch baking dish coated with cooking spray. Place chops over cabbage mixture; top with remaining cabbage mixture. Combine milk and remaining ingredients; pour over cabbage mixture. Cover and bake at 350° for 50 minutes or until chops are tender. Yield: 6 servings (249 calories per serving).

Per Serving: PROTEIN 24.9g FAT 11.1g (Saturated Fat 3.9g)
CARBOHYDRATE 11.6g FIBER 2.6g CHOLESTEROL 73mg
IRON 1.6mg SODIUM 163mg CALCIUM 84mg

PORK CHOPS WITH SWEET POTATO PUREE AND CRANBERRY RELISH

1 tablespoon sugar
1 tablespoon frozen orange juice concentrate, thawed and undiluted
1 cup fresh cranberries
1 tablespoon chopped pecans, toasted
2 medium-size sweet potatoes
2 tablespoons brown sugar
2 teaspoons reduced-calorie margarine
4 (4-ounce) lean boneless center-cut loin pork chops (¾ inch thick)
¼ teaspoon salt
¼ teaspoon pepper
Butter-flavored vegetable cooking spray
Orange zest (optional)
Fresh variegated sage sprigs (optional)

Combine sugar and orange juice concentrate in a small saucepan; add cranberries. Cook over medium heat 8 minutes or until cranberries begin to pop. Remove from heat, and stir in pecans. Cover and chill thoroughly.

Bake potatoes at 400° for 45 minutes or until done. Allow potatoes to cool to touch. Cut potatoes in half, and scoop out pulp; discard peels. Combine potato pulp, brown sugar, and margarine in a medium bowl, stirring until creamy. Cover and keep warm.

Trim fat from chops. Sprinkle chops evenly with salt and pepper. Coat a large nonstick skillet with cooking spray, and place over medium-high heat until hot. Add chops, and cook 5 to 6 minutes on each side or until done.

Pipe sweet potato mixture evenly onto 4 individual serving plates; top with pork chops. Spoon cranberry relish over chops. If desired, garnish with orange zest and fresh sage sprigs. Serve immediately. Yield: 4 servings (425 calories per serving).

Per Serving: PROTEIN 28.0g FAT 15.0g (Saturated Fat 4.4g) CARBOHYDRATE 44.2g FIBER 4.4g CHOLESTEROL 82mg IRON 2.0mg SODIUM 245mg CALCIUM 42mg

Pork Chops with Sweet Potato Puree and Cranberry Relish provides a healthy alternative to holiday favorites.

RIBBED PORK ROAST WITH HERBED CANNELLINI BEANS

1 (8-rib) center rib pork roast (about 4 pounds)
8 cloves garlic, sliced lengthwise into thirds
Vegetable cooking spray
½ teaspoon coarse ground pepper
1 teaspoon vegetable oil
¼ cup shredded carrot
¼ cup minced fresh parsley
1 teaspoon minced fresh rosemary
1 teaspoon minced fresh thyme
2 cloves garlic, minced
2 (16-ounce) cans cannellini beans, drained
¼ cup 1% low-fat milk
2 tablespoons water
1 teaspoon Dijon mustard
Fresh rosemary sprigs (optional)
Fresh thyme sprigs (optional)

Trim fat from roast. Make 24 slits in meaty part of roast; insert sliced garlic in slits. Coat roast with cooking spray; sprinkle with ground pepper. Place roast on a rack in a roasting pan coated with cooking spray. Insert meat thermometer into thickest part of roast, making sure it does not touch bone or fat. Bake at 375° for 1 hour and 35 minutes or until meat thermometer registers 160°. Remove roast from oven, and let stand 10 minutes.

Coat a large nonstick skillet with cooking spray; add oil. Place over medium-high heat until hot. Add carrot, parsley, minced rosemary, minced thyme, and minced garlic; sauté until tender. Add beans, milk, water, and mustard; stir well. Cook over medium heat 10 minutes or until mixture thickens, stirring frequently.

Carve roast into 8 chops, and serve with bean mixture. If desired, garnish with rosemary and thyme sprigs. Yield: 8 servings (300 calories per serving).

Per Serving: PROTEIN 30.3g FAT 13.5g (Saturated Fat 4.7g) CARBOHYDRATE 11.8g FIBER 1.8g CHOLESTEROL 85mg IRON 2.4mg SODIUM 370mg CALCIUM 39mg

SPICED PORK BARBECUE

1 (2-pound) boneless sirloin pork roast
Vegetable cooking spray
2 (14½-ounce) cans no-salt-added whole tomatoes,
    undrained and chopped
1⅓ cups chopped onion
⅓ cup raisins
2 tablespoons no-salt-added tomato paste
2 tablespoons cider vinegar
1 tablespoon minced pickled jalapeño slices
1 teaspoon beef-flavored bouillon granules
¼ teaspoon salt
¼ teaspoon ground cinnamon
⅛ teaspoon ground cloves

Trim fat from roast. Cut roast into 2-inch pieces.
Coat a Dutch oven with cooking spray; place over
medium heat until hot. Add pork; cook until browned
on all sides, turning often. Drain; pat dry with paper
towels. Wipe drippings from pan with a paper towel.

Return pork to pan; add tomato and remaining
ingredients, stirring well. Bring to a boil; cover, reduce heat, and simmer 1½ hours or until pork is very
tender. Uncover and cook over medium-high heat
8 minutes or until liquid evaporates, stirring frequently. Remove from heat; let cool slightly. Shred
pork using two forks. Return pork to pan; cook until
heated. Yield: 8 servings (216 calories per serving).

Per Serving: PROTEIN 24.2g FAT 7.6g (Saturated Fat 0.8g)
CARBOHYDRATE 12.5g FIBER 1.4g CHOLESTEROL 68mg
IRON 1.6mg SODIUM 291mg CALCIUM 50mg

HONEY PORK TENDERLOIN

2 (½-pound) pork tenderloins
⅛ teaspoon ground red pepper
Vegetable cooking spray
⅓ cup reduced-calorie catsup
¼ cup honey
2 tablespoons lemon juice
1 teaspoon low-sodium soy sauce
⅛ teaspoon garlic powder
2 cups cooked long-grain rice (cooked without
    salt or fat)

Trim fat from tenderloins. Cut each tenderloin
crosswise into 4 pieces. Place pieces between 2 sheets
of heavy-duty plastic wrap, and flatten to ¾-inch
thickness, using a meat mallet or rolling pin. Sprinkle
with red pepper.

Coat a large nonstick skillet with cooking spray;
place over medium heat until hot. Add pork, and cook
3 minutes on each side or until browned. Remove
from skillet. Drain and pat dry with paper towels.
Set aside, and keep warm. Wipe skillet dry with a
paper towel.

Combine catsup and next 4 ingredients in skillet; bring mixture to a boil. Add pork; cover, reduce
heat, and simmer 10 minutes or until pork is done.
Serve over cooked rice. Yield: 4 servings (313 calories
per serving).

Per Serving: PROTEIN 25.9g FAT 3.1g (Saturated Fat 1.0g)
CARBOHYDRATE 43.8g FIBER 0.5g CHOLESTEROL 74mg
IRON 2.5mg SODIUM 94mg CALCIUM 20mg

*A tender serving of fowl crowns a
wonderful medley of rice and fruits in
Cornish Hens with Fruited Wild Rice
(page 178). It's a regal feast everyone
will enjoy.*

Poultry

MEXICALI CHICKEN

⅓ cup chopped green onions
¼ cup chopped green pepper
1 teaspoon minced garlic
¾ teaspoon pepper
1 (14½-ounce) can no-salt-added whole tomatoes,
    undrained and chopped
1 (4-ounce) can chopped green chiles, drained
1 cup canned low-sodium chicken broth, undiluted
1 tablespoon fresh lemon juice
4 ounces wagon wheel pasta, uncooked
2 cups chopped cooked chicken (skinned before
    cooking and cooked without salt)
¼ cup chopped fresh cilantro
3 tablespoons sliced ripe olives

Combine first 8 ingredients in a large skillet. Cook, uncovered, over medium-high heat 20 minutes. Cook pasta according to package directions, omitting salt and fat; drain. Add pasta and remaining ingredients to tomato mixture. Cover, reduce heat, and simmer 20 minutes. Yield: 5 servings (258 calories per serving).

Per Serving: PROTEIN 24.4g   FAT 6.6g   (Saturated Fat 1.7g)
CARBOHYDRATE 25.0g   FIBER 2.0g   CHOLESTEROL 61mg
IRON 3.2mg   SODIUM 211mg   CALCIUM 66mg

CHICKEN-DRESSING CASSEROLE

1 cup stone-ground cornmeal
1 teaspoon baking soda
½ teaspoon baking powder
1 cup nonfat buttermilk
¼ cup frozen egg substitute, thawed
Vegetable cooking spray
2 cups chopped cooked chicken (skinned before
    cooking and cooked without salt)
¾ cup chopped onion
¾ cup chopped celery
¾ teaspoon poultry seasoning
½ teaspoon pepper
½ teaspoon sage
¼ teaspoon salt
Dash of hot sauce
2½ cups canned low-sodium chicken broth, undiluted
½ cup frozen egg substitute, thawed

Combine stone-ground cornmeal, baking soda, and baking powder in a medium mixing bowl; make a well in center of mixture. Combine buttermilk and ¼ cup egg substitute; add buttermilk mixture to dry ingredients, stirring just until dry ingredients are moistened.

Spoon batter into an 8-inch cast-iron skillet coated with cooking spray. Bake at 400° for 20 minutes or until golden. Remove cornbread from skillet, and cool slightly on a wire rack.

Crumble cooled cornbread into a large mixing bowl. Add chicken and remaining ingredients, stirring well. Spoon mixture into a 2-quart baking dish coated with cooking spray. Bake, uncovered, at 350° for 1½ hours. Yield: 6 servings (243 calories per serving).

Per Serving: PROTEIN 24.9g   FAT 6.3g   (Saturated Fat 1.6g)
CARBOHYDRATE 21.6g   FIBER 2.9g   CHOLESTEROL 55mg
IRON 2.7mg   SODIUM 454mg   CALCIUM 127mg

CURRIED CHICKEN ORIENTAL

1½ tablespoons low-sodium soy sauce
1½ tablespoons dry sherry
1 teaspoon peeled, grated gingerroot
1 teaspoon minced garlic
¼ teaspoon salt
3 (4-ounce) skinned, boned chicken breast halves,
    cut into thin strips
2 ounces fresh snow pea pods
Vegetable cooking spray
1 teaspoon peanut oil
¼ cup water
½ cup thinly sliced carrot
⅓ cup julienne-cut green pepper
⅓ cup thinly sliced green onions
1 cup sliced fresh mushrooms
1 (8-ounce) can pineapple chunks in juice,
    drained
¼ cup unsalted dry roasted peanuts
2 teaspoons curry powder
1½ tablespoons cornstarch
1½ cups canned low-sodium chicken broth,
    undiluted
2 cups cooked long-grain rice (cooked without
    salt or fat)

Combine first 5 ingredients in a small bowl; stir well. Add chicken, and toss well. Cover and marinate in refrigerator 4 hours, stirring occasionally.

Wash snow peas; trim ends, and remove strings. Set aside.

Coat a wok with cooking spray; heat at medium-high (375°) until hot. Drizzle oil around top of wok, coating sides; heat at medium-high 1 minute. Add chicken and marinade; stir-fry 3 to 4 minutes or until chicken is lightly browned. Remove chicken from wok, and pat chicken dry with paper towels; set aside.

Add ¼ cup water to wok, stirring to de-glaze pan. Add carrot, and stir-fry 2 minutes. Add green pepper and green onions; stir-fry 2 minutes. Add snow peas and mushrooms; stir-fry 1 minute. Add chicken, pineapple, peanuts, and curry powder; toss well. Combine cornstarch and chicken broth, stirring until mixture is smooth.

Add cornstarch mixture to wok; cook, stirring constantly, 1 to 2 minutes or until mixture is thickened and bubbly. Serve over rice. Yield: 4 servings (328 calories per serving).

Per Serving: PROTEIN 25.6g FAT 6.8g (Saturated Fat 1.1g) CARBOHYDRATE 39.7g FIBER 2.8g CHOLESTEROL 49mg IRON 3.3mg SODIUM 387mg CALCIUM 53mg

CHICKEN DIANE

Olive oil-flavored vegetable cooking spray
¾ pound sliced fresh mushrooms
1 cup chopped onion
6 (4-ounce) skinned, boned chicken breast halves
¼ teaspoon salt
¼ teaspoon pepper
2 tablespoons chopped fresh chives
2 tablespoons chopped fresh parsley
¼ cup canned low-sodium chicken broth,
    undiluted
3 tablespoons Cognac
1 tablespoon Dijon mustard

Coat a large nonstick skillet with cooking spray; place over medium-high heat until hot. Add mushrooms and onion; sauté until tender. Remove from skillet, and set aside.

Place chicken between 2 sheets of heavy-duty plastic wrap, and flatten to ¼-inch thickness, using a meat mallet or rolling pin. Sprinkle chicken with salt and pepper. Coat skillet with cooking spray; place over medium-high heat until hot. Add chicken, and cook 4 minutes or until lightly browned. Turn chicken, and spoon reserved mushroom mixture over chicken.

Combine chives and remaining ingredients; pour over chicken. Cover, reduce heat, and simmer 3 minutes or until chicken is tender. Transfer chicken to a serving platter; spoon mushroom mixture over chicken. Yield: 6 servings (154 calories per serving).

Per Serving: PROTEIN 27.7g FAT 2.1g (Saturated Fat 0.4g) CARBOHYDRATE 4.9g FIBER 1.2g CHOLESTEROL 66mg IRON 1.6mg SODIUM 252mg CALCIUM 22mg

RASPBERRY CHICKEN

1 cup canned low-sodium chicken broth, undiluted
4 (4-ounce) skinned, boned chicken breast halves
¼ teaspoon pepper
¼ cup minced shallots
2 tablespoons raspberry vinegar
3 tablespoons low-sugar raspberry preserves
2 tablespoons low-fat sour cream
Fresh raspberries (optional)
Fresh mint sprigs (optional)

Place chicken broth in a large nonstick skillet. Bring to a boil; reduce heat, and simmer 5 minutes or until reduced to ½ cup.

Sprinkle chicken evenly with pepper. Add chicken, shallots, and vinegar to broth in skillet. Cover and cook over medium heat 20 minutes or until chicken is tender. Transfer chicken to serving platter, and keep warm.

Add preserves and sour cream to broth mixture, stirring with a wire whisk; cook, stirring constantly, until mixture is thoroughly heated. Spoon over chicken. If desired, garnish with fresh raspberries and mint sprigs. Yield: 4 servings (154 calories per serving).

Per Serving: PROTEIN 27.3g FAT 2.7g (Saturated Fat 1.0g) CARBOHYDRATE 5.3g FIBER 0.1g CHOLESTEROL 69mg IRON 1.2mg SODIUM 99mg CALCIUM 25mg

Discover a treasury of vegetables hidden inside poultry blankets in Vegetable-Filled Chicken Breasts.

VEGETABLE-FILLED CHICKEN BREASTS

6 (4-ounce) skinned, boned chicken breast halves
12 small fresh asparagus spears
1 cup plus 2 tablespoons (4½ ounces) shredded
   nonfat mozzarella cheese
¾ cup sliced fresh mushrooms
1 cup frozen artichoke hearts, thawed, drained,
   and chopped
1 tablespoon diced pimiento
¼ teaspoon salt
¼ teaspoon pepper
½ cup frozen egg substitute, thawed
¾ cup fine, dry breadcrumbs
2 tablespoons reduced-calorie margarine
Vegetable cooking spray
Dash of paprika
Fresh chives (optional)

Place chicken breasts between 2 sheets of heavy-duty plastic wrap, and flatten to ¼-inch thickness, using a meat mallet or rolling pin. Set aside.

Snap off tough ends of asparagus. Remove scales from stalks with a knife or vegetable peeler, if desired. Arrange asparagus, cheese, and mushrooms evenly on chicken breasts. Top evenly with artichoke and pimiento; sprinkle with salt and pepper. Fold chicken over vegetable mixture, and secure with wooden picks. Dip chicken in egg substitute, and dredge in breadcrumbs.

Melt margarine in a large nonstick skillet over medium heat. Add chicken, and cook 6 to 8 minutes on each side or until browned. Remove chicken from skillet, and place on a baking sheet. Coat chicken with cooking spray; sprinkle with paprika.

Bake at 350° for 15 to 18 minutes or until golden. Transfer chicken to a serving platter, and remove wooden picks. Garnish with fresh chives, if desired. Serve immediately. Yield: 6 servings (248 calories per serving).

Per Serving: PROTEIN 36.1g FAT 5.2g (Saturated Fat 0.9g)
CARBOHYDRATE 13.5g FIBER 1.1g CHOLESTEROL 66mg
IRON 2.0mg SODIUM 489mg CALCIUM 193mg

SALMON-STUFFED CHICKEN BREASTS

1 cup canned low-sodium chicken broth, undiluted
¼ cup chopped shallots
¼ cup chopped celery
¼ cup chopped green pepper
2 teaspoons minced garlic
1 (7½-ounce) can red salmon
3 tablespoons frozen egg substitute, thawed
1 teaspoon chopped fresh tarragon
1 teaspoon dried whole basil
¼ teaspoon salt
¼ teaspoon freshly ground black pepper
⅛ teaspoon ground white pepper
⅛ teaspoon ground red pepper
⅛ teaspoon hot sauce
6 (4-ounce) skinned, boned chicken breast halves
¼ cup Chablis or other dry white wine
½ teaspoon sweet paprika
¼ teaspoon freshly ground black pepper

Combine chicken broth, shallots, celery, green pepper, and garlic in a small saucepan; bring to a boil over medium heat. Reduce heat, and simmer, uncovered, 5 minutes. Remove vegetables, using a slotted spoon; set aside. Reserve broth for another use.

Drain salmon; remove and discard skin and bones. Flake salmon. Combine salmon, drained vegetables, egg substitute, and next 7 ingredients in a bowl, stirring well.

Place chicken between 2 sheets of heavy-duty plastic wrap, and flatten to ¼-inch thickness, using a meat mallet or rolling pin. Divide salmon mixture evenly among chicken breast halves, spooning

mixture onto center of each half. Roll chicken up lengthwise, tucking ends under; secure chicken with wooden picks.

Place chicken rolls, seam side down, in an 11- x 7- x 1½-inch baking dish; drizzle wine over chicken. Sprinkle chicken with paprika and ¼ teaspoon black pepper. Cover and bake at 325° for 40 minutes. Uncover and bake an additional 5 minutes. Transfer chicken to a serving platter, and remove wooden picks. Serve immediately. Yield: 6 servings (189 calories per serving).

Per Serving: PROTEIN 32.2g FAT 4.8g (Saturated Fat 1.2g)
CARBOHYDRATE 2.5g FIBER 0.4g CHOLESTEROL 82mg
IRON 1.7mg SODIUM 198mg CALCIUM 83mg

GRILLED JALAPEÑO CHICKEN

½ cup lime juice
1½ tablespoons minced jalapeño pepper
1 tablespoon vegetable oil
1½ teaspoons garlic powder
6 (6-ounce) skinned chicken breast halves
¼ teaspoon salt
⅛ teaspoon pepper
Vegetable cooking spray
Jalapeño pepper slices (optional)
Lime wedges (optional)

Combine first 4 ingredients in a large heavy-duty, zip-top plastic bag; add chicken. Seal bag, and marinate chicken in refrigerator 1 hour, turning bag occasionally.

Remove chicken from marinade, reserving marinade. Sprinkle chicken with salt and pepper.

Coat grill rack with cooking spray; place rack on grill over medium-hot coals (350° to 400°). Place chicken on rack; grill, covered, 8 minutes on each side or until chicken is done, basting occasionally with marinade. Transfer chicken to a large serving platter. If desired, garnish chicken with jalapeño pepper slices and lime wedges. Yield: 6 servings (176 calories per serving).

Per Serving: PROTEIN 27.7g FAT 5.6g (Saturated Fat 1.3g)
CARBOHYDRATE 2.6g FIBER 0.1g CHOLESTEROL 75mg
IRON 1.0mg SODIUM 164mg CALCIUM 17mg

Guests will take a culinary excursion to the French countryside when you present Poulet au Vinaigre.

POULET AU VINAIGRE

2 cups peeled, coarsely chopped tomato
1 cup red wine vinegar
¾ cup canned low-sodium chicken broth,
  undiluted
2 tablespoons no-salt-added tomato paste
15 cloves garlic
4 (6-ounce) skinned chicken breast halves
1 teaspoon fines herbes
1 bay leaf
Fresh thyme sprigs (optional)
Fresh oregano sprigs (optional)

Combine first 5 ingredients in a medium saucepan; stir well. Cover and simmer over medium-low heat 20 minutes. Add chicken, fines herbes, and bay leaf. Cover and simmer an additional 25 minutes or until chicken is tender.

Transfer chicken to a serving platter, and keep warm. Bring tomato mixture to a boil; cook, uncovered, over medium heat 20 minutes or until mixture is reduced to 1⅓ cups. Remove and discard bay leaf. Remove and discard garlic, if desired. Spoon tomato mixture over chicken. If desired, garnish with fresh thyme and oregano sprigs. Yield: 4 servings (183 calories per serving).

Per Serving: PROTEIN 28.5g FAT 2.1g (Saturated Fat 0.5g)
CARBOHYDRATE 12.4g FIBER 1.4g CHOLESTEROL 66mg
IRON 1.8mg SODIUM 102mg CALCIUM 43mg

ORANGE-GINGER CHICKEN

6 (6-ounce) skinned chicken breast halves
1½ cups unsweetened orange juice
1 cup Chablis or other dry white wine
3 tablespoons minced shallots
1 tablespoon honey
1 teaspoon peeled, minced gingerroot
¼ teaspoon dried whole tarragon
¼ teaspoon ground coriander
¼ teaspoon freshly ground pepper
1 tablespoon plus 1 teaspoon cornstarch
2½ tablespoons water
3 cups cooked long-grain rice (cooked without salt or fat)

Place chicken in a large heavy-duty, zip-top plastic bag. Combine orange juice and next 7 ingredients; pour over chicken. Seal bag, and marinate chicken in refrigerator 3 hours, turning bag occasionally.

Place chicken and marinade in a large nonstick skillet. Bring to a boil over medium heat. Cover, reduce heat, and simmer 20 minutes. Uncover and simmer an additional 10 minutes or until chicken is tender. Transfer chicken to a platter, and keep warm.

Combine cornstarch and water; stir well. Add to marinade; cook, stirring constantly, until thickened and bubbly. Spoon ½ cup rice onto each individual serving plate. Top with chicken; spoon marinade over chicken. Serve immediately. Yield: 6 servings (285 calories per serving).

Per Serving: PROTEIN 28.9g FAT 1.6g (Saturated Fat 0.4g)
CARBOHYDRATE 36.9g FIBER 0.7g CHOLESTEROL 66mg
IRON 2.0mg SODIUM 79mg CALCIUM 35mg

SAUSAGE-STUFFED CHICKEN THIGHS

1½ teaspoons dried Italian seasoning
½ teaspoon pepper
2 teaspoons olive oil
6 chicken thighs (about 1¼ pounds), boned and skinned
Vegetable cooking spray
6 (1-ounce) turkey breakfast sausage links
¼ cup canned low-sodium chicken broth, undiluted
¼ cup Chablis or other dry white wine
⅔ cup canned low-sodium chicken broth, undiluted
⅓ cup Chablis or other dry white wine
1 tablespoon coarse-grained mustard
1 tablespoon Dijon mustard
2 tablespoons chopped green onions
¼ cup nonfat sour cream alternative

Combine first 3 ingredients in a heavy-duty, zip-top plastic bag; add chicken. Seal bag, and shake until chicken is well coated. Marinate in refrigerator at least 4 hours.

Coat a small nonstick skillet with cooking spray; place over medium heat until hot. Add sausage links, and cook until browned, turning frequently. Drain well on paper towels.

Wrap 1 chicken thigh around each sausage link; secure with wooden picks. Place chicken, seam side down, in an 8-inch square baking dish. Pour ¼ cup broth and ¼ cup wine over chicken. Cover and bake at 350° for 40 minutes or until chicken is done. Uncover; broil 5½ inches from heat (with electric oven door partially opened) 5 minutes. Remove picks.

Combine ⅔ cup chicken broth and next 4 ingredients in a small saucepan. Bring to a boil over medium-high heat; boil 10 minutes or until mixture is reduced to 3 tablespoons, stirring occasionally. Remove from heat, and let cool 3 minutes. Whisk in sour cream. Serve with chicken. Yield: 6 servings (197 calories per serving).

Per Serving: PROTEIN 22.5g FAT 9.7g (Saturated Fat 2.3g)
CARBOHYDRATE 2.6g FIBER 0.2g CHOLESTEROL 91mg
IRON 1.7mg SODIUM 355mg CALCIUM 27mg

GLAZED ROASTED CHICKEN

1 (3-pound) broiler-fryer chicken, skinned
1 large carrot, scraped and cut into 3 pieces
1 large stalk celery, cut into 3 pieces
1 small onion, quartered
2 cloves garlic, halved
¼ cup reduced-calorie apple spread
1 tablespoon white wine Worcestershire sauce
1 teaspoon margarine
Fresh rosemary sprigs (optional)
Fresh sage sprigs (optional)

Trim excess fat from chicken. Remove giblets and neck from chicken; reserve for another use. Rinse chicken under cold water; pat dry with paper towels.

Place carrot, celery, onion, and garlic in cavity of chicken. Truss chicken. Place chicken, breast side up, on a rack in a shallow roasting pan; insert meat thermometer into meaty part of thigh, making sure it does not touch bone.

Combine apple spread, Worcestershire sauce, and margarine in a small saucepan. Cook over medium-low heat until spread melts, stirring frequently. Brush chicken with half of spread mixture. Cover and bake at 375° for 45 minutes; uncover and bake an additional 40 minutes or until meat thermometer registers 180°, basting occasionally with remaining spread mixture.

Transfer to a serving platter; remove and discard vegetables from cavity. If desired, garnish with fresh rosemary and sage sprigs. Yield: 6 servings (182 calories per serving).

Per Serving: PROTEIN 23.7g FAT 6.7g (Saturated Fat 1.8g)
CARBOHYDRATE 5.4g FIBER 0g CHOLESTEROL 73mg
IRON 1.0mg SODIUM 113mg CALCIUM 16mg

CORNISH HENS WITH FRUITED WILD RICE

¼ cup chopped dried figs
¼ cup chopped dried apricots
2 tablespoons apricot brandy
¼ cup canned low-sodium chicken broth,
    undiluted
½ cup chopped fresh mushrooms
¼ cup minced shallots
1⅓ cups cooked wild rice (cooked without salt or
    fat)
¼ cup chopped extra-lean cured cooked ham
3 tablespoons chopped walnuts, toasted
2 (1-pound) Cornish hens, skinned
1 teaspoon olive oil
1 teaspoon paprika
1 teaspoon pepper
Apricot wedges (optional)
Fresh thyme (optional)

Combine figs and dried apricots in a small bowl. Bring brandy to a simmer in a small saucepan; pour over fig mixture. Cover and let stand 15 minutes.

Bring chicken broth to a boil in a small skillet over medium-high heat. Add mushrooms and shallots; sauté 5 minutes or until vegetables are tender and liquid has evaporated.

Cut 4 (18- x 15-inch) rectangles of parchment paper; fold each rectangle in half lengthwise, and trim each into a heart shape. Place parchment hearts on 2 large baking sheets, and open out flat. Combine fig mixture, mushroom mixture, rice, ham, and walnuts; stir well. Spoon one-fourth of rice mixture on one side of each parchment heart near the crease.

Remove giblets from hens; reserve for another use. Rinse hens under cold water, and pat dry. Split each hen in half lengthwise, using an electric knife. Place hen halves, cut side down, on rice mixture. Rub hens with olive oil; sprinkle with paprika and pepper.

Fold paper edges over to seal. Starting with rounded edges, pleat and crimp edges together to seal. Bake at 325° for 40 minutes or until hens are done.

Transfer hens and rice mixture to serving plates. If desired, garnish with apricot wedges and thyme. Yield: 4 servings (324 calories per serving).

Per Serving: PROTEIN 30.2g FAT 8.6g (Saturated Fat 1.4g)
CARBOHYDRATE 32.9g FIBER 3.6g CHOLESTEROL 81mg
IRON 3.0mg SODIUM 208mg CALCIUM 46mg

GRECIAN CORNISH HENS

2 (1-pound) Cornish hens, skinned
¼ cup commercial oil-free Italian dressing
¼ cup lemon juice, divided
1¼ cups water
¼ teaspoon salt
⅔ cup basmati rice, uncooked
3 tablespoons pine nuts, toasted
2 tablespoons chopped fresh parsley
2 teaspoons dried whole basil
1 teaspoon dried whole thyme
½ teaspoon pepper
Vegetable cooking spray
12 grape leaves
Lemon slices (optional)

Remove giblets from hens; reserve for another use. Rinse hens under cold water, and pat dry. Split each hen in half lengthwise, using an electric knife.

Place hens in a large heavy-duty, zip-top plastic bag. Combine Italian dressing and 2 tablespoons lemon juice. Pour over hens; seal bag, and shake until hens are well coated. Marinate in refrigerator 8 hours, turning bag occasionally.

Bring 1¼ cups water and salt to a boil in a medium saucepan; stir in rice. Cover, reduce heat, and simmer 20 minutes or until rice is tender and liquid is absorbed.

Combine cooked rice, 1 tablespoon lemon juice, pine nuts, and next 4 ingredients; stir well.

Spoon rice mixture into an 11- x 7- x 1½-inch baking dish coated with cooking spray. Remove hens from marinade; place hens on rice, and drizzle marinade over hens. Cover hens with grape leaves; drizzle remaining 1 tablespoon lemon juice over grape leaves. Cover and bake at 350° for 1 hour or until hens are done.

To serve, remove and discard top layer of grape leaves that may have darkened. Place remaining grape leaves on individual serving plates, and top with rice mixture and hens. Garnish with lemon slices, if desired. Yield: 4 servings (310 calories per serving).

Per Serving: PROTEIN 27.9g FAT 7.8g (Saturated Fat 1.5g)
CARBOHYDRATE 32.0g FIBER 0.9g CHOLESTEROL 76mg
IRON 4.1mg SODIUM 485mg CALCIUM 66mg

CREOLE TURKEY-STUFFED EGGPLANT

2 small eggplants (about ¾ pound each)
Vegetable cooking spray
6 ounces freshly ground raw turkey
½ cup chopped onion
½ cup chopped celery
¼ cup chopped green pepper
2 teaspoons minced garlic
1 cup no-salt-added tomato sauce
2 tablespoons fine, dry breadcrumbs
2 tablespoons frozen egg substitute, thawed
¼ teaspoon dried whole basil
¼ teaspoon dried whole oregano
¼ teaspoon dried whole thyme
¼ teaspoon salt
¼ teaspoon pepper
⅛ teaspoon ground red pepper
1 cup (4 ounces) shredded nonfat Monterey Jack cheese
1 tablespoon freshly grated Parmesan cheese

Prick each eggplant several times with a fork. Place eggplant on a baking sheet, and bake at 350° for 20 minutes. Let cool. Cut each eggplant in half lengthwise; scoop out pulp, leaving ¼-inch-thick shells. Chop pulp; set shells and pulp aside.

Coat a nonstick skillet with cooking spray; place over medium-high heat until hot. Add turkey; cook until browned, stirring until it crumbles. Remove turkey from skillet. Drain; pat dry with paper towels. Wipe drippings from skillet with a paper towel.

Coat skillet with cooking spray. Add onion, celery, green pepper, and garlic; sauté 5 minutes or until tender. Remove from heat; stir in chopped eggplant, turkey, tomato sauce, and next 8 ingredients.

Place eggplant shells in a 13- x 9- x 2-inch baking dish coated with cooking spray. Spoon turkey mixture evenly into shells; cover and bake at 350° for 25 minutes. Sprinkle with cheeses; bake, uncovered, an additional 3 minutes or until mixture is thoroughly heated and cheese melts. Yield: 4 servings (196 calories per serving).

Per Serving: PROTEIN 22.9g FAT 3.0g (Saturated Fat 0.9g)
CARBOHYDRATE 20.9g FIBER 3.2g CHOLESTEROL 31mg
IRON 2.1mg SODIUM 467mg CALCIUM 306mg

TURKEY LASAGNA

Vegetable cooking spray
1 pound freshly ground raw turkey
1½ cups chopped onion
1 teaspoon minced garlic
1 (10-ounce) package frozen chopped spinach, thawed
2 (14½-ounce) cans no-salt-added whole tomatoes, undrained and chopped
2 (6-ounce) cans no-salt-added tomato paste
1 cup water
3 tablespoons chopped fresh basil
1 tablespoon chopped fresh oregano
1 tablespoon minced fresh thyme
½ teaspoon pepper
¼ teaspoon salt
1 (15-ounce) container nonfat ricotta cheese
½ cup frozen egg substitute, thawed
6 lasagna noodles (cooked without salt or fat)
2 cups (8 ounces) shredded nonfat mozzarella cheese, divided
¼ cup freshly grated Parmesan cheese, divided

Coat a large Dutch oven with cooking spray; place over medium-high heat until hot. Add turkey, onion, and garlic; cook until turkey is browned, stirring until it crumbles. Drain turkey mixture, and pat dry with paper towels. Wipe drippings from skillet with a paper towel.

Drain spinach, and press dry between layers of paper towels. Return turkey mixture to skillet. Add spinach, tomato, and next 7 ingredients. Cook over medium heat 15 minutes or until thickened, stirring occasionally. Remove from heat, and set aside.

Combine ricotta cheese and egg substitute in a small bowl; stir well.

Coat a 13- x 9- x 2-inch baking dish with cooking spray. Place 3 lasagna noodles in bottom of dish. Top with half of turkey mixture and half of ricotta cheese mixture. Sprinkle with 1 cup mozzarella cheese and 2 tablespoons Parmesan cheese; repeat layers with remaining noodles, turkey mixture, ricotta cheese mixture, and mozzarella and Parmesan cheeses.

Bake, uncovered, at 325° for 35 to 40 minutes or until thoroughly heated. Let lasagna stand 10 minutes before serving. Yield: 8 servings (317 calories per serving).

Per Serving: PROTEIN 38.0g FAT 3.7g (Saturated Fat 1.4g)
CARBOHYDRATE 36.0g FIBER 4.4g CHOLESTEROL 45mg
IRON 3.8mg SODIUM 471mg CALCIUM 449mg

 DARK POULTRY TALES

Ever wonder why meat on a turkey drumstick is dark yet breast meat is white? Scientists say the color difference is due to a variation in muscle fibers. Slow-to-contract muscle fibers, the kind chickens and turkeys need in their legs in order to run, require fat for fuel. The oxygen a bird needs to burn fat for fuel is stored in myoglobin (red, iron-rich pigment in muscles). Therefore, any muscles that have a high concentration of slow-twitch fibers will naturally be reddish in color.

The wings of chickens and turkeys contain mostly fast-twitch fibers, which are used for quick movements. Their fuel source is stored carbohydrates, or glycogen, which can be broken down without oxygen, making fast-twitch muscle tissue appear white. To confuse matters, the colors are reversed in ducks. The well-exercised wings of the duck are predominantly made up of slow-twitch muscle fibers.

TURKEY SAUSAGE QUICHE IN CRÊPE CUPS

½ cup all-purpose flour
⅓ cup skim milk
¼ cup frozen egg substitute, thawed
1 teaspoon vegetable oil
⅛ teaspoon salt
Vegetable cooking spray
4 ounces smoked turkey sausage, chopped
½ cup chopped green pepper
½ cup chopped onion
1 (8-ounce) carton frozen egg substitute, thawed
½ cup skim milk
2 tablespoons instant nonfat dry milk powder
1 tablespoon all-purpose flour
⅛ teaspoon garlic powder
¾ cup frozen broccoli flowerets, thawed and cut into bite-size pieces
½ cup (2 ounces) shredded reduced-fat sharp Cheddar cheese

Turkey Sausage Quiche in Crêpe Cups holds pleasant surprises for both the eye and the palate.

Combine first 5 ingredients in a medium bowl, stirring with a wire whisk just until no lumps remain. Cover and refrigerate at least 1 hour.

Coat a 7- or 8-inch crêpe pan or skillet with cooking spray; place over medium heat until hot. Pour 3 tablespoons batter into pan, and quickly tilt pan in all directions so batter covers pan in a thin film. Cook 1 minute or until crêpe can be shaken loose from pan. Flip crêpe, and cook about 30 seconds. Remove from pan; place crêpe on a towel to cool. Stack between layers of wax paper to prevent sticking. Repeat until all batter is used.

Coat a large nonstick skillet with cooking spray; place over medium-high heat until hot. Add sausage, green pepper, and onion; sauté 5 to 7 minutes or until green pepper and onion are tender. Remove from heat.

Combine 1 carton egg substitute, ½ cup milk, milk powder, 1 tablespoon flour, and garlic powder in a small bowl; stir until smooth.

Spray 4 (10-ounce) custard cups with cooking spray. Place 1 crêpe in each cup, pressing in center to form a cup. Spoon sausage mixture and broccoli into crêpe shells. Sprinkle with cheese. Pour egg substitute mixture into shells. Place cups on a baking sheet; bake, uncovered, at 400° for 15 minutes. Cover; bake 15 minutes or until a knife inserted in centers comes out clean. Remove from oven; let stand 5 minutes. To remove shells from cups, run a knife around side of each cup, and carefully lift shell out. Yield: 4 servings (268 calories per serving).

Per Serving: PROTEIN 21.3g FAT 8.9g (Saturated Fat 2.9g)
CARBOHYDRATE 24.4g FIBER 1.4g CHOLESTEROL 31mg
IRON 3.2mg SODIUM 579mg CALCIUM 279mg

TURKEY-WILD RICE CASSEROLE

6 ounces wild rice, uncooked
3 cups canned low-sodium chicken broth,
    undiluted
3 cups sliced fresh mushrooms
3 cups chopped cooked turkey breast (skinned
    before cooking and cooked without fat)
⅔ cup commercial oil-free Italian dressing
1 cup low-fat sour cream
Vegetable cooking spray

Rinse wild rice in 3 changes of hot water; drain and set aside. Bring chicken broth to a boil in a medium saucepan; stir in mushrooms. Reduce heat; simmer 5 minutes. Remove mushrooms with a slotted spoon. Add rice to pan; stir well. Cover and cook 1 hour and 5 minutes or until liquid is absorbed.

Combine rice, mushrooms, turkey, dressing, and sour cream; spoon into a 2-quart baking dish coated with cooking spray. Bake, uncovered, at 325° for 45 minutes. Let stand 10 minutes before serving. Yield: 6 servings (298 calories per serving).

Per Serving: PROTEIN 30.6g FAT 6.7g (Saturated Fat 4.0g)
CARBOHYDRATE 28.6g FIBER 1.9g CHOLESTEROL 80mg
IRON 2.7mg SODIUM 382mg CALCIUM 61mg

TURKEY SCALLOPINI

4 (4-ounce) turkey breast cutlets
¼ teaspoon freshly ground pepper
3 tablespoons freshly grated Parmesan cheese
3 tablespoons Italian-seasoned breadcrumbs
Vegetable cooking spray
1½ teaspoons olive oil
¼ cup Chablis or other dry white wine
2 tablespoons fresh lemon juice
2 tablespoons chopped fresh parsley

Place cutlets between 2 sheets of heavy-duty plastic wrap; flatten to ⅛-inch thickness, using a meat mallet or rolling pin. Combine pepper, cheese, and breadcrumbs; dredge cutlets in breadcrumb mixture.

Coat a nonstick skillet with cooking spray; add olive oil. Place over medium-high heat until hot. Add cutlets; cook 2 minutes on each side or until browned.

Add wine and lemon juice; cook 2 minutes or until heated. Transfer to a serving platter; sprinkle with parsley. Yield: 4 servings (178 calories per serving).

Per Serving: PROTEIN 29.0g FAT 5.0g (Saturated Fat 1.7g)
CARBOHYDRATE 2.6g FIBER 0.1g CHOLESTEROL 72mg
IRON 1.6mg SODIUM 214mg CALCIUM 83mg

TURKEY-VEGETABLE TORTILLA DUMPLINGS

1 pound boneless turkey breast, skinned and cut
    into 1-inch-thick slices
2 cups canned low-sodium chicken broth,
    undiluted
½ cup thinly sliced carrot
½ cup chopped onion
½ cup chopped celery
½ teaspoon pepper
¼ teaspoon dried whole rosemary
¼ teaspoon dried whole thyme
¼ teaspoon salt
1 bay leaf
1 tablespoon cornstarch
1 cup skim milk
2 (8-inch) flour tortillas, cut into 1½-inch pieces

Combine first 10 ingredients in a large saucepan; bring to a boil. Reduce heat; simmer, uncovered, over medium heat 45 minutes. Remove turkey with a slotted spoon; keep broth mixture at a simmer. Shred turkey; return turkey to broth mixture.

Combine cornstarch and milk; stir until smooth. Add to broth mixture; cook, stirring constantly, until broth mixture is thickened and bubbly. Reduce heat to low, and add tortilla pieces; simmer, uncovered, 10 minutes. Remove and discard bay leaf. Yield: 4 servings (249 calories per serving).

Per Serving: PROTEIN 29.9g FAT 3.9g (Saturated Fat 1.2g)
CARBOHYDRATE 23.3g FIBER 1.8g CHOLESTEROL 64mg
IRON 2.7mg SODIUM 306mg CALCIUM 124mg

Tempting portions of beef infuse gusto into fresh, crisp Grilled Sirloin Salad (page 190). One bowlful is certain to satisfy the heartiest of appetites.

Salads
& Salad
Dressings

CITRUS SALAD WITH HONEY-LIME DRESSING

¼ cup lime juice
1 tablespoon plus 1 teaspoon honey
1 tablespoon plus 1 teaspoon reduced-calorie chili sauce
1 tablespoon water
Dash of freshly ground pepper
2 cups torn Bibb lettuce
2 cups torn iceberg lettuce
2 cups torn curly endive
2 medium-size pink grapefruit, peeled and sectioned
2 large oranges, peeled and sectioned
½ small ripe avocado, peeled and cut into 18 thin slices

Combine first 5 ingredients in a small bowl; stir with a wire whisk until blended. Cover and chill.

Combine lettuces and endive; toss well. Place 1 cup lettuce mixture on each individual salad plate. Arrange grapefruit sections, orange sections, and avocado on lettuce; drizzle lime mixture evenly over salads. Yield: 6 servings (95 calories per serving).

Per Serving: PROTEIN 1.8g FAT 2.8g (Saturated Fat 0.4g)
CARBOHYDRATE 18.3g FIBER 3.2g CHOLESTEROL 0mg
IRON 0.5mg SODIUM 9mg CALCIUM 38mg

FRUIT SALAD WITH SWEET YOGURT DRESSING

1 (8-ounce) carton plain nonfat yogurt
1 tablespoon unsweetened orange juice
1 tablespoon honey
2 cups sliced fresh strawberries
2 cups fresh blueberries
½ medium cantaloupe, cut into 12 slices

Combine first 3 ingredients in a small bowl; stir well with a wire whisk. Arrange strawberries, blueberries, and cantaloupe on individual salad plates. Top with yogurt mixture. Serve immediately. Yield: 6 servings (104 calories per serving).

Per Serving: PROTEIN 3.5g FAT 0.7g (Saturated Fat 0.2g)
CARBOHYDRATE 23.3g FIBER 4.7g CHOLESTEROL 1mg
IRON 0.5mg SODIUM 39mg CALCIUM 94mg

YOGURT-TOPPED FRUIT SALAD

1½ cups sliced fresh strawberries
2 small bananas, peeled and sliced
1 medium-size orange, peeled and sectioned
6 green leaf lettuce leaves
¼ cup vanilla low-fat yogurt
1 tablespoon creamy peanut butter
1 tablespoon chopped roasted, salted peanuts

Combine first 3 ingredients in a bowl, and toss gently. Spoon onto lettuce-lined salad plates.

Combine yogurt and peanut butter, stirring well. Spoon over fruit. Sprinkle with peanuts; serve immediately. Yield: 6 servings (89 calories per serving).

Per Serving: PROTEIN 2.6g FAT 3.0g (Saturated Fat 0.6g)
CARBOHYDRATE 14.8g FIBER 3.0g CHOLESTEROL 0mg
IRON 0.4mg SODIUM 40mg CALCIUM 33mg

BLACK-EYED PEA SALAD

2 cups water
2 cups frozen black-eyed peas
1 bay leaf
½ cup diced celery
¼ cup diced sweet red pepper
3 tablespoons minced green onions
2 tablespoons chopped fresh parsley
1½ teaspoons chopped fresh oregano
½ teaspoon minced garlic
¼ cup cider vinegar
2 teaspoons water
1 teaspoon vegetable oil
1 teaspoon hot oriental chili sauce
⅛ teaspoon salt

Bring 2 cups water to a boil in a saucepan; add peas and bay leaf. Cover, reduce heat, and simmer 30 minutes. Drain. Remove and discard bay leaf. Combine peas, celery, and next 5 ingredients in a bowl.

Combine vinegar and remaining ingredients; stir with a wire whisk. Pour over vegetable mixture; toss. Cover and chill at least 2 hours. Yield: 6 servings (84 calories per ½-cup serving).

Per Serving: PROTEIN 5.2g FAT 1.7g (Saturated Fat 0.3g)
CARBOHYDRATE 12.9g FIBER 1.6g CHOLESTEROL 0mg
IRON 1.2mg SODIUM 86mg CALCIUM 30mg

A splash of color adds healthful beta carotene to your greenery in Sweet Potato Salad.

SWEET POTATO SALAD

2 medium-size sweet potatoes (about 1 pound)
1 small green pepper, cut into 1-inch pieces
2 tablespoons chopped green onions
1 tablespoon chopped fresh parsley
¼ cup tarragon vinegar
2 teaspoons honey
1 teaspoon water
1 teaspoon vegetable oil
⅛ teaspoon salt
⅛ teaspoon dried whole oregano
Green leaf lettuce (optional)

Wrap sweet potatoes in aluminum foil; prick several times with a fork. Bake at 400° for 45 minutes or until potatoes are soft. Chill thoroughly. Peel and cube potatoes.

Combine potato, pepper, green onions, and parsley in a bowl; toss gently. Combine vinegar and next 5 ingredients in a jar. Cover tightly, and shake vigorously to blend. Pour vinegar mixture over potato mixture, and toss gently. Cover and chill 3 hours.

Line a serving bowl with leaf lettuce, if desired. Spoon potato mixture into bowl, using a slotted spoon. Yield: 6 servings (91 calories per ½-cup serving).

Per Serving: PROTEIN 1.3g FAT 1.0g (Saturated Fat 0.2g)
CARBOHYDRATE 19.8g FIBER 2.4g CHOLESTEROL 0mg
IRON 0.8mg SODIUM 59mg CALCIUM 19mg

MARINATED BLACK BEAN SALAD

½ pound dried black beans
1 cup chopped tomato
¾ cup diced sweet red pepper
¾ cup diced zucchini
¾ cup peeled, diced jicama
½ cup sliced green onions
¼ cup diced avocado
1 tablespoon chopped fresh chives
1 teaspoon seeded, minced jalapeño pepper
½ teaspoon cumin seeds, toasted
¼ cup water
1 tablespoon fat-free Italian salad dressing mix
3 tablespoons fresh lime juice
3 tablespoons balsamic vinegar
1 teaspoon olive oil

Sort and wash beans; place in a Dutch oven. Cover with water to a depth of 3 inches above beans. Bring to a boil; boil 5 minutes. Remove from heat. Cover and let stand 1 hour. Drain. Return beans to pan. Cover with water to a depth of 3 inches above beans. Bring to a boil; cover, reduce heat, and simmer 1 hour. Drain; rinse with cold water. Drain well.

Combine beans and next 9 ingredients in a bowl; toss gently.

Combine water and remaining ingredients, stirring well with a wire whisk. Pour over bean mixture; toss gently. Cover; marinate in refrigerator at least 8 hours. Yield: 11 servings (100 calories per ½-cup serving).

Per Serving: PROTEIN 5.1g FAT 1.4g (Saturated Fat 0.2g)
CARBOHYDRATE 17.7g FIBER 3.4g CHOLESTEROL 0mg
IRON 1.5mg SODIUM 190mg CALCIUM 34mg

ROASTED RED PEPPER AND ASPARAGUS SALAD

2 medium-size sweet red peppers (about ½ pound)
1½ pounds fresh asparagus spears
3 tablespoons red wine vinegar
1 tablespoon water
1 teaspoon dark sesame oil
½ teaspoon freshly ground pepper
¼ teaspoon sugar
⅛ teaspoon salt
8 Bibb lettuce leaves

Cut peppers in half lengthwise; remove and discard seeds and membrane. Place peppers, skin side up, on a baking sheet; flatten with palm of hand. Broil 5½ inches from heat (with electric oven door partially opened) 15 to 20 minutes or until charred. Place in ice water until cool; peel and discard skins. Cut peppers into ¼-inch-wide strips. Cover and chill.

Snap off tough ends of asparagus. Remove scales from spears with a knife or vegetable peeler, if desired. Arrange asparagus in a vegetable steamer over boiling water. Cover and steam 4 minutes or until crisp-tender. Rinse with cold water. Cover and chill.

Combine vinegar and next 5 ingredients in a jar. Cover tightly, and shake vigorously; chill thoroughly.

Arrange asparagus evenly on individual lettuce-lined salad plates. Arrange pepper strips evenly over asparagus. Drizzle vinegar mixture evenly over salads, and serve immediately. Yield: 8 servings (28 calories per serving).

Per Serving: PROTEIN 1.7g FAT 0.8g (Saturated Fat 0.1g)
CARBOHYDRATE 4.8g FIBER 1.8g CHOLESTEROL 0mg
IRON 0.9mg SODIUM 39mg CALCIUM 16mg

ARUGULA, WATERCRESS, AND ENDIVE SALAD

3 cups torn arugula
3 cups torn watercress
3 cups sliced Belgian endive
¼ cup raspberry vinegar
2 tablespoons water
1 teaspoon vegetable oil
⅛ teaspoon dry mustard
⅛ teaspoon dried whole marjoram
2 cups blood orange segments

Combine arugula, watercress, and endive in a large bowl; toss gently. Cover and chill.

Combine vinegar and next 4 ingredients in a jar. Cover tightly, and shake vigorously; chill thoroughly.

Pour vinegar mixture over arugula mixture, and toss gently. Place 1½ cups greens onto each individual salad plate, and top evenly with orange segments. Yield: 6 servings (50 calories per serving).

Per Serving: PROTEIN 1.8g FAT 1.0g (Saturated Fat 0.2g)
CARBOHYDRATE 10.1g FIBER 4.0g CHOLESTEROL 0mg
IRON 0.8mg SODIUM 13mg CALCIUM 91mg

Baby Greens with Warm Goat Cheese, an appetizing prelude to dinner, adds only 85 calories to the menu.

BABY GREENS WITH WARM GOAT CHEESE

3 tablespoons water
1½ tablespoons sherry vinegar
1 teaspoon walnut oil
¾ teaspoon dry mustard
5 cups mixed baby salad greens
2 tablespoons minced fresh parsley
1 teaspoon minced shallots
2 tablespoons finely chopped walnuts
2 ounces goat cheese, cut into 4 slices
Vegetable cooking spray

Combine first 4 ingredients in a small bowl; stir with a wire whisk until blended. Set aside.

Combine greens, parsley, and shallots in a medium bowl; add vinegar mixture, and toss well. Set aside.

Lightly press chopped walnuts into both sides of each cheese slice. Place cheese slices on a baking sheet coated with cooking spray. Bake at 425° for 3 minutes.

Arrange greens evenly on individual salad plates. Place 1 cheese slice on each salad plate. Serve immediately. Yield: 4 servings (85 calories per serving).

Per Serving: PROTEIN 3.5g FAT 6.5g (Saturated Fat 2.3g)
CARBOHYDRATE 2.6g FIBER 0.9g CHOLESTEROL 13mg
IRON 0.8mg SODIUM 200mg CALCIUM 96mg

TOSSED GREENS WITH STRAWBERRIES

3 tablespoons unsweetened orange juice
2 tablespoons balsamic vinegar
1 teaspoon vegetable oil
2½ cups torn leaf lettuce
2 cups torn Bibb lettuce
1 cup sliced fresh strawberries
2 tablespoons thinly sliced green onions
1 tablespoon plus 1 teaspoon sesame seeds, toasted

Combine first 3 ingredients in a small bowl; stir well.

Combine lettuces, strawberries, green onions, and sesame seeds in a large bowl; toss well. Pour orange juice mixture over lettuce mixture, and toss gently. Serve immediately. Yield: 6 servings (36 calories per 1-cup serving).

Per Serving: PROTEIN 1.1g FAT 2.2g (Saturated Fat 0.3g)
CARBOHYDRATE 3.6g FIBER 1.0g CHOLESTEROL 0mg
IRON 0.5mg SODIUM 4mg CALCIUM 12mg

WATERCRESS, ENDIVE, AND PEAR SALAD

2 tablespoons lemon juice
1 tablespoon water
2 teaspoons minced shallots
1 teaspoon walnut oil
¾ teaspoon pepper
2 cups torn watercress
1¼ cups sliced Belgian endive
1½ cups peeled, sliced Bosc pear
2 tablespoons coarsely chopped walnuts

Combine first 5 ingredients in a small bowl; stir well with a wire whisk.

Combine watercress, endive, pear, and walnuts in a large bowl. Pour lemon juice mixture over lettuce mixture, and toss well. Serve immediately. Yield: 5 servings (64 calories per 1-cup serving).

Per Serving: PROTEIN 1.4g FAT 2.8g (Saturated Fat 0.2g)
CARBOHYDRATE 10.1g FIBER 2.0g CHOLESTEROL 0mg
IRON 0.5mg SODIUM 5mg CALCIUM 30mg

GARDEN RICE SALAD

1 cup long-grain rice, uncooked
½ cup frozen English peas
½ cup chopped cucumber
½ cup chopped sweet red pepper
½ cup chopped celery
¼ cup chopped green onions
¼ cup chopped fresh parsley
3 tablespoons sliced ripe olives
½ cup nonfat sour cream alternative
2 tablespoons fresh lemon juice
1½ teaspoons dried Italian seasoning
¼ teaspoon salt

Cook rice according to package directions, omitting salt and fat. Rinse with cold water; drain.

Arrange peas in a vegetable steamer over boiling water. Cover and steam 2 minutes or until tender. Drain. Combine rice, peas, cucumber, and next 5 ingredients in a medium bowl; toss gently. Cover and chill.

Combine sour cream, lemon juice, Italian seasoning, and salt in a bowl; stir well. Cover and chill.

Just before serving, combine rice mixture and sour cream mixture; toss gently. Yield: 10 servings (92 calories per ½-cup serving).

Per Serving: PROTEIN 2.8g FAT 0.6g (Saturated Fat 0.1g)
CARBOHYDRATE 18.4g FIBER 1.1g CHOLESTEROL 0mg
IRON 1.6mg SODIUM 116mg CALCIUM 26mg

TANGY WILD RICE SALAD

1 cup wild rice, uncooked
¾ cup chopped celery
⅓ cup diced dried apricots
2 tablespoons chopped fresh parsley
2 tablespoons slivered almonds
2 tablespoons chopped purple onion
3 tablespoons sherry wine vinegar
1 tablespoon balsamic vinegar
1 teaspoon vegetable oil
¼ teaspoon salt

Cook wild rice according to package directions, omitting salt and fat; drain. Place in a large bowl;

add celery, apricots, parsley, almonds, and onion, stirring well.

Combine vinegars, oil, and salt in a small bowl, stirring well with a wire whisk. Pour over rice mixture, and toss well. Cover and chill at least 2 hours. Yield: 10 servings (90 calories per ½-cup serving).

Per Serving: PROTEIN 3.0g FAT 1.4g (Saturated Fat 0.2g)
CARBOHYDRATE 16.4g FIBER 1.4g CHOLESTEROL 0mg
IRON 0.7mg SODIUM 100mg CALCIUM 16mg

TRI-PASTA SALAD WITH HERBED VINAIGRETTE

3 ounces ziti pasta, uncooked
3 ounces bowtie pasta, uncooked
3 ounces spinach rotini pasta, uncooked
½ cup chopped green pepper
½ cup chopped sweet red pepper
½ cup chopped sweet yellow pepper
½ cup chopped celery
¼ cup chopped carrot
¼ cup sliced pimiento-stuffed olives
2 teaspoons capers
½ cup red wine vinegar
¼ cup water
1 tablespoon chopped fresh basil
1 tablespoon chopped fresh chives
1 tablespoon chopped fresh oregano
1 tablespoon Dijon mustard
2 cloves garlic, minced
1 teaspoon chopped fresh thyme
1 teaspoon olive oil
¼ teaspoon pepper

Cook pastas according to package directions, omitting salt and fat. Drain; rinse under cold water, and drain. Place in a large bowl. Add green pepper and next 6 ingredients; toss well.

Combine vinegar and remaining ingredients in a jar; cover tightly, and shake vigorously. Pour over pasta mixture; toss well. Cover and chill thoroughly. Toss gently before serving. Yield: 8 servings (141 calories per 1-cup serving).

Per Serving: PROTEIN 4.5g FAT 1.6g (Saturated Fat 0.2g)
CARBOHYDRATE 26.9g FIBER 1.5g CHOLESTEROL 0mg
IRON 1.8mg SODIUM 227mg CALCIUM 20mg

ORZO SALAD

1 cup orzo, uncooked
1 (7-ounce) jar sun-dried tomatoes in olive oil
½ cup chopped sweet red pepper
¼ cup chopped green onions
1 (4-ounce) can sliced ripe olives, drained
3 tablespoons chopped fresh parsley
¼ cup red wine vinegar
¼ teaspoon dry mustard

Cook orzo according to package directions, omitting salt and fat; drain.

Drain tomatoes, reserving 1 teaspoon oil. Chop 2 tablespoons tomato. Reserve remaining tomatoes for another use. Combine orzo, tomato, red pepper, and next 3 ingredients in a bowl; toss gently.

Combine reserved 1 teaspoon oil, vinegar, and mustard; stir well with a wire whisk. Pour over orzo mixture; toss gently. Cover and chill at least 2 hours. Yield: 8 servings (116 calories per ½-cup serving).

Per Serving: PROTEIN 3.9g FAT 1.5g (Saturated Fat 0.3g)
CARBOHYDRATE 22.0g FIBER 1.7g CHOLESTEROL 0mg
IRON 1.4mg SODIUM 154mg CALCIUM 19mg

 CHILDREN AND VEGETABLES DO MIX
The National Institutes of Health and the National Cancer Institute recommend that all Americans eat at least five servings of fruits and vegetables daily. That's not so easy for parents to enforce when a child has an aversion to vegetables. Here are ways to serve more greens with fewer groans:
• Provide vegetables the child likes on a regular basis. Most children will eat carrots, peas, and green beans.
• Tuck finely chopped cooked vegetables in a food the child likes. Chopped spinach, slivered cabbage, carrots, green beans, or broccoli can be added to burritos, tacos, chili, sloppy joes, lasagna, or pizza.
• Increase the nutritional value of salads your child likes by adding fresh spinach, tomato, or kidney or garbanzo beans.
• Puree cooked vegetables in a blender and stir them into soups or use them as a sauce.
• Make sure you eat plenty of vegetables. This is most important because children learn more by example than by explanation.

GRILLED SIRLOIN SALAD

½ cup red wine vinegar
2 tablespoons olive oil
1 tablespoon Dijon mustard
2 teaspoons dried whole basil
1 teaspoon sugar
1 teaspoon dried whole oregano
¼ teaspoon garlic powder
¼ teaspoon pepper
1 (¾-pound) lean boneless beef sirloin steak
Vegetable cooking spray
1 medium-size yellow squash, cut in half
   lengthwise
1 medium zucchini, cut in half lengthwise
1 medium-size sweet red pepper, cut in half
   lengthwise and seeded
1 (10-ounce) package frozen artichoke hearts,
   thawed
3 cups torn leaf lettuce
2 cups torn romaine lettuce
1 cup coarsely chopped plum tomato
¼ cup chopped onion
1½ tablespoons freshly grated Parmesan cheese

Combine first 8 ingredients in a small bowl; stir well. Place steak in a heavy-duty, zip-top plastic bag; add half of vinegar mixture, reserving remaining mixture. Seal bag, and shake until steak is well coated. Marinate in refrigerator at least 4 hours, turning bag occasionally.

Remove steak from marinade, discarding marinade. Coat grill rack with cooking spray; place on grill over medium-hot coals (350° to 400°). Place steak, squash, zucchini, and red pepper on rack. Brush vegetables with 1 tablespoon reserved vinegar mixture. Grill, covered, over medium-hot coals 12 to 14 minutes or until vegetables are tender and steak is to desired degree of doneness, turning occasionally. Remove from grill.

Thread artichoke hearts on 3 (10-inch) skewers. Place skewers on rack, and brush artichoke hearts lightly with vinegar mixture. Grill, covered, 3 minutes on each side or until tender. Remove artichoke hearts from grill, and let cool slightly.

Cut steak in half lengthwise. Cut each half into ¼-inch-wide strips. Cut squash, zucchini, and red pepper into 1-inch pieces. Remove artichoke hearts from skewers.

Combine lettuces, tomato, and onion in a large bowl; toss gently.

Add steak and vegetables; toss well. Drizzle with remaining vinegar mixture, and toss well. Sprinkle with Parmesan cheese. Serve immediately. Yield: 7 servings (142 calories per 1½-cup serving).

Per Serving: PROTEIN 13.8g FAT 6.1g (Saturated Fat 1.9g)
CARBOHYDRATE 9.4g FIBER 2.1g CHOLESTEROL 33mg
IRON 2.5mg SODIUM 105mg CALCIUM 57mg

GRILLED FIESTA SALAD

3 (4-ounce) skinned, boned chicken breast halves
¼ cup plus 1 tablespoon lime juice, divided
Vegetable cooking spray
1 teaspoon olive oil
3 tablespoons chopped green onions
1 cup seeded, chopped yellow tomato
1 cup chopped sweet red pepper
2 tablespoons seeded, chopped jalapeño pepper
2 tablespoons water
2 teaspoons honey
2 cups loosely packed shredded red leaf lettuce
1 cup loosely packed shredded iceberg lettuce
1 cup loosely packed shredded Boston lettuce
1 (14½-ounce) can black beans, drained
¼ cup nonfat sour cream alternative
Fresh cilantro sprigs (optional)
Jalapeño pepper slices (optional)

Place chicken in a heavy-duty, zip-top plastic bag; add 2 tablespoons lime juice. Seal bag, and shake until chicken is coated. Marinate in refrigerator 2 hours, turning bag occasionally.

Coat a large nonstick skillet with cooking spray; add olive oil. Place over medium-high heat until hot. Add green onions, and sauté 1 minute. Add tomato and chopped peppers; sauté 2 minutes. Add remaining 3 tablespoons lime juice, water, and honey; cook over medium heat until thoroughly heated. Remove from heat. Set aside, and keep warm.

Remove chicken from marinade; discard marinade. Coat grill rack with cooking spray; place on grill over medium-hot coals (350° to 400°). Place chicken on rack; grill, covered, 5 to 6 minutes on each side or until chicken is done. Cut chicken into thin slices. Set aside, and keep warm.

Combine lettuces in a bowl; toss well. Place 1 cup lettuce mixture on each individual salad plate. Top with black beans. Arrange chicken evenly over beans. Spoon tomato mixture over chicken; top each serving with 1 tablespoon sour cream. If desired, garnish with cilantro sprigs and jalapeño pepper slices. Yield: 4 servings (249 calories per serving).

Per Serving: PROTEIN 27.5g FAT 4.6g (Saturated Fat 0.9g)
CARBOHYDRATE 25.2g FIBER 4.5g CHOLESTEROL 54mg
IRON 3.2mg SODIUM 223mg CALCIUM 58mg

BASIL CHICKEN SALAD

¼ cup plus 2 tablespoons nonfat mayonnaise
2 tablespoons fresh lemon juice
2 teaspoons Dijon mustard
¼ teaspoon hot sauce
⅛ teaspoon white pepper
3 cups chopped cooked chicken breast (skinned before cooking and cooked without salt)
½ cup chopped celery
¼ cup chopped green onions
¼ cup shredded fresh basil
6 cups shredded fresh spinach
1½ tablespoons pine nuts, toasted
Lemon wedges (optional)

Combine first 5 ingredients; stir well. Combine chicken, celery, green onions, and basil in a medium bowl. Add mayonnaise mixture, and toss gently.

Place 1 cup spinach on each individual salad plate. Spoon chicken mixture over spinach. Sprinkle each serving with pine nuts. Garnish with lemon wedges, if desired. Yield: 6 servings (159 calories per serving).

Per Serving: PROTEIN 24.3g FAT 4.1g (Saturated Fat 1.0g)
CARBOHYDRATE 5.6g FIBER 1.4g CHOLESTEROL 62mg
IRON 1.8mg SODIUM 329mg CALCIUM 49mg

POACHED SALMON SALAD

1 (12-ounce) salmon fillet
Vegetable cooking spray
½ cup water
1 teaspoon chicken-flavored bouillon granules
¼ cup plus 2 tablespoons nonfat sour cream alternative
1 tablespoon water
1 tablespoon fresh lemon juice
2 teaspoons minced fresh dillweed
1 teaspoon Dijon mustard
¼ teaspoon sugar
4 cups torn romaine lettuce
16 (⅛-inch-thick) slices cucumber
1 large tomato, cut into 12 wedges
1 hard-cooked egg, cut into 4 wedges
4 green Greek olives
¼ cup chopped onion
2 teaspoons capers

Place fillet in a large nonstick skillet coated with cooking spray. Combine ½ cup water and bouillon granules; pour over fillet. Bring to a boil; cover, reduce heat, and simmer 8 minutes or until fish flakes easily when tested with a fork. Remove fillet from liquid, discarding liquid. Cover fillet, and chill.

Combine sour cream and next 5 ingredients in a small bowl; stir well. Cover and chill thoroughly.

Remove and discard skin from fillet; cut fillet into 4 equal pieces.

Place 1 cup romaine lettuce on each individual salad plate. Top each with 1 piece of salmon. Arrange 4 cucumber slices, 3 tomato wedges, 1 egg wedge, and 1 olive around each piece of salmon. Sprinkle evenly with chopped onion and capers. Serve with sour cream mixture. Yield: 4 servings (224 calories per serving).

Per Serving: PROTEIN 24.3g FAT 9.9g (Saturated Fat 1.9g)
CARBOHYDRATE 8.4g FIBER 2.1g CHOLESTEROL 115mg
IRON 1.8mg SODIUM 370mg CALCIUM 51mg

Take a break from the ordinary with Grilled Tuna Niçoise. A tangy potpourri of vegetables provides the foundation for savory grilled tuna steaks.

GRILLED TUNA NIÇOISE

¼ cup red wine vinegar
1½ tablespoons water
1 tablespoon Dijon mustard
2 teaspoons olive oil, divided
¾ pound fresh green beans
6 small round red potatoes
1 cup thinly sliced sweet red pepper
½ cup thinly sliced purple onion
¼ cup chopped fresh parsley
2 (8-ounce) tuna steaks
Vegetable cooking spray
6 cups torn fresh spinach
1½ cups yellow teardrop tomatoes, cut in half
2 hard-cooked eggs, sliced
6 Niçoise olives

Combine vinegar, water, mustard, and 1 teaspoon olive oil in a small jar. Cover tightly, and shake vigorously to blend.

Wash beans; trim ends, and remove strings. Arrange beans in a vegetable steamer over boiling water. Cover and steam 6 to 8 minutes or until crisp-tender. Drain; let cool slightly, and cut in half.

Wash potatoes; arrange in a vegetable steamer over boiling water. Cover and steam 10 to 12 minutes or until tender. Drain. Let cool; cut into quarters.

Combine green beans, potato, red pepper, onion, and parsley; toss gently. Add vinegar mixture; toss gently. Cover and chill 2 hours.

Brush tuna with remaining 1 teaspoon olive oil. Coat grill rack with cooking spray; place on grill over hot coals (400° to 500°). Place tuna on rack; grill, covered, 5 minutes on each side or until fish flakes easily when tested with a fork. Remove from grill; cut into ¼-inch-thick slices. Set aside; keep warm.

Place 1 cup spinach on each chilled salad plate; top evenly with green bean mixture. Arrange tuna, tomato, egg, and olives evenly over green bean mixture. Yield: 6 servings (224 calories per serving).

Per Serving: PROTEIN 23.0g FAT 7.7g (Saturated Fat 1.8g)
CARBOHYDRATE 16.4g FIBER 4.2g CHOLESTEROL 100mg
IRON 3.5mg SODIUM 171mg CALCIUM 71mg

GARLIC VINAIGRETTE

½ cup cider vinegar
¼ cup water
1 tablespoon reduced-calorie chili sauce
2 teaspoons olive oil
1½ teaspoons prepared horseradish
1 teaspoon prepared mustard
½ teaspoon freshly ground pepper
¼ teaspoon sugar
3 cloves garlic, halved

Combine first 8 ingredients in a small jar; cover tightly, and shake vigorously to blend. Add garlic. Cover and chill at least 2 hours. Remove and discard garlic before serving. Serve with salad greens. Yield: 1 cup (8 calories per tablespoon).

Per Tablespoon: PROTEIN 0.1g FAT 0.6g (Saturated Fat 0.1g)
CARBOHYDRATE 1.0g FIBER 0g CHOLESTEROL 0mg
IRON 0.1mg SODIUM 5mg CALCIUM 2mg

TRIPLE MUSTARD VINAIGRETTE

1½ teaspoons vegetable-flavored bouillon
  granules
1 cup water
1½ teaspoons cornstarch
¼ cup white wine vinegar
¼ cup cider vinegar
1 tablespoon minced fresh basil
1 tablespoon minced fresh chives
2 teaspoons mustard seeds
1 teaspoon dry mustard
1½ teaspoons hot mustard
1 teaspoon olive oil
½ teaspoon cracked black pepper

Combine bouillon granules and water; stir well. Combine cornstarch and ¼ cup bouillon mixture in a small saucepan; stir until smooth. Add remaining bouillon mixture, and bring to a boil. Cook 1 minute, stirring constantly with a wire whisk, until mixture is slightly thickened. Remove from heat, and let cool completely.

Stir in white wine vinegar and remaining ingredients. Cover and chill thoroughly. Serve vinegar mixture with bitter salad greens. Yield: 1¼ cups plus 2 tablespoons (7 calories per tablespoon).

Per Tablespoon: PROTEIN 0.2g FAT 0.4g (Saturated Fat 0g)
CARBOHYDRATE 0.7g FIBER 0g CHOLESTEROL 0mg
IRON 0.1mg SODIUM 62mg CALCIUM 3mg

DIJON-HERB VINAIGRETTE

⅓ cup white wine vinegar
¼ cup plus 1 tablespoon water
2 tablespoons chopped fresh chives
1½ tablespoons minced shallot
1 tablespoon minced fresh dillweed
1 tablespoon Dijon mustard
1 teaspoon minced fresh oregano
1 teaspoon minced fresh thyme
2 teaspoons olive oil
¼ teaspoon sugar

Combine all ingredients in a small jar; cover tightly, and shake vigorously to blend. Chill thoroughly. Serve with salad greens. Yield: ¾ cup (11 calories per tablespoon).

Per Tablespoon: PROTEIN 0.1g FAT 0.8g (Saturated Fat 0.1g)
CARBOHYDRATE 0.6g FIBER 0g CHOLESTEROL 0mg
IRON 0.1mg SODIUM 38mg CALCIUM 3mg

RASPBERRY VINAIGRETTE

¼ cup fresh orange juice
2 tablespoons plus 1 teaspoon water
2 tablespoons red wine vinegar
2 tablespoons raspberry vinegar
1½ tablespoons minced fresh chives
2 teaspoons olive oil
½ teaspoon dried whole dillweed
¼ teaspoon pepper

Combine all ingredients in a small jar; cover tightly, and shake vigorously to blend. Chill thoroughly. Serve vinegar mixture with salad greens. Yield: ¾ cup (10 calories per tablespoon).

Per Tablespoon: PROTEIN 0.1g FAT 0.8g (Saturated Fat 0.1g)
CARBOHYDRATE 0.9g FIBER 0g CHOLESTEROL 0mg
IRON 0.1mg SODIUM 0mg CALCIUM 2mg

SALSA VINAIGRETTE

⅓ cup water
3 tablespoons balsamic vinegar
3 tablespoons white wine vinegar
1 teaspoon sugar
1 teaspoon freshly ground pepper
2 cups peeled, seeded, and finely chopped tomato
½ cup chopped green onions
¼ cup chopped fresh flat-leaf parsley
¼ cup chopped fresh basil
1 teaspoon minced garlic

Combine first 5 ingredients in a medium bowl, stirring well with a wire whisk. Stir in tomato and remaining ingredients. Cover and chill thoroughly. Serve with beef, chicken, or Mexican salad. Yield: 3 cups (3 calories per tablespoon).

Per Tablespoon: PROTEIN 0.1g FAT 0.0g (Saturated Fat 0g) CARBOHYDRATE 0.7g FIBER 0.2g CHOLESTEROL 0mg IRON 0.1mg SODIUM 1mg CALCIUM 2mg

FRESH HERB DRESSING

½ cup tarragon vinegar
¼ cup chopped fresh parsley
3½ tablespoons water
2 tablespoons chopped fresh chives
1 teaspoon sugar
1 teaspoon chopped fresh tarragon
2 teaspoons olive oil
½ teaspoon freshly ground pepper

Combine all ingredients in a small jar; cover tightly, and shake vigorously to blend. Chill thoroughly. Serve with salad greens. Yield: ¾ cup (9 calories per tablespoon).

Per Tablespoon: PROTEIN 0.1g FAT 0.8g (Saturated Fat 0.1g) CARBOHYDRATE 0.6g FIBER 0.1g CHOLESTEROL 0mg IRON 0.2mg SODIUM 1mg CALCIUM 3mg

SPICY COCKTAIL DRESSING

1 (8-ounce) carton nonfat sour cream alternative
¼ cup reduced-calorie chili sauce
1 tablespoon prepared horseradish
¼ teaspoon dry mustard
¼ teaspoon dried whole dillweed

Combine all ingredients in a small bowl; stir well. Cover and chill thoroughly. Serve with seafood salads. Yield: 1 cup plus 2 tablespoons (11 calories per tablespoon).

Per Tablespoon: PROTEIN 0.9g FAT 0.0g (Saturated Fat 0g) CARBOHYDRATE 1.5g FIBER 0g CHOLESTEROL 0mg IRON 0mg SODIUM 12mg CALCIUM 1mg

TOASTED SESAME SEED DRESSING

¼ cup rice wine vinegar
¼ cup water
2 tablespoons low-sodium soy sauce
1 teaspoon sugar
2 teaspoons dark sesame oil
½ teaspoon dry mustard
½ teaspoon crushed red pepper
¼ teaspoon freshly ground pepper
2 tablespoons sesame seeds, toasted
2 tablespoons minced green onions

Combine first 8 ingredients in a small bowl, stirring well with a wire whisk. Stir in sesame seeds and green onions. Cover and chill thoroughly. Serve with salad greens. Yield: ¾ cup plus 2 tablespoons (18 calories per tablespoon).

Per Tablespoon: PROTEIN 0.4g FAT 1.5g (Saturated Fat 0.2g) CARBOHYDRATE 0.6g FIBER 0.1g CHOLESTEROL 0mg IRON 0.2mg SODIUM 57mg CALCIUM 3mg

An excellent partner for easy Toasted Spinach Sandwiches (page 197) is Curried Sweet Potato Strips (page 218) instead of regular fries.

Sandwiches
&
Snacks

SCRAMBLED BREAKFAST SANDWICHES

Vegetable cooking spray
½ cup chopped sweet red pepper
2 tablespoons sliced green onions
1 cup frozen egg substitute, thawed
2 tablespoons grated Parmesan cheese
2 tablespoons skim milk
¼ teaspoon dried Italian seasoning
⅛ teaspoon ground white pepper
8 (¾-ounce) slices Canadian bacon
4 whole wheat English muffins, split and toasted
2 ounces reduced-fat Brie cheese, cubed

Coat a medium nonstick skillet with cooking spray; place over medium-high heat until hot. Add sweet red pepper and green onions; sauté until tender.

Combine egg substitute and next 4 ingredients; beat well with a wire whisk. Pour over pepper mixture in skillet; cook over medium heat until egg substitute mixture is firm but still moist, stirring occasionally.

Place 1 slice of Canadian bacon on each muffin half. Spoon egg substitute mixture evenly over bacon, and top with cheese. Broil 5½ inches from heat (with electric oven door partially opened) 1 minute or until cheese melts. Serve immediately. Yield: 8 servings (163 calories per serving).

Per Serving: PROTEIN 12.3g FAT 3.7g (Saturated Fat 1.7g) CARBOHYDRATE 19.3g FIBER 0.7g CHOLESTEROL 18mg IRON 1.9mg SODIUM 575mg CALCIUM 103mg

GRILLED BLUE CHEESE SANDWICHES

1 cup 1% low-fat cottage cheese
¼ cup torn fresh watercress
¼ cup crumbled blue cheese
2 tablespoons finely chopped walnuts
1 tablespoon nonfat mayonnaise
1 teaspoon low-sodium Worcestershire sauce
2 drops of hot sauce
10 (¾-ounce) slices reduced-calorie whole wheat bread
5 tomato slices (¼ inch thick)
Butter-flavored vegetable cooking spray

Place cottage cheese in container of an electric blender or food processor; cover and process on high speed 30 seconds or until smooth, stopping once to scrape down sides. Transfer to a small bowl. Stir in watercress and next 5 ingredients. Spread cheese mixture evenly over 5 slices of bread, and place tomato slices over cheese mixture. Top with remaining 5 bread slices.

Transfer sandwiches to a sandwich press or hot griddle coated with cooking spray. Cook until bread is lightly browned and cheese melts. Yield: 5 servings (160 calories per serving).

Per Serving: PROTEIN 11.8g FAT 4.0g (Saturated Fat 1.5g) CARBOHYDRATE 21.8g FIBER 4.6g CHOLESTEROL 6mg IRON 0.3mg SODIUM 538mg CALCIUM 62mg

FANCY PEANUT BUTTER AND BANANA SANDWICHES

¼ cup crunchy peanut butter
¼ cup vanilla low-fat yogurt
1 tablespoon honey
2 teaspoons minced crystallized ginger
8 (1-ounce) slices cinnamon-raisin bread
⅓ cup skim milk
1 medium banana, peeled and sliced
1 egg white
Vegetable cooking spray

Combine first 4 ingredients in a small bowl; stir well. Spread 2 tablespoons peanut butter mixture over each of 4 bread slices; top with remaining 4 bread slices. Set aside.

Combine milk, banana, and egg white in container of an electric blender; cover and process on high speed 1 minute or until smooth, stopping once to scrape down sides. Pour into a shallow bowl. Carefully dip sandwiches into milk mixture, and allow excess to drip off.

Place sandwiches on a baking sheet coated with cooking spray. Bake at 425° for 14 minutes; turn sandwiches, and bake an additional 5 minutes or until golden. Serve immediately. Yield: 4 servings (313 calories per serving).

Per Serving: PROTEIN 10.7g FAT 10.0g (Saturated Fat 2.1g) CARBOHYDRATE 47.6g FIBER 3.1g CHOLESTEROL 4mg IRON 1.5mg SODIUM 317mg CALCIUM 101mg

TOASTED SPINACH SANDWICHES

1 (10-ounce) package frozen chopped spinach,
   thawed and drained
½ cup finely chopped celery
¼ cup minced green onions
¼ cup commercial spoonable nonfat salad dressing
¼ cup plain nonfat yogurt
½ teaspoon hot sauce
½ teaspoon fennel seeds, crushed
½ teaspoon garlic powder
8 (¾-ounce) slices reduced-calorie white bread
¼ cup (1 ounce) finely shredded reduced-fat
   Havarti cheese
Butter-flavored vegetable cooking spray

Press spinach between paper towels until barely
moist. Combine spinach and next 7 ingredients in
a medium bowl; stir well.

Spread spinach mixture evenly over 4 slices of
bread; sprinkle evenly with cheese, and top with
remaining 4 bread slices.

Transfer sandwiches to a sandwich press or hot
griddle coated with cooking spray. Cook until bread
is lightly browned and cheese melts. Serve immediately. Yield: 4 servings (155 calories per serving).

Per Serving: PROTEIN 8.9g FAT 2.3g (Saturated Fat 1.1g)
CARBOHYDRATE 28.4g FIBER 6.7g CHOLESTEROL 5mg
IRON 1.7mg SODIUM 561mg CALCIUM 120mg

TRACKING HIDDEN FATS

Although surveys show that many Americans are reducing their consumption of
high-fat meats, the amount of fat coming from other
foods is negating the possible health benefits. Often
these other sources of fat are "hidden." Even when
combination dishes such as pizza and pasta contain
lots of vegetables, large amounts of high-fat cheese,
cream, and meat can contribute more fat to the diet
than many people realize.

Other foods that contain hidden fat include bakery
items such as sweet rolls, cakes, and cookies as well
as whole milk dairy products, particularly cheese.
Limiting the fat from these not-always-obvious
sources can make a major difference in reducing fat
intake to recommended levels.

TOMATO-ZUCCHINI TRIANGLES

Butter-flavored vegetable cooking spray
1 cup diced zucchini
1 cup peeled, seeded, and chopped plum tomato
½ cup chopped onion
1 clove garlic, minced
½ cup nonfat ricotta cheese
¼ cup frozen egg substitute, thawed
3 tablespoons grated Parmesan cheese
2 teaspoons minced fresh oregano
¼ teaspoon cracked pepper
6 sheets commercial frozen phyllo pastry,
   thawed
2 teaspoons reduced-calorie margarine,
   melted

Coat a large skillet with cooking spray; place over
medium-high heat until hot. Add zucchini, tomato,
onion, and garlic; sauté 5 minutes or until liquid
evaporates. Remove from heat; drain well, and press
between paper towels to remove excess moisture.

Combine ricotta cheese and next 4 ingredients in
a medium bowl; stir well. Add vegetable mixture,
stirring well.

Place 1 sheet of phyllo on a damp towel (keep
remaining phyllo covered). Lightly coat phyllo with
cooking spray. Fold phyllo in half crosswise. Lightly
brush with margarine; fold in half lengthwise to
make a strip about 3½ inches wide. Place one-sixth
of zucchini mixture at base of phyllo strip; fold
a bottom corner over filling, making a triangle. Continue folding back and forth into a triangle to end
of strip.

Place triangle, seam side down, on a baking sheet
coated with cooking spray. Lightly brush top with
margarine. Repeat procedure with remaining phyllo,
margarine, and zucchini mixture. Bake at 400° for
15 minutes or until golden. Let triangles cool 5 minutes on wire racks, and serve warm. Yield: 6 servings (119 calories per serving).

Per Serving: PROTEIN 7.8g FAT 2.2g (Saturated Fat 0.8g)
CARBOHYDRATE 18.5g FIBER 0.8g CHOLESTEROL 4mg
IRON 1.1mg SODIUM 89mg CALCIUM 83mg

Perk up a plain roast beef sandwich with sliced beets and the piquant flavors of horseradish, sour cream, and applesauce in Open-Faced Beef Sandwiches.

OPEN-FACED BEEF SANDWICHES

½ cup nonfat sour cream

¼ cup unsweetened applesauce

2 tablespoons prepared horseradish

½ teaspoon cracked pepper

4 (¾-ounce) slices reduced-calorie whole wheat
   bread

1 cup shredded fresh spinach

1 cup canned sliced beets, drained

½ pound thinly sliced cooked roast beef

2 tablespoons minced fresh chives

Combine first 4 ingredients in a small bowl; stir well. Spread 1 tablespoon sour cream mixture over each slice of bread; top each with ¼ cup spinach and ¼ cup beets. Arrange roast beef evenly over beets; sprinkle with chives. Spoon 2 tablespoons sour cream mixture over each sandwich. Yield: 4 servings (175 calories per serving).

Per Serving: PROTEIN 15.9g FAT 5.9g (Saturated Fat 1.8g)
CARBOHYDRATE 15.7g FIBER 3.7g CHOLESTEROL 66mg
IRON 2.8mg SODIUM 595mg CALCIUM 47mg

CATFISH PO-BOYS

Vegetable cooking spray
¼ cup chopped onion
2 tablespoons chopped green pepper
2 tablespoons chopped celery
½ cup seeded, chopped tomato
2 tablespoons minced fresh parsley
½ teaspoon garlic powder
¼ cup plus 1 tablespoon plain nonfat yogurt
3 tablespoons nonfat mayonnaise
¼ teaspoon hot sauce
½ cup crushed corn flakes cereal
¾ teaspoon salt-free lemon-pepper seasoning
¾ teaspoon paprika
¾ pound farm-raised catfish fillets, cut into 1-inch pieces
1 egg white, lightly beaten
1 cup shredded iceberg lettuce
4 reduced-calorie whole wheat buns

Coat a large nonstick skillet with cooking spray; place over medium-high heat until hot. Add onion, green pepper, and celery; sauté until tender. Stir in tomato, parsley, and garlic powder. Transfer mixture to a bowl; let cool slightly. Stir in yogurt, mayonnaise, and hot sauce. Cover and chill thoroughly.

Combine cereal, lemon-pepper seasoning, and paprika. Dip fish pieces in egg white; dredge in cereal mixture. Place on a baking sheet coated with cooking spray. Bake at 500° for 4 minutes. Turn fish, and bake 4 minutes or until crisp and golden.

Place ¼ cup lettuce on bottom half of each bun. Top with fish pieces. Spoon yogurt mixture over fish. Place tops of buns over yogurt mixture. Serve immediately. Yield: 4 servings (256 calories per serving).

Per Serving: PROTEIN 20.9g FAT 5.1g (Saturated Fat 0.9g)
CARBOHYDRATE 30.2g FIBER 2.8g CHOLESTEROL 50mg
IRON 2.7mg SODIUM 563mg CALCIUM 86mg

BROILED CHICKEN SANDWICHES

1 (8-ounce) container plain nonfat yogurt
2 tablespoons lemon juice
1 tablespoon Dijon mustard
1 teaspoon dried tarragon
¼ teaspoon garlic powder
4 (4-ounce) skinned, boned chicken breast halves
8 canned medium-size mild Greek peppers
Vegetable cooking spray
4 green leaf lettuce leaves
4 reduced-calorie whole wheat hamburger buns, split
4 tomato slices (¼ inch thick)

Combine first 5 ingredients in a heavy-duty, zip-top plastic bag. Add chicken. Seal bag; marinate in refrigerator 8 hours, turning bag occasionally.

Remove stems from peppers; discard stems. Cut peppers into ¼-inch slices; set aside.

Remove chicken from marinade, discarding marinade. Place chicken on rack of a broiler pan coated with cooking spray. Broil chicken 5½ inches from heat (with electric oven door partially opened) 6 to 7 minutes on each side or until chicken is done.

Place lettuce leaves on bottom halves of buns. Place chicken breasts on lettuce, and top each with 1 tomato slice. Arrange pepper slices evenly over tomato. Top with remaining bun halves. Yield: 4 servings (240 calories per serving).

Per Serving: PROTEIN 29.6g FAT 4.4g (Saturated Fat 0.9g)
CARBOHYDRATE 18.0g FIBER 2.1g CHOLESTEROL 73mg
IRON 2.0mg SODIUM 532mg CALCIUM 50mg

Pork and Slaw Sandwiches unite traditional dinner partners inside a nutritious whole wheat bun.

PORK AND SLAW SANDWICHES

1 pound lean ground pork
½ cup chopped onion
1 (8-ounce) can no-salt-added tomato sauce
1 tablespoon brown sugar
1 tablespoon low-sodium Worcestershire sauce
1 teaspoon dry mustard
1 teaspoon liquid smoke
½ teaspoon pepper
1½ cups finely shredded red cabbage
½ cup finely chopped Granny Smith apple
½ cup finely shredded carrot
½ cup pineapple low-fat yogurt
¾ teaspoon curry powder
½ teaspoon dry mustard
6 reduced-calorie whole wheat hamburger buns,
    split

Cook pork and onion in a nonstick skillet over medium heat until pork is browned, stirring until it crumbles. Drain and pat dry with paper towels. Wipe drippings from skillet with a paper towel.

Return pork mixture to skillet; add tomato sauce and next 5 ingredients. Bring to a boil; cover, reduce heat and simmer 15 minutes, stirring occasionally. Set aside, and keep warm.

Combine cabbage and next 5 ingredients in a bowl; stir well. Spoon pork mixture evenly onto bottom halves of buns; top evenly with cabbage mixture. Top with remaining bun halves. Serve immediately. Yield: 6 servings (289 calories per serving).

Per Serving: PROTEIN 19.7g   FAT 10.3g   (Saturated Fat 3.7g)
CARBOHYDRATE 28.4g   FIBER 2.7g   CHOLESTEROL 55mg
IRON 1.5mg   SODIUM 296mg   CALCIUM 53mg

LEMON-BASIL TUNA POCKETS

2 (6⅛-ounce) cans 60% less-salt tuna packed in
    spring water, drained
½ cup chopped celery
¼ cup sliced green onions
2 tablespoons chopped fresh basil
2 tablespoons commercial oil-free Italian dressing
2 tablespoons lemon juice
1 tablespoon water
¼ teaspoon salt-free lemon-pepper seasoning
1 clove garlic, minced
6 green leaf lettuce leaves
6 tomato slices (¼ inch thick)
3 (6-inch) whole wheat pita bread rounds, cut in
    half crosswise

Combine first 3 ingredients in a bowl; stir well.
Combine basil and next 5 ingredients; stir well. Pour
over tuna mixture; stir well. Cover and refrigerate
at least 1 hour.

Just before serving, place 1 lettuce leaf and 1
tomato slice in each pita half; spoon tuna mixture
into pitas. Yield: 6 servings (141 calories per serving).

Per Serving: PROTEIN 14.0g   FAT 1.1g   (Saturated Fat 0.2g)
CARBOHYDRATE 17.0g   FIBER 3.2g   CHOLESTEROL 14mg
IRON 1.9mg   SODIUM 200mg   CALCIUM 42mg

DELUXE TURKEY SANDWICHES

½ pound fresh asparagus
3 ounces Neufchâtel cheese, softened
1 tablespoon raspberry vinegar
16 (¾-ounce) slices reduced-calorie oatmeal bread
16 (1-ounce) slices turkey breast
8 (1-ounce) slices nonfat Monterey Jack cheese
Vegetable cooking spray

Snap off tough ends of asparagus. Remove scales
from stalks with a knife or vegetable peeler, if desired. Cut asparagus into 2-inch pieces; arrange in
a vegetable steamer over boiling water. Cover and
steam 8 minutes or until very tender.

Place asparagus, Neufchâtel cheese, and vinegar
in container of an electric blender; cover and process until smooth. Transfer to a bowl; cover and chill
30 minutes.

Spread asparagus mixture over 8 bread slices; top
evenly with turkey and Monterey Jack cheese. Top
with remaining bread slices. Place on a hot griddle
coated with cooking spray. Cook until lightly browned
and cheese melts. Yield: 8 servings (230 calories per
serving).

Per Serving: PROTEIN 31.5g   FAT 4.1g   (Saturated Fat 1.7g)
CARBOHYDRATE 20.1g   FIBER 4.4g   CHOLESTEROL 60mg
IRON 1.1mg   SODIUM 492mg   CALCIUM 219mg

PIMIENTO CHEESE APPLE WEDGES

2 tablespoons (½ ounce) shredded 50% less-fat
    Cheddar cheese
1 tablespoon chopped pecans, toasted
1 tablespoon diced pimiento
1 ounce Neufchâtel cheese, softened
2 drops of hot sauce
4 medium-size Red Delicious apples, cored

Combine first 5 ingredients; spoon evenly into
cavity of each apple. Cut each apple into 6 wedges.
Serve immediately. Yield: 2 dozen (26 calories each).

Per Wedge: PROTEIN 0.4g   FAT 0.9g   (Saturated Fat 0.3g)
CARBOHYDRATE 4.7g   FIBER 1.0g   CHOLESTEROL 1mg
IRON 0.1mg   SODIUM 10mg   CALCIUM 3mg

KING RANCH ROLL-UPS

¼ cup light process cream cheese product, softened
3 tablespoons canned chopped green chiles
2 teaspoons no-salt-added tomato sauce
½ teaspoon chili powder
¼ teaspoon garlic powder
5 (7-inch) flour tortillas
2 (2½-ounce) packages very thinly sliced chicken
2 tablespoons chopped ripe olives

Beat cream cheese in a bowl at medium speed
of an electric mixer until smooth. Add chiles and next
3 ingredients; stir well. Spread over tortillas. Top
with chicken and olives. Roll up tortillas jellyroll
fashion. Cover with plastic wrap; chill 2 hours. Cut
into 1-inch pieces. Yield: 35 roll-ups (27 calories each).

Per Roll-Up: PROTEIN 1.2g   FAT 1.2g   (Saturated Fat 0.3g)
CARBOHYDRATE 3.1g   FIBER 0.2g   CHOLESTEROL 1mg
IRON 0.1mg   SODIUM 26mg   CALCIUM 6mg

INDIVIDUAL PESTO PIZZAS

¼ cup lightly packed fresh basil
1 clove garlic
2 cups torn fresh spinach
2 tablespoons grated Parmesan cheese
2 teaspoons lemon juice
2 whole wheat English muffins, split and toasted
2 (½-ounce) slices Canadian bacon, cut into
   julienne strips
3 tablespoons (¾ ounce) shredded nonfat
   mozzarella cheese
2 teaspoons sliced green onions

Position knife blade in food processor bowl; drop basil and garlic through food chute with processor running, and process 15 seconds or until minced. Add spinach, Parmesan cheese, and lemon juice; process 30 seconds or until smooth, scraping sides of processor bowl once.

Spread spinach mixture evenly over English muffin halves. Divide Canadian bacon strips evenly among muffin halves. Broil 5½ inches from heat (with electric oven door partially opened) 1 minute. Sprinkle evenly with mozzarella cheese; broil an additional minute or until cheese melts. Sprinkle with green onions. Serve immediately. Yield: 4 servings (123 calories per serving).

Per Serving: PROTEIN 7.4g FAT 2.0g (Saturated Fat 1.0g)
CARBOHYDRATE 18.9g FIBER 3.4g CHOLESTEROL 7mg
IRON 1.5mg SODIUM 362mg CALCIUM 144mg

BARBECUED CEREAL SNACK

1½ cups small unsalted pretzels
1 cup low-salt Cheddar cheese goldfish crackers
1 cup corn-and-rice cereal
¾ cup crisp bran cereal squares
2 tablespoons reduced-calorie hickory-flavored
   barbecue sauce
1 tablespoon reduced-calorie margarine, melted
2 tablespoons grated Parmesan cheese
⅛ teaspoon salt

Combine first 4 ingredients in a large bowl. Combine barbecue sauce and margarine; drizzle over pretzel mixture, tossing well. Add Parmesan cheese and salt; toss well.

Spread cereal mixture into a 13- x 9- x 2-inch pan. Bake at 275° for 30 minutes or until crisp. Yield: 4½ cups (68 calories per ½-cup serving).

Per Serving: PROTEIN 1.9g FAT 2.1g (Saturated Fat 0.3g)
CARBOHYDRATE 11.1g FIBER 0.8g CHOLESTEROL 3mg
IRON 0.8mg SODIUM 219mg CALCIUM 18mg

HARVEST POPCORN MIX

1 cup chopped dried apple
2 tablespoons honey
¾ teaspoon pumpkin pie spice
6 cups popped corn (cooked without salt or fat)
Vegetable cooking spray
½ cup raisins

Place dried apple in a large bowl. Combine honey and pumpkin pie spice; pour over dried apple, tossing gently to coat.

Add popcorn, and toss gently to coat. Spread mixture in a single layer in a 15- x 10- x 1-inch jellyroll pan coated with cooking spray. Bake at 200° for 40 minutes, stirring once. Turn oven off, and leave popcorn mixture in oven 1 hour. Remove from oven, and spread on wax paper. Cool completely. Add raisins, and toss gently. Yield: 6½ cups (61 calories per ½-cup serving).

Per Serving: PROTEIN 0.7g FAT 0.3g (Saturated Fat 0g)
CARBOHYDRATE 15.2g FIBER 1.1g CHOLESTEROL 0mg
IRON 0.4mg SODIUM 7mg CALCIUM 6mg

Heat up a mildly flavored beef or chicken dinner with Chunky Southwestern Chili Sauce (page 206). A host of herbs and spices contributes to its fiery vigor.

Sauces
&
Condiments

AMARETTO-PLUM SAUCE

1 pound fresh plums, pitted and coarsely chopped
¼ cup unsweetened orange juice
2 tablespoons brown sugar
2 tablespoons amaretto
3 tablespoons chopped almonds, toasted

Combine first 4 ingredients in a saucepan. Bring to a boil; cover, reduce heat, and simmer 15 minutes or until plums are tender.

Place plum mixture in container of an electric blender or food processor; cover and process until smooth, stopping once to scrape down sides. Stir in chopped almonds. Cover and chill thoroughly. Serve sauce over angel food cake, ice milk, or nonfat frozen yogurt. Yield: 2¼ cups (17 calories per tablespoon).

Per Tablespoon: PROTEIN 0.3g FAT 0.4g (Saturated Fat 0g)
CARBOHYDRATE 3.3g FIBER 0.3g CHOLESTEROL 0mg
IRON 0.1mg SODIUM 0mg CALCIUM 3mg

CITRUS CRANBERRY SAUCE

1 cup chopped fresh cranberries
½ cup plus 1 tablespoon frozen orange juice
    concentrate, thawed and undiluted
¼ cup sugar
2 tablespoons Grand Marnier or other
    orange-flavored liqueur
½ to ¾ teaspoon grated orange rind
½ teaspoon grated lemon rind
¼ teaspoon ground allspice

Combine all ingredients in a small nonaluminum saucepan; bring to a boil. Cover, reduce heat, and simmer 20 minutes, stirring frequently.

Uncover and simmer an additional 5 minutes or until mixture is thickened, stirring frequently. Remove from heat, and let mixture cool completely. Serve over chocolate ice milk, angel food cake, or poached fresh fruit. Yield: 1 cup plus 2 tablespoons (28 calories per tablespoon).

Per Tablespoon: PROTEIN 0.2g FAT 0.0g (Saturated Fat 0g)
CARBOHYDRATE 7.0g FIBER 0.2g CHOLESTEROL 0mg
IRON 0.1mg SODIUM 0mg CALCIUM 4mg

TROPICAL FRUIT SAUCE

1 cup unsweetened orange juice
1½ tablespoons cornstarch
1 tablespoon sugar
2 tablespoons spiced rum
½ cup peeled, diced ripe mango
½ cup diced fresh pineapple
½ teaspoon grated orange rind
½ teaspoon grated lemon rind

Combine orange juice, cornstarch, sugar, and rum in a medium saucepan; stir until smooth. Cook over medium heat, stirring constantly, until thickened. Remove from heat; stir in mango and remaining ingredients. Serve warm or chilled over angel food cake. Yield: 1¾ cups (14 calories per tablespoon).

Per Tablespoon: PROTEIN 0.1g FAT 0.0g (Saturated Fat 0g)
CARBOHYDRATE 3.5g FIBER 0.1g CHOLESTEROL 0mg
IRON 0mg SODIUM 0mg CALCIUM 2mg

 CUTTING EDGE SELECTIONS
A top-notch knife can make kitchen tasks easier. Quality can vary among knives, so it is best to base your purchase on workmanship and the blade's alloy content. For quality workmanship, look for a tempered blade, which makes the knife more durable, and a tang, which is a portion of the blade that runs through the handle. An inexpensive knife has a short tang, increasing the chance the blade and handle will separate. The handle should be made of a material that's a poor conductor of heat, such as wood or a wood and plastic combination.

Below are descriptions of blade alloy content:

TYPES	Advantages	Disadvantages
Carbon Steel	Sharpest edge; chefs' choice.	Easily rusts if not wiped dry immediately after use; stains when left in contact with acidic foods.
High-Carbon Stainless Steel	Won't rust or stain; good for humid climates.	Most expensive; not as sharp as carbon steel.
Stainless Steel	Resists rust and stains.	Dull blade but sharper than superstainless.
Superstainless Steel	Resists rust and stains.	Dullest blade; can't be sharpened.

Indulge in guilt-free ecstasy when you spoon low-fat Chocolate-Cherry Sauce over your favorite ice milk.

CHOCOLATE-CHERRY SAUCE

2 tablespoons sugar
2 tablespoons unsweetened cocoa
1 tablespoon cornstarch
1 cup skim milk
2 tablespoons light-colored corn syrup
1 tablespoon cherry brandy
½ teaspoon vanilla extract
2 tablespoons chopped dried cherries

Combine first 3 ingredients in a small saucepan. Gradually stir in milk, corn syrup, brandy, and vanilla. Cook over medium heat, stirring constantly, 8 minutes or until thickened. Remove from heat. Stir in cherries. Serve warm or at room temperature over angel food cake, ice milk, or nonfat frozen yogurt. Yield: 1¼ cups plus 2 tablespoons (24 calories per tablespoon).

Per Tablespoon: PROTEIN 0.6g FAT 0.2g (Saturated Fat 0.1g)
CARBOHYDRATE 5.0g FIBER 0.2g CHOLESTEROL 0mg
IRON 0.1mg SODIUM 8mg CALCIUM 15mg

CREAMY RASPBERRY-MINT SAUCE

2 cups fresh raspberries
¼ cup plus 2 tablespoons evaporated skimmed milk
3 tablespoons sugar
1 tablespoon minced fresh mint
1 tablespoon Chambord or other raspberry-flavored liqueur
1 teaspoon grated lemon rind

Combine raspberries and milk in container of an electric blender; cover and process until smooth. Place in a wire-mesh strainer; press with back of spoon against the sides of the strainer to squeeze out juice. Discard pulp and seeds remaining in strainer.

Return mixture to blender; add sugar, mint, and liqueur. Cover and process until smooth. Stir in lemon rind. Serve over angel food cake or fresh fruit. Yield: 1½ cups (15 calories per tablespoon).

Per Tablespoon: PROTEIN 0.4g FAT 0.1g (Saturated Fat 0g)
CARBOHYDRATE 3.1g FIBER 0.6g CHOLESTEROL 0mg
IRON 0.1mg SODIUM 4mg CALCIUM 13mg

APPLE BUTTER SAUCE

1 tablespoon reduced-calorie margarine
½ cup peeled, finely chopped apple
2 tablespoons finely chopped onion
2 tablespoons all-purpose flour
½ cup apple cider
¼ cup skim milk
¼ cup apple butter

Melt margarine in a saucepan; add apple and onion. Cook over medium-low heat, stirring constantly, until tender. Add flour; cook, stirring constantly, 1 minute. Add cider, milk, and apple butter. Cook, stirring constantly, until thickened. Serve warm with pork. Yield: 1 cup (23 calories per tablespoon).

Per Tablespoon: PROTEIN 0.3g FAT 0.5g (Saturated Fat 0.1g)
CARBOHYDRATE 4.6g FIBER 0.2g CHOLESTEROL 0mg
IRON 0.1mg SODIUM 9mg CALCIUM 6mg

CHUNKY SOUTHWESTERN CHILI SAUCE

1 (8-ounce) can no-salt-added tomato sauce
½ cup chopped sweet red pepper
½ cup chopped onion
¼ cup chopped fresh cilantro
2 tablespoons brown sugar
2 tablespoons cider vinegar
2 tablespoons golden tequila
2 teaspoons seeded, chopped jalapeño pepper
1 teaspoon ground cumin
1 teaspoon chili powder
½ teaspoon ground cinnamon
¼ teaspoon garlic powder
¼ teaspoon ground red pepper
¾ cup peeled, seeded, and chopped tomato

Combine first 13 ingredients in a saucepan. Bring to a boil; reduce heat, and simmer, uncovered, 20 minutes, stirring frequently. Stir in tomato; simmer 10 minutes. Serve with beef or chicken. Yield: 1½ cups (10 calories per tablespoon).

Per Tablespoon: PROTEIN 0.2g FAT 0.1g (Saturated Fat 0g)
CARBOHYDRATE 2.3g FIBER 0.4g CHOLESTEROL 0mg
IRON 0.3mg SODIUM 4mg CALCIUM 4mg

SHERRIED LEMON SAUCE

Vegetable cooking spray
¼ cup chopped onion
2 tablespoons all-purpose flour
½ cup skim milk, divided
½ cup canned low-sodium chicken broth, undiluted
2 tablespoons dry sherry
2 tablespoons lemon marmalade
Dash of ground white pepper

Coat a small saucepan with cooking spray; place over medium-high heat until hot. Add onion, and sauté until tender.
Combine flour and ¼ cup milk; stir until smooth. Add remaining ¼ cup milk, chicken broth, and sherry; stir well. Add milk mixture to sautéed onion. Cook over medium heat, stirring constantly, until thickened and bubbly. Remove from heat; stir in marmalade and pepper. Serve with chicken or veal. Yield: 1¼ cups (12 calories per tablespoon).

Per Tablespoon: PROTEIN 0.4g FAT 0.1g (Saturated Fat 0g)
CARBOHYDRATE 2.5g FIBER 0.1g CHOLESTEROL 0mg
IRON 0.1mg SODIUM 6mg CALCIUM 9mg

CHUNKY VEGETABLE SAUCE

½ cup plain nonfat yogurt
½ cup nonfat mayonnaise
1 tablespoon red wine vinegar
¼ teaspoon salt
¼ teaspoon liquid smoke
⅛ teaspoon garlic powder
1¼ cups plus 2 tablespoons peeled, seeded, and chopped tomato
¼ cup thinly sliced green onions
¼ cup finely chopped celery

Combine first 6 ingredients in a small bowl. Stir in chopped tomato, green onions, and celery. Serve with fish or poultry. Yield: 1½ cups (8 calories per tablespoon).

Per Tablespoon: PROTEIN 0.3g FAT 0.0g (Saturated Fat 0g)
CARBOHYDRATE 1.6g FIBER 0.1g CHOLESTEROL 0mg
IRON 0mg SODIUM 93mg CALCIUM 11mg

TURKEY-VEGETABLE SPAGHETTI SAUCE

Vegetable cooking spray
2 teaspoons olive oil, divided
½ pound freshly ground raw turkey
1 cup chopped zucchini
¾ cup chopped celery
½ cup chopped carrot
½ cup chopped onion
½ cup chopped green pepper
2 teaspoons chopped garlic
1 (14½-ounce) can no-salt-added whole
 tomatoes, undrained and chopped
1 (6-ounce) can no-salt-added
 tomato paste
3 cups water
¼ cup Burgundy or other dry
 red wine
2 teaspoons dried whole oregano
½ teaspoon salt

Coat a large nonstick skillet with cooking spray; add 1 teaspoon olive oil. Place over medium-high heat until hot. Add ground turkey, and cook until browned, stirring until it crumbles. Remove turkey from skillet. Drain and pat dry with paper towels. Wipe drippings from skillet with a paper towel.

Coat skillet with cooking spray; add remaining 1 teaspoon olive oil. Place over medium-high heat until hot. Add zucchini and next 5 ingredients; cook 5 minutes, stirring frequently.

Add turkey, tomato, tomato paste, water, wine, oregano, and salt to zucchini mixture. Cook, uncovered, over medium-low heat 1 hour, stirring occasionally. Serve over pasta. Yield: 1½ quarts (8 calories per tablespoon).

Per Tablespoon: PROTEIN 0.7g FAT 0.2g (Saturated Fat 0g) CARBOHYDRATE 0.9g FIBER 0.1g CHOLESTEROL 1mg IRON 0.1mg SODIUM 16mg CALCIUM 4mg

FRESH CITRUS-GARLIC MARINADE

⅓ cup fresh orange juice
3 tablespoons honey
2 tablespoons minced garlic (about 6 cloves)
2 tablespoons Chablis or other dry white wine
2 tablespoons fresh lemon juice
2 tablespoons fresh lime juice
¼ teaspoon ground cumin
⅛ teaspoon ground red pepper

Combine all ingredients in a jar. Cover tightly, and shake vigorously.

Use to marinate fish or chicken before grilling. Baste with remaining marinade while grilling. Yield: 1 cup (18 calories per tablespoon).

Per Tablespoon: PROTEIN 0.2g FAT 0.0g (Saturated Fat 0g) CARBOHYDRATE 4.8g FIBER 0g CHOLESTEROL 0mg IRON 0.1mg SODIUM 1mg CALCIUM 5mg

GRAPE AND RHUBARB CHUTNEY

3 cups seedless red grapes, halved
½ pound rhubarb, chopped
½ cup chopped onion
¼ cup raisins
¼ cup firmly packed brown sugar
1 tablespoon grated orange rind
1 teaspoon ground ginger
½ teaspoon ground cinnamon
¼ teaspoon ground allspice
½ cup unsweetened orange juice
¼ cup red wine vinegar

Combine all ingredients in a medium saucepan, stirring well.

Bring mixture to a boil; reduce heat, and simmer, uncovered, 1 hour and 15 minutes or until mixture is thickened, stirring frequently.

Serve grape and rhubarb chutney with beef, pork, or chicken. Yield: 1¾ cups (25 calories per tablespoon).

Per Tablespoon: PROTEIN 0.3g FAT 0.1g (Saturated Fat 0g) CARBOHYDRATE 6.6g FIBER 0.3g CHOLESTEROL 0mg IRON 0.2mg SODIUM 2mg CALCIUM 13mg

The combination of Dijon mustard and ripe mangoes creates a tantalizing taste in spicy Mango Mustard.

MANGO MUSTARD

1 cup peeled, chopped ripe mango
2 tablespoons Dijon mustard
2 teaspoons brown sugar
¼ teaspoon ground allspice
⅛ teaspoon ground ginger
⅛ teaspoon ground cardamom

Combine all ingredients in container of an electric blender; cover and process on high speed until smooth, stopping once to scrape down sides. Serve as a sandwich spread or with grilled chicken or pork. Yield: ¾ cup (15 calories per tablespoon).

Per Tablespoon: PROTEIN 0.1g FAT 0.2g (Saturated Fat 0g) CARBOHYDRATE 3.3g FIBER 0.2g CHOLESTEROL 0mg IRON 0.1mg SODIUM 75mg CALCIUM 5mg

SWEET HOT MUSTARD

½ cup prepared mustard
¼ cup Dijon mustard
3 tablespoons no-sugar-added apricot spread
2 tablespoons currants
¼ teaspoon ground ginger
¼ teaspoon dried crushed red pepper
⅛ teaspoon ground cumin

Combine all ingredients in a small bowl, stirring until mixture is smooth. Serve as a sandwich spread or with chicken or pork. Yield: 1 cup (24 calories per tablespoon).

Per Tablespoon: PROTEIN 0.4g FAT 0.7g (Saturated Fat 0g) CARBOHYDRATE 4.3g FIBER 0.1g CHOLESTEROL 0mg IRON 0.3mg SODIUM 210mg CALCIUM 12mg

GOLDEN GARDEN RELISH

5 cups finely shredded cabbage
2 cups chopped banana pepper
1 cup chopped onion
1 cup thinly sliced celery
½ cup finely chopped sweet red pepper
2 cups white vinegar
¼ cup sugar
2 tablespoons dry mustard
1 teaspoon ground turmeric
¼ teaspoon salt
¼ teaspoon ground white pepper

Combine first 5 ingredients in a large bowl, and toss well.

Combine vinegar, sugar, mustard, turmeric, salt, and white pepper in a small saucepan; stir with a wire whisk until well blended. Bring to a simmer over medium heat. Pour over vegetable mixture; toss well. Let stand at room temperature 20 minutes.

Spoon into hot sterilized jars, leaving ½-inch headspace. Cover at once with metal lids, and screw on bands. Refrigerate at least 3 days before serving. Serve with beef or pork. Yield: 9 half pints (5 calories per tablespoon).

Per Tablespoon: PROTEIN 0.1g FAT 0.1g (Saturated Fat 0g)
CARBOHYDRATE 1.1g FIBER 0.2g CHOLESTEROL 0mg
IRON 0.1mg SODIUM 6mg CALCIUM 3mg

TIME FOR TURMERIC

Considered to be an essential ingredient in pickles and relishes, turmeric is both affordable and readily available. Along with its earthy aroma and slightly bitter taste, this yellow-orange powder can be a substitute for saffron, lending a bright yellow hue to dishes such as paella and bouillabaisse. Most of the turmeric sold in the U.S. is harvested in India from a plant in the ginger family. As with ginger, it is the roots of the turmeric plant that yield the spice.

Look for dried turmeric powder or the fresh root in most supermarkets. Although the spice may be new to American households, manufacturers have long used turmeric to color prepared mustards and as an ingredient in curry powder.

GREEN TOMATO RELISH

2 cups chopped green tomato
1 cup peeled, chopped cooking apple
½ cup chopped unsweetened dates
½ cup chopped onion
¼ cup golden raisins
¼ cup firmly packed brown sugar
1 teaspoon peeled, grated gingerroot
½ teaspoon dry mustard
¼ teaspoon ground allspice
⅛ teaspoon chili powder
⅛ teaspoon ground red pepper
¾ cup white vinegar

Combine all ingredients in medium saucepan, stirring well. Bring mixture to a boil over medium heat; reduce heat, and simmer, uncovered, 25 minutes, stirring occasionally. Transfer mixture to a bowl. Cover and chill at least 4 hours. Serve relish with chicken or pork. Yield: 3¾ cups (14 calories per tablespoon).

Per Tablespoon: PROTEIN 0.1g FAT 0.1g (Saturated Fat 0g)
CARBOHYDRATE 3.5g FIBER 0.3g CHOLESTEROL 0mg
IRON 0.1mg SODIUM 1mg CALCIUM 3mg

WARM PAPAYA RELISH

2½ cups peeled, diced ripe papaya
1 cup chopped onion
¾ cup peeled, seeded, and chopped plum tomato
1 tablespoon seeded, minced jalapeño pepper
¼ cup unsweetened orange juice
2 tablespoons lime juice
3 tablespoons chopped fresh cilantro
2 tablespoons chopped fresh mint

Combine first 6 ingredients in a large nonstick skillet. Cook over medium-low heat 3 to 5 minutes or until thoroughly heated, stirring occasionally. Remove from heat, and stir in cilantro and mint. Serve warm with grilled chicken, fish, or pork. Yield: 4 cups (5 calories per tablespoon).

Per Tablespoon: PROTEIN 0.1g FAT 0.0g (Saturated Fat 0g)
CARBOHYDRATE 1.1g FIBER 0.2g CHOLESTEROL 0mg
IRON 0mg SODIUM 1mg CALCIUM 3mg

PAPAYA SALSA

2 cups peeled, seeded, and finely chopped papaya
2 tablespoons finely chopped fresh mint
2 tablespoons seeded, minced jalapeño pepper
1½ teaspoons peeled, minced gingerroot
2 tablespoons lemon juice
2 tablespoons lime juice
1 tablespoon honey

Combine first 4 ingredients in a medium bowl; toss well. Combine lemon juice, lime juice, and honey; stir well. Pour over papaya mixture; toss gently. Cover and chill at least 2 hours. Yield: 2 cups (7 calories per tablespoon).

Per Tablespoon: PROTEIN 0.1g FAT 0.0g (Saturated Fat 0g)
CARBOHYDRATE 1.9g FIBER 0.2g CHOLESTEROL 0mg
IRON 0mg SODIUM 0mg CALCIUM 3mg

CARIBBEAN FRUIT SALSA

1¼ cups peeled, diced ripe papaya
1 cup peeled, diced ripe mango
½ cup thinly sliced green onions
1 tablespoon chopped serrano pepper
1 tablespoon grated lime rind
½ teaspoon ground ginger
¼ teaspoon ground cumin
⅛ teaspoon ground cardamom
1 cup peeled, diced banana
3 tablespoons lime juice

Combine first 8 ingredients in a large bowl; stir well. Combine banana and lime juice; toss gently. Add banana mixture to papaya mixture, tossing well to combine. Let stand at room temperature 30 minutes. Serve with chicken, pork, or shrimp. Yield: 3¼ cups (8 calories per tablespoon).

Per Tablespoon: PROTEIN 0.1g FAT 0.0g (Saturated Fat 0g)
CARBOHYDRATE 2.1g FIBER 0.3g CHOLESTEROL 0mg
IRON 0mg SODIUM 0mg CALCIUM 2mg

SPICED FRUIT VINEGAR

½ cup fresh blueberries
½ cup fresh raspberries
1 (4-inch) strip orange rind
1 (2-inch) stick cinnamon
6 whole cloves
2 cups white wine vinegar
Additional fresh blueberries (optional)
Additional fresh raspberries (optional)

Place first 5 ingredients in a wide-mouth quart glass jar. Place vinegar in a nonaluminum saucepan; bring to a boil. Pour hot vinegar over berry mixture; cover with lid. Let stand at room temperature at least 3 days.

Pour mixture through a wire-mesh strainer into decorative bottles or jars, discarding berry mixture. If desired, add additional fresh blueberries and raspberries. Seal bottles with a cork or other airtight lid. Use in salad dressings or vinaigrettes. Yield: 2¼ cups (4 calories per tablespoon).

Per Tablespoon: PROTEIN 0.0g FAT 0.0g (Saturated Fat 0g)
CARBOHYDRATE 0.5g FIBER 0.2g CHOLESTEROL 0mg
IRON 0mg SODIUM 1mg CALCIUM 1 mg

You're sure to have big fun on the bayou or anywhere else with Okra and Corn Creole (page 216). This medley of vegetables is guaranteed to send a Cajun tingle down your spine.

Side
Dishes

GINGERED ASPARAGUS

1 pound fresh asparagus spears
Vegetable cooking spray
2 tablespoons low-sodium soy sauce
2 teaspoons sesame seeds, toasted
1 teaspoon peeled, minced gingerroot
Dash of pepper
½ teaspoon grated orange rind

Snap off tough ends of asparagus. Remove scales from stalks with a knife or vegetable peeler, if desired. Cut spears into 2-inch pieces.

Coat a large nonstick skillet with cooking spray. Place over medium-low heat until hot. Add asparagus, soy sauce, sesame seeds, gingerroot, and pepper. Cook, stirring constantly, 5 minutes or until asparagus is crisp-tender. Transfer to a serving bowl, and sprinkle with orange rind. Serve immediately. Yield: 4 servings (32 calories per serving).

Per Serving: PROTEIN 2.6g FAT 1.1g (Saturated Fat 0.1g)
CARBOHYDRATE 4.6g FIBER 1.8g CHOLESTEROL 0mg
IRON 1.0mg SODIUM 244mg CALCIUM 21mg

GREEN BEANS IN SWEET VINAIGRETTE

1 tablespoon plus 1 teaspoon red currant jelly
1 tablespoon cider vinegar
⅛ teaspoon dry mustard
Dash of salt
1 pound fresh green beans
¼ cup finely chopped sweet red pepper

Combine first 4 ingredients in a saucepan; cook over low heat until jelly melts, stirring occasionally.

Wash beans; trim ends, and remove strings. Arrange beans in a vegetable steamer over boiling water. Cover; steam 11 minutes. Add pepper; cover and steam 1 minute or until crisp-tender. Drain; transfer vegetables to a serving bowl. Spoon vinegar mixture over vegetables; toss. Serve immediately. Yield: 6 servings (35 calories per ½-cup serving).

Per Serving: PROTEIN 1.3g FAT 0.1g (Saturated Fat 0g)
CARBOHYDRATE 8.4g FIBER 1.5g CHOLESTEROL 0mg
IRON 0.8mg SODIUM 29mg CALCIUM 27mg

SPICY LIMA BEANS

Vegetable cooking spray
½ cup chopped celery
½ cup chopped onion
½ cup chopped green pepper
1 jalapeño pepper, seeded and diced
1 (10-ounce) package frozen lima beans, thawed
1½ cups diced tomato
1 cup spicy hot vegetable juice cocktail
¼ teaspoon dried whole thyme
⅛ teaspoon hot sauce
1 bay leaf

Coat a large nonstick skillet with cooking spray; place over medium-high heat until hot. Add celery, onion, and peppers; sauté 3 to 5 minutes or until crisp-tender.

Add lima beans and remaining ingredients; stir well. Bring to a boil; cover, reduce heat, and simmer 12 minutes or until lima beans are tender, stirring occasionally. Remove and discard bay leaf. Yield: 8 servings (65 calories per ½-cup serving).

Per Serving: PROTEIN 3.4g FAT 0.3g (Saturated Fat 0g)
CARBOHYDRATE 12.8g FIBER 1.6g CHOLESTEROL 0mg
IRON 1.5mg SODIUM 148mg CALCIUM 22mg

SELENIUM SUCCESS

Although selenium doesn't garner as much attention as other minerals, researchers are convinced this nutrient plays a key role in good health. That is why the most recent edition of the Food and Nutrition Board's Recommended Dietary Allowances includes selenium.

Along with vitamin E, selenium works to neutralize damaging compounds called free radicals, creating antioxidant abilities. Perhaps more importantly, preliminary evidence seems to support selenium as a potent cancer fighter. Studies show that people with low blood levels of selenium are at high risk for nonmelanoma skin cancer. To tap into the health benefits of selenium, reach for these foods: seafood, kidney, liver, and, to a small extent, lean meats, mushrooms, and asparagus.

Italian Broccoli and Tomatoes is a tasty addition to dinner, and it can be prepared in less than 30 minutes.

ITALIAN BROCCOLI AND TOMATOES

1 pound fresh broccoli
2 medium tomatoes, cut into 8 wedges
2 tablespoons water
½ teaspoon garlic powder
½ teaspoon dried whole oregano
½ cup (2 ounces) shredded nonfat mozzarella
   cheese
2 tablespoons sliced ripe olives

Trim off large leaves of broccoli, and remove tough ends of lower stalks. Wash broccoli thoroughly, and cut into small spears. Arrange broccoli in a vegetable steamer over boiling water. Cover and steam 5 to 8 minutes or until crisp-tender. Drain; place in saucepan. Add tomato, water, garlic powder, and oregano; stir gently. Cook, uncovered, over medium-low heat 10 to 15 minutes or until thoroughly heated, stirring occasionally. Sprinkle with cheese and olives. Remove from heat. Cover and let stand 2 to 3 minutes or until cheese melts. Yield: 8 servings (37 calories per ½-cup serving).

Per Serving: PROTEIN 3.8g FAT 0.9g (Saturated Fat 0.2g)
CARBOHYDRATE 4.9g FIBER 1.9g CHOLESTEROL 1mg
IRON 0.8mg SODIUM 111mg CALCIUM 76mg

APPLE SWEET-SOUR CABBAGE

Vegetable cooking spray
½ cup sliced green onions
4 cups shredded red cabbage
2 medium-size Red Delicious apples, sliced
3 tablespoons brown sugar
¼ teaspoon salt
⅛ teaspoon pepper
½ cup unsweetened apple juice
¼ cup plus 2 tablespoons cider vinegar

Coat a large nonstick skillet with cooking spray; place over medium-high heat until hot. Add green onions, and sauté 2 to 3 minutes or until tender. Add shredded red cabbage and remaining ingredients; toss well. Cook, uncovered, over medium heat 15 to 18 minutes or until cabbage is tender, stirring occasionally. Yield: 7 servings (65 calories per ½-cup serving).

Per Serving: PROTEIN 0.8g FAT 0.4g (Saturated Fat 0.1g)
CARBOHYDRATE 16.2g FIBER 2.4g CHOLESTEROL 0mg
IRON 0.7mg SODIUM 92mg CALCIUM 37mg

ANISE CARROTS

¾ pound baby carrots, cut in half lengthwise
¼ cup unsweetened apple juice
1 tablespoon brown sugar
1 teaspoon cornstarch
⅛ teaspoon anise seeds
Dash of salt

Arrange carrot in a vegetable steamer over boiling water. Cover and steam 6 minutes or until carrot is tender; drain. Transfer to a serving platter, and keep warm.

Combine apple juice and remaining ingredients in a small saucepan; stir until smooth. Cook, stirring constantly, over medium heat until mixture is thickened and bubbly. Pour over carrot, and toss gently. Yield: 4 servings (52 calories per ½-cup serving).

Per Serving: PROTEIN 0.8g FAT 0.2g (Saturated Fat 0g)
CARBOHYDRATE 12.5g FIBER 2.5g CHOLESTEROL 0mg
IRON 0.6mg SODIUM 65mg CALCIUM 25mg

CAULIFLOWER PIE

10 cups cauliflower flowerets (about 1 medium head)
Butter-flavored vegetable cooking spray
1 (8-ounce) container nonfat sour cream alternative
½ cup frozen egg substitute, thawed
½ cup (2 ounces) shredded reduced-fat Cheddar cheese
1 (2-ounce) jar diced pimiento, drained
¼ teaspoon salt
¼ teaspoon ground white pepper
⅓ cup soft whole wheat breadcrumbs
¼ teaspoon paprika

Arrange cauliflower in a vegetable steamer over boiling water. Cover and steam 8 minutes or until tender. Drain well. Arrange in a shallow 1½-quart round casserole coated with cooking spray.

Combine sour cream and next 5 ingredients in a bowl; stir well. Pour sour cream mixture over cauliflower. Combine breadcrumbs and paprika; toss gently. Sprinkle over sour cream mixture. Coat breadcrumb mixture with cooking spray. Bake, uncovered, at 375° for 20 minutes or until hot and bubbly. Yield: 10 servings (66 calories per serving).

Per Serving: PROTEIN 6.4g FAT 1.4g (Saturated Fat 0.7g)
CARBOHYDRATE 7.3g FIBER 2.2g CHOLESTEROL 4mg
IRON 0.9mg SODIUM 155mg CALCIUM 82mg

MUSTARD CAULIFLOWER AND PEAS

3 tablespoons nonfat mayonnaise
2 teaspoons prepared mustard
¼ teaspoon onion powder
¼ teaspoon dried whole dillweed
Dash of pepper
4 cups cauliflower flowerets
2 cups fresh Sugar Snap peas, trimmed

Combine first 5 ingredients in a small bowl; stir well. Set aside.

Arrange cauliflower in a vegetable steamer over boiling water. Cover and steam 2 minutes; add peas.

Cover and steam an additional 4 minutes or until vegetables are tender; drain. Transfer to a serving bowl.

Spoon mayonnaise mixture over vegetable mixture, and toss well. Serve immediately. Yield: 10 servings (28 calories per ½-cup serving).

Per Serving: PROTEIN 1.8g FAT 0.2g (Saturated Fat 0g)
CARBOHYDRATE 5.5g FIBER 1.9g CHOLESTEROL 0mg
IRON 0.8mg SODIUM 79mg CALCIUM 27mg

GARDEN SCALLOPED CORN

2 (16½-ounce) cans no-salt-added cream-style corn
⅔ cup crushed unsalted crackers
⅔ cup chopped green pepper
⅔ cup finely shredded carrot
½ cup chopped celery
¼ cup plus 2 tablespoons sliced green onions
1 (4-ounce) jar diced pimiento, drained
1 cup frozen egg substitute, thawed
⅓ cup evaporated skimmed milk
2 tablespoons reduced-calorie margarine, melted
1 teaspoon sugar
½ teaspoon salt
½ teaspoon hot sauce
Vegetable cooking spray
½ cup (2 ounces) shredded 50% less-fat Cheddar cheese
½ teaspoon paprika

Combine first 13 ingredients in a large bowl; stir well. Pour mixture into a 2-quart shallow baking dish coated with cooking spray. Bake, uncovered, at 350° for 1 hour and 10 minutes or until set. Sprinkle with cheese and paprika. Bake an additional 5 minutes or until cheese melts. Yield: 12 servings (126 calories per serving).

Per Serving: PROTEIN 5.9g FAT 3.1g (Saturated Fat 0.8g)
CARBOHYDRATE 21.5g FIBER 1.6g CHOLESTEROL 3mg
IRON 1.2mg SODIUM 239mg CALCIUM 65mg

FENNEL-SWEET POTATO BAKE

2 fennel bulbs (about 2½ pounds)
4 medium-size sweet potatoes, peeled and cut into 2-inch pieces
Vegetable cooking spray
¼ cup plus 2 tablespoons canned low-sodium chicken broth, undiluted
1½ teaspoons olive oil
1 teaspoon onion powder
¼ teaspoon pepper
2½ tablespoons chopped fresh parsley

Trim tough outer stalks from fennel. Cut bulbs in half lengthwise; remove cores. Cut fennel into 1-inch pieces. Place fennel and potato in an 11- x 7- x 1½-inch baking dish coated with cooking spray.

Combine chicken broth and oil in a small bowl, stirring with a wire whisk. Drizzle over vegetables, tossing to coat. Sprinkle with onion powder and pepper. Cover and bake at 375° for 30 minutes. Stir gently; sprinkle with parsley. Cover and bake an additional 30 to 35 minutes or until vegetables are tender. Yield: 8 servings (140 calories per serving).

Per Serving: PROTEIN 3.0g FAT 1.5g (Saturated Fat 0.2g)
CARBOHYDRATE 29.8g FIBER 3.6g CHOLESTEROL 0mg
IRON 1.8mg SODIUM 22mg CALCIUM 64mg

MUSHROOM AND LEEK SAUTÉ

1 tablespoon plus 1 teaspoon reduced-calorie margarine
2 cups sliced leeks
1 pound fresh mushrooms, quartered
2 tablespoons low-sodium soy sauce
½ teaspoon dried whole oregano
¼ teaspoon pepper

Heat margarine in a nonstick skillet over medium-high heat until margarine melts. Add leeks; sauté 3 minutes. Add mushrooms and remaining ingredients; sauté 4 minutes or until mushrooms are tender. Yield: 7 servings (47 calories per ½-cup serving).

Per Serving: PROTEIN 1.8g FAT 1.7g (Saturated Fat 0.2g)
CARBOHYDRATE 7.1g FIBER 1.2g CHOLESTEROL 0mg
IRON 1.4mg SODIUM 141mg CALCIUM 22mg

OKRA AND CORN CREOLE

Vegetable cooking spray
1 cup chopped green pepper
½ cup chopped onion
2½ cups fresh corn cut from cob (about 3 ears)
½ cup water
2 (14½-ounce) cans no-salt-added whole tomatoes,
    undrained and chopped
2 tablespoons no-salt-added tomato paste
½ teaspoon sugar
¼ teaspoon salt
¼ teaspoon pepper
¼ teaspoon hot sauce
2 cups sliced fresh okra

Coat a large nonstick skillet with cooking spray;
place over medium-high heat until hot. Add green
pepper and onion; sauté 3 minutes or until tender.

Add corn and water to vegetables in skillet, stirring well. Cover and cook over medium heat 5 minutes; stir gently, and cook an additional 5 minutes.
Add chopped tomato and next 5 ingredients. Bring
to a boil; cover, reduce heat, and simmer 10 minutes, stirring occasionally. Add okra; cover and
simmer 5 to 7 minutes or until okra is tender. Yield:
12 servings (56 calories per ½-cup serving).

Per Serving: PROTEIN 2.2g FAT 0.5g (Saturated Fat 0.1g)
CARBOHYDRATE 12.5g FIBER 1.9g CHOLESTEROL 0mg
IRON 0.8mg SODIUM 66mg CALCIUM 40mg

CREAMY SLICED POTATOES

1¼ pounds round red potatoes, cut into
    ¼-inch-thick slices
1 tablespoon reduced-calorie margarine
1½ tablespoons all-purpose flour
1 cup skim milk
¼ teaspoon salt
¼ teaspoon dried whole dillweed
⅛ teaspoon pepper
¼ cup nonfat sour cream alternative

Cook potato in a large saucepan in boiling water to cover 10 to 15 minutes or until tender. Drain.
Place in a medium bowl; set aside, and keep warm.

Melt margarine in a small saucepan over low heat;
add flour, stirring until smooth. Cook 1 minute, stirring constantly with a wire whisk. Gradually add
milk; cook over medium heat, stirring constantly,
until mixture is thickened and bubbly. Stir in salt,
dillweed, and pepper. Remove from heat, and stir
in sour cream. Add sour cream mixture to potato;
toss gently. Serve warm. Yield: 8 servings (90 calories
per ½-cup serving).

Per Serving: PROTEIN 3.0g FAT 1.1g (Saturated Fat 0.2g)
CARBOHYDRATE 17.4g FIBER 1.1g CHOLESTEROL 1mg
IRON 0.3mg SODIUM 111mg CALCIUM 43mg

POTATO AND BRUSSELS SPROUTS GRATIN

3 cups thinly sliced baking potato
1 (10-ounce) package frozen brussels sprouts,
    thawed and halved
Vegetable cooking spray
1 tablespoon reduced-calorie margarine
2 tablespoons all-purpose flour
1½ cups skim milk
½ teaspoon onion powder
¼ teaspoon salt
¼ teaspoon dried whole thyme
⅛ teaspoon pepper
¼ cup freshly grated Parmesan cheese

Place potato slices and brussels sprouts in an
11- x 7- x 1½-inch baking dish coated with cooking spray.

Melt margarine in a saucepan over low heat; add
flour, stirring until smooth. Cook 1 minute, stirring
constantly with a wire whisk. Gradually add milk.
Cook over medium heat, stirring constantly, an additional 10 minutes or until thickened and bubbly.
Stir in onion powder, salt, thyme, and pepper.

Pour over potato mixture. Cover and bake at 375°
for 50 minutes or until potato is tender. Sprinkle with
cheese; bake, uncovered, an additional 10 minutes
or until golden. Serve immediately. Yield: 6 servings
(146 calories per serving).

Per Serving: PROTEIN 7.6g FAT 2.9g (Saturated Fat 1.1g)
CARBOHYDRATE 24.1g FIBER 3.5g CHOLESTEROL 4mg
IRON 2.0mg SODIUM 242mg CALCIUM 165mg

Round out a healthy meal by serving Individual Sweet Potato Casseroles, a light variation of a classic side dish.

INDIVIDUAL SWEET POTATO CASSEROLES

4 cups peeled, cubed sweet potato
¼ cup unsweetened apple juice
1½ tablespoons brown sugar
2 tablespoons nonfat buttermilk
2 tablespoons nonfat sour cream alternative
1 teaspoon grated orange rind
¼ teaspoon orange extract
⅛ teaspoon ground cinnamon
⅛ teaspoon ground coriander
⅛ teaspoon ground nutmeg
2 egg whites
Vegetable cooking spray
1 teaspoon crushed gingersnap cookie
1 teaspoon chopped pecans

Cook sweet potato in a large saucepan in boiling water to cover 15 minutes or until tender. Drain.

Position knife blade in food processor bowl; add potato. Process until smooth; transfer to a large bowl. Add apple juice and next 8 ingredients, stirring to combine. Let cool to room temperature.

Beat egg whites at high speed of an electric mixer until stiff peaks form; gently fold egg whites into potato mixture.

Spoon mixture evenly into 4 (¾-cup) ramekins coated with cooking spray. Sprinkle evenly with crushed cookie and chopped pecans.

Place ramekins in a 9-inch square pan; pour hot water into pan to depth of 1 inch. Bake at 325° for 30 minutes. Serve immediately. Yield: 4 servings (188 calories per serving).

Per Serving: PROTEIN 4.8g FAT 1.1g (Saturated Fat 0.2g)
CARBOHYDRATE 39.7g FIBER 4.1g CHOLESTEROL 1mg
IRON 1.0mg SODIUM 59mg CALCIUM 55mg

CURRIED SWEET POTATO STRIPS

3 small sweet potatoes, peeled (about 1½ pounds)
1 tablespoon plus 1 teaspoon vegetable oil
1 tablespoon unsweetened apple juice
½ teaspoon curry powder
Vegetable cooking spray

Cut each potato lengthwise into 14 thin wedges; place in a large heavy-duty, zip-top plastic bag. Add oil, apple juice, and curry powder to bag. Seal bag, and shake until potato wedges are well coated.

Remove potato wedges from bag, and place in a single layer on a 15- x 10- x 1-inch jellyroll pan coated with cooking spray. Bake at 400° for 45 minutes or until crisp and lightly browned, stirring every 10 minutes. Serve immediately. Yield: 4 servings (189 calories per serving).

Per Serving: PROTEIN 2.3g FAT 5.2g (Saturated Fat 0.9g)
CARBOHYDRATE 34.2g FIBER 4.2g CHOLESTEROL 0mg
IRON 0.9mg SODIUM 18mg CALCIUM 32mg

SPAGHETTI SQUASH ITALIANO

1 (2¼-pound) spaghetti squash
Vegetable cooking spray
1 teaspoon reduced-calorie margarine
1 cup chopped onion
¼ cup chopped green pepper
1 teaspoon minced garlic
2 cups peeled, chopped tomato
1 (8-ounce) can no-salt-added tomato sauce
¼ cup Chablis or other dry white wine
½ teaspoon dried Italian seasoning
½ teaspoon pepper
1 tablespoon grated Parmesan cheese
Fresh basil sprigs (optional)

Wash squash; cut in half lengthwise. Remove and discard seeds. Place squash, cut side down, in a 13- x 9- x 2-inch baking dish coated with cooking spray. Bake at 350° for 45 minutes or until tender; let cool. Using a fork, remove spaghetti-like strands; discard shells. Place squash strands in a 13- x 9- x 2-inch baking dish coated with cooking spray.

Coat a large nonstick skillet with cooking spray; add margarine. Place over medium-high heat until margarine melts. Add onion, green pepper, and garlic; sauté until tender. Stir in tomato; cook, uncovered, until thoroughly heated, stirring frequently. Add tomato sauce, wine, Italian seasoning, and pepper; stir well. Cover, reduce heat, and simmer 15 minutes.

Spoon tomato sauce mixture over squash; sprinkle with cheese. Bake, uncovered, at 350° for 20 to 25 minutes or until thoroughly heated. Garnish with fresh basil sprigs, if desired. Serve immediately. Yield: 8 servings (53 calories per ½-cup serving).

Per Serving: PROTEIN 1.5g FAT 1.1g (Saturated Fat 0.2g)
CARBOHYDRATE 10.1g FIBER 1.7g CHOLESTEROL 0mg
IRON 0.6mg SODIUM 40mg CALCIUM 33mg

STREUSEL-TOPPED BUTTERNUT SQUASH

1 (1½-pound) butternut squash
½ cup unsweetened applesauce
⅓ cup maple brown sugar low-fat yogurt
¼ teaspoon salt
¼ teaspoon ground cinnamon
Vegetable cooking spray
½ cup wheat bran flakes cereal, slightly crushed
3 tablespoons brown sugar
¼ teaspoon ground cinnamon
2 teaspoons reduced-calorie margarine, melted

Wash squash; cut in half lengthwise. Place, cut side down, in an 11- x 7- x 1½-inch baking dish. Add water to pan to depth of ½ inch. Cover and bake at 400° for 50 minutes or until squash is tender. Drain. Let cool. Remove and discard seeds. Scoop out pulp, and place in a medium bowl; discard shells.

Add applesauce, yogurt, salt, and ¼ teaspoon cinnamon. Beat at medium speed of an electric mixer until smooth. Spoon mixture into a 1-quart baking dish coated with cooking spray.

Combine cereal and remaining ingredients in a small bowl; stir well. Sprinkle over squash mixture. Bake, uncovered, at 400° for 15 to 20 minutes or until thoroughly heated. Yield: 5 servings (104 calories per ½-cup serving).

Per Serving: PROTEIN 2.2g FAT 1.5g (Saturated Fat 0.3g)
CARBOHYDRATE 23.2g FIBER 2.2g CHOLESTEROL 1mg
IRON 2.4mg SODIUM 200mg CALCIUM 71mg

WINTER VEGETABLE SAUTÉ

2 (16-ounce) cans whole beets, drained
Vegetable cooking spray
1 teaspoon vegetable oil
2 cups julienne-cut carrot
2 cups julienne-cut parsnip
7 green onions, cut into ½-inch pieces
½ teaspoon dried whole thyme
¼ teaspoon salt
⅛ teaspoon pepper

Cut beets into julienne strips; set aside 2 cups. Reserve remaining beets for another use.

Coat a large nonstick skillet with cooking spray; add oil. Place over medium-high heat until hot. Add carrot and remaining ingredients; sauté 3 to 5 minutes or until vegetables are crisp-tender. Add 2 cups beets; stir gently. Cook until thoroughly heated, stirring gently. Yield: 12 servings (34 calories per ½-cup serving).

Per Serving: PROTEIN 0.7g   FAT 0.5g   (Saturated Fat 0.1g)
CARBOHYDRATE 7.1g   FIBER 1.2g   CHOLESTEROL 0mg
IRON 0.5mg   SODIUM 124mg   CALCIUM 20mg

ZUCCHINI AND SPROUTS SAUTÉ

Olive oil-flavored vegetable cooking spray
1 teaspoon olive oil
1 cup julienne-cut green pepper
2 cloves garlic, minced
2 cups julienne-cut zucchini
2 cups fresh bean sprouts
½ teaspoon dried whole dillweed
¼ teaspoon salt
⅛ teaspoon pepper

Coat a large nonstick skillet with cooking spray; add olive oil. Place over medium-high heat until hot. Add green pepper and garlic; sauté 5 minutes or until pepper is crisp-tender. Add zucchini, and sauté 3 minutes. Stir in bean sprouts and remaining ingredients; sauté 5 minutes or until vegetables are tender. Yield: 5 servings (32 calories per ½-cup serving).

Per Serving: PROTEIN 1.8g   FAT 1.2g   (Saturated Fat 0.2g)
CARBOHYDRATE 4.9g   FIBER 1.0g   CHOLESTEROL 0mg
IRON 0.8mg   SODIUM 122mg   CALCIUM 18mg

VEGETABLE STIR-FRY

Olive oil-flavored vegetable cooking spray
1 medium onion, cut into thin wedges
1½ cups julienne-cut carrots
1½ cups fresh Sugar Snap peas, trimmed
1 cup chopped sweet red pepper
½ cup canned low-sodium chicken broth,
   undiluted
2 tablespoons low-sodium soy sauce
2 teaspoons cornstarch
1 teaspoon sugar
¼ teaspoon ground ginger
⅛ teaspoon ground red pepper

Coat a wok or large nonstick skillet with cooking spray. Heat at medium-high (375°) until hot. Add onion; stir-fry 3 minutes. Add carrot; stir-fry 2 minutes. Add peas and sweet red pepper; stir-fry 4 to 5 minutes or until vegetables are crisp-tender.

Combine chicken broth and remaining ingredients, stirring with a wire whisk until smooth; add to vegetable mixture. Cook, stirring constantly, until mixture is thickened. Serve immediately. Yield: 8 servings (42 calories per ½-cup serving).

Per Serving: PROTEIN 1.5g   FAT 0.4g   (Saturated Fat 0g)
CARBOHYDRATE 8.3g   FIBER 2.0g   CHOLESTEROL 0mg
IRON 0.9mg   SODIUM 111mg   CALCIUM 22mg

 MAGNIFICENT MAGNESIUM
A fairly common mineral, magnesium doesn't net much attention by the news media. But study after study supports this nutrient as being an important part of good nutrition. A recent report finds that a magnesium-rich diet can lower both total blood cholesterol and the harmful LDL cholesterol levels. And a preliminary report suggests that too little magnesium in the diet may be one culprit behind chronic fatigue syndrome.

Research is too preliminary to make concrete recommendations about how much magnesium to include in the diet. But researchers say it can't hurt to enjoy magnesium-rich foods such as green leafy vegetables, whole grains, almonds, and legumes, especially black beans, kidney beans, navy beans, and soybeans.

FRESH CITRUS FRUIT COCKTAIL

2 medium-size oranges, peeled, sectioned, and
   coarsely chopped
1 medium-size pink grapefruit, peeled, sectioned,
   and coarsely chopped
2 kiwifruit, peeled and coarsely chopped
¼ teaspoon grated orange rind
¼ teaspoon grated lime rind
3 tablespoons fresh orange juice
2 tablespoons honey
1 tablespoon fresh lime juice

Combine first 3 ingredients in a medium bowl,
and toss gently.
   Combine orange rind and remaining ingredients
in a small bowl; stir with a wire whisk until blended.
Pour orange juice mixture over fruit mixture, and
toss gently. Yield: 5 servings (81 calories per ½-cup
serving).

Per Serving: PROTEIN 1.2g FAT 0.3g (Saturated Fat 0.1g)
CARBOHYDRATE 19.9g FIBER 3.3g CHOLESTEROL 0mg
IRON 0.3mg SODIUM 1mg CALCIUM 31mg

YOGURT-TOPPED BROILED GRAPEFRUIT

2 large pink grapefruit
1 teaspoon sugar
¼ cup no-sugar-added strawberry spread
¼ cup vanilla low-fat yogurt

Cut grapefruit in half crosswise; remove seeds,
and loosen sections. Place grapefruit, cut side up,
on rack of a broiler pan.
   Sprinkle each grapefuit half with ¼ teaspoon
sugar. Spread 1 tablespoon strawberry spread over
each grapefruit half. Broil 5½ inches from heat (with
electric oven door partially opened) 6 minutes or
until thoroughly heated and sugar melts. Top each
grapefruit half with 1 tablespoon yogurt. Serve
immediately. Yield: 4 servings (104 calories per
serving).

Per Serving: PROTEIN 1.6g FAT 0.3g (Saturated Fat 0.1g)
CARBOHYDRATE 26.4g FIBER 0.9g CHOLESTEROL 1mg
IRON 0.1mg SODIUM 9mg CALCIUM 41mg

BAKED FRUIT COMPOTE

1 (20-ounce) can pineapple chunks in juice,
   undrained
1 (16-ounce) can apricot halves in light syrup,
   undrained
1 (16-ounce) can sliced peaches in light syrup,
   drained
1 (16-ounce) can seedless green grapes in light
   syrup, drained
¼ cup firmly packed brown sugar
1 tablespoon plus 1 teaspoon cornstarch
¼ teaspoon ground cinnamon
¼ teaspoon ground allspice
Poached baby pears (optional)

Drain pineapple, reserving ½ cup juice. Drain
apricot halves, reserving ¼ cup liquid. Combine pineapple, apricots, peaches, and grapes in a 13- x 9- x 2-
inch baking dish.
   Combine reserved fruit juices, brown sugar, and
next 3 ingredients in a small saucepan, stirring well.
Cook over medium heat, stirring constantly, until
thickened and bubbly. Remove from heat, and pour
over fruit; stir gently. Bake, uncovered, at 375° for
25 to 30 minutes or until bubbly. Serve warm.
Garnish with poached baby pears, if desired. Yield:
10 servings (111 calories per ½-cup serving).

Per Serving: PROTEIN 0.7g FAT 0.3g (Saturated Fat 0g)
CARBOHYDRATE 28.3g FIBER 1.0g CHOLESTEROL 0mg
IRON 1.0mg SODIUM 11mg CALCIUM 18mg

---

*Stir up a sea of exceptional flavor
and elegance with Shrimp and
Corn Chowder (page 226). Tempting
pieces of shrimp float atop the thick,
creamy chowder.*

Soups
&
Stews

CHILLED APRICOT-PEAR SOUP

1 (16-ounce) can apricot halves in juice
1 (16-ounce) can pear halves in juice
1 (8-ounce) carton vanilla low-fat yogurt
½ cup skim milk
2 tablespoons Grand Marnier or other
    orange-flavored liqueur
½ teaspoon ground cinnamon
¼ teaspoon ground nutmeg
⅛ teaspoon ground cloves
Fresh apricot slices (optional)
Fresh mint sprigs (optional)

Drain canned fruit, reserving 1 cup juice. Combine canned fruit, reserved 1 cup juice, and next 6 ingredients in container of an electric blender; cover and process 1 minute or until smooth, stopping once to scrape down sides. Cover and chill 2 hours.

To serve, ladle soup into individual bowls. If desired, garnish with fresh apricot slices and mint sprigs. Yield: 4½ cups (115 calories per ¾-cup serving).

Per Serving: PROTEIN 3.2g FAT 0.6g (Saturated Fat 0.4g)
CARBOHYDRATE 23.1g FIBER 1.5g CHOLESTEROL 2mg
IRON 0.6mg SODIUM 40mg CALCIUM 105mg

BEET AND CARROT SOUP

2 cups peeled, diced beets
2 cups diced carrot
1 cup finely chopped onion
3 cups canned low-sodium chicken broth,
    undiluted
½ cup unsweetened orange juice
1 tablespoon lemon juice
¼ teaspoon ground nutmeg
⅛ teaspoon ground allspice
3 tablespoons plus 1 teaspoon plain nonfat
    yogurt
Grated orange rind (optional)

Combine first 4 ingredients in a medium saucepan. Bring to a boil; cover, reduce heat, and simmer 30 minutes or until vegetables are tender. Remove from heat, and let cool 10 minutes.

Transfer vegetables to container of an electric blender, using a slotted spoon; reserve broth. Cover and process vegetable mixture until smooth, stopping once to scrape down sides. Add pureed mixture, orange juice, and next 3 ingredients to broth, stirring well with a wire whisk. Cover and chill thoroughly.

To serve, ladle soup into individual bowls. Top each serving with 2 teaspoons yogurt. Garnish with grated orange rind, if desired. Yield: 5 cups (94 calories per 1-cup serving).

Per Serving: PROTEIN 3.8g FAT 1.2g (Saturated Fat 0.3g)
CARBOHYDRATE 18.4g FIBER 2.8g CHOLESTEROL 0mg
IRON 1.5mg SODIUM 113mg CALCIUM 50mg

BEANS AND GREENS SOUP

Vegetable cooking spray
1½ cups chopped onion
1½ cups chopped carrot
1 clove garlic, minced
4 cups water
1 (15-ounce) can pinto beans, rinsed and
    drained
¼ cup chopped fresh parsley
1 teaspoon chicken-flavored bouillon granules
½ teaspoon dried whole thyme
¼ teaspoon ground red pepper
1 bay leaf
3 cups coarsely chopped kale
¾ cup diced lean smoked turkey ham
Fresh parsley sprigs (optional)

Coat a large Dutch oven with cooking spray; place over medium-high heat until hot. Add onion, carrot, and garlic; sauté until vegetables are crisp-tender.

Add water and next 6 ingredients; stir well. Bring to a boil; cover, reduce heat, and simmer 10 minutes. Add kale and ham. Cover and cook an additional 5 minutes or until thoroughly heated. Remove and discard bay leaf. Ladle soup into individual bowls. Garnish with parsley sprigs, if desired. Yield: 1½ quarts (206 calories per 1½-cup serving).

Per Serving: PROTEIN 14.2g FAT 2.8g (Saturated Fat 0.8g)
CARBOHYDRATE 33.4g FIBER 6.2g CHOLESTEROL 0mg
IRON 3.4mg SODIUM 907mg CALCIUM 124mg

ROBUST THREE-BEAN SOUP

Olive oil-flavored vegetable cooking spray
1 cup chopped onion
½ cup chopped green pepper
1 clove garlic, minced
1 (16-ounce) can kidney beans, drained
1 (14½-ounce) can no-salt-added whole tomatoes, undrained and chopped
1 (10-ounce) package frozen baby lima beans, thawed
1 (10-ounce) package frozen cut green beans, thawed
2 cups water
½ cup Burgundy or other dry red wine
¼ cup chopped fresh parsley
1 tablespoon low-sodium Worcestershire sauce
1 teaspoon beef-flavored bouillon granules
1 teaspoon dried whole basil
½ teaspoon dried whole thyme
¼ teaspoon salt
¼ teaspoon pepper

Coat a Dutch oven with cooking spray; place over medium-high heat until hot. Add onion, green pepper, and garlic; sauté 2 minutes or until onion and pepper are tender.

Add kidney beans and remaining ingredients, stirring well. Bring mixture to a boil; cover, reduce heat, and simmer 40 minutes or until vegetables are tender. Yield: 2 quarts (120 calories per 1-cup serving).

Per Serving: PROTEIN 7.0g FAT 0.5g (Saturated Fat 0.1g)
CARBOHYDRATE 23.1g FIBER 3.5g CHOLESTEROL 0mg
IRON 3.0mg SODIUM 331mg CALCIUM 65mg

CHICKEN AND BLACK BEAN SOUP

¾ cup dried black beans
2 (13¾-ounce) cans no-salt-added chicken broth
2 cups water
1 teaspoon dried whole oregano
½ teaspoon ground cumin
Vegetable cooking spray
1 cup chopped purple onion
¾ cup chopped green pepper
¾ cup chopped sweet red pepper
2 cloves garlic, minced
2¼ cups peeled, seeded, and chopped tomato
2 cups chopped cooked chicken breast (skinned before cooking and cooked without salt)
1 cup frozen whole kernel corn, thawed
¼ cup dry sherry
1 teaspoon chicken-flavored bouillon granules

Sort and wash beans; place beans in a large Dutch oven. Cover with water to a depth of 2 inches above beans; let soak overnight. Drain beans. Combine beans, broth, water, oregano, and cumin in pan; bring to a boil. Cover, reduce heat, and simmer 1 hour or until beans are tender, stirring occasionally.

Coat a nonstick skillet with cooking spray; place over medium-high heat until hot. Add onion, peppers, and garlic; sauté until tender. Add onion mixture, tomato, and remaining ingredients to bean mixture. Cover; simmer 30 minutes or until vegetables are tender. Yield: 2½ quarts (160 calories per 1-cup serving).

Per Serving: PROTEIN 15.4g FAT 3.0g (Saturated Fat 0.7g)
CARBOHYDRATE 18.4g FIBER 3.7g CHOLESTEROL 28mg
IRON 1.9mg SODIUM 158mg CALCIUM 37mg

IRON: TOO MUCH OF A GOOD THING?

In 1992, a Finnish study suggested that iron may play a role in the development of heart disease in men. The study, which monitored serum levels of ferritin (an iron-storing protein) in 1,931 men for five years, found that those with levels considered normal were more than twice as likely to have heart attacks than those with lower levels. One possible explanation was that in the blood vessels, iron helped oxidize LDL cholesterol, turning it into a form that was more likely to clog arteries.

Studies in the U.S. haven't confirmed a relationship between iron levels and heart attacks. Iron could be a marker for something else that causes the problem, such as a diet high in red meat. So for now, don't give up iron-rich foods but note that iron supplements usually aren't necessary except under a doctor's orders.

SPICY CHICKEN AND
RICE SOUP

4 (6-ounce) skinned chicken breast halves
2 cups sliced carrot
1 cup chopped onion
½ cup sliced celery
1 bay leaf
5 cups water
2 (14½-ounce) cans no-salt-added whole tomatoes,
    undrained and chopped
½ cup chopped green pepper
1 teaspoon ground cumin
½ teaspoon ground coriander
½ teaspoon crushed red pepper
¼ teaspoon garlic powder
¼ teaspoon ground cinnamon
¼ teaspoon ground allspice
⅓ cup long-grain rice, uncooked
¼ cup currants
1 tablespoon plus 2 teaspoons chopped fresh
    parsley

Combine chicken, carrot, onion, celery, bay leaf, and water in a large Dutch oven. Bring to a boil; cover, reduce heat, and simmer 25 minutes or until chicken is tender. Remove chicken from broth; skim fat from broth, reserving broth. Bone chicken, and cut into bite-size pieces.

Add chicken, tomato, green pepper, cumin, coriander, red pepper, garlic powder, cinnamon, and allspice to broth in pan. Bring mixture to a boil; cover, reduce heat, and simmer 15 minutes. Stir in uncooked rice and currants. Cover and simmer an additional 25 minutes or until rice is tender. Ladle soup into individual bowls, and sprinkle each serving with ½ teaspoon chopped fresh parsley. Yield: 2½ quarts (148 calories per 1-cup serving).

Per Serving: PROTEIN 17.6g FAT 2.1g (Saturated Fat 0.6g)
CARBOHYDRATE 14.5g FIBER 1.9g CHOLESTEROL 43mg
IRON 1.6mg SODIUM 68mg CALCIUM 55mg

SCANDINAVIAN CREAMY
VEGETABLE SOUP

2 cups sliced carrot
1 cup frozen English peas, thawed
1 cup cauliflower flowerets
1 cup chopped celery
½ cup chopped onion
2 cups canned low-sodium chicken broth,
    undiluted
2 cups thinly sliced romaine lettuce
¼ cup plus 2 tablespoons all-purpose flour
2½ cups skim milk, divided
2 tablespoons chopped fresh parsley
½ teaspoon dried whole dillweed
¼ teaspoon salt
⅛ teaspoon ground white pepper

Combine first 6 ingredients in a Dutch oven. Bring to a boil; cover, reduce heat, and simmer 10 minutes or until vegetables are tender. Add lettuce; cook, uncovered, 1 minute.

Combine flour and 1 cup milk, stirring until smooth. Add flour mixture, remaining 1½ cups milk, parsley, dillweed, salt, and pepper to vegetable mixture. Cook, stirring constantly, 5 minutes or until mixture is thickened and bubbly. Ladle soup into individual bowls. Yield: 2 quarts (97 calories per 1-cup serving).

Per Serving: PROTEIN 5.9g FAT 0.8g (Saturated Fat 0.2g)
CARBOHYDRATE 17.2g FIBER 3.2g CHOLESTEROL 2mg
IRON 1.5mg SODIUM 184mg CALCIUM 130mg

Let the vibrant colors of Pork-Pepper Soup entice you to experience its equally outstanding taste.

PORK-PEPPER SOUP

1 pound lean boneless pork loin (½ inch thick)
Vegetable cooking spray
1 cup chopped onion
2 cloves garlic, minced
1 jalapeño pepper, seeded and sliced
1 cup sliced carrot
2 cups canned low-sodium chicken broth,
    undiluted
1 cup water
¼ cup chopped fresh parsley
2 tablespoons low-sodium soy sauce
½ teaspoon dried whole basil
¼ teaspoon dried whole thyme
¼ teaspoon pepper
1 small green pepper, cut into thin strips
1 small sweet red pepper, cut into thin strips
1 small sweet yellow pepper, cut into thin strips
2 tablespoons pine nuts, toasted

Trim fat from pork; cut pork into ½-inch cubes. Coat a large Dutch oven with cooking spray; place over medium heat until hot. Add pork, and cook until pork is browned on all sides, stirring frequently. Drain and pat dry with paper towels. Wipe drippings from pan with a paper towel.

Coat pan with cooking spray; place over medium-high heat until hot. Add onion, garlic, and jalapeño pepper; sauté until tender. Add pork, carrot, and next 7 ingredients. Bring mixture to a boil; cover, reduce heat, and simmer 30 minutes or until pork is tender. Add pepper strips; cover and cook an additional 10 minutes or until pepper is tender. Stir in toasted pine nuts. Yield: 1½ quarts (185 calories per 1-cup serving).

Per Serving: PROTEIN 18.6g FAT 8.6g (Saturated Fat 2.4g)
CARBOHYDRATE 9.2g FIBER 2.1g CHOLESTEROL 45mg
IRON 2.6mg SODIUM 248mg CALCIUM 29mg

SALMON CHOWDER

½ pound fresh green beans
2 cups peeled, cubed potato
1 cup chopped onion
3 cups water
½ cup clam juice
1 tablespoon minced fresh tarragon
1 teaspoon chicken-flavored bouillon granules
¼ teaspoon ground white pepper
⅛ teaspoon garlic powder
1 pound salmon fillets, cut into ¾-inch pieces
⅓ cup all-purpose flour
2 cups skim milk, divided
¾ to 1 teaspoon grated lemon rind

Wash green beans; trim ends, and remove strings. Cut beans into ¾-inch pieces. Combine beans and next 8 ingredients in a Dutch oven. Bring mixture to a boil; cover, reduce heat, and simmer 15 minutes. Add salmon; cover and cook an additional 5 minutes.

Combine flour and ½ cup milk in a small bowl, stirring with a wire whisk until smooth. Gradually add flour mixture and remaining 1½ cups milk to salmon mixture. Cook, stirring constantly, 15 minutes or until mixture is slightly thickened. Remove mixture from heat, and stir in grated lemon rind.

Ladle chowder into individual bowls. Yield: 9 cups (154 calories per 1-cup serving).

Per Serving: PROTEIN 14.7g FAT 3.3g (Saturated Fat 0.7g) CARBOHYDRATE 16.0g FIBER 1.5g CHOLESTEROL 21mg IRON 1.1mg SODIUM 175mg CALCIUM 84mg

SHRIMP AND CORN CHOWDER

1 poblano pepper
1 large sweet red pepper
Vegetable cooking spray
½ cup chopped onion
2 cloves garlic, minced
2 (10-ounce) packages frozen whole kernel corn, thawed
2 cups 1% low-fat milk, divided
⅔ cup evaporated skimmed milk
1½ teaspoons cornstarch
3 tablespoons water
¼ teaspoon salt
1 pound unpeeled medium-size fresh shrimp
2 tablespoons minced fresh cilantro
Fresh cilantro sprigs (optional)

Cut peppers in half lengthwise; remove and discard seeds and membrane. Place peppers, skin side up, on a baking sheet; flatten with palm of hand. Broil 5½ inches from heat (with electric oven door partially opened) 15 minutes or until charred. Place peppers in ice water; chill 5 minutes. Remove from water; peel and discard skins. Dice peppers; set aside.

Coat a nonstick skillet with cooking spray; place over medium-high heat until hot. Add onion and garlic; sauté until tender.

Position knife blade in food processor bowl; add onion mixture and corn. Process until smooth. Transfer pureed mixture to a large saucepan; stir in 1 cup 1% milk. Cook over medium heat, stirring constantly, 15 minutes. Stir in remaining 1 cup 1% milk. Cover and cook over medium-low heat 10 minutes, stirring occasionally.

Pour corn mixture into a wire-mesh strainer; press with back of spoon against the sides of the strainer to squeeze out liquid. Discard pulp remaining in strainer. Return corn mixture to saucepan, and stir in evaporated milk.

Combine cornstarch and water; add to corn mixture, and stir well. Add diced pepper and salt; stir well. Bring to a boil; reduce heat, and simmer, uncovered, 20 minutes or until thickened, stirring frequently.

Peel and devein shrimp. Add shrimp to corn mixture; cook over medium heat 3 to 5 minutes or until shrimp turns pink. Stir in minced cilantro. Ladle chowder into individual serving bowls, and garnish with cilantro sprigs, if desired. Yield: 1½ quarts (222 calories per 1-cup serving).

Per Serving: PROTEIN 19.9g FAT 2.9g (Saturated Fat 0.9g) CARBOHYDRATE 31.9g FIBER 1.3g CHOLESTEROL 91mg IRON 2.5mg SODIUM 261mg CALCIUM 224m

BEEF AND BEAN PICADILLO

1¼ pounds lean boneless top round steak (½ inch thick)
Vegetable cooking spray
1½ cups chopped onion
1 tablespoon seeded, chopped jalapeño pepper
2 cloves garlic, minced
3 cups water
1 (14½-ounce) can no-salt-added whole tomatoes, undrained and chopped
2 tablespoons Burgundy or other dry red wine
1 teaspoon beef-flavored bouillon granules
½ teaspoon ground red pepper
½ teaspoon ground cinnamon
½ teaspoon ground cloves
¼ teaspoon ground allspice
1 (16-ounce) can black beans, drained
1 cup peeled, chopped apple
3 tablespoons raisins

Trim fat from steak; cut steak into 1-inch pieces. Coat a Dutch oven with cooking spray; place over medium-high heat until hot. Add steak; cook until browned on all sides, stirring frequently. Drain and pat dry with paper towels. Wipe drippings from pan with a paper towel.

Coat pan with cooking spray; place over medium-high heat until hot. Add onion, jalapeño pepper, and garlic; sauté until onion is tender.

Add steak, water, tomato, red wine, bouillon granules, red pepper, cinnamon, cloves, and all-spice, stirring well. Bring mixture to a boil; cover, reduce heat, and simmer 1 hour and 40 minutes. Add beans, apple, and raisins. Cover and simmer an additional 10 minutes or until steak and apple are tender. Yield: 5 cups (290 calories per 1-cup serving).

Per Serving: PROTEIN 31.4g FAT 5.6g (Saturated Fat 1.8g)
CARBOHYDRATE 29.1g FIBER 4.2g CHOLESTEROL 65mg
IRON 4.1mg SODIUM 382mg CALCIUM 65mg

ORIENTAL BEEF-VEGETABLE STEW

1 pound lean boneless top round steak (½ inch thick)
Vegetable cooking spray
1 medium onion, sliced
2 cloves garlic, minced
1 (14½-ounce) can no-salt-added whole tomatoes, undrained and chopped
2½ cups water
2 tablespoons low-sodium soy sauce
1 tablespoon brown sugar
2 teaspoons peeled, grated gingerroot
1½ cups sliced carrot
1 cup sliced fresh mushrooms
½ cup fresh bean sprouts
1 (4-ounce) jar sliced pimiento, drained
1½ cups broccoli flowerets

Trim fat from steak; cut steak into 1-inch pieces. Coat a Dutch oven with cooking spray; place over medium-high heat until hot. Add steak; cook until browned on all sides, stirring frequently. Drain and pat dry with paper towels. Wipe drippings from pan with a paper towel.

Coat pan with cooking spray; place over medium-high heat until hot. Add onion and garlic; sauté until onion is tender.

Add steak, tomato, water, soy sauce, brown sugar, and gingerroot, stirring well. Bring to a boil; cover, reduce heat, and simmer 1½ hours.

Add sliced carrot; cover and cook 20 minutes. Stir in sliced mushrooms, bean sprouts, and pimiento; cover and cook 15 minutes. Add broccoli, and cook an additional 15 minutes or until meat and broccoli are tender. Yield: 7 cups (141 calories per 1-cup serving).

Per Serving: PROTEIN 17.2g FAT 3.1g (Saturated Fat 1.0g)
CARBOHYDRATE 11.7g FIBER 2.3g CHOLESTEROL 37mg
IRON 2.5mg SODIUM 199mg CALCIUM 48mg

With a skillful blend of herbs and spices, a classic combination of chicken and vegetables becomes a superb Indian-style dish in Curried Chicken-Vegetable Stew.

CURRIED CHICKEN-VEGETABLE STEW

3 (6-ounce) skinned chicken breast halves
¾ cup chopped onion
3 cloves garlic, minced
½ teaspoon dried crushed red pepper
3 cups water
1 (14½-ounce) can no-salt-added whole tomatoes, undrained and chopped
2 cups cubed zucchini
2 cups cubed yellow squash
1 cup sliced carrot
1 medium-size sweet red pepper, seeded and cut into strips
½ cup no-salt-added tomato sauce
3 tablespoons no-salt-added tomato paste
1 teaspoon ground ginger
½ teaspoon salt
½ teaspoon ground cumin
½ teaspoon ground coriander
¼ teaspoon ground fenugreek

Combine chicken breast halves, chopped onion, minced garlic, crushed red pepper, and water in a large Dutch oven. Bring mixture to a boil; cover, reduce heat, and simmer 25 minutes or until chicken is tender.

Remove chicken breast halves from broth; skim fat from broth, reserving broth. Bone chicken, and cut into bite-size pieces.

Combine reserved broth, cooked chicken, chopped tomato, and remaining ingredients in pan; stir well.

Bring mixture to a boil; cover, reduce heat, and simmer 30 minutes or until vegetables are tender. Ladle chicken and vegetable stew into individual bowls. Yield: 9 cups (136 calories per 1½-cup serving).

Per Serving: PROTEIN 16.2g FAT 1.9g (Saturated Fat 0.5g)
CARBOHYDRATE 14.6g FIBER 3.3g CHOLESTEROL 37mg
IRON 2.0mg SODIUM 257mg CALCIUM 63mg

CHICKEN POSOLE

3 (6-ounce) skinned chicken breast halves
1 medium onion, sliced
3 cloves garlic, minced
1 teaspoon chicken-flavored bouillon granules
¼ teaspoon pepper
4 cups water
1 (16-ounce) can white hominy, drained
½ cup chopped sweet red pepper
½ cup chopped sweet yellow pepper
1 tablespoon chili powder
1 teaspoon ground cumin
1 teaspoon dried whole oregano
1 teaspoon dried whole coriander
¼ teaspoon salt
1¾ cups seeded, chopped tomato
1½ cups finely shredded iceberg lettuce
¼ cup plus 2 tablespoons sliced radish

Combine first 6 ingredients in a Dutch oven. Bring to a boil; cover, reduce heat, and simmer 35 minutes or until chicken is tender. Remove chicken from broth; skim fat from broth, reserving broth. Bone chicken, and chop.

Combine reserved broth, chicken, hominy, sweet red pepper, sweet yellow pepper, chili powder, ground cumin, oregano, coriander, and salt in pan, stirring well. Bring to a boil; cover, reduce heat, and simmer 20 minutes. Stir in chopped tomato; cook, uncovered, 5 minutes. Ladle soup into individual bowls. Top each serving with ¼ cup chopped lettuce and 1 tablespoon sliced radish. Yield: 1½ quarts (171 calories per 1-cup serving).

Per Serving: PROTEIN 18.0g FAT 3.2g (Saturated Fat 0.7g)
CARBOHYDRATE 17.7g FIBER 4.0g CHOLESTEROL 42mg
IRON 2.2mg SODIUM 434mg CALCIUM 44mg

LAMB AND APPLES INDIENNE

1 pound lean boneless lamb
Vegetable cooking spray
1 medium onion, sliced
1 cup sliced celery
½ cup chopped sweet red pepper
2 cloves garlic, minced
2 cups canned low-sodium chicken broth,
    undiluted
1 teaspoon curry powder
½ teaspoon ground cumin
¼ teaspoon ground allspice
⅛ to ¼ teaspoon ground white pepper
2 medium-size Granny Smith apples, peeled,
    cored, and sliced
2 cups peeled, cubed sweet potato
¼ cup sliced green onions

Trim fat from lamb; cut lamb into 1-inch pieces. Coat a Dutch oven with cooking spray; place over

medium-high heat until hot. Add lamb, and cook until browned on all sides, stirring occasionally. Drain and pat dry with paper towels. Wipe drippings from pan with a paper towel.

Coat pan with cooking spray; place over medium-high heat until hot. Add onion, celery, red pepper, and garlic; sauté until crisp-tender.

Add lamb, chicken broth, and next 4 ingredients; stir well. Bring to a boil; cover, reduce heat, and simmer 45 minutes. Add apple and sweet potato, stirring well. Cover and cook an additional 20 minutes or until lamb and vegetables are tender.

Ladle soup into individual bowls. Sprinkle each serving with 2 teaspoons sliced green onions. Yield: 1½ quarts (204 calories per 1-cup serving).

Per Serving: PROTEIN 16.7g FAT 4.4g (Saturated Fat 1.3g)
CARBOHYDRATE 25.1g FIBER 4.1g CHOLESTEROL 45mg
IRON 2.5mg SODIUM 94mg CALCIUM 38mg

RUSTIC TURKEY AND MACARONI STEW

1 pound turkey tenderloins
½ teaspoon cracked pepper
Olive oil-flavored vegetable cooking spray
1 teaspoon olive oil
1½ cups chopped onion
1 clove garlic, minced
2 cups coarsely chopped carrot
2 cups coarsely chopped celery
¼ cup chopped fresh parsley
½ teaspoon dried whole thyme
1 bay leaf
3 cups canned low-sodium chicken broth,
    undiluted
½ cup Chablis or other dry white wine
1 tablespoon balsamic vinegar
½ cup elbow macaroni, uncooked
¼ cup sliced ripe olives
2 tablespoons plus 1 teaspoon freshly grated
    Parmesan cheese

Cut turkey into 1-inch pieces, and sprinkle with pepper. Coat a large Dutch oven with cooking spray; add olive oil. Place over medium heat until hot. Add turkey, and cook until turkey is browned on all sides, stirring frequently. Drain and pat dry with paper towels. Wipe drippings from pan with a paper towel.

Coat pan with cooking spray; place over medium-high heat until hot. Add onion and garlic; sauté until tender.

Add turkey, carrot, and next 7 ingredients, stirring well. Bring to a boil; cover, reduce heat, and simmer 25 minutes or until vegetables are tender. Add macaroni and olives; cover and cook an additional 10 minutes or until macaroni is tender. Remove and discard bay leaf. Ladle stew into individual bowls. Sprinkle each serving with 1 teaspoon cheese. Yield: 7 cups (174 calories per 1-cup serving).

Per Serving: PROTEIN 18.0g FAT 3.8g (Saturated Fat 1.1g)
CARBOHYDRATE 16.9g FIBER 2.9g CHOLESTEROL 37mg
IRON 2.4mg SODIUM 193mg CALCIUM 78mg

TURKEY MEATBALL STEW

1 pound freshly ground raw turkey
½ cup soft breadcrumbs
1 tablespoon chopped fresh parsley
1 teaspoon white wine Worcestershire sauce
½ teaspoon dried whole marjoram
¼ teaspoon salt
¼ teaspoon dried whole sage
¼ teaspoon pepper
Vegetable cooking spray
1 teaspoon vegetable oil
2 cups sliced carrot
½ cup chopped onion
½ teaspoon dried whole thyme
2 cups canned low-sodium chicken broth,
    undiluted
1 cup water
2 cups sliced fresh mushrooms
1 (8-ounce) package frozen Sugar Snap peas,
    thawed

Combine first 8 ingredients in a medium bowl; stir well. Shape into 24 meatballs.

Coat a Dutch oven with cooking spray; add oil. Place over medium heat until hot. Add meatballs, and cook 6 to 8 minutes or until browned, stirring frequently. Drain and pat dry with paper towels. Wipe drippings from pan with a paper towel.

Return meatballs to pan; add carrot, onion, thyme, chicken broth, and water. Bring to a boil; cover, reduce heat, and simmer 40 minutes or until vegetables are tender. Add mushrooms and peas; stir well. Cover and simmer 10 minutes or until thoroughly heated. Yield: 1½ quarts (166 calories per 1-cup serving).

Per Serving: PROTEIN 19.3g FAT 3.5g (Saturated Fat 0.9g)
CARBOHYDRATE 13.1g FIBER 3.2g CHOLESTEROL 49mg
IRON 2.9mg SODIUM 204mg CALCIUM 53mg

End a distinctive dinner with heavenly Chocolate Mint Pudding (page 235). Indulging in this creamy chocolate fantasy won't leave you feeling guilty because it's so low in fat.

Desserts

AUTUMN FRUIT IN SPICED SAUCE

¼ cup raisins
1½ tablespoons brandy
Vegetable cooking spray
1 tablespoon reduced-calorie margarine
1⅓ cups chopped red cooking apple
1⅓ cups chopped fresh pear
¾ cup sugar
3 tablespoons cornstarch
¾ cup unsweetened apple juice
¾ cup water
1 tablespoon lemon juice
¾ teaspoon ground cinnamon
½ teaspoon ground nutmeg
2⅓ cups vanilla low-fat frozen yogurt

Combine raisins and brandy in a bowl; set aside.

Coat a medium nonstick skillet with cooking spray; add margarine. Place over medium-high heat until margarine melts. Add apple and pear; sauté 3 to 4 minutes or until tender. Set aside.

Combine sugar and cornstarch in a medium saucepan. Stir in apple juice and next 4 ingredients. Cook over medium heat, stirring constantly with a wire whisk, until mixture comes to a boil; boil 1 minute, stirring constantly. Remove from heat; stir in raisin mixture and apple mixture.

Scoop ⅓ cup frozen yogurt into each individual dessert bowl, and top each with ½ cup apple mixture. Serve immediately. Yield: 7 servings (228 calories per serving).

Per Serving: PROTEIN 2.1g FAT 2.6g (Saturated Fat 1.0g)
CARBOHYDRATE 49.9g FIBER 1.9g CHOLESTEROL 6mg
IRON 0.4mg SODIUM 38mg CALCIUM 70mg

BANANA-CITRUS TRIFLE

8 ounces commercial angel food cake
3⅓ cups sliced banana (about 5 medium)
1 tablespoon lime juice
3 medium-size oranges
¼ cup sugar
¼ cup water
1½ teaspoons grated orange rind
1½ teaspoons grated lime rind
1½ cups vanilla low-fat yogurt

Cut cake into ¼-inch-thick slices; set aside. Combine banana slices and lime juice; set aside.

Peel and section oranges, catching juice in a small saucepan. Set sections aside. Add sugar and water to saucepan, stirring well. Bring to a boil; cook, uncovered, 4 to 5 minutes or until mixture is reduced to ⅓ cup. Remove from heat, and stir in grated rinds. Pour over banana slices, and toss gently.

Arrange half of cake slices in a 2-quart trifle bowl. Spoon half of banana mixture over cake slices. Spread half of yogurt over banana mixture, and arrange half of orange sections over yogurt. Repeat layering procedure with remaining cake, banana mixture, yogurt, and orange sections. Cover and chill 6 hours. Yield: 8 servings (219 calories per serving).

Per Serving: PROTEIN 4.8g FAT 1.0g (Saturated Fat 0.5g)
CARBOHYDRATE 50.9g FIBER 4.1g CHOLESTEROL 2mg
IRON 0.4mg SODIUM 70mg CALCIUM 124mg

CHAMPAGNE BERRY PARFAITS

2 cups fresh strawberries
1 cup champagne
⅓ cup sugar
1½ cups fresh strawberries, halved
1½ cups fresh blackberries
1 cup fresh blueberries
1 cup fresh raspberries
1 quart vanilla nonfat frozen yogurt, softened

Place 2 cups strawberries in container of an electric blender or food processor; cover and process until smooth. Transfer strawberry puree to a saucepan. Add champagne and sugar; stir. Bring to a boil; reduce heat, and cook, uncovered, 30 minutes or until mixture is reduced to 1 cup, stirring occasionally.

Combine strawberry halves, blackberries, blueberries, and raspberries in a medium bowl. Pour champagne mixture over berries, and toss gently.

Spoon ¼ cup yogurt into each of 8 parfait glasses. Top each with ¼ cup berry mixture. Repeat layers with remaining yogurt and fruit mixture. Cover and freeze 30 minutes. Yield: 8 servings (174 calories per ½-cup serving).

Per Serving: PROTEIN 4.5g FAT 0.6g (Saturated Fat 0g)
CARBOHYDRATE 40.9g FIBER 6.5g CHOLESTEROL 0mg
IRON 0.7mg SODIUM 65mg CALCIUM 156mg

CHERRIES JUBILEE

1 cup unsweetened cherry juice blend
¼ cup sugar
2 tablespoons cornstarch
2 teaspoons grated lemon rind
1 teaspoon ground cinnamon
4 cups frozen unsweetened dark sweet cherries, thawed
½ teaspoon almond extract
⅓ cup amaretto
1 quart vanilla ice milk

Combine first 5 ingredients in a large skillet, stirring well. Bring to a boil, stirring constantly. Reduce heat, and simmer 2 to 3 minutes or until mixture is thickened, stirring occasionally. Remove from heat; stir in cherries and almond extract.

Place amaretto in a small, long-handled pan; heat just until warm. Ignite with a long match; pour over cherry mixture. Stir gently until flame dies down.

Scoop ½ cup ice milk into each individual dessert bowl. Spoon cherry mixture evenly over ice milk. Serve immediately. Yield: 8 servings (204 calories per serving).

Per Serving: PROTEIN 3.5g FAT 3.3g (Saturated Fat 1.9g) CARBOHYDRATE 42.0g FIBER 0.4g CHOLESTEROL 9mg IRON 0.7mg SODIUM 56mg CALCIUM 104mg

PEACH COBBLER

½ cup firmly packed brown sugar
½ cup water
1 tablespoon cornstarch
¾ teaspoon ground cinnamon
3½ cups sliced frozen peaches, thawed
2½ teaspoons margarine
1 teaspoon lemon juice
½ teaspoon vanilla extract
Vegetable cooking spray
1 cup all-purpose flour
1¼ teaspoons baking powder
¼ teaspoon salt
½ cup sugar
⅔ cup skim milk
3 tablespoons margarine, softened
2½ cups vanilla nonfat frozen yogurt

Combine first 4 ingredients in a large saucepan, stirring well. Add peaches, stirring well. Cook over medium heat, stirring constantly, 6 to 8 minutes or until mixture is thickened and bubbly. Add 2½ teaspoons margarine, lemon juice, and vanilla; stir until margarine melts. Transfer to an 11- x 7- x 1½-inch baking dish coated with cooking spray. Set aside.

Combine flour and next 3 ingredients in a bowl; stir well. Add milk and 3 tablespoons margarine; beat at medium speed of an electric mixer until smooth. Pour over peach mixture. Bake at 350° for 45 minutes or until lightly browned. Let stand 5 minutes. Spoon into individual serving bowls. Top each with ¼ cup yogurt. Serve immediately. Yield: 10 servings (249 calories per serving).

Per Serving: PROTEIN 4.2g FAT 4.6g (Saturated Fat 0.9g) CARBOHYDRATE 49.7g FIBER 1.6g CHOLESTEROL 0mg IRON 1.0mg SODIUM 190mg CALCIUM 128mg

PLUM AND WALNUT CRISP

½ cup sugar
2 tablespoons cornstarch
1½ teaspoons grated lemon rind
4 pounds purple plums, pitted and quartered
2 tablespoons fresh lemon juice
¾ cup regular oats, uncooked
¼ cup all-purpose flour
¼ cup firmly packed brown sugar
¼ cup reduced-calorie margarine
¼ cup chopped walnuts
Vegetable cooking spray

Combine first 3 ingredients in a large bowl; stir well. Add plums, and toss gently to coat. Add lemon juice, and toss gently. Let stand 30 minutes.

Combine oats, flour, and brown sugar in a small bowl. Cut in margarine with a pastry blender until mixture resembles coarse meal. Stir in walnuts.

Spoon plum mixture into a 2½-quart casserole coated with cooking spray. Cover; bake at 400° for 40 minutes. Sprinkle oat mixture over plums. Bake, uncovered, 15 minutes or until lightly browned. Serve warm. Yield: 12 servings (180 calories per serving).

Per Serving: PROTEIN 2.4g FAT 4.3g (Saturated Fat 0.5g) CARBOHYDRATE 36.0g FIBER 3.3g CHOLESTEROL 0mg IRON 0.7mg SODIUM 39mg CALCIUM 13mg

Cranberry and Lime Layered Parfait is a refreshing fusion of two intriguing flavors.

CRANBERRY AND LIME LAYERED PARFAIT

4 cups fresh cranberries
¾ cup sugar
⅓ cup cranberry juice cocktail
2 tablespoons fresh lemon juice
1½ teaspoons grated lemon rind
¾ cup sugar, divided
3 tablespoons cornstarch
2 cups skim milk
1 teaspoon vanilla extract
¾ teaspoon unflavored gelatin
2 tablespoons cold water
6 ounces light process cream cheese product
⅓ cup sifted powdered sugar
1 tablespoon grated lime rind
1 tablespoon fresh lime juice
3 egg whites
⅛ teaspoon cream of tartar
¼ cup water
Additional fresh cranberries (optional)
Lime zest (optional)

Combine first 5 ingredients in a large saucepan. Cook over medium heat 10 to 15 minutes or until mixture is thickened, stirring frequently. Pour mixture through a wire-mesh strainer into a bowl, discarding pulp. Set strained mixture aside.

Combine ¼ cup sugar and cornstarch in a medium saucepan; gradually stir in milk. Bring to a boil; reduce heat, and cook, stirring constantly, 1 minute. Remove from heat, and stir in vanilla. Gently fold into cranberry mixture. Cover and chill 1 hour.

Sprinkle gelatin over cold water in a small saucepan; let stand 1 minute. Cook over low heat, stirring until gelatin dissolves, about 2 minutes.

Combine cream cheese and powdered sugar in container of an electric blender; cover and process until smooth. Add gelatin mixture, lime rind, and lime juice; cover and process until smooth. Set aside.

Beat egg whites and cream of tartar at high speed of an electric mixer until stiff peaks form.

Combine remaining ½ cup sugar and ¼ cup water in a small saucepan. Bring to a boil; cook, without stirring, until candy thermometer registers 238° (about 7 minutes).

Gradually pour sugar mixture in a thin stream over beaten egg whites while beating constantly at high speed. Continue to beat until egg white mixture is cool and set.

Gently fold egg white mixture into lime mixture. Layer half of cranberry mixture and all of lime mixture evenly in 12 (¾-cup) parfait glasses. Cover and chill 15 minutes. Spoon remaining half of cranberry mixture evenly over lime mixture. Cover and chill 2 hours. If desired, garnish with additional fresh cranberries and lime zest. Yield: 12 servings (188 calories per serving).

Per Serving: PROTEIN 3.3g FAT 2.5g (Saturated Fat 1.5g) CARBOHYDRATE 39.3g FIBER 0.1g CHOLESTEROL 9mg IRON 0.2mg SODIUM 107mg CALCIUM 74mg

CHOCOLATE MINT PUDDING

½ cup sugar
⅓ cup unsweetened cocoa
¼ cup cornstarch
3 cups 1% low-fat milk
1 tablespoon crème de menthe
1 teaspoon vanilla extract
3 peppermint candy pieces, coarsely crushed

Combine first 3 ingredients in a medium saucepan. Gradually add milk, stirring with a wire whisk until smooth. Cook over medium-low heat, stirring constantly, 25 to 30 minutes or until mixture is thickened. Remove from heat; stir in liqueur and vanilla.

Spoon mixture into individual dessert dishes. Cover and chill thoroughly. Just before serving, sprinkle evenly with crushed peppermint. Yield: 7 servings (152 calories per ½-cup serving).

Per Serving: PROTEIN 4.6g FAT 1.7g (Saturated Fat 1.0g) CARBOHYDRATE 28.5g FIBER 0g CHOLESTEROL 4mg IRON 0.8mg SODIUM 55mg CALCIUM 135mg

CHOCOLATE RUM MOUSSE

½ cup sugar
¼ cup cornstarch
¼ cup unsweetened cocoa
1 teaspoon unflavored gelatin
3 cups skim milk
2 tablespoons Kahlúa or other coffee-flavored liqueur
1 teaspoon vanilla extract
2 egg whites
Dash of cream of tartar
⅓ cup sugar
2½ tablespoons water
Orange curls (optional)

Combine first 4 ingredients in a large saucepan. Gradually stir in milk and liqueur, stirring with a wire whisk until smooth. Cook over medium heat, stirring constantly, until mixture comes to a boil. Reduce heat, and simmer, stirring constantly, 2 minutes. Remove from heat; stir in vanilla. Cover with plastic wrap, gently pressing directly on surface of chocolate mixture. Let cool.

Beat egg whites and cream of tartar at high speed of an electric mixer until stiff peaks form.

Combine ⅓ cup sugar and water in a small saucepan. Bring mixture to a boil; cook, without stirring, until candy thermometer registers 238° (about 7 minutes).

Gradually pour sugar mixture in a thin stream over beaten egg whites while beating constantly at high speed. Continue to beat until egg white mixture is cool and set.

Fold chocolate mixture into egg white mixture. Spoon into individual dessert dishes. Cover with plastic wrap, gently pressing directly on surface of mousse. Chill at least 4 hours. Garnish with orange curls, if desired. Yield: 10 servings (117 calories per ½-cup serving).

Per Serving: PROTEIN 4.1g FAT 0.4g (Saturated Fat 0.3g) CARBOHYDRATE 24.3g FIBER 0g CHOLESTEROL 2mg IRON 0.4mg SODIUM 52mg CALCIUM 94mg

ESPRESSO GRANITÁ

1 cup sugar
²/₃ cup water
2 tablespoons Kahlûa or other coffee-flavored
   liqueur
2 tablespoons Grand Marnier or other
   orange-flavored liqueur
1 (3-inch) stick cinnamon
3 cups strong brewed espresso

Combine first 5 ingredients in a small saucepan. Bring mixture to a boil; reduce heat, and simmer 5 minutes, stirring frequently. Remove from heat, and let cool slightly. Remove and discard cinnamon stick. Add espresso, and stir well. Cover and chill thoroughly.

Pour mixture into freezer can of a 2-quart hand-turned or electric freezer. Freeze according to manufacturer's instructions. Let ripen 1 hour, if desired. Scoop granitá into individual dessert bowls. Serve immediately. Yield: 5 cups (85 calories per ½-cup serving).

Per Serving: PROTEIN 0.1g FAT 0.0g (Saturated Fat 0g) CARBOHYDRATE 21.8g FIBER 0g CHOLESTEROL 0mg IRON 0.3mg SODIUM 2mg CALCIUM 1mg

BLUEBERRY-BUTTERMILK SHERBET

3 cups fresh blueberries
1 cup nonfat buttermilk
1 cup skim milk
½ cup sugar
½ cup unsweetened grape juice

Position knife blade in food processor bowl; add blueberries, and process until smooth. Transfer to a wire-mesh strainer; press with back of spoon against the sides of the strainer to squeeze out juice. Discard pulp in strainer. Combine blueberry juice, buttermilk, and remaining ingredients, stirring until sugar dissolves.

Pour mixture into freezer can of a 2-quart hand-turned or electric freezer. Freeze according to manufacturer's instructions. Let ripen l hour, if desired. Scoop sherbet into individual dessert bowls. Serve immediately. Yield: 4 cups (95 calories per ½-cup serving).

Per Serving: PROTEIN 2.3g FAT 0.4g (Saturated Fat 0.1g) CARBOHYDRATE 21.2g FIBER 0g CHOLESTEROL 2mg IRON 0.3mg SODIUM 51mg CALCIUM 82mg

CANTALOUPE SORBET

½ cup sugar
½ cup water
2 teaspoons grated lemon rind
9 cups cubed cantaloupe (about 2 medium)
¼ cup fresh lemon juice

Combine first 3 ingredients in a small saucepan. Bring to a boil; cook over medium heat, stirring constantly, until sugar dissolves. Remove from heat, and let cool slightly.

Position knife blade in food processor bowl; add cantaloupe. Process until smooth. Transfer to a large bowl; add sugar mixture and lemon juice, stirring well. Cover and chill thoroughly.

Pour mixture into freezer can of a 2-quart hand-turned or electric freezer. Freeze according to manufacturer's instructions. Let ripen 1 hour, if desired.

Scoop sorbet into individual dessert bowls. Serve immediately. Yield: 1½ quarts (75 calories per ½-cup serving).

Per Serving: PROTEIN 1.1g FAT 0.3g (Saturated Fat 0.2g) CARBOHYDRATE 18.6g FIBER 1.4g CHOLESTEROL 0mg IRON 0.2mg SODIUM 11mg CALCIUM 14mg

Create a bouquet of frozen treats: (clockwise from top left) Espresso Granitá, Sangria Sorbet, Blueberry-Buttermilk Sherbet, Pineapple-Orange Frozen Yogurt (page 238), Raspberry-Lemon Frozen Yogurt (page 238), and Cantaloupe Sorbet.

SANGRIA SORBET

1 cup water

½ cup sugar

2 tablespoons Grand Marnier or other orange-flavored liqueur

2 teaspoons grated lemon rind

2 teaspoons grated orange rind

¼ cup fresh lemon juice

¼ cup fresh orange juice

2¼ cups lemon-flavored sparkling mineral water, chilled

2 cups Burgundy or other dry red wine, chilled

Combine first 5 ingredients in a small saucepan. Bring to a boil; cook over medium heat, stirring constantly, until sugar dissolves. Remove from heat, and let cool slightly. Add lemon juice and orange juice, stirring well. Cover and chill thoroughly.

Combine chilled juice mixture, mineral water, and wine; stir well.

Pour mixture into freezer can of a 2-quart hand-turned or electric freezer. Freeze according to manufacturer's instructions. Let ripen 1 hour, if desired. Scoop sorbet into individual dessert bowls. Serve immediately. Yield: 7 cups (54 calories per ½-cup serving).

Per Serving: PROTEIN 0.1g FAT 0.0g (Saturated Fat 0g) CARBOHYDRATE 8.7g FIBER 0g CHOLESTEROL 0mg IRON 0.2mg SODIUM 12mg CALCIUM 6mg

PINEAPPLE-ORANGE FROZEN YOGURT

1 envelope unflavored gelatin
¼ cup cold water
2 (8-ounce) cartons plain nonfat yogurt
1 (6-ounce) can frozen orange juice concentrate, thawed and undiluted
¾ cup cold water
1 (8-ounce) can pineapple chunks in juice, drained
⅓ cup sugar

Sprinkle gelatin over ¼ cup cold water in a small saucepan; let stand 1 minute. Cook over low heat, stirring until gelatin dissolves, about 2 minutes.

Place gelatin mixture, yogurt, and remaining ingredients in container of an electric blender; cover and process until smooth, stopping once to scrape down sides. Pour mixture into freezer can of a 1-gallon hand-turned or electric freezer. Freeze according to manufacturer's instructions. Let ripen 1 hour, if desired. Scoop frozen yogurt into individual dessert bowls. Serve immediately. Yield: 7 cups (64 calories per ½-cup serving).

Per Serving: PROTEIN 2.6g FAT 0.1g (Saturated Fat 0g) CARBOHYDRATE 13.4g FIBER 0.2g CHOLESTEROL 1mg IRON 0.1mg SODIUM 26mg CALCIUM 69mg

RASPBERRY-LEMON FROZEN YOGURT

1 envelope unflavored gelatin
¼ cup cold water
2 (8-ounce) cartons plain nonfat yogurt
1 (10-ounce) package frozen raspberries in light syrup, thawed and drained
1 (6-ounce) can frozen lemonade concentrate, thawed and undiluted
¾ cup cold water
⅓ cup sugar

Sprinkle gelatin over ¼ cup cold water in a small saucepan; let stand 1 minute. Cook over low heat, stirring until gelatin dissolves, about 2 minutes.

Combine gelatin mixture, yogurt, and remaining ingredients in container of an electric blender; cover

and process until mixture is smooth, stopping once to scrape down sides.

Pour mixture into freezer can of a 2-quart hand-turned or electric freezer. Freeze according to manufacturer's instructions. Let ripen 1 hour, if desired. Scoop frozen yogurt into individual dessert bowls. Serve immediately. Yield: 1½ quarts (84 calories per ½-cup serving).

Per Serving: PROTEIN 2.8g FAT 0.1g (Saturated Fat 0.1g) CARBOHYDRATE 18.5g FIBER 1.0g CHOLESTEROL 1mg IRON 0.2mg SODIUM 30mg CALCIUM 78mg

FROZEN RUM-CURRANT LOAF

2 cups skim milk
2 cups evaporated skimmed milk
⅔ cup sugar
½ cup frozen egg substitute, thawed
2 tablespoons dark rum
2 teaspoons vanilla extract
½ cup currants
¼ cup slivered almonds, toasted and chopped

Combine first 3 ingredients in a large saucepan; bring to a boil. Remove from heat. Gradually stir about one-fourth of hot mixture into egg substitute; add to remaining hot mixture, stirring constantly. Cook over low heat, stirring constantly, 2 minutes or until mixture is slightly thickened. Remove from heat; stir in rum, vanilla, and currants. Cover and chill at least 8 hours.

Pour mixture into freezer can of a 2-quart hand-turned or electric freezer. Freeze according to manufacturer's instructions. Stir in almonds.

Line 2 (8½- x 4½- x 3-inch) loafpans with heavy-duty aluminum foil. Spoon frozen mixture evenly into prepared loafpans, and cover with foil. Freeze until firm.

Remove top piece of aluminum foil. Invert each loaf onto a serving platter, and remove remaining foil. Let stand 5 minutes at room temperature. Cut each loaf into 6 equal slices, using an electric knife. Serve immediately. Yield: 12 servings (137 calories per serving).

Per Serving: PROTEIN 6.4g FAT 1.9g (Saturated Fat 0.3g) CARBOHYDRATE 24.3g FIBER 0.4g CHOLESTEROL 3mg IRON 0.6mg SODIUM 88mg CALCIUM 191mg

CINNAMON SOUFFLÉS

Vegetable cooking spray
¼ cup plus 3 tablespoons sugar, divided
1½ tablespoons cornstarch
1½ teaspoons ground cinnamon
⅛ teaspoon freshly ground nutmeg
¾ cup 1% low-fat milk
2 teaspoons vanilla extract
½ cup frozen egg substitute, thawed
5 egg whites
½ teaspoon cream of tartar
⅓ cup sugar
Freshly ground nutmeg (optional)

Coat 10 individual (¾-cup) soufflé dishes or custard cups with cooking spray. Sprinkle dishes evenly with 3 tablespoons sugar, carefully shaking to coat bottom and sides of each dish; set aside.

Combine ¼ cup sugar, cornstarch, cinnamon, and ⅛ teaspoon nutmeg in a medium saucepan. Gradually add milk, stirring with a wire whisk until well blended. Cook over medium heat, stirring constantly, until mixture is thickened and bubbly. Remove from heat. Add vanilla; stir well. Gradually stir about one-fourth of hot mixture into egg substitute; add to remaining hot mixture, stirring constantly.

Beat egg whites and cream of tartar in a large bowl at high speed of an electric mixer until soft peaks form. Gradually add ⅓ cup sugar, 1 tablespoon at a time, beating until stiff peaks form.

Gently fold one-fourth of egg white mixture into cinnamon mixture. Gently fold remaining egg white mixture into cinnamon mixture. Spoon evenly into prepared dishes. Bake at 350° for 18 to 20 minutes or until soufflés are puffed. Sprinkle with freshly ground nutmeg, if desired. Serve immediately. Yield: 10 servings (81 calories per serving).

Per Serving: PROTEIN 3.5g FAT 0.4g (Saturated Fat 0.1g)
CARBOHYDRATE 15.6g FIBER 0.1g CHOLESTEROL 1mg
IRON 0.4mg SODIUM 64mg CALCIUM 32mg

GRAND MARNIER SOUFFLÉS

Vegetable cooking spray
¼ cup plus 2 tablespoons sugar, divided
1½ tablespoons cornstarch
¾ cup skim milk
2 teaspoons grated orange rind
2 tablespoons Grand Marnier
2 egg yolks, lightly beaten
6 egg whites
½ teaspoon cream of tartar
⅓ cup sugar
1 tablespoon powdered sugar
Orange curls (optional)

Coat 10 individual (¾-cup) soufflé dishes or custard cups with cooking spray. Sprinkle dishes evenly with 2 tablespoons sugar, carefully shaking to coat bottom and sides of each dish; set aside.

Combine ¼ cup sugar and cornstarch in a medium saucepan. Gradually add milk, stirring with a wire whisk until well blended. Cook over medium heat, stirring constantly, until mixture is thickened and bubbly. Remove from heat. Add orange rind and liqueur; stir well. Gradually stir about one-fourth of hot mixture into egg yolks; add to remaining hot mixture, stirring constantly.

Beat egg whites and cream of tartar in a large bowl at high speed of an electric mixer until soft peaks form. Gradually add ⅓ cup sugar, 1 tablespoon at a time, beating until stiff peaks form.

Gently fold one-fourth of egg white mixture into orange mixture. Gently fold remaining egg white mixture into orange mixture. Spoon into prepared dishes. Bake at 350° for 18 to 20 minutes or until soufflés are puffed. Sift powdered sugar over soufflés. Garnish with orange curls, if desired. Serve immediately. Yield: 10 servings (92 calories per serving).

Per Serving: PROTEIN 3.2g FAT 1.3g (Saturated Fat 0.4g)
CARBOHYDRATE 17.2g FIBER 0g CHOLESTEROL 44mg
IRON 0.2mg SODIUM 53mg CALCIUM 29mg

ESPRESSO DREAM PIE

1 envelope unflavored gelatin
2 tablespoons Kahlûa or other coffee-flavored
    liqueur
1 cup evaporated skimmed milk
½ cup frozen egg substitute, thawed
¼ cup sugar
1 tablespoon instant espresso powder
¼ teaspoon ground cinnamon
1 teaspoon vanilla extract
3 egg whites
⅛ teaspoon cream of tartar
½ cup sugar
¼ cup water
1 cup frozen lite whipped topping, thawed
Chocolate Crumb Crust
2 tablespoons grated semisweet chocolate

Sprinkle gelatin over liqueur in a saucepan; let stand 2 minutes. Add evaporated milk and next 4 ingredients. Cook over medium-low heat, stirring constantly with a wire whisk, 5 minutes or until thickened. Remove from heat; stir in vanilla. Chill 25 minutes or until consistency of unbeaten egg white.

Beat egg whites and cream of tartar at high speed of an electric mixer until stiff peaks form.

Combine ½ cup sugar and water in a saucepan. Bring to a boil; cook, without stirring, until candy thermometer registers 238°. Pour sugar mixture in a thin stream over egg whites while beating at high speed. Beat until mixture is cool and set.

Gently fold one-fourth of egg white mixture into espresso mixture. Gently fold in remaining egg white mixture and whipped topping. Spoon into Chocolate Crumb Crust. Cover and chill at least 2 hours. Just before serving, sprinkle with grated chocolate. Yield: 10 servings (214 calories per serving).

Chocolate Crumb Crust

¼ cup reduced-calorie margarine, melted
1½ tablespoons unsweetened cocoa
1 cup fine, dry breadcrumbs
⅓ cup sugar
2 tablespoons water
⅛ teaspoon ground cinnamon
Vegetable cooking spray

Combine margarine and cocoa in a small bowl, stirring well. Stir in breadcrumbs and next 3 ingredients. Firmly press crumb mixture evenly into bottom and up sides of a 10-inch deep-dish pieplate coated with cooking spray. Bake at 350° for 15 minutes. Cool crust completely on a wire rack. Yield: 1 (10-inch) crust.

Per Serving: PROTEIN 6.4g FAT 5.0g (Saturated Fat 1.5g)
CARBOHYDRATE 36.9g FIBER 0.5g CHOLESTEROL 2mg
IRON 0.9mg SODIUM 193mg CALCIUM 96mg

STRAWBERRY-RHUBARB PIE

1 cup all-purpose flour
1 teaspoon sugar
¼ cup reduced-calorie margarine, cut into small
    pieces and chilled
2 to 3 tablespoons ice water
Vegetable cooking spray
1 cup sugar
3 tablespoons cornstarch
½ teaspoon grated orange rind
⅓ cup unsweetened orange juice
2½ cups sliced fresh rhubarb
1½ cups halved fresh strawberries
3 tablespoons all-purpose flour
3 tablespoons brown sugar
2 tablespoons quick-cooking oats, uncooked
½ teaspoon ground cinnamon
2 tablespoons reduced-calorie margarine, cut into
    small pieces and chilled

Combine 1 cup flour and 1 teaspoon sugar in a large bowl; cut in ¼ cup margarine with a pastry blender until mixture resembles coarse meal. Sprinkle ice water, 1 tablespoon at a time, over surface; toss with a fork until dry ingredients are moistened and mixture is crumbly. Shape into a ball. Gently press between 2 sheets of heavy-duty plastic wrap to a 4-inch circle. Chill at least 25 minutes.

Roll dough to a 12-inch circle between sheets of plastic wrap. Place in freezer 5 minutes or until top sheet of plastic wrap can be removed easily. Invert and fit dough into a 9-inch pieplate coated with cooking spray; remove remaining sheet of plastic wrap. Fold edges of dough under and flute. Set aside.

Combine 1 cup sugar and cornstarch in a medium saucepan; stir well. Stir in orange rind and orange juice. Bring to a boil, and cook, stirring constantly, 1 minute. Remove from heat; add rhubarb and strawberries, stirring gently. Spoon into prepared pastry shell.

Combine 3 tablespoons flour and next 3 ingredients in a small bowl; cut in 2 tablespoons margarine with a pastry blender until mixture resembles coarse meal. Sprinkle over rhubarb mixture. Bake at 400° for 30 minutes. Let pie cool completely on a wire rack. Yield: 10 servings (212 calories per serving).

Per Serving: PROTEIN 2.2g FAT 4.8g (Saturated Fat 0.7g)
CARBOHYDRATE 41.6g FIBER 1.4g CHOLESTEROL 0mg
IRON 1.0mg SODIUM 70mg CALCIUM 42mg

JEWELLED FRUIT TART

1 cup sifted cake flour
2 tablespoons sugar
½ teaspoon baking powder
2 teaspoons grated lemon rind
¼ cup margarine
2 tablespoons ice water
¾ cup plain nonfat yogurt
3 ounces Neufchâtel cheese, softened
¼ cup sifted powdered sugar
3 ounces nonfat cream cheese product, softened
1 teaspoon grated lemon rind
1 teaspoon fresh lemon juice
¼ cup reduced-calorie apple spread
1 medium nectarine, halved, pitted, and thinly
    sliced
2 small purple plums, halved, pitted, and thinly
    sliced
1 cup seedless green grapes

Combine first 4 ingredients in a bowl; cut in margarine with a pastry blender until mixture resembles coarse meal. Sprinkle ice water, 1 tablespoon at a time, over surface; toss with a fork until dry ingredients are moistened and mixture is crumbly. Shape into a ball. Gently press dough between 2 sheets of heavy-duty plastic wrap to a 4-inch circle. Chill at least 1 hour.

Roll dough to an 11-inch circle between sheets of plastic wrap. Place in freezer 20 minutes or until plastic wrap can be removed easily. Remove top sheet of plastic wrap. Invert and fit dough into an ungreased 9-inch tart pan; remove remaining sheet of plastic wrap. Prick bottom and sides of pastry with a fork. Bake at 375° for 15 minutes or until lightly browned. Remove from oven, and cool completely.

Spoon yogurt onto several layers of heavy-duty paper towels; spread to ½-inch thickness. Cover with additional paper towels; let stand 5 minutes. Scrape yogurt into a bowl, using a rubber spatula.

Beat Neufchâtel cheese at medium speed of an electric mixer until smooth. Add powdered sugar, and beat well. Stir in drained yogurt, cream cheese, lemon rind, and lemon juice. Spoon mixture into prepared crust.

Place apple spread in a small saucepan; bring to a boil, stirring with a wire whisk until smooth. Arrange nectarine, plums, and grapes over tart. Brush with warm apple spread. Cover and chill 1 to 2 hours. Yield: 12 servings (173 calories per serving).

Per Serving: PROTEIN 4.3g FAT 6.9g (Saturated Fat 2.2g)
CARBOHYDRATE 24.1g FIBER 1.0g CHOLESTEROL 8mg
IRON 0.9mg SODIUM 167mg CALCIUM 81mg

 EASY VANILLA EXTRACT
Using real (not artificial) vanilla extract in lower fat desserts can add richness and deepen flavor without adding calories. To truly appreciate the heady aroma and rich taste of vanilla, try homemade.

Start with vanilla beans, which are available at most supermarkets; one vanilla bean will make ¼ cup (2 ounces) of extract. Cut each bean into quarters; using a small sharp knife or scissors, split the sections open lengthwise. Put the pieces in a clean jar with an airtight lid, and add ¼ cup vodka per bean. Cover and shake the jar well. Let the beans steep for four weeks, shaking the jar occasionally.

Next, filter the extract into a clean bottle through a funnel lined with a paper coffee filter, and store tightly capped. This mixture isn't as concentrated as commercially made extract, so you may want to use slightly more than the amount called for in a recipe. At only 11 calories per teaspoon, this can be a guilt-free, flavorful addition to enjoy.

CHOCOLATE CHIP CHESS TARTLETS

¼ cup margarine, softened
½ cup sugar
¼ cup frozen egg substitute, thawed
¼ cup all-purpose flour
⅛ teaspoon salt
1 tablespoon bourbon
½ cup semisweet chocolate morsels
¼ cup chopped pecans
Tartlet Shells

Beat margarine at medium speed of an electric mixer until creamy; gradually add sugar, beating well. Add egg substitute; beat well. Add flour and salt; beat until well blended.

Stir in bourbon, semisweet chocolate morsels, and chopped pecans. Spoon mixture evenly into Tartlet Shells. Bake at 350° for 30 minutes or until tartlets are lightly browned. Yield: 18 tartlets (166 calories each).

Tartlet Shells

1½ cups sifted cake flour
3 ounces Neufchâtel cheese, softened
⅓ cup margarine, softened
Vegetable cooking spray

Combine first 3 ingredients in a bowl, stirring until blended. Shape dough into 18 balls; cover and chill. Place in muffin pans coated with cooking spray, shaping each ball halfway up sides of muffin cup to form a shell. Yield: 18 tartlet shells.

Per Tartlet: PROTEIN 2.1g FAT 10.3g (Saturated Fat 2.9g)
CARBOHYDRATE 17.3g FIBER 0.4g CHOLESTEROL 4mg
IRON 1.0mg SODIUM 109mg CALCIUM 11mg

APPLE BISCUIT TATIN

¼ cup firmly packed dark brown sugar
2 tablespoons reduced-calorie margarine
6 large Granny Smith apples (about 2½ pounds), peeled, cored, and cut into eighths
2 tablespoons cornstarch
2 teaspoons ground cinnamon
2 tablespoons brown sugar
1 cup sifted cake flour
¼ cup yellow cornmeal
1 teaspoon baking powder
½ teaspoon baking soda
¼ cup sugar
¼ cup margarine
¼ cup plain nonfat yogurt
¼ cup skim milk

Combine ¼ cup brown sugar and 2 tablespoons reduced-calorie margarine in a 10-inch cast-iron skillet. Cook over medium heat until mixture bubbles, stirring frequently.

Combine apple, cornstarch, and cinnamon in a large bowl; toss gently. Layer apple mixture in skillet; sprinkle with 2 tablespoons brown sugar.

Combine flour and next 4 ingredients in a bowl, stirring well. Cut in ¼ cup margarine with a pastry blender until mixture resembles coarse meal. Add yogurt and milk, stirring with a fork just until dry ingredients are moistened.

Drop dough by spoonfuls over apple mixture. Bake at 375° for 35 to 45 minutes or until apples are tender and crust is golden. (Shield with aluminum foil to prevent excessive browning, if necessary.) Serve warm. Yield: 10 servings (211 calories per serving).

Per Serving: PROTEIN 1.9g FAT 6.5g (Saturated Fat 1.2g)
CARBOHYDRATE 38.2g FIBER 2.8g CHOLESTEROL 0mg
IRON 1.4mg SODIUM 156mg CALCIUM 64mg

BANANA CAKE

Vegetable cooking spray
2½ cups plus 1 tablespoon sifted cake flour, divided
1½ teaspoons baking powder
½ teaspoon baking soda
1½ cups mashed ripe banana (about 4 medium)
¾ cup sugar
⅓ cup nonfat buttermilk
¼ cup vegetable oil
1 egg yolk
2 teaspoons vanilla extract
3 egg whites
¼ teaspoon cream of tartar
1 tablespoon powdered sugar

Coat a 13- x 9- x 2-inch baking dish with cooking spray; dust with 1 tablespoon cake flour, and set aside.

Combine remaining 2½ cups flour, baking powder, and soda in a large mixing bowl, stirring well. Set aside.

Position knife blade in food processor bowl; add banana and next 5 ingredients. Process until smooth. Set aside.

Beat egg whites and cream of tartar at high speed of an electric mixer just until stiff peaks form.

Add banana mixture to dry ingredients; stir gently until almost smooth. Fold one-third of beaten egg white into batter. Gently fold in remaining egg white.

Spoon batter into prepared pan. Bake at 350° for 30 minutes or until cake springs back when lightly touched. Remove from oven, and let cool completely on a wire rack. Sift powdered sugar over cooled cake. Yield: 12 servings (217 calories per serving).

Per Serving: PROTEIN 3.5g FAT 5.4g (Saturated Fat 1.1g) CARBOHYDRATE 39.0g FIBER 0.9g CHOLESTEROL 18mg IRON 1.9mg SODIUM 98mg CALCIUM 47mg

CARROT SPICE CAKE

Vegetable cooking spray
1 tablespoon all-purpose flour
2½ cups sifted cake flour
2½ teaspoons baking powder
¼ teaspoon baking soda
1½ teaspoons ground cinnamon
½ teaspoon ground ginger
¼ teaspoon ground nutmeg
⅛ teaspoon ground cloves
1½ cups finely shredded carrot
½ cup sugar
½ cup firmly packed dark brown sugar
½ cup nonfat buttermilk
¼ cup frozen egg substitute, thawed
¼ cup vegetable oil
1 teaspoon vanilla extract
1 (15¼-ounce) can crushed pineapple in juice, well drained
4 egg whites
¼ teaspoon cream of tartar
1 tablespoon powdered sugar

Coat a 13- x 9- x 2-inch baking dish with cooking spray; dust with 1 tablespoon flour, and set aside.

Combine cake flour and next 6 ingredients in a large mixing bowl; stir well. Set aside.

Position knife blade in food processor bowl. Add carrot and next 6 ingredients. Process 10 seconds or until thoroughly combined. Add to dry ingredients, and stir just until blended. Stir in pineapple.

Beat egg whites and cream of tartar at high speed of an electric mixer until stiff peaks form. Fold ½ cup beaten egg whites into batter. Fold in remaining egg whites.

Pour batter into prepared pan. Bake at 350° for 25 to 27 minutes or until cake springs back when lightly touched. Remove from oven, and let cool completely on a wire rack. Dust powdered sugar over cooled cake. Yield: 12 servings (229 calories per serving).

Per Serving: PROTEIN 4.2g FAT 4.9g (Saturated Fat 0.9g) CARBOHYDRATE 42.4g FIBER 0.8g CHOLESTEROL 0mg IRON 2.4mg SODIUM 129mg CALCIUM 80mg

CHOCOLATE ESPRESSO PUDDING CAKE

1 cup sifted cake flour
1½ teaspoons baking powder
½ teaspoon baking soda
½ cup sugar
2 tablespoons unsweetened cocoa
1 tablespoon instant espresso powder
½ cup evaporated skimmed milk
¼ cup vegetable oil
1 teaspoon vanilla extract
½ cup firmly packed dark brown sugar
3 tablespoons unsweetened cocoa
2 teaspoons instant espresso powder
1 cup boiling water

Combine first 6 ingredients in a bowl; stir well. Combine milk, oil, and vanilla; add to dry ingredients, and stir. Spoon into an 8-inch square pan.

Combine brown sugar, 3 tablespoons cocoa, and 2 teaspoons espresso powder. Sprinkle over batter. Pour water over batter. (Do not stir.) Bake at 350° for 30 minutes or until cake springs back when touched. Serve warm. Yield: 12 servings (161 calories per serving).

Per Serving: PROTEIN 2.3g FAT 4.9g (Saturated Fat 1.0g)
CARBOHYDRATE 26.8g FIBER 0g CHOLESTEROL 1mg
IRON 1.4mg SODIUM 88mg CALCIUM 75mg

GINGER MOLASSES CAKE

Vegetable cooking spray
1 tablespoon all-purpose flour
¾ cup sugar
½ cup molasses
3 tablespoons vegetable oil
1 egg, lightly beaten
1 tablespoon minced crystallized ginger
2 tablespoons brandy
2 cups sifted cake flour
1½ teaspoons baking powder
½ teaspoon baking soda
½ teaspoon ground ginger
¼ teaspoon ground white pepper
1 cup boiling water
2 teaspoons powdered sugar

Coat a 6-cup bundt pan with cooking spray, and sprinkle with 1 tablespoon all-purpose flour. Set pan aside.

Combine ¾ cup sugar, molasses, and oil; beat at medium speed of an electric mixer until smooth. Add egg, and beat well. Add crystallized ginger and brandy; beat well.

Combine cake flour and next 4 ingredients; add to molasses mixture alternately with water, beginning and ending with flour mixture. Mix after each addition. (Batter will be thin.)

Pour batter into prepared pan. Bake at 325° for 55 minutes or until a wooden pick inserted in center comes out clean. Cool in pan on a wire rack 10 minutes; remove from pan, and let cool completely on wire rack. Sift powdered sugar over cooled cake. Yield: 12 servings (190 calories per serving).

Per Serving: PROTEIN 2.1g FAT 4.1g (Saturated Fat 0.8g)
CARBOHYDRATE 36.5g FIBER 0g CHOLESTEROL 18mg
IRON 2.4mg SODIUM 83mg CALCIUM 77mg

CARAMEL PEACH CAKE

¼ cup margarine, softened
½ cup sugar
1 egg
1 cup all-purpose flour
¾ teaspoon baking powder
½ teaspoon baking soda
½ teaspoon ground allspice
½ cup low-fat sour cream
¾ cup chopped frozen peaches, thawed
3 tablespoons chopped almonds, toasted
¾ teaspoon vanilla extract
¼ teaspoon almond extract
Vegetable cooking spray
2 tablespoons margarine
2 tablespoons brown sugar
1 tablespoon skim milk
½ cup sifted powdered sugar
¼ teaspoon vanilla extract

Beat ¼ cup margarine at medium speed of an electric mixer until creamy; gradually add ½ cup sugar, beating well. Add egg, and beat until well blended.

For a superb finale to dinner or a moist between-meal indulgence, serve Caramel Peach Cake.

Combine flour, baking powder, soda, and allspice; stir well. Add flour mixture to margarine mixture alternately with sour cream, beginning and ending with flour mixture. Mix after each addition. Stir in peaches, almonds, ¾ teaspoon vanilla extract, and almond extract.

Pour batter into a 6-cup nonstick Bundt pan coated with cooking spray. Bake at 350° for 45 minutes or until a wooden pick inserted in center comes out clean. Cool in pan on a wire rack 10 minutes; remove from pan, and let cake cool completely on wire rack.

Melt 2 tablespoons margarine in a small saucepan. Add brown sugar, and cook over medium heat, stirring constantly, until sugar dissolves. Remove from heat; add milk, stirring well.

Add powdered sugar and ¼ teaspoon vanilla extract; beat at medium speed of electric mixer until mixture is smooth. Drizzle powdered sugar mixture over cooled cake. Yield: 10 servings (232 calories per serving).

Per Serving: PROTEIN 3.1g FAT 10.5g (Saturated Fat 2.6g)
CARBOHYDRATE 31.7g FIBER 0.9g CHOLESTEROL 27mg
IRON 0.9mg SODIUM 157mg CALCIUM 56mg

SWEET POTATO CHEESECAKE

Vegetable cooking spray
3 tablespoons graham cracker crumbs
2 (8-ounce) packages Neufchâtel cheese, softened
    and cut into cubes
½ cup 1% low-fat cottage cheese
½ cup low-fat sour cream
1 cup mashed, cooked sweet potato
¾ cup firmly packed dark brown sugar
2 tablespoons praline liqueur
1½ teaspoons pumpkin pie spice
2 teaspoons vanilla extract
¾ cup frozen egg substitute, thawed
½ cup sugar
¼ cup water
⅓ cup finely chopped pecans, toasted

Coat a 9-inch springform pan with cooking spray. Sprinkle graham cracker crumbs evenly over bottom of pan. Set aside.

Position knife blade in food processor bowl. Add Neufchâtel cheese, cottage cheese, and sour cream; process until smooth, scraping sides of processor bowl once. Add sweet potato and next 4 ingredients; process until smooth, scraping sides of processor bowl occasionally. Slowly pour egg substitute through food chute with processor running, blending just until combined. Spoon over graham cracker crumbs.

Bake at 300° for 50 minutes (center will be soft but will firm when chilled). Turn off oven; leave cheesecake in oven 30 minutes. Remove from oven; let cool to room temperature on a wire rack. Cover and chill 8 hours.

Combine ½ cup sugar and water in a saucepan. Cook over medium heat 12 minutes or until mixture is golden, stirring frequently. Stir in pecans. Rapidly spread mixture onto a baking sheet coated with cooking spray. Let cool completely. Break pecan mixture into pieces. Position knife blade in food processor bowl; add pecan pieces. Pulse 8 times or until mixture is finely chopped. Just before serving, sprinkle pecan mixture over cheesecake. Yield: 16 servings (203 calories per serving).

Per Serving: PROTEIN 5.6g FAT 9.9g (Saturated Fat 5.2g)
CARBOHYDRATE 23.5g FIBER 0.7g CHOLESTEROL 25mg
IRON 0.7mg SODIUM 177mg CALCIUM 52mg

TRIPLE DELIGHT CHEESECAKE

Vegetable cooking spray
¼ cup chocolate wafer crumbs
2 (8-ounce) packages Neufchâtel cheese, softened
    and divided
½ cup sugar, divided
½ cup frozen egg substitute, thawed and divided
¼ teaspoon vanilla extract
1 cup low-fat sour cream, divided
1 (1-ounce) square semisweet chocolate, melted
¼ cup firmly packed dark brown sugar
2 teaspoons all-purpose flour
½ teaspoon vanilla extract
2 tablespoons chopped pecans
2 egg whites, lightly beaten
¼ teaspoon vanilla
1 tablespoon amaretto
1 (1-ounce) square semisweet chocolate, melted
Fresh raspberries (optional)
Fresh mint sprigs (optional)

Coat an 8-inch springform pan with cooking spray. Sprinkle chocolate wafer crumbs evenly over bottom of pan. Set aside.

Combine 6 ounces Neufchâtel cheese and ¼ cup sugar in a medium bowl; beat at medium speed of mixer until creamy. Add ¼ cup egg substitute and ¼ teaspoon vanilla; beat until well blended. Stir in ¼ cup sour cream and 1 ounce melted chocolate. Spoon mixture over wafer crumbs.

Combine 6 ounces Neufchâtel cheese, brown sugar, and flour in a bowl; beat at medium speed of mixer until creamy. Add remaining ¼ cup egg substitute and ½ teaspoon vanilla; beat until well blended. Stir in pecans. Spoon over chocolate mixture.

Combine remaining 4 ounces Neufchâtel cheese and remaining ¼ cup sugar; beat at medium speed of mixer until creamy. Add egg whites; beat until well blended. Stir in remaining ¾ cup sour cream, ¼ teaspoon vanilla, and amaretto. Spoon gently over pecan mixture.

Bake at 300° for 1 hour (center will be soft but will firm when chilled). Turn off oven, and leave cheesecake in oven 15 minutes. Remove from oven, and let cool to room temperature on a wire rack. Cover and chill 8 hours.

To serve, place 1 ounce melted chocolate in a zip-top plastic bag. Cut ⅛-inch off corner of bag; pipe onto individual dessert plates. Place cheesecake on plates. If desired, garnish with raspberries and mint sprigs. Yield: 12 servings (227 calories per serving).

Per Serving: PROTEIN 6.5g FAT 14.2g (Saturated Fat 8.3g)
CARBOHYDRATE 19.8g FIBER 0.1g CHOLESTEROL 38mg
IRON 0.6mg SODIUM 193mg CALCIUM 61mg

ORANGE-FILLED KISSES

4 egg whites
1 cup sifted powdered sugar
Orange Filling

Beat egg whites at high speed of an electric mixer until foamy. Gradually add sugar, 1 tablespoon at a time, beating until stiff peaks form and sugar dissolves (2 to 4 minutes). Drop by level teaspoonfuls onto cookie sheets lined with aluminum foil. Bake at 250° for 1 hour. Cool slightly on cookie sheets. Remove to wire racks; cool completely.

Just before serving, spread 1 teaspoon Orange Filling on bottoms of 19 cookies. Top with remaining cookies. Yield: 19 kisses (31 calories each).

Orange Filling

2 tablespoons margarine, softened
1 cup sifted powdered sugar
2 teaspoons skim milk
1 teaspoon grated orange rind

Beat margarine at medium speed of an electric mixer until creamy; gradually add sugar, beating well. Add milk and orange rind; stir well. Yield: ⅓ cup plus 1 tablespoon.

Per Kiss: PROTEIN 0.4g FAT 0.6g (Saturated Fat 0.1g)
CARBOHYDRATE 6.4g FIBER 0g CHOLESTEROL 0mg
IRON 0mg SODIUM 13mg CALCIUM 1mg

PEPPERMINT MERINGUE COOKIES

2 egg whites
½ cup sugar
½ teaspoon peppermint extract
⅓ cup semisweet chocolate mini-morsels
Vegetable cooking spray

Beat egg whites at high speed of an electric mixer until foamy. Gradually add sugar, 1 tablespoon at a time, beating until stiff peaks form and sugar dissolves (2 to 4 minutes). Fold in peppermint extract and chocolate morsels.

Drop egg white mixture by level tablespoonfuls, 2 inches apart, onto cookie sheets coated with cooking spray. Bake at 200° for 2 hours or until dry. Remove from cookie sheets, and let cookies cool completely on a wire rack. Yield: 25 cookies (29 calories each).

Per Cookie: PROTEIN 0.4g FAT 0.8g (Saturated Fat 0.5g)
CARBOHYDRATE 5.3g FIBER 0g CHOLESTEROL 0mg
IRON 0.1mg SODIUM 4mg CALCIUM 1mg

OATMEAL KRISPIES

⅓ cup margarine, softened
½ cup firmly packed brown sugar
⅓ cup frozen egg substitute, thawed
½ teaspoon vanilla extract
¾ cup all-purpose flour
½ teaspoon baking soda
¼ teaspoon salt
1½ cups quick-cooking oats, uncooked
½ cup semisweet chocolate mini-morsels
½ cup crisp rice cereal
Vegetable cooking spray

Beat margarine at medium speed of an electric mixer until creamy; gradually add brown sugar, beating well. Add egg substitute and vanilla, and beat well.

Combine flour, baking soda, and salt; add to margarine mixture, mixing well. Stir in uncooked oats, semisweet chocolate mini-morsels, and crisp rice cereal.

Drop dough by level tablespoonfuls, 2 inches apart, onto cookie sheets coated with vegetable cooking spray. Bake at 350° for 8 to 10 minutes or until cookies are lightly browned. Cool slightly on cookie sheets. Remove to wire racks, and let cookies cool completely. Yield: 40 cookies (57 calories each).

Per Cookie: PROTEIN 1.1g FAT 2.5g (Saturated Fat 0.8g)
CARBOHYDRATE 8.1g FIBER 0.4g CHOLESTEROL 0mg
IRON 0.4mg SODIUM 49mg CALCIUM 8mg

Cooking Light 1994 Menu Plans

This plan for seven days of calorie-controlled meals provides a healthful approach to weight loss. Follow the plan precisely, or use it as a model for planning your own balanced meals by substituting foods of comparable calories and nutrients. Refer to the Calorie/Nutrient Chart on pages 250–261 for these values. The menu items marked with an asterisk are included in the menu or recipe sections and can be located in the Index. When planning your own menus, remember that of the total calories provided, at least 50 percent of the calories should be from carbohydrate, about 20 percent from protein, and no more than 30 percent from fat. In addition, it is recommended that less than 10 percent of the calories come from saturated fat.

Most women can safely lose weight while eating 1,200 calories per day; most men can lose while eating 1,600. Once weight is lost, modify the menu plan according to the calories needed to maintain your ideal weight. If you feel that you are losing weight too slowly, keep in mind that eating fewer calories to speed up weight loss may rob you of the nutrients your body needs to stay healthy. Also, your metabolism may slow down to accommodate a limited food supply. Exercise is the key to speedier weight loss.

1200 calories		Day 1	1600 calories	
BREAKFAST				
1 serving	163	*Scrambled Breakfast Sandwiches	1 serving	163
½ cup	48	*Bountiful Fresh Fruit Cup	½ cup	48
1 cup	52	*Cafe Mexicana	1 cup	52
½ cup	56	Orange juice	½ cup	56
	319			**319**
LUNCH				
1 serving	142	*Grilled Sirloin Salad	1 serving	142
¾ cup	42	Cantaloupe	¾ cup	42
1 muffin	131	*Cornmeal-Zucchini Muffins	1 muffin	131
	—	*Chocolate Squares with Peppermint Ice Milk	1 serving	260
	315			**575**
DINNER				
1 serving	298	*Turkey-Wild Rice Casserole	1 serving	298
1 serving	32	*Gingered Asparagus	1 serving	32
1 cup	52	*Romaine Salad with Avocado Dressing	1 cup	52
1 roll	72	Whole wheat roll	1 roll	72
	454			**454**
SNACK				
2 cookies	114	Oatmeal cookies	3 cookies	171
	—	Skim milk	1 cup	86
	Total 1202			**Total 1605**
(Calories from Fat: 26%)			(Calories from Fat: 22%)	

1200 calories		Day 2	1600 calories	
BREAKFAST				
1 serving	191	*Jalapeño Brunch Scramble	1 serving	191
1 cup	79	Honeydew melon	1 cup	79
	—	Grits	½ cup	73
	—	Skim milk	1 cup	86
	270			**429**
LUNCH				
1 cup	148	*Spicy Chicken and Rice Soup	1 cup	148
1 serving	160	*Grilled Blue Cheese Sandwiches	1 serving	160
	—	Whole wheat crackers	4 each	100
	—	*Garden Dip	3 tablespoons	36
	—	Celery sticks	¾ cup	27
	—	*Autumn Spice Squares	1 serving	90
	308			**561**
DINNER				
1 serving	152	*Oven-Barbecued Pork	1 serving	152
1 serving	189	*Curried Sweet Potato Strips	1 serving	189
½ cup	65	*Spicy Lima Beans	½ cup	65
½ cup	59	*Carrot-Waldorf Salad	½ cup	59
	465			**465**
SNACK				
1 cookie	61	*Ginger Crinkles	1 cookie	61
1 cup	86	Skim milk	1 cup	86
	Total 1190			**Total 1602**
(Calories from Fat: 18%)			(Calories from Fat: 18%)	

1200 calories		Day 3	1600 calories	
BREAKFAST				
1 muffin	156	*Fresh Apple Muffins	1 muffin	156
1 cup	86	Skim milk	1 cup	86
½ cup	56	Orange juice	½ cup	56
	298			**298**
LUNCH				
1 serving	240	*Broiled Chicken Sandwiches	1 serving	240
½ cup	91	*Sweet Potato Salad	½ cup	91
1 cookie	57	*Oatmeal Krispies	2 cookies	114
	388			**445**
DINNER				
1 serving	337	*Smothered Beef and Mushrooms	1 serving	337
	—	Cooked rice	½ cup	108
½ cup	41	Butternut squash	½ cup	41
1 cup	36	*Tossed Greens with Strawberries	1 cup	36
	—	Whole wheat roll	1 roll	72
	—	*Lemon-Cheese Squares	1 serving	173
	414			**767**
SNACK				
3 wedges	78	*Pimiento Cheese Apple Wedges	3 wedges	78
	Total 1178			**Total 1588**
(Calories from Fat: 18%)			(Calories from Fat: 18%)	

1200 calories		Day 4	1600 calories	
		BREAKFAST		
1 pancake	113	*Gingerbread Pancakes	2 pancakes	226
1 tablespoon	6	Reduced-calorie maple syrup	3 tablespoons	18
2 links	154	*Country-Style	2 links	154
		Sausage Links		
½ cup	58	Apple juice	1 cup	117
	331			515
		LUNCH		
1 serving	141	*Lemon-Basil Tuna Pockets	1 serving	141
1 serving	104	*Fruit Salad with	1 serving	104
		Sweet Yogurt Dressing		
	—	*Carrot Spice Cake	1 serving	229
	245			474
		DINNER		
1 serving	284	*Linguine with Asparagus and	1 serving	284
		Goat Cheese		
1 serving	50	*Arugula, Watercress, and	1 serving	50
		Endive Salad		
1 roll	102	*Poppy Seed Fan Tans	1 roll	102
	436			436
		SNACK		
1 bar	89	*Crunchy Cereal Bars	1 bar	89
1 cup	91	*Citrus Spritzer	1 cup	91
	Total 1192			**Total 1605**
(Calories from Fat: 21%)			(Calories from Fat: 20%)	

1200 calories		Day 6	1600 calories	
		BREAKFAST		
1 muffin	128	*Fruity Yogurt Muffins	2 muffins	256
1 each	109	Medium banana	1 each	109
1 cup	86	Skim milk	1 cup	86
	323			451
		LUNCH		
1 cup	160	*Chicken and Black Bean Soup	1 cup	160
1 cup	64	*Watercress, Endive,	1 cup	64
		and Pear Salad		
1 slice	97	*Sesame-Cheese Batter Bread	1 slice	97
	—	Angel food cake	1 slice	147
	321			468
		DINNER		
1 serving	182	*Glazed Roasted Chicken	1 serving	182
½ cup	56	*Okra and Corn Creole	½ cup	56
	—	Steamed green beans	½ cup	22
½ cup	84	*Black-Eyed Pea Salad	½ cup	84
1 roll	72	Whole wheat dinner roll	1 roll	72
	—	Reduced-calorie margarine	1 teaspoon	17
	394			433
		SNACK		
	—	*Amaretto Tea Scones	1 scone	84
1 cup	159	*Hot Spiced Cider	1 cup	159
	Total 1197			**Total 1595**
(Calories from Fat: 18%)			(Calories from Fat: 17%)	

1200 calories		Day 5	1600 calories	
		BREAKFAST		
1 bagel	112	*Caraway Bagels	2 bagels	224
1 teaspoon	17	Reduced-calorie margarine	2 teaspoons	34
1(8-ounce) carton	127	Plain nonfat yogurt	1(8-ounce) carton	127
½ cup	22	Fresh strawberries	1 cup	44
	278			429
		LUNCH		
1 serving	230	*Deluxe Turkey Sandwiches	1 serving	230
1 serving	34	*Zippy Deviled Eggs	1 serving	34
	—	Carrot sticks	½ cup	24
½ cup	57	Seedless green grapes	½ cup	57
	321			345
		DINNER		
1 serving	270	*Easy Lamb Chops Jalapeño	1 serving	270
½ cup	120	*Basmati Rice Pilaf	½ cup	120
1 cup	50	*Strawberry-Spinach Salad	1 cup	50
	—	*Autumn Fruit in Spiced Sauce	1 serving	228
	440			668
		SNACK		
½ cup	61	*Harvest Popcorn Mix	½ cup	61
1 cup	98	*Island Tea	1 cup	98
	Total 1198			**Total 1601**
(Calories from Fat: 18%)			(Calories from Fat: 17%)	

1200 calories		Day 7	1600 calories	
		BREAKFAST		
1 slice	136	*Raisin-Bran Loaf	2 slices	272
1 cup	86	Skim milk	1 cup	86
½ cup	47	Grapefruit juice	1 cup	94
	269			452
		LUNCH		
1 serving	119	*Tomato-Zucchini Triangles	1 serving	119
1 serving	95	*Citrus Salad with	1 serving	95
		Honey-Lime Dressing		
	—	*Sangria Sorbet	1 cup	108
	214			322
		DINNER		
1 serving	229	*Grilled Ginger Salmon Fillets	1 serving	229
½ cup	90	*Creamy Sliced Potatoes	½ cup	90
1 cup	24	Steamed broccoli	1 cup	24
1 serving	79	*Spicy Orange Salad	1 serving	79
	—	Small kaiser roll	1 each	92
1 cup	133	*Frosty Cappuccino	1 cup	133
	555			647
		SNACK		
1 cup	160	*Peanutty Banana Shake	1 cup	160
	Total 1198			**Total 1581**
(Calories from Fat: 22%)			(Calories from Fat: 20%)	

Calorie/Nutrient Chart

FOOD	APPROXIMATE MEASURE	FOOD ENERGY (CALORIES)	PROTEIN (GRAMS)	FAT (GRAMS)	SATURATED FAT (GRAMS)	CARBOHYDRATE (GRAMS)	FIBER (GRAMS)	CHOLESTEROL (MILLIGRAMS)	IRON (MILLIGRAMS)	SODIUM (MILLIGRAMS)	CALCIUM (MILLIGRAMS)
Apple											
Fresh, with skin	1 medium	81	0.2	0.5	0.08	21.0	4.3	0	0.2	0	10
Juice, unsweetened	½ cup	58	0.1	0.1	0.02	14.5	0.2	0	0.5	4	9
Applesauce, unsweetened	½ cup	52	0.2	0.1	0.01	13.8	1.8	0	0.1	2	4
Apricot											
Fresh	1 each	18	0.4	0.1	0.01	4.1	0.8	0	0.2	0	5
Canned, in juice	½ cup	58	0.8	0.0	0.00	15.0	0.5	0	0.4	5	15
Canned, in light syrup	½ cup	75	0.7	0.1	—	19.0	0.5	—	0.3	1	12
Canned, peeled, in water	½ cup	25	0.8	0.0	0.00	6.2	1.7	0	0.6	12	9
Dried, uncooked	1 each	17	0.3	0.0	0.00	4.3	0.5	0	0.3	1	3
Nectar	½ cup	70	0.5	0.1	0.01	18.0	0.8	0	0.5	4	9
Artichoke											
Whole, cooked	1 each	53	2.6	0.2	0.04	12.4	1.1	0	1.6	79	47
Hearts, cooked	½ cup	37	1.8	0.1	0.03	8.7	0.8	0	1.1	55	33
Arugula	3 ounces	21	2.2	0.5	—	3.1	—	0	—	23	136
Asparagus, fresh, cooked	½ cup	23	2.3	0.3	0.06	4.0	0.9	0	0.6	4	22
Avocado	1 medium	322	3.9	30.6	4.88	14.8	4.2	0	2.0	20	22
Bacon											
Canadian-style	1 ounce	45	5.8	2.0	0.63	0.5	0.0	14	0.2	399	2
Cured, broiled	1 ounce	163	8.6	14.0	4.93	0.2	0.0	24	0.5	452	3
Turkey, cooked	1 ounce	60	4.0	4.0	—	8.0	—	20	—	400	—
Bamboo shoots, cooked	½ cup	7	0.9	0.1	0.03	1.1	0.4	0	0.1	2	7
Banana											
Mashed	½ cup	101	1.1	0.5	0.20	25.8	3.2	0	0.3	1	7
Whole	1 medium	109	1.2	0.5	0.22	27.6	3.5	0	0.4	1	7
Barley											
Dry	½ cup	352	9.9	1.2	0.24	77.7	15.6	0	2.5	9	29
Cooked	½ cup	97	1.8	0.3	0.07	22.2	—	0	1.0	2	9
Basil, fresh, raw	¼ cup	1	0.1	0.0	—	0.1	—	0	0.1	0	3
Bean sprouts, raw	½ cup	16	1.6	0.1	0.01	3.1	0.6	0	0.5	3	7
Beans, cooked and drained											
Black	½ cup	114	7.6	0.5	0.12	20.4	3.6	0	1.8	1	23
Cannellini	½ cup	112	7.7	0.4	0.06	20.2	3.2	0	2.6	2	25
Garbanzo	½ cup	134	7.3	2.1	0.22	22.5	2.9	0	2.4	6	40
Great Northern	½ cup	132	9.3	0.5	0.16	23.7	3.8	0	2.4	2	76
Green, fresh	½ cup	22	1.2	0.2	0.40	4.9	1.1	0	0.8	2	29
Green, canned, regular pack	½ cup	14	0.8	0.1	0.01	3.1	0.9	0	0.5	171	18
Kidney or red	½ cup	112	7.7	0.4	0.06	20.2	3.2	0	2.6	2	25
Lima, frozen, baby	½ cup	94	6.0	0.3	0.06	17.5	4.8	0	1.8	26	25
Pinto, canned	½ cup	94	5.5	0.4	0.08	17.5	2.6	0	1.9	184	44
Wax, canned	½ cup	14	0.8	0.1	0.01	3.1	0.8	0	0.5	171	18
White	½ cup	127	8.0	0.6	0.15	23.2	3.9	0	2.5	2	65
Beef, trimmed of fat											
Flank steak, broiled	3 ounces	207	21.6	12.7	5.43	0.0	0.0	60	2.2	71	5
Ground, extra-lean, broiled	3 ounces	218	21.5	13.9	5.46	0.0	0.0	71	2.0	60	6
Ground, ultra-lean, broiled	3 ounces	146	20.8	7.0	2.75	1.5	—	72	—	238	—
Liver, braised	3 ounces	137	20.7	4.2	1.62	2.9	—	331	5.7	60	6
Round, bottom, braised	3 ounces	189	26.9	8.2	2.92	0.0	0.0	82	2.9	43	4
Round, eye of, cooked	3 ounces	156	24.7	5.5	2.12	0.0	0.0	59	1.7	53	4
Round, top, lean, broiled	3 ounces	162	27.0	5.3	1.84	0.0	0.0	71	2.4	52	5

Dash (—) indicates insufficient data available

FOOD	APPROXIMATE MEASURE	FOOD ENERGY (CALORIES)	PROTEIN (GRAMS)	FAT (GRAMS)	SATURATED FAT (GRAMS)	CARBOHYDRATE (GRAMS)	FIBER (GRAMS)	CHOLESTEROL (MILLIGRAMS)	IRON (MILLIGRAMS)	SODIUM (MILLIGRAMS)	CALCIUM (MILLIGRAMS)
Beef (*continued*)											
Sirloin, broiled	3 ounces	177	25.8	7.4	3.03	0.0	0.0	76	2.9	56	9
Tenderloin, roasted	3 ounces	173	24.0	7.9	3.09	0.0	0.0	71	3.0	54	6
Beets											
Fresh, diced, cooked	½ cup	26	0.9	0.4	0.01	5.7	0.8	0	0.5	42	9
Canned, regular pack	½ cup	31	0.8	0.1	0.02	7.5	0.7	0	0.5	201	16
Beverages											
Beer	12 fluid ounces	146	1.1	0.0	0.00	13.1	0.7	0	0.1	18	18
Beer, light	12 fluid ounces	95	0.7	0.0	0.00	4.4	—	0	0.1	10	17
Brandy, bourbon, gin, rum, vodka, or whiskey, 80 proof	1 fluid ounce	65	0.0	0.0	0.00	0.0	0.0	0	0.0	0	0
Champagne	6 fluid ounces	135	0.5	0.0	0.00	2.1	0.0	0	0.9	7	5
Club soda	8 fluid ounces	0	0.0	0.0	0.00	0.0	0.0	0	—	48	11
Coffee, black	1 cup	5	0.2	0.0	0.00	0.9	—	0	1.0	5	5
Coffee liqueur	1 fluid ounce	99	0.0	0.1	0.03	13.9	—	0	0.0	2	0
Cognac brandy	1 fluid ounce	69	—	—	—	—	—	—	—	—	—
Crème de menthe liqueur	1 fluid ounce	110	0.0	0.1	0.00	12.3	—	0	0.0	1	0
Sherry, sweet	1 fluid ounce	39	0.1	0.0	—	2.0	0.0	0	0.1	4	2
Vermouth, dry	1 fluid ounce	35	0.0	0.0	0.00	1.6	0.0	0	0.1	5	2
Vermouth, sweet	1 fluid ounce	45	0.0	0.0	0.00	4.7	0.0	0	0.1	8	2
Wine, port	6 fluid ounces	279	0.2	0.0	0.00	21.3	0.0	0	0.7	7	7
Wine, red	6 fluid ounces	121	0.4	0.0	0.00	0.5	0.0	0	1.4	18	12
Wine, white, dry	6 fluid ounces	117	0.2	0.0	0.00	1.1	0.0	0	0.9	7	16
Blackberries, fresh	½ cup	37	0.5	0.3	0.01	9.2	5.3	0	0.4	0	23
Blueberries, fresh	½ cup	41	0.5	0.3	0.02	10.2	3.3	0	0.1	4	4
Bouillon, dry											
Beef-flavored cubes	1 cube	3	0.1	0.0	—	0.2	—	—	—	400	—
Beef-flavored granules	1 teaspoon	10	0.5	1.1	0.30	0.5	—	—	—	945	—
Chicken-flavored cubes	1 cube	10	0.2	0.2	—	1.1	—	1	0.1	1152	—
Chicken-flavored granules	1 teaspoon	10	0.5	1.1	0.30	0.5	—	—	—	819	—
Bran											
Oat, dry, uncooked	½ cup	153	8.0	3.0	0.28	23.5	6.0	0	2.6	1	31
Oat, unprocessed	½ cup	114	8.0	3.3	0.62	30.8	7.4	0	2.5	2	27
Wheat, crude	½ cup	65	4.7	1.3	0.19	19.4	12.7	0	3.2	1	22
Bread											
Bagel, plain	1 each	161	5.9	1.5	0.21	30.5	1.2	—	1.4	196	23
Biscuit, homemade	1 each	127	2.3	6.4	1.74	14.9	0.6	2	0.6	224	65
Bun, hamburger or hot dog	1 each	136	3.2	3.4	0.52	22.4	0.1	13	0.8	112	19
Cornbread	2-ounce square	154	3.5	6.0	3.36	21.1	1.2	56	0.7	273	96
English muffin	1 each	182	5.9	3.6	1.93	30.9	0.8	32	1.5	234	41
French	1 slice	73	2.3	0.5	0.16	13.9	0.6	1	0.6	145	11
Light, wheatberry or 7-grain	1 slice	40	2.0	1.0	—	7.0	2.8	0	0.7	105	20
Pita, whole wheat	1 medium	122	2.4	0.9	0.10	23.5	4.4	0	4.4	—	39
Pumpernickel	1 slice	76	2.8	0.4	0.05	16.4	1.8	0	0.7	176	26
Raisin	1 slice	66	1.6	0.7	0.16	13.4	0.9	1	0.3	91	18
Rye	1 slice	61	2.3	0.3	0.04	13.0	1.5	0	0.4	139	19
White	1 slice	67	2.2	0.8	0.19	12.6	0.5	1	0.6	127	18
Whole wheat	1 slice	56	2.4	0.7	0.12	11.0	2.1	1	0.5	121	23
Breadcrumbs											
Fine, dry	½ cup	196	6.3	2.2	0.52	36.7	2.1	2	1.7	368	61
Seasoned	½ cup	214	8.4	1.5	—	41.5	0.3	—	1.9	1590	59
Breadstick, plain	1 each	17	0.4	0.5	—	2.7	—	—	0.2	20	1
Broccoli, fresh, chopped, cooked or raw	½ cup	12	1.3	0.1	0.02	2.3	1.4	0	0.4	12	21
Broth											
Beef, canned, diluted	1 cup	31	4.8	0.7	0.34	2.6	0.0	24	0.5	782	0
Beef, no-salt-added	1 cup	22	0.5	0.0	0.00	1.9	0.0	0	0.0	7	0
Chicken, low-sodium	1 cup	22	0.4	0.0	—	2.0	0.0	0	0.0	4	0
Chicken, no-salt-added	1 cup	16	1.0	1.0	—	0.0	—	—	—	67	—
Brussels sprouts, fresh, cooked	½ cup	30	2.0	0.4	0.08	6.8	3.4	0	0.9	16	28

FOOD	APPROXIMATE MEASURE	FOOD ENERGY (CALORIES)	PROTEIN (GRAMS)	FAT (GRAMS)	SATURATED FAT (GRAMS)	CARBOHYDRATE (GRAMS)	FIBER (GRAMS)	CHOLESTEROL (MILLIGRAMS)	IRON (MILLIGRAMS)	SODIUM (MILLIGRAMS)	CALCIUM (MILLIGRAMS)
Bulgur, uncooked	½ cup	239	8.6	0.9	0.16	53.1	12.8	0	1.7	12	24
Butter											
Regular	1 tablespoon	102	0.1	11.5	7.17	0.0	0.0	31	0.0	117	3
Whipped	1 tablespoon	68	0.1	7.7	4.78	0.0	0.0	21	0.0	78	2
Cabbage											
Bok choy	1 cup	9	1.0	0.1	0.02	1.5	0.7	0	0.6	45	73
Common varieties, raw, shredded	½ cup	8	0.4	0.1	0.01	1.9	0.8	0	0.2	6	16
Cake, without frosting											
Angel food	2-ounce slice	147	3.2	0.1	—	33.7	0.0	0	0.2	83	54
Pound	1-ounce slice	305	3.6	17.5	10.19	33.7	0.4	134	0.5	245	27
Sponge, cut into 12 slices	1 slice	183	3.6	5.0	1.48	30.8	0.3	221	0.8	99	44
Yellow, cut into 12 slices	1 slice	190	2.8	7.5	1.92	28.0	0.3	40	0.2	157	79
Candy											
Fudge, chocolate	1 ounce	113	0.8	3.4	—	21.3	0.1	0	0.3	54	22
Gumdrops	1 ounce	98	0.0	0.2	0.03	24.8	0.0	0	0.1	10	2
Hard	1 each	27	0.0	0.0	0.00	6.8	0.0	0	0.1	2	1
Jelly beans	1 ounce	104	0.0	0.1	0.09	26.4	0.0	0	0.3	3	3
Milk chocolate	1 ounce	153	2.4	8.7	5.13	16.4	—	7	0.4	23	58
Cantaloupe, raw, diced	½ cup	28	0.7	0.2	0.12	6.7	0.9	0	0.2	7	9
Capers	1 tablespoon	4	0.4	0.0	—	0.6	—	0	—	670	—
Carambola (starfruit)	1 medium	42	0.7	0.4	—	9.9	1.5	0	0.3	3	5
Carrot											
Raw	1 medium	31	0.7	0.1	0.02	7.3	2.3	0	0.4	25	19
Cooked, sliced	½ cup	33	0.8	0.1	0.22	7.6	1.4	0	0.4	48	22
Juice, canned	½ cup	66	1.6	0.2	0.05	15.3	1.6	0	0.8	48	40
Catsup											
Regular	1 tablespoon	18	0.3	0.1	0.01	4.3	0.3	0	0.1	178	4
No-salt-added	1 tablespoon	15	0.0	0.0	—	4.0	—	—	—	6	—
Reduced-calorie	1 tablespoon	7	0.0	0.0	—	1.2	—	—	0.0	3	0
Cauliflower											
Raw, flowerets	½ cup	12	1.0	0.1	0.01	2.5	1.2	0	0.3	7	14
Cooked, flowerets	½ cup	15	1.2	0.1	0.02	2.8	1.4	0	0.2	4	17
Caviar	1 tablespoon	40	3.9	2.9	0.07	0.6	0.0	94	—	240	—
Celeriac, raw, shredded	½ cup	30	1.2	0.2	0.06	7.2	1.0	0	0.5	78	34
Celery, raw, diced	½ cup	10	0.4	0.1	0.02	2.2	1.0	0	0.2	52	24
Cereal											
Bran flakes	½ cup	64	2.5	0.4	0.06	15.3	2.7	0	5.6	182	10
Bran, whole	½ cup	104	6.0	1.5	0.12	32.7	14.9	0	6.7	387	30
Corn flakes	½ cup	44	0.9	0.0	0.00	9.8	0.1	0	0.7	140	0
Crispy rice	½ cup	55	0.9	0.1	—	12.4	0.2	0	0.3	103	3
Granola	½ cup	242	5.8	8.9	—	34.7	—	—	1.8	66	29
Puffed wheat	½ cup	22	0.9	0.1	0.01	4.8	0.2	0	0.3	0	2
Raisin bran	½ cup	77	2.7	0.5	—	18.6	3.4	0	3.0	179	9
Shredded wheat miniatures	½ cup	76	2.3	0.5	0.08	17.0	2.0	0	0.9	2	8
Toasted oat	½ cup	44	1.7	0.7	0.13	7.8	0.4	0	1.8	123	19
Whole-grain wheat flakes	½ cup	79	1.9	0.2	0.04	18.6	1.4	0	0.6	150	6
Cheese											
American, processed	1 ounce	106	6.3	8.9	5.58	0.5	0.0	27	0.1	405	175
American, processed, light	1 ounce	50	6.9	2.0	—	1.0	0.0	—	—	407	198
American, processed, skim	1 ounce	69	6.0	4.0	—	2.0	0.0	15	—	407	198
Blue	1 ounce	100	6.1	8.1	5.30	0.7	0.0	21	0.1	395	150
Brie	1 ounce	95	5.9	7.8	4.94	0.1	0.0	28	0.1	178	52
Camembert	1 ounce	85	5.6	6.9	4.33	0.1	0.0	20	0.1	239	110
Cheddar	1 ounce	114	7.0	9.4	5.98	0.4	0.0	30	0.2	176	204
Cheddar, 40% less-fat	1 ounce	71	5.0	4.1	2.40	6.0	—	15	0.1	195	192
Cheddar, light, processed	1 ounce	50	6.9	2.0	—	1.0	0.0	—	—	442	198

Dash (—) indicates insufficient data available

FOOD	APPROXIMATE MEASURE	FOOD ENERGY (CALORIES)	PROTEIN (GRAMS)	FAT (GRAMS)	SATURATED FAT (GRAMS)	CARBOHYDRATE (GRAMS)	FIBER (GRAMS)	CHOLESTEROL (MILLIGRAMS)	IRON (MILLIGRAMS)	SODIUM (MILLIGRAMS)	CALCIUM (MILLIGRAMS)
Cheese (*continued*)											
Cheddar, reduced-fat, sharp	1 ounce	86	8.3	5.4	3.15	1.2	—	19	0.1	205	251
Colby, reduced-fat	1 ounce	85	8.2	5.5	3.23	0.7	—	19	0.1	163	223
Cottage, dry curd, no-salt-added	½ cup	62	12.5	0.3	0.20	1.3	0.0	5	0.2	9	23
Cottage, nonfat	½ cup	70	15.0	0.0	0.00	3.0	—	5	—	419	60
Cottage, low-fat (1% milkfat)	½ cup	81	14.0	1.1	0.72	3.1	0.0	5	0.2	459	69
Cottage, low-fat (2% milkfat)	½ cup	102	15.5	2.2	1.38	4.1		9	0.2	459	77
Cottage (4% milkfat)	½ cup	108	13.1	4.7	2.99	2.8	0.0	16	0.1	425	63
Cream, light	1 ounce	62	2.9	4.8	2.86	1.8	—	16	0.0	160	38
Cream, nonfat	1 ounce	24	4.0	0.0	—	1.0	0.0	5	0.0	170	80
Farmer	1 ounce	40	4.0	3.0	—	1.0	—	—	—	—	30
Feta	1 ounce	75	4.0	6.0	4.24	1.2	0.0	25	0.2	316	139
Fontina	1 ounce	110	7.3	8.8	5.44	0.4	0.0	33	0.1	—	156
Gouda	1 ounce	101	7.1	7.8	4.99	0.6	0.0	32	0.1	232	198
Gruyère	1 ounce	117	8.4	9.2	5.36	0.1	0.0	31	—	95	287
Monterey Jack	1 ounce	106	6.9	8.6	5.41	0.2	0.0	22	0.2	152	211
Monterey Jack, reduced-fat	1 ounce	83	8.4	5.4	3.15	0.5	—	19	0.1	181	227
Mozzarella, part-skim	1 ounce	72	6.9	4.5	2.86	0.8	0.0	16	0.1	132	183
Mozzarella, whole milk	1 ounce	80	5.5	6.1	3.73	0.6	0.0	22	0.0	106	147
Muenster	1 ounce	104	6.6	8.5	5.42	0.3	0.0	27	0.1	178	203
Neufchâtel	1 ounce	74	2.8	6.6	4.20	0.8	0.0	22	0.1	113	21
Parmesan, grated	1 ounce	129	11.8	8.5	5.40	1.1	0.0	22	0.3	528	390
Provolone	1 ounce	100	7.2	7.5	4.84	0.6	0.0	20	0.1	248	214
Ricotta, lite	1 ounce	20	3.0	1.0	0.60	1.0	—	4	—	20	34
Ricotta, nonfat	1 ounce	20	4.0	0.0	—	2.0	—	3	—	15	48
Ricotta, part-skim	1 ounce	39	3.2	2.2	1.39	1.5	0.0	9	0.1	35	77
Romano, grated	1 ounce	110	9.0	7.6	4.85	1.0	0.0	29	—	340	302
Swiss	1 ounce	107	8.1	7.8	5.04	1.0	0.0	26	0.0	74	272
Swiss, reduced-fat	1 ounce	85	9.6	5.0	2.78	0.5	—	18	0.1	44	334
Cherries											
Fresh, sweet	½ cup	52	0.9	0.7	0.16	12.0	1.7	0	0.3	0	11
Sour, in light syrup	½ cup	94	0.9	0.1	0.03	24.3	0.1	0	1.7	9	13
Sour, unsweetened	½ cup	39	0.8	0.2	0.05	9.4	1.8	0	0.2	2	12
Chicken, skinned, boned, and roasted											
White meat	3 ounces	147	26.1	3.8	1.07	0.0	0.0	72	0.9	65	13
Dark meat	3 ounces	174	23.3	8.3	2.26	0.0	0.0	79	1.1	79	13
Liver	3 ounces	134	20.7	4.6	1.56	0.7	0.0	537	7.2	43	12
Chili sauce	1 tablespoon	18	0.4	0.1	0.03	4.2	0.1	0	0.1	228	3
Chives, raw, chopped	1 tablespoon	1	0.1	0.0	0.00	0.1	0.1	0	0.0	0	2
Chocolate											
Chips, semisweet	¼ cup	215	1.7	15.2	—	24.2	0.4	0	1.1	1	13
Sweet	1 ounce	150	1.2	9.9	—	16.4	0.1	0	0.4	9	27
Syrup, fudge	1 tablespoon	62	0.9	2.6	1.55	10.1	0.1	2	0.2	17	24
Unsweetened, baking	1 ounce	141	3.1	14.7	8.79	8.5	0.7	0	2.0	1	23
Chutney, apple	1 tablespoon	41	0.2	0.0	—	10.5	—	—	0.2	34	5
Cilantro, fresh, minced	1 tablespoon	1	0.1	0.0	0.00	0.3	0.2	0	0.2	1	5
Clams											
Raw	½ cup	92	15.8	1.2	0.12	3.2	0.0	42	17.3	69	57
Canned, drained	½ cup	118	20.4	1.6	0.15	4.1	0.0	54	22.4	90	74
Cocoa powder, unsweetened	1 tablespoon	24	1.6	0.7	0.44	2.6	—	0	0.9	2	8
Coconut											
Fresh, grated	1 cup	460	4.3	43.5	38.61	19.8	11.7	0	3.2	26	18
Dried, sweetened, shredded	1 cup	463	2.7	32.8	29.08	44.0	4.9	0	1.8	242	14
Dried, unsweetened, shredded	1 cup	526	5.5	51.4	45.62	18.8	4.2	0	2.6	30	21
Cookies											
Brownie	2-ounce bar	243	2.7	10.1	3.13	39.0	—	10	1.3	153	25
Chocolate	1 each	72	1.0	3.4	0.90	9.4	0.0	13	0.4	61	18
Chocolate chip, homemade	1 each	69	0.9	4.6	—	6.8	0.2	7	0.3	30	7
Fig bar	1 each	60	0.5	1.0	0.26	11.0	—	—	0.5	60	10

FOOD	APPROXIMATE MEASURE	FOOD ENERGY (CALORIES)	PROTEIN (GRAMS)	FAT (GRAMS)	SATURATED FAT (GRAMS)	CARBOHYDRATE (GRAMS)	FIBER (GRAMS)	CHOLESTEROL (MILLIGRAMS)	IRON (MILLIGRAMS)	SODIUM (MILLIGRAMS)	CALCIUM (MILLIGRAMS)
Cookies (continued)											
Fortune	1 each	23	0.3	0.2	—	5.0	0.1	—	0.1	—	1
Gingersnaps	1 each	36	0.5	1.3	0.33	5.4	0.0	3	0.4	11	14
Oatmeal, plain	1 each	57	0.9	2.7	0.68	7.2	0.4	9	0.3	46	13
Sugar wafers	1 each	47	0.6	2.4	0.48	5.9	0.0	7	0.1	61	4
Vanilla creme	1 each	83	0.8	3.6	—	12.1	—	—	0.4	61	3
Vanilla wafers	1 each	17	0.2	0.9	0.17	2.1	0.0	2	0.1	22	2
Corn											
Fresh, kernels, cooked	½ cup	89	2.6	1.0	0.16	20.6	3.0	0	0.5	14	2
Cream-style, regular pack	½ cup	92	2.2	0.5	0.08	23.2	1.5	0	0.5	365	4
Cornmeal											
Degermed, yellow	1 cup	505	11.7	2.3	0.31	107.2	7.2	0	5.7	4	7
Self-rising	1 cup	407	10.1	4.1	0.58	85.7	—	0	7.0	1521	440
Cornstarch	1 tablespoon	31	0.0	0.0	0.00	7.3	0.1	0	0.0	1	0
Couscous, cooked	½ cup	100	3.4	0.1	0.03	20.8	—	0	0.3	4	7
Crab											
Blue, cooked	3 ounces	87	17.2	1.5	0.19	0.0	0.0	85	0.8	237	88
Imitation	3 ounces	87	10.2	1.1	—	8.7	0.0	17	0.3	715	11
King, cooked	3 ounces	82	16.5	1.3	0.11	0.0	0.0	45	0.6	912	50
Crackers											
Butter	1 each	17	0.0	1.0	—	2.0	—	—	0.1	32	4
Graham, plain	1 square	30	0.5	0.5	—	5.5	—	—	0.2	48	1
Melba rounds, plain	1 each	11	0.4	0.2	—	2.0	—	—	0.1	34	0
Saltine	1 each	13	0.3	0.4	—	2.1	—	—	0.1	43	5
Whole wheat	1 each	33	0.7	1.3	0.33	4.7	0.3	0	0.0	60	0
Cranberry											
Fresh, whole	½ cup	23	0.2	0.1	0.01	6.0	0.6	0	0.1	0	3
Juice cocktail, reduced-calorie	½ cup	22	0.0	0.0	0.00	5.6	—	0	0.0	4	11
Juice cocktail, regular	½ cup	75	0.0	0.1	0.00	19.2	—	0	0.2	5	4
Sauce, sweetened	¼ cup	105	0.1	0.1	0.01	26.9	0.2	0	0.1	20	3
Cream											
Half-and-half	1 tablespoon	20	0.4	1.7	1.08	0.7	0.0	6	0.0	6	16
Sour	1 tablespoon	31	0.5	3.0	1.88	0.6	0.0	6	0.0	8	17
Sour, nonfat	1 tablespoon	10	1.0	0.0	—	1.0	—	0	—	10	—
Sour, reduced-calorie	1 tablespoon	20	0.4	1.8	1.12	0.6	0.0	6	0.0	6	16
Whipping, unwhipped	1 tablespoon	51	0.3	5.5	3.43	0.4	0.0	20	0.0	6	10
Creamer, non-dairy, powder	1 teaspoon	11	0.1	0.7	0.64	1.1	0.0	0	0.0	4	16
Croutons, seasoned	1 ounce	139	3.0	5.0	—	18.9	—	—	0.3	—	20
Cucumbers, raw, whole	1 medium	32	1.3	0.3	0.08	7.1	2.4	0	0.7	5	34
Currants	1 tablespoon	25	0.4	0.0	0.00	6.7	0.1	0	0.3	1	8
Dandelion greens, raw	1 cup	25	1.5	0.4	—	5.1	0.9	0	1.7	42	103
Dates, pitted, unsweetened	5 each	114	0.8	0.2	0.08	30.5	3.6	0	0.5	1	13
Doughnut											
Cake type	1 each	156	1.8	7.4	1.92	20.6	0.5	24	0.5	200	16
Plain, yeast	1 each	166	2.5	10.7	2.60	15.1	0.9	10	0.6	94	15
Egg											
White	1 each	16	3.4	0.0	0.00	0.3	0.0	0	0.0	52	2
Whole	1 each	77	6.5	5.2	1.61	0.6	0.0	213	0.7	66	25
Yolk	1 each	61	2.8	5.2	1.61	0.3	0.0	213	0.6	7	23
Substitute	¼ cup	30	6.0	0.0	0.00	1.0	—	0	1.1	90	20
Eggplant, cooked without salt	½ cup	13	0.4	0.1	0.02	3.2	0.5	0	0.2	1	3
Extract, vanilla	1 teaspoon	15	0.0	0.0	—	1.5	0.0	0	0.0	0	0
Fennel, leaves, raw	½ cup	13	1.2	0.2	—	2.3	0.2	0	1.2	4	45

Dash (—) indicates insufficient data available

FOOD	APPROXIMATE MEASURE	FOOD ENERGY (CALORIES)	PROTEIN (GRAMS)	FAT (GRAMS)	SATURATED FAT (GRAMS)	CARBOHYDRATE (GRAMS)	FIBER (GRAMS)	CHOLESTEROL (MILLIGRAMS)	IRON (MILLIGRAMS)	SODIUM (MILLIGRAMS)	CALCIUM (MILLIGRAMS)
Figs											
Fresh	1 medium	37	0.4	0.2	0.03	9.9	1.9	0	0.2	1	18
Dried	1 each	48	0.6	0.2	0.04	12.2	3.2	0	0.4	2	27
Fish, cooked											
Cod	3 ounces	89	19.4	0.7	0.14	0.0	0.0	47	0.4	66	12
Flounder	3 ounces	100	20.5	1.3	0.31	0.0	0.0	58	0.3	89	15
Grouper	3 ounces	100	21.1	1.1	0.25	0.0	0.0	40	1.0	45	18
Haddock	3 ounces	95	20.6	0.8	0.14	0.0	0.0	63	1.1	74	36
Halibut	3 ounces	119	22.7	2.5	0.35	0.0	0.0	35	0.9	59	51
Mackerel	3 ounces	134	20.1	5.4	1.53	0.0	0.0	62	0.6	56	11
Mahimahi	3 ounces	93	20.2	0.8	0.20	0.0	0.0	80	1.2	96	—
Perch	3 ounces	100	21.1	1.0	0.20	0.0	0.0	98	1.0	67	87
Pollock	3 ounces	96	20.0	1.0	0.20	0.0	0.0	82	0.2	99	5
Pompano	3 ounces	179	20.1	10.3	3.83	0.0	0.0	54	0.6	65	37
Salmon, sockeye	3 ounces	184	23.2	9.3	1.63	0.0	0.0	74	0.5	56	6
Scrod	3 ounces	89	19.4	0.7	0.14	0.0	0.0	47	0.4	66	12
Snapper	3 ounces	109	22.4	1.5	0.31	0.0	0.0	40	0.2	48	34
Sole	3 ounces	100	20.5	1.3	0.31	0.0	0.0	58	0.3	89	15
Swordfish	3 ounces	132	21.6	4.4	1.20	0.0	0.0	43	0.9	98	5
Trout	3 ounces	128	22.4	3.7	0.71	0.0	0.0	62	2.1	29	73
Tuna, canned in oil, drained	3 ounces	168	24.8	7.0	1.30	0.0	0.0	15	1.2	301	11
Tuna, canned in water, drained	3 ounces	111	25.2	0.4	0.14	0.0	0.0	—	2.7	303	10
Flour											
All-purpose, unsifted	1 cup	455	12.9	1.2	0.19	95.4	3.4	0	5.8	2	19
Bread, sifted	1 cup	495	16.4	2.3	0.33	99.4	—	0	6.0	3	21
Cake, sifted	1 cup	395	8.9	0.9	0.14	85.1	—	0	8.0	2	15
Rye, light, sifted	1 cup	374	8.6	1.4	0.15	81.8	14.9	0	1.8	2	21
Whole wheat, unsifted	1 cup	407	16.4	2.2	0.39	87.1	15.1	0	4.7	6	41
Frankfurter											
All-meat	1 each	138	4.9	12.6	4.63	1.1	0.0	22	0.5	482	5
Chicken	1 each	113	5.7	8.6	—	3.0	—	44	0.9	603	42
Turkey	1 each	103	5.6	8.5	2.65	1.1	—	42	0.8	488	60
Fruit bits, dried	1 ounce	93	1.3	0.0	—	20.0	—	0	0.5	24	—
Fruit cocktail, canned, packed in juice	½ cup	57	0.6	0.0	0.00	14.6	0.8	0	0.2	5	10
Garlic, raw	1 clove	4	0.2	0.0	0.00	1.0	0.0	0	0.1	1	5
Gelatin											
Flavored, prepared with water	½ cup	81	1.5	0.0	—	18.6	0.0	0	0.0	54	0
Unflavored	1 teaspoon	10	2.6	0.0	—	0.0	—	—	—	3	—
Ginger											
Fresh, grated	1 teaspoon	1	0.0	0.0	0.00	0.3	0.0	0	0.0	0	0
Crystallized	1 ounce	96	0.1	0.1	—	24.7	0.2	0	6.0	17	65
Grapefruit											
Fresh	1 medium	77	1.5	0.2	0.03	19.3	1.5	0	0.2	0	29
Juice, unsweetened	½ cup	47	0.6	0.1	0.02	11.1	0.0	0	2.5	1	9
Grapes, green, seedless	1 cup	114	1.1	0.9	0.30	28.4	2.6	0	0.4	3	18
Grape juice, Concord	½ cup	60	0.0	0.0	—	14.9	—	—	0.0	11	4
Grits, cooked	½ cup	73	1.7	0.2	0.40	15.7	—	0	0.8	0	0
Ham											
Cured, roasted, extra-lean	3 ounces	123	17.8	4.7	1.54	1.3	0.0	45	1.3	1023	7
Reduced-fat, low-salt	3 ounces	104	15.3	4.2	—	1.8	—	42	—	658	—
Hominy, white or yellow	½ cup	58	1.2	0.7	0.10	11.4	2.0	0	0.5	168	8
Honey	1 tablespoon	64	0.1	0.0	0.00	17.5	0.0	0	0.1	1	1
Honeydew, raw, diced	1 cup	59	0.8	0.2	0.08	15.6	1.5	0	0.1	17	10
Horseradish, prepared	1 tablespoon	6	0.2	0.0	0.01	1.4	0.1	0	0.1	14	9
Hot sauce, bottled	¼ teaspoon	0	0.0	0.0	—	0.0	—	0	0.0	9	0
Ice, cherry	½ cup	82	0.2	0.0	—	10.3	—	—	—	0	—

FOOD	APPROXIMATE MEASURE	FOOD ENERGY (CALORIES)	PROTEIN (GRAMS)	FAT (GRAMS)	SATURATED FAT (GRAMS)	CARBOHYDRATE (GRAMS)	FIBER (GRAMS)	CHOLESTEROL (MILLIGRAMS)	IRON (MILLIGRAMS)	SODIUM (MILLIGRAMS)	CALCIUM (MILLIGRAMS)
Ice cream											
Vanilla, regular	½ cup	134	2.3	7.2	4.39	15.9	0.0	30	0.0	58	88
Vanilla, gourmet	½ cup	175	2.0	11.8	7.37	16.0	0.0	44	0.1	54	75
Ice milk, vanilla	½ cup	92	2.6	2.8	1.76	14.5	0.0	9	0.1	52	88
Jams and Jellies											
Regular	1 tablespoon	54	0.1	0.0	0.01	14.0	0.2	0	0.2	2	4
Reduced-calorie	1 tablespoon	29	0.1	0.0	—	7.4	—	0	0.0	16	1
Jicama	1 cup	49	1.6	0.2	0.07	10.5	0.7	0	0.7	7	18
Kiwifruit	1 each	44	1.0	0.5	0.08	8.9	2.6	0	0.4	0	20
Kumquat	1 each	12	0.2	0.0	0.00	3.1	0.7	0	0.1	1	8
Lamb											
Ground, cooked	3 ounces	241	21.0	16.7	6.91	0.0	—	82	1.5	69	19
Leg, roasted	3 ounces	162	24.1	6.6	2.35	0.0	—	76	1.8	58	7
Loin or chop, broiled	3 ounces	184	25.5	8.3	2.96	0.0	—	81	1.7	71	16
Rib, broiled	3 ounces	200	23.6	11.0	3.95	0.0	—	77	1.9	72	14
Lard	1 tablespoon	116	0.0	12.8	5.03	0.0	0.0	12	0.0	0	0
Leeks, bulb, raw	½ cup	32	0.8	0.2	0.03	7.3	0.6	0	1.0	10	31
Lemon											
Fresh	1 each	22	1.3	0.3	0.04	11.4	0.4	0	0.6	3	66
Juice	1 tablespoon	3	0.1	0.0	0.01	1.0	—	0	0.0	3	2
Lemonade, sweetened	1 cup	99	0.2	0.0	0.01	26.0	0.2	0	0.4	7	7
Lentils, cooked	½ cup	115	8.9	0.4	0.05	19.9	4.0	0	3.3	2	19
Lettuce											
Belgian endive	1 cup	14	0.9	0.1	0.02	2.9	—	0	0.5	6	—
Boston or Bibb, shredded	1 cup	7	0.7	0.1	0.02	1.3	0.4	0	0.2	3	—
Curly endive or escarole	1 cup	8	0.6	0.1	0.02	1.7	0.4	0	0.4	11	26
Iceberg, chopped	1 cup	7	0.5	0.1	0.01	1.1	0.5	0	0.3	5	10
Radicchio, raw	1 ounce	7	0.4	0.1	—	1.3	—	0	—	6	6
Romaine, chopped	1 cup	9	0.9	0.1	0.01	1.3	1.0	0	0.6	4	20
Lime											
Fresh	1 each	20	0.4	0.1	0.01	6.8	0.3	0	0.4	1	21
Juice	1 tablespoon	4	0.1	0.0	0.00	1.4	—	0	0.0	0	1
Lobster, cooked, meat only	3 ounces	83	17.4	0.5	0.09	1.1	0.0	61	0.3	323	52
Luncheon meats											
Bologna, all meat	1 slice	90	3.3	8.0	3.01	0.8	0.0	16	0.4	289	3
Deviled ham	1 ounce	78	4.3	6.7	—	0.0	0.0	—	0.3	—	1
Salami	1 ounce	71	3.9	5.7	2.29	0.6	0.0	18	0.8	302	4
Turkey ham	1 ounce	34	5.5	1.2	0.45	0.3	—	19	0.4	286	2
Turkey pastrami	1 ounce	33	5.4	1.2	0.43	0.1	—	18	0.4	283	2
Lychees, raw	1 each	6	0.1	0.0	—	1.6	0.0	0	0.0	0	0
Mango, raw	½ cup	54	0.4	0.2	0.05	14.0	1.2	0	0.1	2	8
Margarine											
Regular	1 tablespoon	101	0.1	11.4	2.23	0.1	0.0	0	0.0	133	4
Reduced-calorie, stick	1 tablespoon	50	0.1	5.6	0.93	0.1	0.0	0	0.0	139	3
Marshmallows, miniature	½ cup	73	0.5	0.0	0.00	18.5	0.0	0	0.4	9	4
Mayonnaise											
Regular	1 tablespoon	99	0.2	10.9	1.62	0.4	0.0	8	0.1	78	2
Nonfat	1 tablespoon	12	0.0	0.0	—	3.0	—	0	0.0	190	—
Reduced-calorie	1 tablespoon	44	0.1	4.6	0.70	0.7	0.0	6	0.0	88	1
Milk											
Buttermilk	1 cup	98	7.8	2.1	1.35	11.7	0.0	10	0.1	257	284
Buttermilk, nonfat	1 cup	88	8.8	0.8	0.64	12.0	—	8	—	256	288
Chocolate, low-fat 1%	1 cup	158	8.1	2.5	1.55	26.1	0.1	8	0.6	153	288

Dash (—) indicates insufficient data available

FOOD	APPROXIMATE MEASURE	FOOD ENERGY (CALORIES)	PROTEIN (GRAMS)	FAT (GRAMS)	SATURATED FAT (GRAMS)	CARBOHYDRATE (GRAMS)	FIBER (GRAMS)	CHOLESTEROL (MILLIGRAMS)	IRON (MILLIGRAMS)	SODIUM (MILLIGRAMS)	CALCIUM (MILLIGRAMS)
Milk (*continued*)											
Chocolate, low-fat 2%	1 cup	180	8.0	5.0	3.10	25.8	0.1	18	0.6	150	285
Condensed, sweetened	1 cup	982	24.2	26.3	16.77	166.5	0.0	104	0.5	389	869
Evaporated, skim, canned	1 cup	200	19.3	0.5	0.31	29.1	0.0	10	0.7	294	742
Low-fat, 1% fat	1 cup	102	8.0	2.5	1.61	11.6	0.0	10	0.1	122	300
Low-fat, 2% fat	1 cup	122	8.1	4.7	2.93	11.7	0.0	20	0.1	122	298
Nonfat dry	⅓ cup	145	14.5	0.3	0.20	20.8	0.0	8	0.1	214	503
Powder, malted, chocolate	1 tablespoon	84	1.1	0.7	—	18.4	—	—	0.3	47	13
Skim	1 cup	86	8.3	0.4	0.28	11.9	0.0	5	0.1	127	301
Whole	1 cup	149	8.0	8.1	5.05	11.3	0.0	34	0.1	120	290
Millet, cooked	½ cup	143	4.2	1.2	0.21	28.4	—	0	0.8	2	4
Mint, fresh, raw	¼ cup	1	0.1	0.0	—	0.1	—	0	0.1	0	4
Molasses, cane, light	1 tablespoon	52	0.0	0.0	—	13.3	0.0	0	0.9	3	34
Mushrooms											
Fresh	½ cup	9	0.7	0.1	0.02	1.6	0.5	0	0.4	1	2
Canned	½ cup	19	1.5	0.2	0.02	3.9	—	0	0.6	—	—
Shiitake, dried	1 each	14	0.3	0.0	0.01	2.6	0.4	0	0.1	0	0
Mussels, blue, cooked	3 ounces	146	20.2	3.8	0.02	6.3	0.0	48	5.7	314	28
Mustard											
Dijon	1 tablespoon	18	0.0	1.0	—	1.0	0.0	0	—	446	—
Prepared, yellow	1 tablespoon	12	0.7	0.7	0.03	1.0	0.2	0	0.3	196	13
Nectarine, fresh	1 each	67	1.3	0.6	0.07	16.1	2.2	0	0.2	0	7
Nuts											
Almonds, chopped	1 tablespoon	48	1.6	4.2	0.40	1.7	0.9	0	0.3	1	22
Cashews, dry roasted, unsalted	1 tablespoon	49	1.3	4.0	0.78	2.8	0.5	0	0.5	1	4
Hazelnuts, chopped	1 tablespoon	45	0.9	4.5	0.32	1.1	0.3	0	0.2	0	14
Macadamia, roasted, unsalted	1 tablespoon	60	0.6	6.4	0.96	1.1	0.1	0	0.1	1	4
Peanuts, roasted, unsalted	1 tablespoon	53	2.4	4.5	0.62	1.7	0.8	0	0.2	1	8
Pecans, chopped	1 tablespoon	50	0.6	5.0	0.40	1.4	0.5	0	0.2	0	3
Pine	1 tablespoon	52	2.4	5.1	0.78	1.4	0.1	0	0.9	0	3
Pistachio nuts	1 tablespoon	46	1.6	3.9	0.49	2.0	0.9	0	0.5	0	11
Walnuts, black	1 tablespoon	47	1.9	4.4	0.28	0.9	0.5	0	0.2	0	5
Oats											
Cooked	1 cup	145	6.1	2.3	0.42	25.3	2.1	0	1.6	374	19
Rolled, dry	½ cup	156	6.5	2.6	0.45	27.1	4.2	0	1.7	2	21
Oil											
Canola	1 tablespoon	117	0.0	13.6	0.97	0.0	0.0	0	0.0	0	0
Corn	1 tablespoon	121	0.0	13.6	1.73	0.0	0.0	0	0.0	0	0
Olive	1 tablespoon	119	0.0	13.5	1.82	0.0	0.0	0	0.1	0	0
Peanut	1 tablespoon	119	0.0	13.5	2.28	0.0	0.0	0	0.0	0	0
Safflower	1 tablespoon	121	0.0	13.6	1.24	0.0	0.0	0	0.0	0	0
Sesame	1 tablespoon	121	0.0	13.6	1.92	0.0	0.0	0	0.0	0	0
Okra, cooked	½ cup	26	1.5	0.1	0.04	5.8	0.6	0	0.3	4	50
Olives											
Green, stuffed	1 each	4	0.0	0.4	—	0.1	—	—	—	290	—
Ripe	1 medium	5	0.0	0.4	0.08	0.3	0.1	0	0.1	35	4
Onions											
Green	1 tablespoon	2	0.1	0.0	0.00	0.5	0.2	0	0.1	1	5
Raw, chopped	½ cup	32	1.0	0.1	0.02	7.3	1.6	0	0.2	3	17
Cooked, yellow or white	½ cup	23	0.7	0.1	0.02	5.3	—	0	0.1	2	12
Orange											
Fresh	1 medium	62	1.2	0.2	0.02	15.4	5.8	0	0.1	0	52
Juice	½ cup	56	0.8	0.1	0.01	13.4	0.2	0	0.1	1	11
Mandarin, canned, packed in juice	½ cup	46	0.7	0.0	0.00	12.0	0.1	0	0.4	6	14
Mandarin, canned, packed in light syrup	½ cup	77	0.6	0.1	0.02	20.4	0.1	0	0.5	8	9
Mandarin, canned, packed in water	½ cup	37	0.0	0.0	—	8.4	—	—	0.4	11	—
Oysters, raw	3 ounces	59	6.0	2.1	0.54	3.3	0.0	47	5.7	95	38

FOOD	APPROXIMATE MEASURE	FOOD ENERGY (CALORIES)	PROTEIN (GRAMS)	FAT (GRAMS)	SATURATED FAT (GRAMS)	CARBOHYDRATE (GRAMS)	FIBER (GRAMS)	CHOLESTEROL (MILLIGRAMS)	IRON (MILLIGRAMS)	SODIUM (MILLIGRAMS)	CALCIUM (MILLIGRAMS)
Papaya											
Fresh, cubed	½ cup	27	0.4	0.1	0.03	6.9	1.2	0	0.1	2	17
Nectar, canned	½ cup	71	0.3	0.3	0.06	18.1	—	0	0.4	6	13
Parsley, raw	1 tablespoon	1	0.1	0.0	0.00	0.3	0.2	0	0.2	1	5
Parsnips, cooked, diced	½ cup	63	1.0	0.2	0.04	15.1	2.1	0	0.4	8	29
Passion fruit	1 medium	17	0.4	0.1	—	4.2	2.0	0	0.3	5	2
Pasta, cooked											
Macaroni or lasagna noodles	½ cup	99	3.3	0.5	0.07	19.8	1.1	0	1.0	1	5
Medium egg noodles	½ cup	106	3.8	1.2	0.25	19.9	1.8	26	1.3	6	10
Rice noodles	½ cup	138	3.1	1.3	—	28.6	—	0	2.2	—	40
Spaghetti or fettuccine	½ cup	99	3.3	0.5	0.07	19.8	1.1	0	1.0	1	5
Spinach noodles	½ cup	100	3.8	1.0	0.15	18.9	1.4	0	1.8	22	46
Whole wheat	½ cup	100	3.7	1.4	0.18	19.8	2.5	0	1.0	1	12
Peaches											
Fresh	1 medium	37	0.6	0.1	0.01	9.7	1.4	0	0.1	0	4
Canned, packed in juice	½ cup	55	0.8	0.0	0.00	14.3	0.6	0	0.3	5	7
Canned, packed in light syrup	½ cup	69	0.6	0.0	0.00	18.6	0.4	0	0.5	6	4
Canned, packed in water	½ cup	29	0.5	0.1	0.01	7.5	0.4	0	0.4	4	2
Juice	½ cup	57	0.0	0.0	—	13.6	—	—	—	5	—
Peanut butter											
Regular	1 tablespoon	95	4.6	8.3	1.38	2.6	1.0	0	0.3	79	5
No-salt-added	1 tablespoon	95	4.6	8.3	1.38	2.6	1.0	0	0.3	3	5
Pear											
Fresh	1 medium	97	0.6	0.7	0.03	24.9	4.3	0	0.4	0	18
Canned, packed in juice	½ cup	62	0.4	0.1	0.00	16.0	1.1	0	0.3	5	11
Canned, packed in light syrup	½ cup	71	0.2	0.0	—	19.6	3.1	0	0.3	6	6
Nectar, canned	½ cup	64	0.4	0.2	—	16.1	0.4	—	0.1	1	4
Peas											
Black-eyed, cooked	½ cup	90	6.7	0.7	0.17	15.0	1.5	0	1.2	3	23
English, cooked	½ cup	62	4.1	0.2	0.04	11.4	3.5	0	1.2	70	19
Snow pea pods, cooked or raw	½ cup	34	2.6	0.2	0.03	5.6	2.2	0	1.6	3	34
Split, cooked	½ cup	116	8.2	0.4	0.05	20.7	2.3	0	1.3	2	14
Peppers											
Chile, hot, green, chopped	1 tablespoon	4	0.2	0.0	0.00	0.9	0.2	0	0.1	1	2
Jalapeño, green	1 each	4	0.2	0.0	0.00	0.9	0.2	0	0.1	1	2
Sweet, raw, green, red, or yellow	1 medium	19	0.6	0.4	0.05	3.9	1.2	0	0.9	2	4
Phyllo pastry, raw	1 sheet	57	1.3	1.1	0.17	10.0	—	0	0.6	92	2
Pickle											
Dill, sliced	¼ cup	4	0.2	0.1	0.02	0.9	0.5	0	0.4	553	10
Relish, chopped, sour	1 tablespoon	3	0.1	0.1	—	0.4	0.2	0	0.2	207	4
Sweet, sliced	¼ cup	57	0.2	0.2	0.04	14.1	0.4	0	0.5	276	5
Pie, baked, 9-inch diameter, cut into 8 slices											
Apple, fresh	1 slice	409	3.3	15.3	5.22	67.7	3.5	12	0.8	229	37
Chocolate meringue	1 slice	354	6.8	13.4	5.38	53.8	0.5	109	1.2	307	130
Egg custard	1 slice	248	7.3	11.6	4.07	28.6	0.3	149	0.9	229	129
Peach	1 slice	327	3.2	11.0	2.74	55.1	0.8	0	1.0	339	35
Pecan	1 slice	478	5.8	20.3	4.31	71.1	0.5	141	2.4	324	51
Pumpkin	1 slice	181	4.0	6.8	2.24	27.0	0.8	61	1.1	210	78
Pimiento, diced	1 tablespoon	4	0.2	0.1	0.01	1.0	—	0	0.3	3	1
Pineapple											
Fresh, diced	½ cup	38	0.3	0.3	0.02	9.6	1.2	0	0.3	1	5
Canned, packed in juice	½ cup	75	0.5	0.1	0.01	19.6	0.9	0	0.3	1	17
Canned, packed in light syrup	½ cup	66	0.5	0.2	0.01	16.9	0.6	0	0.5	1	18
Juice, unsweetened	½ cup	70	0.4	0.1	0.01	17.2	0.1	0	0.3	1	21
Plum, fresh	1 medium	35	0.5	0.4	0.03	8.3	1.3	0	0.1	0	3
Popcorn, hot-air popped	1 cup	23	0.8	0.3	0.04	4.6	0.9	0	0.2	0	1
Poppy seeds	1 tablespoon	47	1.6	3.9	0.43	2.1	0.5	0	0.8	2	127

Dash (—) indicates insufficient data available

FOOD	APPROXIMATE MEASURE	FOOD ENERGY (CALORIES)	PROTEIN (GRAMS)	FAT (GRAMS)	SATURATED FAT (GRAMS)	CARBOHYDRATE (GRAMS)	FIBER (GRAMS)	CHOLESTEROL (MILLIGRAMS)	IRON (MILLIGRAMS)	SODIUM (MILLIGRAMS)	CALCIUM (MILLIGRAMS)
Pork, cooked											
Chop, center-loin	3 ounces	204	24.2	11.1	—	0.0	0.0	77	0.9	59	5
Roast	3 ounces	204	22.7	11.7	4.07	0.0	0.0	77	1.0	59	8
Sausage link or patty	1 ounce	105	5.6	8.8	3.06	0.3	0.0	24	0.3	367	9
Spareribs	3 ounces	338	24.7	25.7	10.00	0.0	0.0	103	1.5	79	40
Tenderloin	3 ounces	141	24.5	4.1	1.41	0.0	0.0	79	1.3	57	8
Potatoes											
Baked, with skin	1 each	218	4.4	0.2	0.05	50.4	3.6	0	2.7	16	20
Boiled, diced	½ cup	67	1.3	0.1	0.02	15.6	1.2	0	0.2	4	6
Potato chips											
Regular	10 each	105	1.3	7.1	1.81	10.4	1.0	0	0.2	94	5
No-salt-added	10 each	105	1.3	7.1	1.81	10.4	1.0	0	0.2	1	5
Pretzel sticks, thin	10 each	25	0.5	0.5	—	4.4	0.0	—	0.3	83	4
Prunes											
Dried, pitted	1 each	20	0.2	0.0	0.00	5.3	0.6	0	0.2	0	4
Juice	½ cup	91	0.8	0.0	0.00	22.3	1.3	0	1.5	5	15
Pumpkin											
Canned	½ cup	42	1.3	0.3	0.18	9.9	2.0	0	1.7	6	32
Seeds, dry	1 ounce	153	7.0	13.0	2.46	5.0	0.6	0	4.2	5	12
Radish, fresh, sliced	½ cup	10	0.3	0.3	0.01	2.1	0.3	0	0.2	14	12
Raisins	1 tablespoon	27	0.3	0.0	0.01	7.2	0.5	0	0.2	1	4
Raisins, golden	1 tablespoon	31	0.4	0.1	0.02	8.2	0.5	0	0.2	1	5
Raspberries											
Black, fresh	½ cup	33	0.6	0.4	0.01	7.7	5.0	0	0.4	0	15
Red, fresh	½ cup	30	0.6	0.3	0.01	7.1	4.6	0	0.3	0	14
Rhubarb											
Raw, diced	½ cup	13	0.5	0.1	0.02	2.8	0.4	0	0.1	2	52
Cooked, with sugar	½ cup	157	0.5	0.1	0.01	42.1	—	0	0.3	1	196
Rice, cooked without salt or fat											
Brown	½ cup	110	2.5	0.9	—	23.2	0.3	1	0.5	1	8
White, long-grain	½ cup	108	2.0	0.1	—	24.0	0.5	0	0.9	0	10
Wild	½ cup	83	3.3	0.3	0.04	17.5	—	0	0.5	2	2
Rice cake, plain	1 each	36	0.7	0.2	0.00	7.7	0.1	0	0.2	1	1
Roll											
Croissant	1 each	272	4.6	17.3	10.67	24.6	0.8	47	1.1	384	32
Hard	1 each	156	4.9	1.6	0.35	29.8	0.1	2	1.1	312	24
Kaiser, small	1 each	92	3.0	1.8	—	16.0	0.1	—	1.3	192	7
Plain, brown-and-serve	1 each	82	2.2	2.0	0.34	13.7	0.1	2	0.5	141	13
Whole wheat	1 each	72	2.3	1.8	0.51	12.0	0.8	9	0.5	149	16
Rutabaga, cooked, cubed	½ cup	29	0.9	0.2	0.02	6.6	0.9	0	0.4	15	36
Salad dressing											
Blue cheese	1 tablespoon	84	0.4	9.2	—	0.3	0.0	0	0.0	216	3
Blue cheese, low-calorie	1 tablespoon	59	0.9	5.8	1.40	0.8	—	11	0.1	171	24
French	1 tablespoon	96	0.3	9.4	—	2.9	0.0	8	0.1	205	6
French, low-calorie	1 tablespoon	20	0.0	0.0	0.00	4.0	—	0	—	120	—
Italian	1 tablespoon	84	0.1	9.1	—	0.6	0.0	0	0.0	172	1
Italian, no-oil, low-calorie	1 tablespoon	8	0.1	0.0	—	1.8	0.0	0	0.0	161	1
Thousand Island	1 tablespoon	59	0.1	5.6	0.94	2.4	0.3	—	0.1	109	2
Thousand Island, low-calorie	1 tablespoon	24	0.1	1.6	0.25	2.5	0.2	2	0.1	153	2
Salsa, commercial	1 tablespoon	3	0.1	0.0	—	0.5	—	—	0.0	42	1
Salt, iodized	1 teaspoon	0	0.0	0.0	0.00	0.0	0.0	0	0.0	2343	15
Sauerkraut, canned	½ cup	22	1.1	0.2	0.04	5.0	1.3	0	1.7	780	35
Scallops, raw, large	3 ounces	75	14.3	0.6	0.07	2.0	0.0	28	0.2	137	20
Sesame seeds, dry, whole	1 teaspoon	17	0.5	1.5	0.21	0.7	0.1	0	0.4	0	29
Sherbet											
Lime or raspberry	½ cup	104	0.9	0.9	—	23.8	0.0	0	0.0	67	39
Orange	½ cup	135	1.1	1.9	1.19	29.3	0.0	7	0.1	44	52

FOOD	APPROXIMATE MEASURE	FOOD ENERGY (CALORIES)	PROTEIN (GRAMS)	FAT (GRAMS)	SATURATED FAT (GRAMS)	CARBOHYDRATE (GRAMS)	FIBER (GRAMS)	CHOLESTEROL (MILLIGRAMS)	IRON (MILLIGRAMS)	SODIUM (MILLIGRAMS)	CALCIUM (MILLIGRAMS)
Shortening	1 tablespoon	113	0.0	12.6	2.36	0.0	0.0	0	0.0	0	0
Shrimp											
Fresh, cooked, peeled, and deveined	3 ounces	84	17.8	0.9	0.25	0.0	0.0	166	2.6	191	33
Canned, drained	3 ounces	102	19.6	1.7	0.32	0.9	0.0	147	2.3	144	50
Soup, condensed, made with water											
Beef broth	1 cup	31	4.8	0.7	0.34	2.6	0.0	24	0.5	782	0
Chicken noodle	1 cup	75	4.0	2.4	0.65	9.3	0.2	7	0.7	1106	17
Chili, beef	1 cup	170	6.7	6.6	—	21.4	1.4	13	2.1	1035	43
Cream of chicken	1 cup	117	2.9	7.3	2.07	9.0	0.1	10	0.6	986	34
Cream of mushroom	1 cup	129	2.3	9.0	2.44	9.0	0.4	2	0.5	1032	46
Cream of potato	1 cup	73	1.7	2.3	1.22	11.0	—	5	0.5	1000	20
Onion	1 cup	58	3.7	1.7	—	8.2	—	0	0.7	1053	27
Tomato	1 cup	85	2.0	1.9	0.37	16.6	0.5	0	1.7	871	12
Vegetable, beef	1 cup	78	5.4	2.0	0.83	9.8	0.2	5	1.2	956	17
Soy sauce											
Regular	1 tablespoon	8	0.8	0.0	0.00	1.2	0.0	0	0.3	829	2
Low-sodium	1 tablespoon	6	0.0	0.0	0.00	0.0	—	0	0.0	390	—
Reduced-sodium	1 tablespoon	8	0.8	0.0	0.00	1.2	0.0	0	0.3	484	2
Spinach											
Fresh	1 cup	12	1.6	0.2	0.03	2.0	2.2	0	1.5	44	55
Canned, regular pack	½ cup	22	2.3	0.4	0.00	3.4	1.1	0	1.8	373	97
Cooked	½ cup	21	2.7	0.2	0.04	3.4	2.4	0	3.2	63	122
Squash, cooked											
Acorn	½ cup	57	1.1	0.1	0.03	14.9	1.2	0	1.0	4	45
Butternut	½ cup	41	0.8	0.1	0.02	10.7	1.2	0	0.6	4	42
Spaghetti	½ cup	22	0.5	0.2	0.05	5.0	1.0	0	0.3	14	16
Summer	½ cup	18	0.8	0.3	0.06	3.9	1.4	0	0.3	1	24
Squid, raw	4 ounces	104	17.7	1.6	0.41	3.5	0.0	264	0.8	50	36
Strawberries, fresh	1 cup	45	0.9	0.6	0.03	10.5	3.9	0	0.6	1	21
Sugar											
Granulated	1 tablespoon	48	0.0	0.0	0.00	12.4	0.0	0	0.0	0	0
Brown, packed	1 tablespoon	51	0.0	0.0	—	13.3	0.0	0	0.5	4	12
Powdered	1 tablespoon	29	0.0	0.0	0.00	7.5	0.0	0	0.0	0	0
Sunflower kernels	¼ cup	205	8.2	17.8	1.87	6.8	2.4	0	2.4	1	42
Sweet potatoes											
Whole, baked	½ cup	103	1.7	0.1	0.02	24.3	3.0	0	0.4	10	28
Mashed	½ cup	172	2.7	0.5	0.10	39.8	4.9	0	0.9	21	34
Syrup											
Chocolate-flavored	1 tablespoon	49	0.6	0.2	0.00	11.0	—	0	0.3	12	3
Corn, dark or light	1 tablespoon	60	0.0	0.0	0.00	15.4	0.0	0	0.8	14	9
Maple, reduced-calorie	1 tablespoon	30	0.0	0.2	0.00	7.8	0.0	0	0.0	41	0
Pancake	1 tablespoon	50	0.0	0.0	0.00	12.8	0.0	0	0.2	2	20
Taco shell	1 each	52	0.7	2.8	—	5.9	—	—	—	62	—
Tangerine											
Fresh	1 medium	38	0.5	0.1	0.02	9.6	1.6	0	0.1	1	12
Juice, unsweetened	½ cup	53	0.6	0.2	0.02	12.5	0.1	0	0.2	1	22
Tapioca, dry	1 tablespoon	32	0.0	0.0	—	8.4	0.1	0	0.2	0	2
Tofu											
Firm	4 ounces	164	17.9	9.9	1.43	4.9	1.4	0	11.9	16	232
Soft	4 ounces	60	7.0	3.0	—	2.0	—	0	1.4	5	100
Tomato											
Fresh	1 medium	26	1.0	0.4	0.06	5.7	1.6	0	0.6	11	6
Cooked	½ cup	30	1.3	0.3	0.04	6.8	0.9	0	0.7	13	10
Juice, regular	1 cup	41	1.8	0.1	0.02	10.3	0.9	0	1.4	881	22
Juice, no-salt-added	1 cup	41	1.8	0.1	0.02	10.3	0.9	—	1.4	24	22
Paste, regular	1 tablespoon	14	0.6	0.1	0.02	3.1	0.7	0	0.5	129	6

Dash (—) indicates insufficient data available

FOOD	APPROXIMATE MEASURE	FOOD ENERGY (CALORIES)	PROTEIN (GRAMS)	FAT (GRAMS)	SATURATED FAT (GRAMS)	CARBOHYDRATE (GRAMS)	FIBER (GRAMS)	CHOLESTEROL (MILLIGRAMS)	IRON (MILLIGRAMS)	SODIUM (MILLIGRAMS)	CALCIUM (MILLIGRAMS)
Tomato (*continued*)											
Paste, no-salt-added	1 tablespoon	11	0.5	0.0	—	2.6	—	—	0.2	6	4
Sauce, regular	½ cup	37	1.6	0.2	0.03	8.8	1.8	0	0.9	741	17
Sauce, no-salt-added	½ cup	40	1.2	0.0	—	9.2	1.6	—	—	24	—
Stewed, canned	½ cup	30	0.9	1.1	0.20	5.2	0.2	0	0.4	187	10
Whole, canned, peeled	½ cup	22	0.9	0.0	—	5.2	0.8	—	0.5	424	38
Whole, canned, no-salt-added	½ cup	22	0.9	0.0	—	5.2	0.8	—	0.5	15	38
Tortilla											
Chips, plain	10 each	135	2.1	7.3	1.05	16.0	0.2	0	0.7	24	3
Corn, 6″ diameter	1 each	67	2.1	1.1	0.12	12.8	1.6	0	1.4	53	42
Flour, 6″ diameter	1 each	111	2.4	2.3	0.56	22.2	0.9	0	0.8	0	27
Turkey, skinned, boned, and roasted											
White meat	3 ounces	134	25.3	2.7	0.87	0.0	0.0	59	1.1	54	16
Dark meat	3 ounces	159	24.3	6.1	2.06	0.0	0.0	72	2.0	67	27
Smoked	3 ounces	126	20.4	4.9	1.45	0.0	0.0	48	2.3	586	9
Turnip greens, cooked	½ cup	14	0.8	0.2	0.04	3.1	2.2	0	0.6	21	99
Turnips, cooked, cubed	½ cup	14	0.6	0.1	0.01	3.8	1.6	0	0.2	39	17
Veal, cooked											
Ground	3 ounces	146	20.7	6.4	2.59	0.0	—	88	0.8	71	14
Leg	3 ounces	128	23.9	2.9	1.04	0.0	—	88	0.8	58	5
Loin	3 ounces	149	22.4	5.9	2.19	0.0	—	90	0.7	82	18
Vegetable juice cocktail											
Regular	1 cup	46	1.5	0.2	0.03	11.0	0.5	0	1.0	883	27
Low-sodium	1 cup	48	2.4	0.2	—	9.7	—	—	1.7	48	34
Venison, roasted	3 ounces	134	25.7	2.7	1.06	0.0	—	95	3.8	46	6
Vinegar, distilled	1 tablespoon	2	0.0	0.0	0.00	0.8	0.0	0	0.0	0	0
Water chestnuts, canned, sliced	½ cup	35	0.6	0.0	0.01	8.7	0.4	0	0.6	6	3
Watercress, fresh	½ cup	2	0.4	0.0	0.00	0.2	0.4	0	0.0	7	20
Watermelon, raw, diced	1 cup	51	1.0	0.7	0.35	11.5	0.9	0	0.3	3	13
Wheat bran, crude	1 tablespoon	8	0.6	0.2	0.02	2.4	1.6	0	0.4	0	3
Wheat germ	1 tablespoon	26	1.7	0.7	0.12	3.7	1.1	0	0.5	1	3
Whipped cream	1 tablespoon	26	0.2	2.8	1.71	0.2	0.0	10	0.0	3	5
Whipped topping, non-dairy, frozen	1 tablespoon	15	0.1	1.2	1.02	1.1	0.0	0	0.0	1	0
Wonton wrappers	1 each	6	0.2	0.1	0.03	0.9	0.0	5	0.1	12	1
Worcestershire sauce											
Regular	1 tablespoon	12	0.3	0.0	0.00	2.7	0.0	0	0.0	147	15
Low-sodium	1 tablespoon	12	0.0	0.0	0.00	3.0	—	0	—	57	—
Yeast, active, dry	1 package	20	2.6	0.1	0.01	2.7	2.2	0	1.1	4	3
Yogurt											
Coffee and vanilla, low-fat	1 cup	193	11.2	2.8	1.84	31.3	0.0	11	0.2	150	388
Frozen, low-fat	½ cup	99	3.0	2.0	1.41	18.0	—	10	—	35	100
Frozen, nonfat	½ cup	82	3.4	0.0	0.00	18.1	—	0	—	60	129
Fruit varieties, low-fat	1 cup	225	9.0	2.6	1.68	42.3	0.2	9	0.1	120	313
Plain, low-fat	1 cup	143	11.9	3.5	2.27	16.0	0.0	14	0.2	159	415
Plain, nonfat	1 cup	127	13.0	0.4	0.26	17.4	0.0	5	0.2	173	452
Zucchini											
Raw	½ cup	9	0.7	0.1	0.02	1.9	0.3	0	0.3	2	10
Cooked, diced	½ cup	17	0.7	0.1	0.01	4.1	0.5	0	0.4	3	14

Source of Data: Computrition, Inc., Chatsworth, California. Primarily comprised of *Composition of Foods: Raw, Processed, Prepared.* Agriculture Handbook No. 8 Series. United States Department of Agriculture, Human Nutrition Information Service, 1976–1991.

Recipe Index

Almonds
Bread, Golden Almond Turban, 118
Milk, Warm Vanilla-Almond, 35
Ambrosia, Fresh Melon, 41
Appetizers. *See also* Snacks.
Bread and Wild Mushrooms, Grilled, 99
Bruschetta with Basil, 55
Chicken Curry in Phyllo Baskets, 101
Chicken Pancakes with Fruit Salsa, 101
Corn Biscotti Appetizers, 97
Dips
Garden Dip, 80
Garlic and Pepper Dip, Roasted, 96
Pepperoncini-Cheese Dip, 51
Eggplant Chutney and Pita Chips, 96
Pastry Beef Rolls, 100
Popovers, Tex-Mex Appetizer, 97
Salmon Torte, Scandinavian, 102
Scallop Puffs in Zucchini, 102
Seafood Fondue, Marinated, 103
Shrimp and Peppers, Pickled, 102
Spinach-Ricotta Strudel, Herbed, 100
Spreads
Eggplant Spread with Pita Chips, Roasted, 66
Three-Cheese Spread, 96
Tuna and Sun-Dried Tomato Crostini, 98
Tuna Niçoise Canapés, 69
Turkey and Sun-Dried Tomato Pâté, Smoked, 90
Turkey Dumplings, Chinese, 103
Vegetable Sushi, 98
Apples
Brown Betty, Apple-Cherry, 77
Cabbage, Apple Sweet-Sour, 214
Fruit Cup, Bountiful Fresh, 39
Indienne, Lamb and Apples, 229
Mix, Harvest Popcorn, 202
Muffins, Fresh Apple, 110
Sauce, Apple Butter, 206
Spread, Apple-Maple, 35
Tatin, Apple Biscuit, 242
Wedges, Pimiento Cheese Apple, 201
Apricot-Pear Soup, Chilled, 222
Artichoke and Spinach Stuffed Shells, 143
Asparagus
Gingered Asparagus, 212
Lasagna, Asparagus, 140
Linguine with Asparagus and Goat Cheese, 141
Linguini with Asparagus and Shiitake Mushrooms, 136
Lobster with Asparagus, Honey-Mustard, 128
Salad, Roasted Red Pepper and Asparagus, 186
Avocado Dressing, Romaine Salad with, 77

Bacon
Biscuits, Bacon-Cornmeal, 109
Sandwiches, Scrambled Breakfast, 196
Bananas
Cake, Banana, 243
Frosty Fruit, 35
Pancakes, Banana, 112
Plantains, Black Beans and Rice with Baked, 146
Sandwiches, Fancy Peanut Butter and Banana, 196
Shake, Peanutty Banana, 105
Skewers, Grilled Honey Fruit, 68
Trifle, Banana-Citrus, 232
Barley
Pepperpot, Caribbean, 64
Tomatoes, Barley with, 132
Beans
Baked Beans, Hearty, 83
Black and White Beans with Orzo Primavera, 147
Black Beans and Rice with Baked Plantains, 146
Burritos, Caramelized Onion, Black Bean, and Orange, 146
Cannellini Beans, Ribbed Pork Roast with Herbed, 169
Green Beans in Sweet Vinaigrette, 212
Lima Beans, Spicy, 212
Picadillo, Beef and Bean, 227
Risotto, Greek White Bean, 148
Salads
Black Bean Salad, Marinated, 186
Christmas Confetti, 91
Scallops with Black Beans, Grilled, 129
Soup, Beans and Greens, 222
Soup, Chicken and Black Bean, 223
Soup, Robust Three-Bean, 223
Tostadas, Bean-Goat Cheese, 147
White Bean and Radicchio Gratin, 148
White Beans, Sautéed Kale and, 54
Beef
Corned Beef-Cabbage Pie, 78
Pastry Beef Rolls, 100
Picadillo, Beef and Bean, 227
Ragoût, Smothered, 76
Salad, Grilled Sirloin, 190
Sandwiches, Open-Faced Beef, 198
Steaks
Flank Steak with Onion Marmalade, Broiled, 160
Smothered Beef and Mushrooms, 161
Stir-Fry, Tangy Beef, 159
Tenderloin, Cognac-Marinated Beef, 161
Stew, Harvest, 87
Stew, Oriental Beef-Vegetable, 227
Beef, Ground
Peppers, Pizza-Style Stuffed, 158
Pie, Golden Shepherd's, 159
Pie, Tamale, 158
Beet and Carrot Soup, 222
Beverages
Alcoholic
Cafe Mexicana, 106
Cappuccino, Frosty, 52
Punch, Spiked Jamaican Fruit, 65
Strawberry Sparkler, 56
Tropical Mimosas, 105
Berry Cooler, Sparkling, 74
Cider, Hot Spiced, 106
Citrus Spritzer, 106
Fruit Sparkler, Triple, 44
Jumbled Up Bubbly, 82
Lemonade, Warm Apple, 37
Pink Elephants, 105
Raspberry Buttermilk Sipper, 105
Shake, Peanutty Banana, 105
Tea, Island, 106
Tea, Orange Spice, 54
Tea, Spiced Cranberry, 62
Tea, Spiced Peach, 41
Vanilla-Almond Milk, Warm, 35
Biscotti Appetizers, Corn, 97
Biscotti, Spiced Ginger, 71
Biscuits
Bacon-Cornmeal Biscuits, 109
Cornmeal Daisy Biscuits, 37
Cornmeal Drop Biscuits, 54
Irish Soda Drop Biscuits, 79
Blueberry-Buttermilk Sherbet, 236
Breads. *See also* specific types.
Bruschetta with Basil, 55
Cornbread Wedges, 158
Corn Sticks, Hot Pepper, 109
Grilled Bread and Wild Mushrooms, 99
Mustard Breadsticks, Easy, 113
Popovers, Barely Sweet, 110
Popovers, Corn, 64
Popovers, Tex-Mex Appetizer, 97

Breads (continued)
    Raisin-Bran Loaf, 35
    Scones, Amaretto Tea, 108
    Spoonbread, Southern, 112
    Yeast
        Bagels, Caraway, 113
        Breadsticks, Crisp Rosemary-
            Pepper, 74
        Character Bread, 116
        Cornmeal Bread, 61
        Fan Tans, Poppy Seed, 115
        Focaccia, Sweet Onion, 59
        Parmesan Ribbon Bread, 116
        Rolls, Kaiser, 114
        Rolls, Overnight Molasses Pan, 114
        Rolls, Overnight Whole Wheat
            Pan, 88
        Rolls, Whole Wheat Dinner, 115
        Sesame-Cheese Batter Bread, 44
        Sweet Bread, Italian, 39
        Turban Bread, Golden Almond, 118
Broccoli
    Italian Broccoli and Tomatoes, 213
    Phyllo Stacks, Broccoli-Feta, 148
    Salad, Broccoli-Potato Caesar, 62
    Vinaigrette, Quick Broccoli, 49
Brussels Sprouts Gratin, Potato and, 216
Bulgur
    Spicy Bulgur, 132
    Tabbouleh Skillet, 132
    Triple Grain Skillet, 133
Burritos, Caramelized Onion, Black Bean,
    and Orange, 146

Cabbage
    Apple Sweet-Sour Cabbage, 214
    Casserole, Pork Chop and
        Cabbage, 167
    Pie, Corned Beef-Cabbage, 78
    Relish, Golden Garden, 209
    Slaw Sandwiches, Pork and, 200
Cakes. See also Breads, Cookies.
    Banana Cake, 243
    Caramel Peach Cake, 244
    Carrot Spice Cake, 243
    Cheesecake, Sweet Potato, 246
    Cheesecake, Triple Delight, 246
    Chocolate Espresso Pudding
        Cake, 244
    Coffee Cake, Raisin-Pear, 112
    Ginger Molasses Cake, 244
    Squares, Autumn Spice, 88
Cantaloupe. See Melons.
Carrots
    Anise Carrots, 214
    Cake, Carrot Spice, 243
    Salad, Carrot-Waldorf, 43
    Soup, Beet and Carrot, 222
    Topping, Ham Steaks with
        Orange-Carrot, 166

Casseroles
    Chicken-Dressing Casserole, 172
    Corn, Garden Scalloped, 215
    Fruit Compote, Baked, 220
    Macaroni with Eggplant, Olives, and
        Thyme, 150
    Pork Chop and Cabbage Casserole, 167
    Potato and Brussels Sprouts
        Gratin, 216
    Sweet Potato Casseroles,
        Individual, 217
    Tofu Pizza Casserole, 156
    Turkey-Wild Rice Casserole, 182
    Vegetable Hash, Baked, 154
Cauliflower and Peas, Mustard, 214
Cauliflower Pie, 214
Cheese
    Breads
        Batter Bread, Sesame-Cheese, 44
        Parmesan Ribbon Bread, 116
    Dip, Garden, 80
    Dip, Pepperoncini-Cheese, 51
    Greens with Warm Goat Cheese,
        Baby, 187
    Grouper, Pineapple-Goat Cheese, 121
    Linguine, Vegetable-Cheese, 56
    Linguine with Asparagus and Goat
        Cheese, 141
    Phyllo Stacks, Broccoli-Feta, 148
    Pimiento Cheese Apple Wedges, 201
    Potato and Brussels Sprouts Gratin, 216
    Sandwiches, Grilled Blue Cheese, 196
    Spreads
        Spiced Cheese Spread, 47
        Three-Cheese Spread, 96
    Squares, Lemon-Cheese, 79
    Tortellini with Red and Yellow Tomato,
        Cheese, 137
    Tostadas, Bean-Goat Cheese, 147
    White Bean and Radicchio Gratin, 148
Cheesecakes. See Cakes.
Cherries
    Brown Betty, Apple-Cherry, 77
    Jubilee, Cherries, 233
    Sauce, Chocolate-Cherry, 205
Chicken
    Breasts, Salmon-Stuffed Chicken, 175
    Breasts, Vegetable-Filled Chicken, 174
    Casserole, Chicken-Dressing, 172
    Curried Chicken Oriental, 172
    Diane, Chicken, 173
    Fettuccini, Greek, 140
    Jalapeño Chicken, Grilled, 175
    Mexicali Chicken, 172
    Orange-Ginger Chicken, 177
    Pancakes with Fruit Salsa, Chicken, 101
    Phyllo Baskets, Chicken Curry in, 101
    Posole, Chicken, 229
    Poulet Au Vinaigre, 176
    Ragoût, Smothered, 76

Raspberry Chicken, 173
Roasted Chicken, Glazed, 178
Roll-Ups, King Ranch, 201
Roulades with Chunky Tomato Sauce,
    Steamed Chicken, 73
Salads
    Basil Chicken Salad, 191
    Black-Eyed Pea Salad, Chicken and, 58
    Grilled Fiesta Salad, 190
Sandwiches, Broiled Chicken, 199
Satay Trio, 67
Soup, Chicken and Black Bean, 223
Soup, Spicy Chicken and Rice, 224
Spaghettini, Grilled Chicken, 144
Stew, Curried Chicken-Vegetable, 228
Thighs, Sausage-Stuffed Chicken, 177
Chili Sauce, Chunky Southwestern, 206
Chili-Style Lamb Chops, 164
Chocolate
    Brownie Drops, Cocoa, 59
    Cake, Chocolate Espresso Pudding, 244
    Cheesecake, Triple Delight, 246
    Crust, Chocolate Crumb, 240
    Meringue Hearts, Chocolate, 56
    Mousse, Chocolate Rum, 235
    Pudding, Chocolate Mint, 235
    Sauce, Chocolate-Cherry, 205
    Squares with Peppermint Ice Milk,
        Chocolate, 85
    Tartlets, Chocolate Chip Chess, 242
Chowder, Salmon, 226
Chowder, Shrimp and Corn, 226
Chutney
    Eggplant Chutney and Pita Chips, 96
    Grape and Rhubarb Chutney, 207
    Tropical Chutney, Haddock with, 121
Cinnamon Soufflés, 239
Coconut Macaroons, Easy, 91
Coconut Rice, Papaya Shrimp with, 130
Coffee
    Cafe Mexicana, 106
    Cappuccino, Frosty, 52
Coleslaw. See Cabbage or Salads.
Cookies
    Biscotti, Spiced Ginger, 71
    Cereal Bars, Crunchy, 47
    Cocoa Brownie Drops, 59
    Coconut Macaroons, Easy, 91
    Ginger Crinkles, 44
    Oatmeal Krispies, 247
    Orange-Filled Kisses, 247
    Peppermint Meringue Cookies, 247
    Sugar Bunnies, 82
Corn
    Biscotti Appetizers, Corn, 97
    Chowder, Shrimp and Corn, 226
    Creole, Okra and Corn, 216
    Popovers, Corn, 64
    Quesadillas, Corn, Zucchini, and
        Black-Eyed Pea, 149

Corn (continued)
    Salad, Corn Relish, 85
    Salsa, Grilled Amberjack with
        Pepper-Corn, 120
    Scalloped Corn, Garden, 215
    Sticks, Hot Pepper Corn, 109
Cornish Hens
    Grecian Cornish Hens, 179
    Wild Rice, Cornish Hens with
        Fruited, 178
Couscous, Oriental, 132
Crab
    Flounder, Crabmeat-Stuffed, 121
    Noodles with Crabmeat, Chinese
        Curly, 141
    Ravioli with Parslied Tomato Sauce,
        Crabmeat, 142
    Timbales, Crabmeat, 127
Crackers
    Grahams, Animal, 108
    Whole Wheat Batter Crackers, 108
Cranberries
    Parfait, Cranberry and Lime
        Layered, 234
    Relish, Pork Chops with Sweet Potato
        Puree and Cranberry, 169
    Sauce, Citrus Cranberry, 204
    Sauce, Salmon with Cranberry-
        Leek, 124
    Tea, Spiced Cranberry, 62
    Vinaigrette, Poached Pear Salad with
        Cranberry-Port, 71
Crêpe Cups, Turkey Sausage Quiche
    in, 180
Cucumber and Tomato Salad, Minted, 68
Currants. See Raisins.
Curry
    Chicken Oriental, Curried, 172
    Stew, Curried Chicken-Vegetable, 228
    Sweet Potato Strips, Curried, 218

Desserts. See also specific types.
    Apple-Cherry Brown Betty, 77
    Banana-Citrus Trifle, 232
    Cherries Jubilee, 233
    Chocolate
        Meringue Hearts, Chocolate, 56
        Mousse, Chocolate Rum, 235
        Pudding, Chocolate Mint, 235
        Squares with Peppermint Ice Milk,
            Chocolate, 85
    Frozen
        Berry Parfaits, Champagne, 232
        Espresso Granitá, 236
        Pineapple-Orange Frozen
            Yogurt, 238
        Raspberry-Lemon Frozen
            Yogurt, 238
        Rum-Currant Loaf, Frozen, 238
    Fruit in Spiced Sauce, Autumn, 232

Lemon-Cheese Squares, 79
Mango-Lime Ice, 65
Parfait, Cranberry and Lime
    Layered, 234
Plum and Walnut Crisp, 233
Sauces
    Amaretto-Plum Sauce, 204
    Chocolate-Cherry Sauce, 205
    Citrus Cranberry Sauce, 204
    Fruit Sauce, Peaches with, 74
    Fruit Sauce, Tropical, 204
    Raspberry-Mint Sauce,
        Creamy, 205
Soufflés, Cinnamon, 239
Soufflés, Grand Marnier, 239
Sundaes, Pineapple Mint Julep, 54
Tatin, Apple Biscuit, 242
Dumplings
    Turkey Dumplings, Chinese, 103
    Turkey-Vegetable Tortilla
        Dumplings, 182

Eggplant
    Chutney and Pita Chips, Eggplant, 96
    Ditalini Pasta, Eggplant and, 136
    Macaroni with Eggplant, Olives, and
        Thyme, 150
    Pizza Loaf, Mediterranean, 52
    Ratatouille, Grouper with Roasted, 122
    Spread with Pita Chips, Roasted
        Eggplant, 66
    Turkey-Stuffed Eggplant, Creole, 179
Eggs
    Deviled Eggs, Zippy, 85
    Jalapeño Brunch Scramble, 155
    Sandwiches, Scrambled
        Breakfast, 196

Fettuccini
    Greek Fettuccini, 140
    Spinach Fettuccini, Creamy, 140
Fillings and Toppings
    Orange-Carrot Topping, Ham Steaks
        with, 166
    Orange Filling, 247
    Potato Topping, 159
Fish. See also specific types and Seafood.
    Amberjack with Pepper-Corn Salsa,
        Grilled, 120
    Catfish, Herbed Grilled, 83
    Catfish Po-Boys, 199
    Flounder, Crabmeat-Stuffed, 121
    Grouper, Pineapple-Goat Cheese, 121
    Grouper with Roasted
        Ratatouille, 122
    Haddock with Tropical Chutney, 121
    Mahimahi with Tomatillo Salsa,
        Baked, 123
    Marlin, Three-Peppercorn, 123
    Sea Bass and Vegetables, Baked, 120

Seafood Fondue, Marinated, 103
Seasoned Fish and Tomatoes, 48
Snapper, Oriental Red, 124
Snapper Veracruzana, Baked, 125
Sole with Roasted Garlic-Potato
    Puree, 125
Swordfish, Orange Julep, 126
Fruit. See also specific types.
    Autumn Fruit in Spiced Sauce, 232
    Chutney, Haddock with Tropical, 121
    Cocktail, Fresh Citrus Fruit, 220
    Compote, Baked Fruit, 220
    Cup, Bountiful Fresh Fruit, 39
    Frosty Fruit, 35
    Lemon-Lime Marinated Fruit, 91
    Marinade, Fresh Citrus-Garlic, 207
    Muffins, Fruity Yogurt, 47
    Punch, Spiked Jamaican Fruit, 65
    Salad with Sweet Yogurt Dressing,
        Fruit, 184
    Salad, Yogurt-Topped Fruit, 184
    Salsa, Caribbean Fruit, 210
    Salsa, Fruit, 101
    Sauce, Citrus Cranberry, 204
    Sauce, Peaches with Fruit, 74
    Sauce, Tropical Fruit, 204
    Skewers, Grilled Honey Fruit, 68
    Sparkler, Triple Fruit, 44
    Tart, Jewelled Fruit, 241
    Trifle, Banana-Citrus, 232
    Vinegar, Spiced Fruit, 210
    Wild Rice, Cornish Hens with
        Fruited, 178

Grape and Rhubarb Chutney, 207
Grapefruit
    Cocktail, Fresh Citrus Fruit, 220
    Yogurt-Topped Broiled
        Grapefruit, 220
Greens. See also specific types.
    Baby Greens with Warm Goat
        Cheese, 187
    Kale and White Beans, Sautéed, 54
    Mixed Greens with Strawberry-
        Mustard Dressing, 64
    Soup, Beans and Greens, 222
    Tossed Greens with Strawberries, 188
Grits, Seared, 41

Ham. See also Pork.
    Steaks with Orange-Carrot Topping,
        Ham, 166
Hominy, Hearty Mushroom, 150
Honey
    Dressing, Citrus Salad with
        Honey-Lime, 184
    Fruit Skewers, Grilled Honey, 68
    Lobster with Asparagus,
        Honey-Mustard, 128
    Pork Tenderloin, Honey, 170

Honeydew. *See* Melons.
Hors d'Oeuvres. *See* Appetizers.

Ice Milks and Sherbets
    Blueberry-Buttermilk Sherbet, 236
    Cantaloupe Sorbet, 236
    Peppermint Ice Milk, 85
    Sangria Sorbet, 237

Kiwifruit
    Cocktail, Fresh Citrus Fruit, 220

Lamb
    Chops, Chili-Style Lamb, 164
    Chops Jalapeño, Easy Lamb, 164
    Indienne, Lamb and Apples, 229
    Mediterranean Pizza Loaf, 52
    Rack of Lamb, Classic, 165
    Satay Trio, 67
Lasagna, Asparagus, 140
Lasagna, Turkey, 180
Leek Sauce, Salmon with
        Cranberry-, 124
Leek Sauté, Mushroom and, 215
Lemon
    Marinated Fruit, Lemon-Lime, 91
    Pockets, Lemon-Basil Tuna, 201
    Sauce, Sherried Lemon, 206
    Squares, Lemon-Cheese, 79
    Yams, Lemon Nutmeg, 70
    Yogurt, Raspberry-Lemon
        Frozen, 238
Lime
    Dressing, Citrus Salad with
        Honey-Lime, 184
    Ice, Mango-Lime, 65
    Marinated Fruit, Lemon-Lime, 91
    Parfait, Cranberry and Lime
        Layered, 234
Linguine
    Asparagus and Goat Cheese, Linguine
        with, 141
    Asparagus and Shiitake Mushrooms,
        Linguini with, 136
    Vegetable-Cheese Linguine, 56
Lobster, Capellini with, 139
Lobster with Asparagus,
        Honey-Mustard, 128

Macaroni
    Eggplant, Olives, and Thyme,
        Macaroni with, 150
    Stew, Rustic Turkey and
        Macaroni, 230
Mangoes
    Ice, Mango-Lime, 65
    Mustard, Mango, 208
    Salsa, Tomato-Mango, 147
Marinades. *See* Sauces.
Meatball Stew, Turkey, 230

Melons
    Ambrosia, Fresh Melon, 41
    Cantaloupe Sorbet, 236
    Salad, Gingered Melon, 59
Meringues
    Chocolate Meringue Hearts, 56
    Orange-Filled Kisses, 247
    Peppermint Meringue Cookies, 247
Mint
    Pudding, Chocolate Mint, 235
    Salad, Minted Cucumber and
        Tomato, 68
    Sauce, Creamy Raspberry-
        Mint, 205
    Sundaes, Pineapple Mint Julep, 54
Muffins
    Apple Muffins, Fresh, 110
    Cornmeal-Zucchini Muffins, 110
    Sweet Potato Muffins, 41
    Yogurt Muffins, Fruity, 47
Mushrooms
    Beef and Mushrooms,
        Smothered, 161
    Bread and Wild Mushrooms,
        Grilled, 99
    Hominy, Hearty Mushroom, 150
    Linguini with Asparagus and Shiitake
        Mushrooms, 136
    Puffs, Stuffed Potato, 152
    Salad, Roasted Mushroom and
        Fennel, 73
    Sauté, Mushroom and Leek, 215
Mussels Medley, Shrimp and, 130
Mustard
    Breadsticks, Easy Mustard, 113
    Cauliflower and Peas, Mustard, 214
    Dressing, Mixed Greens with
        Strawberry-Mustard, 64
    Lobster with Asparagus,
        Honey-Mustard, 128
    Mango Mustard, 208
    Sweet Hot Mustard, 208
    Vinaigrette, Dijon-Herb, 193
    Vinaigrette, Triple Mustard, 193

Noodles and Vegetables, Spicy
        Peanut, 151
Noodles with Crabmeat, Chinese
        Curly, 141

Oatmeal Krispies, 247
Okra and Corn Creole, 216
Omelets
    Frittata, Three-Pepper, 38
Onions
    Burritos, Caramelized Onion, Black
        Bean, and Orange, 146
    Focaccia, Sweet Onion, 59
    Marmalade, Broiled Flank Steak with
        Onion, 160

Salmon with Caramelized Onions,
        Steamed, 124
Oranges
    Burritos, Caramelized Onion, Black
        Bean, and Orange, 146
    Cocktail, Fresh Citrus Fruit, 220
    Filling, Orange, 247
    Kisses, Orange-Filled, 247
    Salad, Jack-O'-Lantern, 87
    Salad, Spicy Orange, 52
    Swordfish, Orange Julep, 126
    Tea, Island, 106
    Topping, Ham Steaks with
        Orange-Carrot, 166
    Yogurt, Pineapple-Orange Frozen, 238
Orzo
    Pork, Tequila Sunrise, 167
    Primavera, Black and White Beans with
        Orzo, 147
    Salad, Orzo, 189
Oysters and Pasta Shells, 143

Pancakes
    Banana Pancakes, 112
    Chicken Pancakes with Fruit
        Salsa, 101
    Gingerbread Pancakes, 111
Papaya
    Relish, Warm Papaya, 209
    Salsa, Papaya, 210
    Shrimp with Coconut Rice, Papaya, 130
Pastas. *See also* specific types.
    Capellini, Adobe Shrimp and, 138
    Capellini, Grilled Vegetables and, 136
    Capellini with Cilantro Pesto, 138
    Capellini with Lobster, 139
    Chicken, Mexicali, 172
    Ditalini Pasta, Eggplant and, 136
    Oysters and Pasta Shells, 143
    Penne Pasta Primavera, 137
    Ravioli with Parslied Tomato Sauce,
        Crabmeat, 142
    Salad with Herbed Vinaigrette,
        Tri-Pasta, 189
    Spaghettini, Grilled Chicken, 144
    Stuffed Shells, Artichoke and
        Spinach, 143
    Tetrazzini Toss, Turkey, 144
    Tortellini with Red and Yellow Tomato,
        Cheese, 137
Peaches
    Cake, Caramel Peach, 244
    Cobbler, Peach, 233
    Mimosas, Tropical, 105
    Peaches with Fruit Sauce, 74
    Tea, Spiced Peach, 41
Peanut Butter
    Eggstra Special PB and J's, 80
    Sandwiches, Fancy Peanut Butter and
        Banana, 196

Peanut Butter (*continued*)
Sauce, Peanut, 67
Shake, Peanutty Banana, 105
Pears
Coffee Cake, Raisin-Pear, 112
Fruit Cup, Bountiful Fresh, 39
Salad, Watercress, Endive, and
Pear, 188
Salad with Cranberry-Port Vinaigrette,
Poached Pear, 71
Soup, Chilled Apricot-Pear, 222
Peas
Black-Eyed
Quesadillas, Corn, Zucchini, and
Black-Eyed Pea, 149
Rice, Black-Eyed Peas and, 135
Salad, Black-Eyed Pea, 184
Salad, Chicken and Black-Eyed
Pea, 58
Mustard Cauliflower and Peas, 214
Peppermint Ice Milk, 85
Peppermint Meringue Cookies, 247
Peppers
Dip, Pepperoncini-Cheese, 51
Dip, Roasted Garlic and Pepper, 96
Frittata, Three-Pepper, 38
Jalapeño
Brunch Scramble, Jalapeño, 155
Chicken, Grilled Jalapeño, 175
Lamb Chops Jalapeño, Easy, 164
Pepperpot, Caribbean, 64
Pickled Shrimp and Peppers, 102
Rice Quiche in Pepper Cups, 156
Salad, Roasted Red Pepper and
Asparagus, 186
Salsa, Grilled Amberjack with
Pepper-Corn, 120
Soup, Pork-Pepper, 225
Stuffed Peppers, Pizza-Style, 158
Phyllo
Beef Rolls, Pastry, 100
Broccoli-Feta Phyllo Stacks, 148
Chicken Curry in Phyllo Baskets, 101
Corned Beef-Cabbage Pie, 78
Pork, Pastry-Wrapped, 70
Spinach-Ricotta Strudel,
Herbed, 100
Pies and Pastries
Cauliflower Pie, 214
Cobbler, Peach, 233
Corned Beef-Cabbage Pie, 78
Crusts
Chocolate Crumb Crust, 240
Tartlet Shells, 242
Espresso Dream Pie, 240
Raspberry Cream Pie, 49
Shepherd's Pie, Golden, 159
Strawberry-Rhubarb Pie, 240
Strudel, Herbed Spinach-Ricotta, 100
Tamale Pie, 158

Tarts
Chocolate Chip Chess Tartlets, 242
Fruit Tart, Jewelled, 241
Potato Tart, Tuscan, 153
Pineapple
Grouper, Pineapple-Goat
Cheese, 121
Skewers, Grilled Honey Fruit, 68
Sundaes, Pineapple Mint Julep, 54
Yogurt, Pineapple-Orange
Frozen, 238
Pizza
Casserole, Tofu Pizza, 156
Mediterranean Pizza Loaf, 52
Pesto Pizzas, Individual, 202
Plum and Walnut Crisp, 233
Plum Sauce, Amaretto-, 204
Popcorn Mix, Harvest, 202
Pork. *See also* Bacon, Ham, Sausage.
Barbecued Pork, Oven-, 53
Barbecue, Spiced Pork, 170
Brochettes, Sesame Pork, 166
Chops
Casserole, Pork Chop and
Cabbage, 167
Sweet Potato Puree and Cranberry
Relish, Pork Chops with, 169
Patties, Cajun, 166
Roasts
Cannellini Beans, Ribbed Pork
Roast with Herbed, 169
Pastry-Wrapped Pork, 70
Sandwiches, Pork and Slaw, 200
Satay Trio, 67
Soup, Pork-Pepper, 225
Tenderloin, Honey Pork, 170
Tequila Sunrise Pork, 167
Potatoes
Creamy Sliced Potatoes, 216
Gratin, Potato and Brussels
Sprouts, 216
Puffs, Stuffed Potato, 152
Puree, Sole with Roasted Garlic-
Potato, 125
Ragoût, Mexican Potato, 151
Salad, Broccoli-Potato
Caesar, 62
Tart, Tuscan Potato, 153
Topping, Potato, 159
Vichyssoise with Pesto, 46
Potatoes, Sweet
Bake, Fennel-Sweet Potato, 215
Browns, Sweet Potato, 37
Casseroles, Individual Sweet
Potato, 217
Cheesecake, Sweet Potato, 246
Curried Sweet Potato Strips, 218
Muffins, Sweet Potato, 41
Puree and Cranberry Relish, Pork
Chops with Sweet Potato, 169

Salad, Sweet Potato, 185
Yams, Lemon Nutmeg, 70
Pretzels
Barbecued Cereal Snack, 202
Spicy Nibbles, 82
Pumpkin
Bisque, Pumpkin, 60
Stew, Harvest, 87

Quiches
Rice Quiche in Pepper Cups, 156
Turkey Sausage Quiche in Crêpe
Cups, 180

Ragoût
Chunky Vegetable Ragoût, 153
Mexican Potato Ragoût, 151
Smothered Ragoût, 76
Raisins
Coffee Cake, Raisin-Pear, 112
Currant Loaf, Frozen Rum-, 238
Loaf, Raisin-Bran, 35
Raspberries
Chicken, Raspberry, 173
Cooler, Sparkling Berry, 74
Pie, Raspberry Cream, 49
Sauce, Creamy Raspberry-Mint, 205
Sipper, Raspberry Buttermilk, 105
Vinaigrette, Raspberry, 193
Yogurt, Raspberry-Lemon
Frozen, 238
Relishes
Cranberry Relish, Pork Chops with
Sweet Potato Puree and, 169
Garden Relish, Golden, 209
Green Tomato Relish, 209
Papaya Relish, Warm, 209
Rhubarb Chutney, Grape and, 207
Rhubarb Pie, Strawberry-, 240
Rice
Basmati Rice, Fragrant, 67
Black Beans and Rice with Baked
Plantains, 146
Black-Eyed Peas and Rice, 135
Brown Rice, Southwestern, 133
Coconut Rice, Papaya Shrimp
with, 130
Grecian Cornish Hens, 179
Paella, Vegetable, 154
Pilaf, Basmati Rice, 77
Quiche in Pepper Cups, Rice, 156
Risotto, Greek White Bean, 148
Risotto, Herbed, 135
Salad, Garden Rice, 188
Soup, Spicy Chicken and Rice, 224
Spanish Rice, Easy, 134
Spicy Yellow Rice, 49
Stir-Fry, Tangy Beef, 159
Sushi, Vegetable, 98
Triple Grain Skillet, 133

Rice (continued)
  Wild Rice
    Casserole, Turkey-Wild Rice, 182
    Cornish Hens with Fruited Wild
      Rice, 178
    Garden Wild Rice, 135
    Salad, Tangy Wild Rice, 188
Rolls and Buns. *See also* Breads.
  Kaiser Rolls, 114
  Molasses Pan Rolls, Overnight, 114
  Poppy Seed Fan Tans, 115
  Whole Wheat Dinner Rolls, 115
  Whole Wheat Pan Rolls, Overnight, 88

Salad Dressings
  Avocado Dressing, Romaine Salad
    with, 77
  Cocktail Dressing, Spicy, 194
  Herb Dressing, Fresh, 194
  Honey-Lime Dressing, Citrus Salad
    with, 184
  Sesame Seed Dressing, Toasted, 194
  Strawberry-Mustard Dressing, Mixed
    Greens with, 64
  Vinaigrette
    Broccoli Vinaigrette, Quick, 49
    Cranberry-Port Vinaigrette,
      Poached Pear Salad with, 71
    Dijon-Herb Vinaigrette, 193
    Garlic Vinaigrette, 193
    Herbed Vinaigrette, Tri-Pasta Salad
      with, 189
    Mustard Vinaigrette, Triple, 193
    Raspberry Vinaigrette, 193
    Salsa Vinaigrette, 194
    Sweet Vinaigrette, Green
      Beans in, 212
  Yogurt Dressing, Fruit Salad with
    Sweet, 184
Salads
  Bean
    Black Bean Salad, Marinated, 186
    Christmas Confetti, 91
  Chicken
    Basil Chicken Salad, 191
    Black-Eyed Pea Salad, Chicken
      and, 58
    Grilled Fiesta Salad, 190
  Fruit
    Citrus Salad with Honey-Lime
      Dressing, 184
    Fruit Salad with Sweet Yogurt
      Dressing, 184
    Jack-O'-Lantern Salad, 87
    Lemon-Lime Marinated Fruit, 91
    Melon Salad, Gingered, 59
    Orange Salad, Spicy, 52
    Pear Salad with Cranberry-Port
      Vinaigrette, Poached, 71
    Yogurt-Topped Fruit Salad, 184

  Green
    Arugula, Watercress, and Endive
      Salad, 186
    Mixed Greens with Strawberry-
      Mustard Dressing, 64
    Romaine Salad with Avocado
      Dressing, 77
    Tossed Greens with
      Strawberries, 188
    Warm Goat Cheese, Baby Greens
      with, 187
    Watercress, Endive, and Pear
      Salad, 188
  Mushroom and Fennel Salad,
    Roasted, 73
  Orzo Salad, 189
  Pasta Salad with Herbed Vinaigrette,
    Tri-, 189
  Potato Salad, Sweet, 185
  Rice Salad, Garden, 188
  Salmon Salad, Poached, 191
  Sirloin Salad, Grilled, 190
  Slaw Sandwiches, Pork and, 200
  Tuna Niçoise, Grilled, 192
  Vegetable
    Broccoli-Potato Caesar Salad, 62
    Carrot-Waldorf Salad, 43
    Corn Relish Salad, 85
    Cucumber and Tomato Salad,
      Minted, 68
    Pea Salad, Black-Eyed, 184
    Red Pepper and Asparagus Salad,
      Roasted, 186
    Strawberry-Spinach Salad, 47
    Tangy Vegetable Salad, 79
    Wild Rice Salad, Tangy, 188
Salmon
  Chicken Breasts, Salmon-Stuffed, 175
  Chowder, Salmon, 226
  Cranberry-Leek Sauce, Salmon
    with, 124
  Fillets, Grilled Ginger Salmon, 123
  Salad, Poached Salmon, 191
  Steamed Salmon with Caramelized
    Onions, 124
  Torte, Scandinavian Salmon, 102
Salsas
  Fruit Salsa, Caribbean, 210
  Papaya Salsa, 210
  Pepper-Corn Salsa, Grilled Amberjack
    with, 120
  Tomatillo Salsa, Baked Mahimahi
    with, 123
  Vinaigrette, Salsa, 194
Sandwiches
  Beef Sandwiches, Open-Faced, 198
  Blue Cheese Sandwiches, Grilled, 196
  Catfish Po-Boys, 199
  Chicken Sandwiches, Broiled, 199
  PB and J's, Eggstra Special, 80

  Peanut Butter and Banana Sandwiches,
    Fancy, 196
  Pork and Slaw Sandwiches, 200
  Scrambled Breakfast Sandwiches, 196
  Spinach Sandwiches, Toasted, 197
  Tomato-Zucchini Triangles, 197
  Tuna Pockets, Lemon-Basil, 201
  Turkey Sandwiches, Deluxe, 201
  Turkey Sandwiches on Cornmeal
    Bread, 61
Sauces. *See also* Desserts/Sauces.
  Apple Butter Sauce, 206
  Buttermilk Marinade, 163
  Chili Sauce, Chunky
    Southwestern, 206
  Citrus-Garlic Marinade, Fresh, 207
  Lemon Sauce, Sherried, 206
  Peanut Sauce, 67
  Pesto Pizzas, Individual, 202
  Pesto, Vichyssoise with, 46
  Salsa, Fruit, 101
  Salsa, Tomato-Mango, 147
  Seafood
    Pepper Sauce, Roasted, 127
  Spaghetti Sauce, Turkey-
    Vegetable, 207
  Tomato Sauce, Steamed Chicken
    Roulades with Chunky, 73
  Vegetable Sauce, Chunky, 206
Sausage Links, Country-Style, 36
Sausage-Stuffed Chicken Thighs, 177
Scallops
  Grilled Scallops with Black Beans, 129
  Puffs in Zucchini, Scallop, 102
  Stir-Fried Scallops and
    Vegetables, 128
Seafood. *See also* specific types and Fish.
  Fondue, Marinated Seafood, 103
  Pepperpot, Caribbean, 64
Sherbets. *See* Ice Milks and Sherbets.
Shrimp
  Cakes, Sautéed Shrimp, 90
  Capellini, Adobe Shrimp and, 138
  Chowder, Shrimp and Corn, 226
  Fondue, Marinated Seafood, 103
  Grits, Shrimp and, 40
  Medley, Shrimp and Mussels, 130
  Papaya Shrimp with Coconut
    Rice, 130
  Pepperpot, Caribbean, 64
  Pickled Shrimp and Peppers, 102
Snacks
  Apple Wedges, Pimiento Cheese, 201
  Cereal Snack, Barbecued, 202
  Pizzas, Individual Pesto, 202
  Popcorn Mix, Harvest, 202
  Roll-Ups, King Ranch, 201
  Spicy Nibbles, 82
Soufflés, Cinnamon, 239
Soufflés, Grand Marnier, 239

Soups. *See also* Chili, Chowders, Stews.
   Apricot-Pear Soup, Chilled, 222
   Beans and Greens Soup, 222
   Bean Soup, Robust Three-, 223
   Beet and Carrot Soup, 222
   Chicken and Black Bean Soup, 223
   Chicken and Rice Soup, Spicy, 224
   Pork-Pepper Soup, 225
   Pumpkin Bisque, 60
   Vegetable Soup, Scandinavian
     Creamy, 224
   Vichyssoise with Pesto, 46
Spinach
   Fettuccini, Creamy Spinach, 140
   Salad, Strawberry-Spinach, 47
   Sandwiches, Toasted Spinach, 197
   Strudel, Herbed Spinach-Ricotta, 100
   Stuffed Shells, Artichoke and
     Spinach, 143
Spreads. *See also* Appetizers/Spreads.
   Apple-Maple Spread, 35
   Cheese Spread, Spiced, 47
   Mustard, Mango, 208
   Mustard, Sweet Hot, 208
Squash. *See also* Zucchini.
   Butternut Squash, Streusel-Topped, 218
   Spaghetti Squash Italiano, 218
Stews. *See also* Chili, Chowders, Soups.
   Beef and Bean Picadillo, 227
   Beef-Vegetable Stew, Oriental, 227
   Chicken Posole, 229
   Chicken-Vegetable Stew, Curried, 228
   Harvest Stew, 87
   Lamb and Apples Indienne, 229
   Pepperpot, Caribbean, 64
   Ragoût, Chunky Vegetable, 153
   Ragoût, Mexican Potato, 151
   Ragoût, Smothered, 76
   Turkey and Macaroni Stew, Rustic, 230
   Turkey Meatball Stew, 230
Strawberries
   Dressing, Mixed Greens with
     Strawberry-Mustard, 64
   Frosty Fruit, 35
   Parfaits, Champagne Berry, 232
   Pie, Strawberry-Rhubarb, 240
   Salad, Strawberry-Spinach, 47
   Sparkler, Strawberry, 56
   Tossed Greens with Strawberries, 188

Tamale Pie, 158
Tea
   Cranberry Tea, Spiced, 62
   Island Tea, 106
   Orange Spice Tea, 54
   Peach Tea, Spiced, 41
Tofu
   Casserole, Tofu Pizza, 156
   Noodles and Vegetables, Spicy
     Peanut, 151

Tomatoes
   Barley with Tomatoes, 132
   Cacciatore, Braised Veal, 164
   Crostini, Tuna and Sun-Dried
     Tomato, 98
   Fish and Tomatoes, Seasoned, 48
   Italian Broccoli and Tomatoes, 213
   Okra and Corn Creole, 216
   Pâté, Smoked Turkey and Sun-Dried
     Tomato, 90
   Relish, Green Tomato, 209
   Rice, Easy Spanish, 134
   Salad, Minted Cucumber and
     Tomato, 68
   Salsa, Tomato-Mango, 147
   Sauce, Crabmeat Ravioli with Parslied
     Tomato, 142
   Sauce, Steamed Chicken Roulades with
     Chunky Tomato, 73
   Tortellini with Red and Yellow Tomato,
     Cheese, 137
   Triangles, Tomato-Zucchini, 197
   Veracruzana, Baked Snapper, 125
Tortillas. *See also* Burritos.
   Dumplings, Turkey-Vegetable
     Tortilla, 182
   Jalapeño Brunch Scramble, 155
   Quesadillas, Corn, Zucchini, and
     Black-Eyed Pea, 149
   Roll-Ups, King Ranch, 201
   Tostadas, Bean-Goat Cheese, 147
Tuna
   Canapés, Tuna Niçoise, 69
   Crostini, Tuna and Sun-Dried
     Tomato, 98
   Niçoise, Grilled Tuna, 192
   Pockets, Lemon-Basil Tuna, 201
   Provençal, Seared Tuna, 127
Turkey
   Casserole, Turkey-Wild Rice, 182
   Dumplings, Chinese Turkey, 103
   Dumplings, Turkey-Vegetable
     Tortilla, 182
   Eggplant, Creole Turkey-Stuffed, 179
   Hash, Savory Turkey, 43
   Lasagna, Turkey, 180
   Pâté, Smoked Turkey and Sun-Dried
     Tomato, 90
   Quiche in Crêpe Cups, Turkey
     Sausage, 180
   Sandwiches, Deluxe Turkey, 201
   Sandwiches on Cornmeal Bread,
     Turkey, 61
   Sauce, Turkey-Vegetable
     Spaghetti, 207
   Scallopini, Turkey, 182
   Stew, Rustic Turkey and
     Macaroni, 230
   Stew, Turkey Meatball, 230
   Toss, Turkey Tetrazzini, 144

Vanilla-Almond Milk, Warm, 35
Veal
   Bavarian Veal, 162
   Cacciatore, Braised Veal, 164
   Milano, Easy Veal, 162
   Roasted Veal with Root Vegetables, 162
Vegetables. *See also* specific types.
   Capellini, Grilled Vegetables and, 136
   Chicken Breasts, Vegetable-Filled, 174
   Dumplings, Turkey-Vegetable
     Tortilla, 182
   Fennel-Sweet Potato Bake, 215
   Hash, Baked Vegetable, 154
   Hash, Savory Turkey, 43
   Kale and White Beans, Sautéed, 54
   Linguine, Vegetable-Cheese, 56
   Noodles and Vegetables, Spicy
     Peanut, 151
   Paella, Vegetable, 154
   Pasta Primavera, Penne, 137
   Provençal, Seared Tuna, 127
   Ragoût, Chunky Vegetable, 153
   Relish, Golden Garden, 209
   Salads
     Garden Rice Salad, 188
     Tangy Vegetable Salad, 79
   Sauce, Chunky Vegetable, 206
   Sauce, Turkey-Vegetable
     Spaghetti, 207
   Sauté, Winter Vegetable, 219
   Scallops and Vegetables, Stir-Fried, 128
   Sea Bass and Vegetables, Baked, 120
   Soup, Scandinavian Creamy
     Vegetable, 224
   Stew, Curried Chicken-Vegetable, 228
   Stew, Oriental Beef-Vegetable, 227
   Stir-Fry, Vegetable, 219
   Sushi, Vegetable, 98
   Veal with Root Vegetables, Roasted, 162
Vinegar, Spiced Fruit, 210

Watermelon. *See* Melons.
Wild Rice. *See* Rice/Wild Rice.

Yogurt
   Dressing, Fruit Salad with Sweet
     Yogurt, 184
   Frozen Yogurt, Pineapple-Orange, 238
   Frozen Yogurt, Raspberry-Lemon, 238
   Fruit Salad, Yogurt-Topped, 184
   Grapefruit, Yogurt-Topped Broiled, 220
   Muffins, Fruity Yogurt, 47

Zucchini
   Muffins, Cornmeal-Zucchini, 110
   Quesadillas, Corn, Zucchini, and
     Black-Eyed Pea, 149
   Sauté, Zucchini and Sprouts, 219
   Scallop Puffs in Zucchini, 102
   Triangles, Tomato-Zucchini, 197

Subject Index

Aerobic conditioning
  benefits of, 8, 11
  exercises for, 20, 21
  using hand weights during, 21
  heart rate and, 18
  warm-up and cool-down phases
    during, 20
Alcohol, 11
  computer analysis of, 17
  cooking with, 17
  effects of, 11
  heart disease and intake of, 11
  recommendations, 11
Alcoholism
  blood cholesterol levels and, 9
  effect of family on, 68
American Academy of Pediatrics, 10
American Cancer Society, 16, 23
American College of Sports Medicine, 18
American Dietetic Association, 10
American Heart Association (AHA), 8, 11,
  16, 18, 19, 23
American Lung Association, 23
Anencephaly, reducing risk of, 10
Antioxidants, 9, 212
  function of, 212
  sources of, 212
Atherosclerosis, decreasing risk of, 138

Beta carotene, 9, 10
Bicycle symbol, 14
Blood cholesterol levels. See Cholesterol,
  blood.
Body fat. See Fat, body.
Bran, 133
Breads, temperatures for baking, 61
Breakfast
  consumption of, 109
  menus for, 248, 249

Calcium, 10
  bone loss of, 10
  computer analysis of, 17
  daily recommendations, 17
  nutrition labeling of, 27, 28
  sources of, 10
Calorie/Nutrient Chart, 250
Calories
  amounts needed, 17
  calculating percentage of, 17, 82
  calculation of requirements, 17
  computer analysis of, 17
  daily percentages from different
    nutrients, 16, 17, 32, 82, 248
  in nutrients, 17, 26

nutrition labeling of, 26, 27
  for weight loss, 17, 248
Cancer, 9
  antioxidants and, 212
  fiber and prevention of, 8, 113
  reducing risk of, 15, 16, 23, 113
  smoking and, 23
  weight control and, 8
Carbohydrates
  calories in, 17, 26
  complex (starches), 15, 43
  computer analysis of, 17
  daily amounts of, 17, 26
  as energy source, 17, 26
  nutrition labeling of, 26, 27
  percentage suggestions on, 17,
    32, 248
Cardiovascular disease. See Heart
  disease.
Cardiovascular system, exercise
  and, 18
Caseinate, 28
Centers for Disease Control and
  Prevention (CDC), 11, 18
Cheese. See Dairy products.
Chicken. See Poultry.
Children
  blood cholesterol levels in, 8
  calcium for, 10
  establishing good nutrition practices
    for, 8, 15, 16, 189
  and fitness, 91
  and secondhand smoke, 23
  serving size of food for, 15
  weight control for, 91
Cholesterol, blood, 9, 18
  exercise and, 18
  heart disease and, 8, 9, 11
  lipoproteins and, 9
  lowering levels of, 8, 9, 113, 219
  magnesium and, 219
  reducing levels in children, 8
  saturated fat intake and, 9, 16
Cholesterol, dietary
  computer analysis of, 17
  daily amounts of, 17, 26
  recommendations for, 26
  reducing level in food, 24
Chronic fatigue syndrome,
  magnesium intake and, 219
Computer analysis, 17
Cooking equipment, 25
Cooking methods, 43
  low-fat, 25
Cool-down phase, 20

Daily Value. See Percent Daily Value.
Dairy products, 16, 43
  as calcium source, 10
  low-fat, 10, 24, 25, 43
  as protein source, 43, 150
  serving size of, 15
Diabetes, 8
  reducing risk of, 11
Dietary fiber. See Fiber.
Dietary Guidelines, 14, 16
Dietitian, registered, 15, 17
Duck. See Poultry.

Eating habits, 15, 16, 23, 68, 189
  breakfast and, 109
Endosperm, nutrients in, 133
Environmental Protection Agency
  (EPA), 23
Exercise, 8, 11, 14, 18, 19. See also
  Aerobic conditioning, Flexibility,
  Strength training, and Stretching.
  avoiding injury during, 19, 20
  benefits of, 8, 10, 11, 18, 20, 22, 137
  biochemical changes during, 11
  and bone density, 11
  breathing and, 19
  children and, 10
  heart rate and, 19
  metabolic changes from, 248
  monitoring pulse during, 19, 65
  motivation and, 19
  muscle toning, 137
  program of, 18, 19, 20, 21
  proper techniques for, 20, 21
  recommendations for, 8, 11
  stress and, 11
  walking, 18, 19
  warm-up and cool-down phases
    during, 18, 20
  weight control and, 8, 91, 248
Exercise equipment, 14, 29
  Exerlopers™, 29
  hand weights, 20,21
  stair stepper, 19, 21
  stationary bicycle, 19, 20
  treadmill, 21
  Twist 'N Ski™, 29
  Wave Webs™, 29
Expert Panel on Detection, Evaluation,
  and Treatment of High Blood
  Cholesterol in Adults, 9

Family rituals, importance of, 68
Farmers market, 62
Fat-off ladle, 25

Fat, body, 8, 11
Fat, dietary, 15, 16, 22, 43, 197. *See also*
    Polyunsaturated fat, Saturated fat,
    and Unsaturated fat.
    avoiding excess, 43, 197
    blood cholesterol and, 16
    budget for, 16, 82
    calories in, 17, 26
    computer analysis of, 17
    daily amounts of, 26, 82
    function in the body of, 16
    heart disease and, 16, 22
    hidden sources of, 197
    percentage suggestions on, 17, 27,
        82, 248
    protein sources and, 15
    nutrition labeling of, 26, 27
    reduced-fat cooking, 24, 25, 43
    reducing intake of, 8, 10, 16, 22,
        43, 197
    sources of, 15, 16, 24
    weight loss and, 8
Ferritin, blood levels of, 223
Fiber, 15, 113
    dietary guidelines for, 17, 26, 27, 113
    dietary preventive aspects of, 8,
        27, 113
    function in the body of, 113
    increasing intake of, 113
    nutrition labeling of, 26
    sources of, 113
    water-insoluble, 113
    water-soluble, 113
Fish, selection of, 120
Fitness, 18
    benefits of, 18
    components of, 11
    symbol, 14
Flexibility, exercises for, 20
Folic acid, 10
    benefits of, 10
Food and Drug Administration
    (FDA), 26, 27
Food co-ops, 62
Food groups, 14, 15
Food Guide Pyramid, 14, 15
Food labeling, 26, 27, 28, 29
Free radicals, 212
Fruits, 189
    benefits of, 8
    consumption of, 189
    as fiber source, 113
    intake of, 8
    nutrients in, 10, 113
    serving size of, 15

Genetics. *See* Heredity.
Germ, nutrients in, 9, 133
Goals, 22
    setting of, 19

Grains, 10, 133, 219. *See also* specific
        types.
    as complementary protein food, 150
    as fiber source, 113
    increasing intake of, 15, 113
    nutrients in, 10, 133
    shopping for, 62
Grid nutrients. *See* Nutrients, computer
        analysis of.
Grill, cooking on, 25

Hand weights, 21
Health food stores, 62
Heart disease, 8, 18, 22
    alcohol and, 11
    blood cholesterol levels and, 8, 9, 16
    exercise and, 9, 11, 18, 22
    obesity and, 8
    reducing risk of, 8, 9, 10, 11, 15,
        16, 22
    smoking and, 23
    vitamin E and, 9, 10
    weight control and, 8
Heart rate, 18. *See also* Maximum heart
        rate (MHR) and Target heart rate
        (THR).
    to determine, 65
    exercise and, 18
Herbs and spices, 43. *See also* specific
        types.
Heredity, and blood cholesterol
        levels, 9
High blood pressure, 11, 18
    exercise and, 18
Hostility, heart disease risk and, 23
Hypertension. *See* High blood pressure.

Immune system, laughter and, 22
Injury, decreasing risk of during
        exercise, 19, 20, 21
Ingredient substitutions, 24
Iron, 10, 223
    computer analysis of, 17
    daily amounts of, 17
    heart disease and intake of, 10, 223
    nutrition labeling of, 27

Kitchen equipment, 25, 204
Knives, selecting quality, 204

Labeling, 26, 27, 28, 29
    of health claims, 28
    of nutrients, 26, 27
    of nutrient claims, 28
Laughter, 22
Legumes, 15, 43
    as complementary protein food, 150
    nutrients in, 10, 150, 219
    shopping for, 62
Lifestyle, positive changes in, 22

Lipoproteins
    high-density (HDLs), 9, 11
    low-density (LDLs), 9, 219, 223

Magnesium, 219
    sources of, 219
Maximum heart rate (MHR), to
        determine, 65
Meals, balanced, 32, 248
Meats, 223. *See also* specific types.
    labeling of, 26
    nutrients in, 10, 16, 223
    serving size of, 15
Metabolism
    effects on from dieting, 8, 248
    and exercise, 18
Milk and milk products, 16. *See also*
        Dairy products.
    as calcium source, 10
Minerals, 10, 15. *See also* specific
        types.
Monounsaturated fat, sources of, 16
Motivation, benefits of, 22
Multiple Risk Factor Intervention Trial
        (MR FIT), 9, 11
Muscle fibers in poultry, 180
Muscles
    strengthening of, 20
    stretching of, 19
    toning of, 18, 20

National Cancer Institute, 8, 10
National Heart, Lung, and Blood
        Institute, 9
National Institutes of Health (NIH),
        8, 189
National Labeling and Education Act
        (NLEA), 26, 27, 28
Niacin, 27
Nutrients, 17. *See also* specific types.
    balanced mix of, 14, 32, 94
    daily percentages of different, 17
Nutrients, computer analysis of, 17
    calcium, 17
    calories, 17
    carbohydrates, 17
    cholesterol, 17
    daily amounts of, 17
    fat, 17
    fiber, 17
    iron, 17
    protein, 17
    sodium, 17
Nutrition
    children and, 8, 10, 15, 16, 189
    symbol, 14
Nutrition labeling. *See* Labeling.

Obesity, heart disease risk
        and, 8

Oils, 9, 16, 138
  preventing rancidity of, 138
  storage of, 138
Osteoporosis, prevention of, 10

Percent Daily Value, 26, 27
Polyunsaturated fat, 16
Poultry
  muscle fibers in, 180
  nutrition labeling of, 26
Pressure cooker, 25
Protein
  animal, 15
  calories in, 17, 26
  complementary, 150
  computer analysis of, 17
  daily amounts of, 17
  nutrition labeling of, 26, 27
  percentage suggestions on, 17,
    32, 248
  sources of, 15, 150

Recipe modification, 24
Recommended Dietary Allowances
  (RDAs), 17, 212
Riboflavin, nutrition labeling
  of, 27
Rice, 15

Saffron, 209
Salt. *See* Sodium.
Saturated fat, 8, 9, 10, 22
  cancer risk and intake of, 8
  heart disease risk and intake of, 27
  nutrition labeling of, 27
  recommendations for, 16, 17, 26, 27,
    32, 248
  reducing intake of, 10, 16
  sources of, 9, 16

Selenium, 212
Serving sizes, 15
  labeling of, 26, 27
Shopping, 16, 43
Smoking, 11, 23
  heart disease and, 9, 11, 23
  passive, 23
Snacks, suggestions for, 43
Sodium
  computer analysis of, 17
  daily amounts of, 17, 26, 27
  reducing intake of, 24
Soybeans, 219
Spina bifida, reducing risk of, 10
Steaming basket, 25
Strength training, 20
  benefits of, 11
Stress
  exercise and, 11, 18
  heart disease and, 22
  and high-density lipoprotein
    levels, 9
Stretching, 20
  benefits of, 11, 20
  exercises for, 20
Stroke, 8, 9

Target heart rate (THR), 19, 65
  to determine, 65
Thiamine, 27
Trans-fatty acids, 9
Turkey. *See* Poultry.
Turmeric, 209

U.S. Department of Agriculture (USDA),
  14, 15, 17, 26
U.S. Public Health Service, 10, 11, 18
Unsaturated fat, 9

Vanilla extract, making, 241
Vegetable cooking spray, 43
Vegetables, 15
  consumption of, 189
  as fiber source, 113
  increasing intake of, 8, 15, 189
  nutrients in, 10
Vegetarian lifestyle
  complementary proteins, 150
Vinegar, balsamic, 98
Vitamins, 15, 16
  labeling requirements for food, 27
  vitamin A, 9, 16
  vitamin Bs, 27
  vitamin C, 9, 10
  vitamin D, 16
  vitamin E, 9, 10, 16, 212
  vitamin K, 16

Walking, 14, 18
  benefits of, 18
  program for, 19
Warm-up phase, 20
  benefits of, 19
  in exercise program, 18
Weight control, 8, 91, 109, 248
  alcohol intake and, 11
  blood cholesterol and, 9
  breakfast and, 109
  calorie requirement for, 17, 248
  for children, 91
  exercise and, 8, 11, 248
  fat intake and, 8
  heart disease and, 8, 11
Weight training, 18
Wok, 25
Workout. *See* Exercise, program of.

Yogurt cheesemaker, 25

Acknowledgments and Credits

Oxmoor House wishes to thank the following individuals and merchants:

Annieglass, Santa Cruz, CA
Applause Dance & Aerobic Wear, Birmingham, AL
Barbara Eigen Arts, Jersey City, NJ
Biot, New York, NY
Birmingham Botanical Gardens, Birmingham, AL
Bridgewater/Boston International, Newton, MA
Bromberg's, Birmingham, AL
Cassis & Co., New York, NY
Christine's, Birmingham, AL
Dansk International Designs Ltd., Mount Kisco, NY
Mr. and Mrs. James Edwards, Grove Hill, AL
ExerScience™ by NordicTrack, Chaska, MN
Fioriware, Zanesville, OH
Fitz and Floyd/Omnibus International, New York, NY
Fresh World Produce, Birmingham, AL
Goldsmith/Corot, Inc., New York, NY
Gorham, Providence, RI
Haldon, Irving, TX
Mrs. Katherine Hamilton, Grove Hill, AL
Hydro-Fit, Inc., Eugene, OR
J.R. Brooks and Son, Inc., Homestead, FL
Julie Cline Ceramics, Oakland, CA
Izabel Lam, Long Island City, NY
Los Angeles Pottery, Los Angeles, CA
Martin & Son Wholesale Florist, Birmingham, AL
Nordic Fitness Products of Alabama, Birmingham, AL
Perdido Beach Resort, Orange Beach, AL
Pillivuyt, Silinas, CA
Plateman, San Francisco, CA
Sasaki, Secaucus, NJ
Stonefish Pottery, Providence, RI
Swid Powell, New York, NY
Taitu, Dallas, TX
The Holly Tree, Birmingham, AL
Towle, Newbury Port, MA
Toni Tully, Birmingham, AL
Union Street Glass, Oakland, CA
Vietri, Hillsborough, NC
Jarinda Wiechman, Birmingham, AL
Wilton Armetale, Mount Joy, PA
Yamazaki, Lyndhurst, NJ

Photographers

Ralph Anderson: pages 17, 24, 29, 45, 53, 95, 99, 104, 107, 111, 117, 139, 142, 145, 149, 152, 155, 171, 181, 195, 198, 200, 203, 205

Jim Bathie: front cover, back cover, frontispiece, pages 6, 7, 12, 13, 20, 21, 30, 31, 33, 34, 36, 38, 40, 42, 46, 48, 50, 55, 58, 60, 63, 66, 69, 72, 75, 76, 81, 84, 86, 89, 92, 93, 119, 122, 126, 129, 131, 134, 157, 160, 163, 165, 168, 174, 176, 183, 185, 187, 192, 208, 211, 213, 217, 221, 225, 228, 231, 234, 237, 245

Sylvia Martin: page 78

Photo Stylists

Kay Clarke: front cover, back cover, frontispiece, pages 6, 7, 12, 13, 30, 31, 33, 34, 36, 38, 40, 42, 46, 48, 50, 58, 60, 63, 66, 69, 72, 75, 76, 78, 81, 84, 86, 89, 92, 93, 119, 122, 126, 129, 131, 134, 157, 160, 163, 165, 168, 174, 176, 183, 185, 187, 192, 208, 211, 213, 217, 221, 225, 228, 231, 234, 237, 245

Virginia Cravens: pages 17, 24, 29, 45, 53, 95, 99, 104, 107, 111, 117, 139, 142, 145, 149, 152, 155, 171, 181, 195, 198, 200, 203, 205

Angie Neskaug Sinclair: page 55